Critical Essays on

SIR ARTHUR CONAN DOYLE

CRITICAL ESSAYS
ON
BRITISH LITERATURE

Zack Bowen, General Editor
University of Miami

Critical Essays on
SIR ARTHUR CONAN DOYLE

edited by

HAROLD OREL

G. K. Hall & Co. / New York
Maxwell Macmillan Canada / Toronto
Maxwell Macmillan International / New York Oxford Singapore Sydney

G. K. Hall & Co.	Maxwell Macmillan Canada, Inc.
Macmillan Publishing Company	1200 Eglinton Avenue East
866 Third Avenue	Suite 200
New York, New York 10022	Don Mills, Ontario M3C 3N1

Macmillan Publishing Company is part of the Maxwell Communication Group of Companies.

Library of Congress Cataloging-in-Publication Data
Critical essays on Sir Arthur Conan Doyle/edited by Harold Orel.
    p.   cm.—(Critical essays on British literature)
    Includes bibliographical references and index.
    ISBN 0-8161-8865-3 (alk. paper)
    1. Doyle, Arthur Conan, Sir, 1859–1930—Criticism and interpretation.   2. Holmes, Sherlock (Fictitious character)
    I. Orel, Harold, 1926–   II. Series.
    PR4624.C75 1992
    823'.8—dc20   92-229
                                                   CIP

10 9 8 7 6 5 4 3 2 1

Printed in the United States of America

To Bill and Elaine House

Contents

◆

General Editor's Note

♦

The Critical Essays on British Literature series provides a variety of approaches to both classical and contemporary writers of Britain and Ireland. The formats of the volumes in the series vary with the thematic designs of individual editors, and with the amount and nature of existing reviews—criticism augmented, where appropriate, by original essays by recognized authorities. It is hoped that each volume will be unique in developing a new overall perspective on its particular subject.

Harold Orel's introduction and selection of essays cover evaluations of Doyle's contemporaries as well as the historical evaluations and scholarship of more recent critics of Doyle's work; the purposeful treatment by Holmes's admirers of Doyle's detective-story characters as real people; and the literary and social importance of the large body of writing Doyle did besides the Holmes stories. This volume makes a genuine contribution in considering the entire career of Arthur Conan Doyle and his place in literature.

ZACK BOWEN
University of Miami

Publisher's Note

◆

Producing a volume that contains both newly commissioned and reprinted material presents the publisher with the challenge of balancing the desire to achieve stylistic consistency with the need to preserve the integrity of works first published elsewhere. In the Critical Essays series, essays commissioned especially for a particular volume are edited to be consistent with G. K. Hall's house style; reprinted essays appear in the style in which they were first published, with only typographical errors corrected. Consequently, shifts in style from one essay to another are the result of our efforts to be faithful to each text as it was originally published.

Introduction

HAROLD OREL

Since Sherlock Holmes made his first appearance in 1887, more than a full century has elapsed; the Great Detective seems to have become immortal. He is certainly much written about. *The World Bibliography of Sherlock Holmes and Doctor Watson*, compiled by Ronald Burt De Waal,[1] was followed by a companion volume, *The International Sherlock Holmes*.[2] These two bibliographies list more than 12000 items, and a third volume is being prepared.

Studies of Holmes's cases, the iconography of Holmes, parodies and travesties, as well as works on contemporary history and sociology, are so numerous that one can hardly credit the fact that Doyle wrote only 60 stories—56 short stories and 4 novels—and two pastiches about Holmes and Watson. More than 50 Sherlockian periodicals are published today. Workshops on Holmes's achievements are regularly offered at American universities. A three-volume paper edition of 1,848 pages was published in the People's Republic of China in the late 1980s. A large alcove devoted to Holmes publications, set aside in Tokyo's largest bookstore to celebrate the one hundredth year since he was first introduced to the public (1987), did a thriving business. The societies devoted to Holmes include the Baker Street Irregulars, the Red Circle, Mrs. Hudson's Cliff Dwellers, the Montague Street Lodgers, the Noble Bachelors, the Scowrers and Molly Maguires, the Blind German Mechanics, the Cremona Fiddlers, the Clients of Sherlock Holmes, the Nashville Scholars of the Three Pipe Problems, the Devil's Foot Society, the Giant Rats of Sumatra, the Five Orange Pips, the Three Garridebs, the Priory Scholars, *und so weiter*.

More than 500 films and radio and television adaptations have been made.

Some Holmes enthusiasts have accumulated collections of more than 20,000 items. Several actors have found it possible to make a living from impersonating either Holmes or Doyle talking about Holmes. Tourists in

London often find their way to the second floor of the Sherlock Holmes pub on Northumberland Street, only a 10-minute walk from Trafalgar Square. There they can inspect the reproduction of the sitting room at 221B Baker Street, originally prepared by the London borough of St. Marylebone for the Festival of Britain in 1951, at which it was probably the most popular single exhibit. At least three other sitting-room replicas are tourist attractions in other countries.

In 1953 a large number of Englishmen and women dressed in Victorian costumes turned out for the opening of the Baker Street line on the Underground. In 1968 six women tried to force their way into a dinner of Baker Street Irregulars, all of whom were men; their effort was frustrated by a vigorous counteroffensive. The women thereupon formed their own national organization, the Adventuresses of Sherlock Holmes; their journal, *The Serpentine Muse*, has a wider readership than just their membership. As the *New York Times* noted, "As with the Baker Street Irregulars, membership is limited: petitioners are rarely admitted at their first request."[3]

It may be that the best way to begin these prefatory remarks to a collection of essays and reviews based on the life and career of Sir Arthur Conan Doyle is to examine the extraordinary game, played by most members of the BSI (Baker Street Irregulars), that posits as its basic assumption a conviction that Sherlock Holmes and Dr. Watson are historical figures, and that Doyle is a figment of their imagination—or at best acts as Dr. Watson's literary agent. The *Baker Street Journal*, founded in 1946, makes this assumption very plain, and indeed its contents in issue after issue simply continue a tradition established by the popular book *Profile by Gaslight* (1944). Long essays to this effect were written for that volume by Heywood Broun, Stephen Vincent Benét, Rex Stout, Christopher Morley, Dorothy Sayers, and Alexander Woollcott.

But did not this pretence begin as an attitude in the 1890s? A half-century before the publication of *Profile by Gaslight*, Andrew Lang meticulously destroyed Holmes's explanation of which candidate for the Fortescue Scholarship copied the examination papers in "The Adventure of the Three Students." Lang demonstrated that the story's explanation could not be believed; he demanded to know if Holmes were hiding the true explanation. (Doyle never responded to the challenge, but then, so far as Lang was concerned, Doyle's opinion was irrelevant to the problem posed.)

In 1912 Ronald A. Knox, at the time an undergraduate at Oxford University and later one of England's leading Roman Catholic prelates, delivered to the Gryphon Club of Trinity College a lecture entitled "Studies in the Literature of Sherlock Holmes." It was cast in the form of a satire on contemporary German scholarship, and it postulated 11 basic parts of a Sherlock Holmes story; it even made space for a Deutero-Holmes and a Deutero-Watson.

Doyle was amazed that Knox had got so much more out of his stories than he had put into them, though it was difficult for him to remain amused as the rules of the New Scholarship were hammered into place. These rules insisted that all characters in the stories really lived; that one must never mention the fact that they were real people; and that all questions of the Canon had to be treated with seriousness. As Dorothy Sayers wrote in 1946, 16 years after Doyle had died, "The rule of the game is that it must be played as solemnly as a county cricket match at Lord's. The slightest touch of extravagance or burlesque ruins the atmosphere."[4]

Thus, a plaque commemorating the first meeting of Sherlock Holmes and Dr. Watson has been set up in St. Bartholomew's Hospital in London. A steep elevation near Tulsa, Oklahoma, is today named Holmes Peak, despite a four-year struggle with the U.S. Board on Geographic Names and, for that matter, the Catholic diocese of Tulsa, which owned part of the hill. A letter was written to the pope, reminding him that Sherlock Holmes had rendered a number of valuable services to the Vatican; the question was promptly settled in Holmes's favor.

Cait Murphy has collected these and similar stories of how far Holmes devotees are prepared to go, and in her wonderful essay "The Game's Still Afoot" she describes how a number of dedicated readers were so impressed by the unfortunate wounding of Dr. Watson by a Jezail bullet at the battle of Maiwand (1880)—a bullet that shattered his bone and grazed the subclavian artery—that they voted to erect a statue in Afghanistan, on the battlefield of Maiwand. They had actually worked out an agreement with the government of that nation in 1977 when the Russians invaded, putting a halt to their plans. (The money for the statue had already been committed.) Some of the Maiwand Jezails (such is their name in Nebraska) wanted to hire someone who would fly into Maiwand, touching down briefly but long enough to permit the inflation of a portable monument there. The project didn't fly, alas, but this inspired project may yet rise again.[5]

Scholars are intrigued by the question of how many times Dr. Watson married, since the Holmes stories seem to suggest confusingly that the good doctor married more than once. For that matter, we are not sure whether Watson was really struck in the shoulder by a Jezail bullet; though the opening paragraphs of A Study in Scarlet identify the location as the shoulder, later stories in the Holmes canon speak of the wound as being in the leg. A dread prospect looms before us: the wording of any plaque attached to a statue to be erected in Maiwand will either have to fudge the issue or ignore it altogether.

The Holmes stories represent little more than 10 percent of Doyle's total output. Doyle could have written more Holmes stories than he did; no one had the formula more firmly under control. Though he complained about the mechanical aspects of plot construction, he experienced few difficulties in developing ideas suitable for the length of a contribution to the *Strand Magazine.*

Moreover, he was offered impressive sums of money to continue writing them, far more than the $5,000 to $8,000 per story that made him—shortly after the appearance of *The Hound of the Baskervilles* in 1901–2—the highest-priced writer of fiction in England. George H. Doran, the Canadian-born American publisher, once proposed to Doyle that, since he declined to write further Sherlock Holmes adventures in anything like their old form, he might undertake to write a biography of Dr. Watson, the friend and Boswell of Sherlock Holmes, and thus create a perfectly legitimate vehicle for further cases. Doyle responded that the idea was good—indeed, the best he had heard for the revival of Sherlock Holmes—but that he could not take himself away from his psychic work. And shortly afterward he died.

When Raymond Blathwayt, one of the pioneers of the celebrity interview, published his record of an encounter with Doyle, Doyle remarked that he had based Holmes on Dr. Joe Bell of the medical faculty at Edinburgh University.[6] He had been greatly impressed by Dr. Bell's ability, while sitting in the patients' waiting room "with a face like a Red Indian," to diagnose an individual as he or she came in, even before the person had uttered a word. "So I got the idea for Sherlock Holmes," Doyle went on. Even then Doyle was tiring of his creation: "Sherlock is utterly inhuman, no heart, but with a beautifully logical intellect." He was quick to add that the best detective in fiction was Edgar Allan Poe's Monsieur Dupin and, after him, Monsieur Le Cocq, Gaboriau's hero. "The great defect in the detective of fiction," Doyle told Blathwayt, "is that he obtains results without any obvious reason. That is not fair, it is not art."[7] Doyle's affections were dedicated to his historical novels; his love for them should not be underestimated. He boasted time and again of *The White Company* as the best thing he had ever written. "I endeavoured in that to reconstruct the whole of the fourteenth century," he added, and he noted that Scott had always avoided this historical period. Indeed, he said, he had read 150 books in preparation for writing *The White Company*.[8]

In an interview with Harry How that same year, Doyle "revealed" his trick of literary construction in *The Adventures of Sherlock Holmes*: invariably first to conceive the end of the story and then to write up to it.[9] His art lay in the ingenious way in which he concealed from the reader what the climax would be. A Holmes story took him about one week to write, and the ideas came at all manner of times—when out walking, cricketing, tricycling, or playing tennis. He worked between the hours of breakfast and lunch, and again in the evening from five to eight, writing some 3000 words a day. He was so confident that his next story was unsolvable that he even bet his wife a shilling that she would not guess the true solution of it until she got to the end of the chapter.

Early in 1893, toward the end of winter, Doyle made up his mind about his popular fictional hero. In a conversation with Silas K. Hocking, author of *Her Benny* (a tale of Liverpool streets, written for children, that sold more than a million copies), Doyle confessed, "The fact is, he has got to be an 'old man of the sea' about my neck, and I intend to make an end of him. If I don't he'll make an end of me."[10]

At the time, Hocking, Doyle, and the archbishop of Canterbury were staying at the Rifel Alp Hotel, above Zermatt. They went for a walk to the Findelan Glacier. "How are you going to do it?" Hocking asked Doyle. "I haven't decided yet," Doyle laughed. "But I'm determined to put an end to him somehow." "Rather rough on an old friend," Hocking said, "who has brought you fame and fortune." The archbishop, Edward White Benson, made a strong case for the continuance of Holmes. Finally, Hocking said, "If you are determined on making an end of Holmes, why not bring him out to Switzerland and drop him down a crevasse? It would save funeral expenses." Doyle laughed. "Not a bad idea."[11] "Shortly thereafter, Holmes, in "The Adventure of the Final Problem," disappeared over the Reichenbach Falls. The news of Holmes's supposed death, locked in the arms of Dr. Moriarty as the two men fell into the swirling waters of the falls, caused consternation when The *Strand Magazine* appeared in December 1893. The strong public reaction against this heartless act, which Greenhough Smith, Doyle's editor, and George Newnes, Doyle's publisher, had both tried to avert, was without parallel in English literary history. A Holmes story by itself could raise the *Strand Magazine's* circulation by more than 100,000 copies. Now, realizing that no more Holmes stories would be written, some 20,000 readers canceled their subscriptions. The Prince of Wales expressed dismay. In Piccadilly and in the City, young men wore mourning bands of black for Sherlock Holmes. One woman sent Doyle a letter of remonstrance that began with the salutation "You brute." Years later, in his autobiography *Memories and Adventures*, Doyle admitted he had been "utterly callous" but, he defiantly went on, was "only glad to have a chance of opening out into new fields of imagination, for the temptation of high prices made it difficult to get one's thoughts away from Holmes."[12]

For years there was no shaking Doyle's conviction that Sherlock Holmes was "merely a mechanical creature, not a man of flesh and blood,—and easy to create because he was soulless. One story by Edgar Allan Poe would be worth a dozen such."[13]

Doyle was moving on to greener pastures and believed that little more could be done with Holmes—or, to be more precise, he did not want to do that little more. He was also modest about the value or originality of Holmes as a literary creation. He always gave full credit to his illustrator, Sidney Paget, and to William Gillette, the actor-manager who wrote the long-running play based on the Holmes stories. Trying to figure out a plot twist that would interest the audience, Gillette, while working on the script, cabled Doyle from America, "May I marry Sherlock Holmes?" Doyle's response was a cable: "You may marry him, murder him, or do anything you like with him."

In 1921 Arthur Guiterman, a minor critic, tried to identify Holmes with his creator. Doyle was extremely annoyed at this "interpretation." He sent a verse letter to *London Opinion*, the journal in which Guiterman had made the observation. Into his normally equable temperament a darker hint of ill-temper might be seen to move:

> Sure, there are limits when one cries with acidity,
> Where are the limits of human stupidity? . . .
> Pray master this, my esteemed commentator,
> That the created is not the creator.
> Just grasp this fact with your cerebral tentacle,
> That the doll and its maker are never identical.[14]

The savagery of the thrust was surely related to Doyle's abiding suspicion that, in spending so much time on the Holmes-Watson stories, he had diverted his best creative talents away from an entirely different kind of fiction.

Some Baker Street Irregulars have expressed uneasiness about what happened to Holmes after Doyle resurrected him in 1903, with the publication of *The Hound of the Baskervilles*. They have argued that the final period of Holmes's life was weakly plotted and heavily reliant on ideas that had already been used in better ways; that an inartistic sense of macabre effects had seemed to come to the fore; and that revolting illnesses, exotic poisons, and so forth, proliferated in stories written right up to Holmes's final appearance.[15]

Still another reason lay beneath Doyle's conviction that his historical romances, as a whole, constituted a superior body of work. He was uneasily aware that Holmes's knowledge of chemistry was more superficial than an author needed as a basis for Holmes's solutions to difficult cases. Holmes resembled Doyle in that he knew some simple inorganic chemistry and just enough organic chemistry to understand how the body worked. Dr. Watson told us, in *A Study in Scarlet*, that Holmes knew a good deal about belladonna, opium, and poisons generally, and had a practical but limited knowledge of geology, an unsystematic sense of anatomy, and no interest in astronomy. Later stories contradicted this listing of what Holmes knew and didn't know, but there is no evidence that Holmes benefited from electricity; he owned no colorimeter; and he never used the basic absorption spectroscope, which was in wide use by the 1880s. Dr. Watson must have been mistaken when he claimed that Holmes invented "a reagent which is precipitated by haemoglobin and by nothing else," or that Holmes *at a glance* could distinguish the ash of any known brand of either cigar or tobacco.[16]

When Holmes diluted a drop of blood in a liter of water, the degree of dilution had to be one part to 50,000 (1/50 ml in 1,000 ml), yet Holmes declared flatly that "the proportion of blood cannot be more than one in a million."[17]

Holmes did not bother to refer problems to the analytical laboratories of his day. He did not depend on fingerprint identification, though Galton's identification system was well known. In "The Engineer's Thumb" he confused an amalgam with an alloy. He talked about a blue carbuncle despite the fact that carbuncles are a variety of garnet, and always red, never blue. He spoke of a 40-gram weight of crystallized charcoal when every diamond merchant would have measured its weight in carats.[18]

In *Memories and Adventures* Doyle confessed with some chagrin that he had been mistaken in writing, in "The Adventure of the Priory School," that Holmes could tell by looking at a bicycle track on a damp moor which way it was heading. "I had so many remonstrances upon this point," Doyle wrote, "varying from pity to anger, that I took out my bicycle and tried. I had imagined that the observations of the way in which the track of the hind wheel overlaid the track of the front one when the machine was not running dead straight would show the direction. I found that my correspondents were right and I was wrong, for this would be the same whichever way the cycle was moving."[19]

Hence, it is most likely that Doyle grew tired, over the years, of being criticized for getting his details wrong, particularly since Holmes insisted that whereas others might see, *he* observed, and observed accurately. Doyle, who could be a dedicated researcher when it came to details about a South American jungle or a period of medieval history, simply didn't care enough about Holmes to spend the time needed for authenticating his scientific data. After all, he believed that Holmes's character admitted of no light or shade. That was tiresome enough in itself. But Doyle, on more than one occasion, said that Dr. Watson never showed one gleam of humor or made one single joke; Holmes and Watson were not real characters.

So much for Doyle's ability to judge fairly the quality of what he had written in the Holmes-Watson canon. Though the wisdom of vox populi may often be questioned, the pleasure of six generations of readers will not be significantly reduced even if additional factual errors are discovered in the stories, or if a larger number of details turn out, on closer examination, to be ungenerous with the truth. Doyle, though a giant in the flesh and one of the most colorful of all Victorian authors, will doubtless continue to seem less vivid, for many of his readers, than any of the 60 Holmes stories.

I

Opening the first part of this anthology is an elegantly written speculation about the problems created by an inconsistent use of Dr. Watson's first name.

Dorothy L. Sayers was a prime mover in the campaign to eliminate Arthur Conan Doyle from all considerations of the "Canon," and she proceeds here (and elsewhere) on the basis of an assumption that most textual inconsistencies will yield to a rational approach. Goodwill is often unable to clear up the mystery, and anyhow, Holmes himself would approve of her assumption. It sweeps away cobwebs. One feels reassured that ambiguities and unresolved tensions in the text will ultimately be eliminated. And one derives additional reassurance from Sayers's argument that Dr. Watson sometimes rendered evidence inadequately or produced only a partial transcript of what went on.

A much-needed corrective to the usual patronizing treatments of Dr. Watson can be found in Peter V. Conroy's stimulating essay. After all, Watson is also one of the great fictional creations of the Victorian age. His intellectual powers are less than those of Holmes, but then, so are everyone else's. Watson, Conroy reminds us, is not only a competent doctor and Holmes's most loyal friend but also the very capable chronicler of Holmes's exploits. What a dreary comedown it would be if Holmes narrated all his own stories—or, an equally depressing thought, Inspector Lestrade, or Mrs. Hudson! The art of Dr. Watson's storytelling receives here a generous (and long-overdue) encomium. Inevitably Conroy's treatment reminds us that much of the power of the Holmes stories derives from the skill with which Doyle characterizes the good doctor.

Recent scholarship suggests that Holmes's personality and methodology can profitably be set against a larger historical setting, a context of Victorian history. Stephen Knight's investigation of "the Great Detective" can be taken in conjunction with a provocative sociological inquiry conducted by Christopher Clausen. These two essays define Holmes as a commentary by Doyle (however indirect) on the darker side of Victorian life. There was certainly much to deplore in industrial England, a savagery of doctrine and practice that constituted, in Knight's phrase, an "economic world-view" of "city workers, clerks and businessmen who patronised *The Strand*." A Victorian might even despair at the knowledge that so much evil had been so triumphant in a society supposedly dedicated to the ideals of science and progress. Knight's emphasis on anxiety as an underestimated factor of Victorian life is surely justified, though whether sexual tensions are as significant in Doyle's fiction as they were in the short stories of any number of practitioners—George Gissing, Ella D'Arcy, George Egerton, Hubert Crackanthorpe, Rudyard Kipling, and Thomas Hardy, among many others—is more debatable. It is noteworthy that Knight stresses the role played by the audience "in the constitution of cultural ideology."

Clausen's angle of approach suggests that he has far more on his mind than simply nostalgia or an appreciation of Doyle's entertainment values. Clausen argues convincingly that the solutions to appalling crimes cannot be conceived by detectives like Lestrade, who are wedded to the orthodoxies of their profession and the platitudes of their age. Holmes stands outside the system. His eccentricities emphasize the need of modern heroes to separate themselves from the assumptions held by less imaginative contemporaries (Dr. Watson among them). Yet he never questions the aristocracy or industrialism; he refuses to indict institutions; he does not threaten the established order even as he pursues clues, identifies malefactors, and brings them to justice. Clausen ends by remarking that the decline in artistic merit of the later stories was related to an increasing public faith in the police, as well as to a growing conviction that crime would not deal a mortal blow to civilization after all.

The remaining five essays in this part examine significant and rarely explored aspects of the Holmes-Watson stories that so frequently elicit love letters rather than serious criticism. Paul Barolsky, disturbed by what he regards as a strange neglect of a major consideration, examines the relationship of Holmes to the fin de siècle. Though one may scoff at the notion of Holmes as a "closet aesthete," the evidence amassed by Barolsky, linking the detective to Des Esseintes and Dorian Gray, is formidable. Holmes regards his profession as an art; he often speaks in the language patterns of an aesthete of the 1890s; he uses drugs to stimulate the senses; he relates details to overall impressions (his method resembles that of Bernard Berenson, who in turn was influenced by Pater); and he enjoys using "theatrical gifts." The essay concludes with an examination of the ways in which Holmes's ability to penetrate disguises looks forward to Nabokov's fictions.

Kim Herzinger's observation that dilettantism in Sherlock Holmes studies is defensible (she does a pretty good job of defending it) is based on the premise that Holmes repeatedly succeeds "in the resolution of cases beyond the mere commonplace," and does so by creating his own world "entirely." Detection, instead of being bound by the restrictions of law, has been converted by Holmes to an art. "Holmes is aroused by one thing, not by any thing," Herzinger states, "and it marks him as a dilettante, just as the kinds of cases he chooses mark him as an aesthete, an aesthete of detection." (The point resembles, but in subtle respects differs from, Barolsky's listing of the ways in which Holmes's character and method have affinities to those of the declared aesthetes of the 1890s.) Herzinger's essay, filled with provocative opinions and aperçus, redirects our attention to reader response, "the matter of [Holmes's] appeal."

Dr. Pasquale Accardo's analysis of how Dr. Joseph Bell influenced Doyle's concept of ideal medical practice is as good as any that has reached print. More important, the observation-and-deduction methodology of Dr. Bell was best put to use by Holmes himself. It is salutary to remember, as Dr. Accardo asks us to do, that Holmes's observations were not infallible; his diagnoses were frequently mistaken. But Holmes's willingness to risk doing something, to act boldly even when logic fails, is an integral element of his personality and, we should add, as Dr. Accardo does, accounts for many of his successes.

Barrie Hayne, in a full-length critique of the degree to which Holmes's behavior and conversation fulfill classic definitions of comedy, begins with a consideration of Watson's common sense, the necessary counterforce to Holmes's "fanciful or intuitive side." Holmes and Watson may be bonded in a "comic marriage," but it is only ostensibly that Watson seems comic (in terms of his obtuseness). Holmes, as Hayne does well to remind us, is a character of humors. Even as he guys the police he is capable of self-irony, and on occasion exhibits an attractive insouciance. The essay avoids exaggerated claims and recognizes the problems that may arise from underestimating the serious tone of cases based on the perpetration of serious crimes. Hayne reaches a strong finale in his argument that a "large sense of fun" runs through the stories, and that the society Doyle describes, though reared on reason, is "not always proof against the attacks of the irrational."

Lydia Alix Fillingham identifies a number of historical events that affected the imaginations of many Victorians: the creation of the Criminal Investigations Department, the astonishing growth of Mormonism in the New World, the proliferation of secret societies and brotherhoods throughout Europe, assassinations and bombings in Europe, and the increasingly violent history of Ireland in the latter years of the century. She notes accurately the interest of other writers in these themes, and the names of Robert Louis Stevenson and H. F. Wood, which she cites, might be augmented by dozens of others (including that of Henry James). They were becoming alarmed by a large, unstable, and anonymous population that was developing within the metropolitan areas of the kingdom; the growth of states within the State seemed to threaten stability. "Holmes's reticence incarnates and justifies the minimalist impulse of the Liberal state," Fillingham writes. Crime in Holmes's day could not be fought successfully until more information became available to the members of London's police force. Ultimately, the more efficient organization of the bureaucracy was to become intimately linked with the development of computerlike devices and filing systems; until the needed tools were at hand, however, Holmes, as an extragovernmental agent, was a necessary means whereby the "right questions" might be asked "to extract information already held by the bureaucracy." In other words, Holmes helped to "reconcile bureaucracy and the Liberal ideology."

II

Any fair-minded treatment must make room for the proposition that Doyle, as the author of *all* the Holmes stories, had a larger range of interests and exhibited more diverse talents than those stories were able to demonstrate. He was a writer of several historical romances that held their own in a strongly competitive market, and (it is worth repeating) he thought much more highly of them than he did of the Holmes stories. He was a novelist who touched on a number of modern social issues. He wrote histories of both the Boer War and the Great War that were not only popular but praised highly by military experts, reviewers, and the general public. He was an active practitioner in the short story genre. He pioneered in the field of science fiction. He wrote poetry that many people liked. He pursued contemporary political and ethical questions and wrote voluminously on criminal cases and what he considered to be miscarriages of justice. And all this gave way to the subject matter of spiritualism, on which he wrote a good deal and for which he gathered the materials of an impressive history.

Horace Green, in reviewing *Our Second American Adventure*, recalled that Tolstoy, "to the last," was ashamed of *Anna Karenina*.[20] Even though it was Tolstoy's most popular novel and exhibited a high degree of artistry, the Russian regarded it as a by-product, preferring instead the sermons he recorded, in narrative form, as *Resurrection* and *The Kreutzer Sonata*. A similar chagrin was present in Doyle's responses to interviewers who persisted in wanting to talk about a phase of his life that he had wanted to end only five years after the first Holmes story was published.

The Holmes stories will always form the most substantial contribution made by Doyle to world literature. Libraries throughout the world will retain Holmes collections long after most fictional works by Doyle's contemporaries have been discarded, sold off, or pulped. Nevertheless, Doyle wrote for a public that eagerly awaited whatever his subject matter might turn out to be, and many of his devoted readers shared his view as to the relative merits of his fictions. The importance of Holmes, in other words, was instantly recognized, but the possibility that the Holmes stories surpassed in literary value anything that Doyle wrote, or might write in the future, was not taken seriously by a large number of common readers until after the Great War.

The second part of this anthology reprints a representative selection of reviews and articles focusing on those "other writings." Such a gathering has not been made before, and perforce these writings constitute a miniaturized reception study of an extraordinarily popular writer, one whose active career as an author spanned almost a half-century. They demonstrate the respect reviewers felt for Doyle's talents, even when the reviewers believed that those talents were not worthily employed or when they argued that Doyle was operating below the level of his own best endeavor. Max Beerbohm, who had a genius for detecting literary fraud, regarded Doyle with good-humored affection, despite his conviction that Doyle was treating historical matters too liberally. George Bernard Shaw, customarily less forgiving of theatrical claptrap than Beerbohm, paid his respects to a playwright-actor collaboration that worked its magic successfully (in his review of *A Story of Waterloo*); assessed at their due worth the "ready-made feeling and prearranged effects" of such plays, wishing them a safe journey to the music hall, "which is their proper place now that we no longer have a 'Gallery of Illustration' "; but felt constrained to add, "I enjoy them, and am entirely in favour of their multiplication so long as it is understood that they are not the business of fine actors and first-class theatres." And Andrew Lang, possibly England's most influential reviewer before the advent of Arnold Bennett, spoke admiringly of Doyle's "old-fashioned notion that a novelist should tell us a plain tale," while enumerating, as a responsible critic should, the limitations of Doyle's artistic technique.

In all these notices of Doyle's publications one may sense more than the homage owed to a professional man of letters whose hits outnumbered his misses and who continued to turn out "product" year after year, in the manner of such professional entertainers as Hall Caine, Marie Corelli, Anthony Hope, and Rudyard Kipling. (These are the names on Lang's list, but there were many others whose action-filled narratives dominated the pages of mass-circulation periodicals in the 1880s and 1890s.) Practically all the critics genuinely liked Doyle as a personality, as a living force who made the commercial world of publishing a more colorful and exciting milieu. Their codicils and reservations did not subtract from their overall admiration. The anonymous commentator in the New York periodical *Critic* (20 July 1895) who wrote that Sherlock Holmes was not known to this generation "as well as Detective Bucket was to a previous generation" and who added that "It was not by one character that Dickens and Thackeray were known, but by a whole library full" was charmed by Doyle's diffidence about the modest fees he had earned on a lecture tour to the United States. Thackeray and Dickens had made money, and Doyle added, "When we have another Thackeray and Dickens, they may do the same."[21] (Doyle was not placing himself in that category; the critic liked him all the more for refusing to do so).

Critics regularly noted Doyle's failings: his lack of subtlety, his lapses from a strict standard of grammatical usage, his repetition of epithets as a shorthand device for characterization. But his virtues were inseparably bound up with his weaknesses as a literary artist, and were more important. An anonymous reviewer of *The Great Boer War* was appalled by the "distressing frequency" with which Doyle's infinitives fell apart but conceded that Doyle was both lucid and vigorous. As the song said, it "gets there all the same" by means "not too easy to analyse," and he acknowledged that Doyle had the art, "so conspicuous in Froude and Macaulay and J. R. Green, of luring the reader on, even when he is weary, from one paragraph to the next."[22] (Doyle was in the very best of company, placed there by a critic who perceived the rough-and-ready blemishes of a military history written under the pressures of a publishing deadline.)

James Payn's admiration of *The White Company* led him to the remarkable statement (one that must have pleased Doyle) "I have read nothing of the kind so good since *Ivanhoe*, with which it has many points of resemblance." Yet it is curious, and perhaps illuminating, that contemporary reviewers were less interested in comparing Doyle with the great romancers of the past than in comparing Doyle's latest work with his previous record of publications. Laurence Hutton thought that *The Refugees* "invited comparison with his own admirable work in the same kind." David Christie Murray, though he spoke of Edgar Allan Poe, Charles Reade, and Stanley Weyman, was most concerned by writing problems inevitable in the re-creation of past times— problems Doyle had confronted, and not always successfully solved, in novels prior to the writing of *Rodney Stone*.

The anonymous reviewer of *A Duet with an Occasional Chorus* did not enjoy the colorlessness of the main characters, the digressions about Poets' Corner and "the matrimonial relations of Mr. and Mrs. Carlyle," and the slenderness of the materials used. The critic apparently did not know enough about Doyle's life to respond to the strong autobiographical notes that were struck repeatedly throughout the narrative, but he did know Doyle's previous writings well. "The result," he wrote, "is a book, which is certainly quite unworthy of Mr. Conan Doyle's reputation, and which, indeed, considering the sort of work that he has accustomed his numerous admirers to expect from him, is, we cannot refrain from saying, a rather daring experiment on the docility of his public."

It is understandable that the occasion of the publication of a collected edition of Doyle's novels in 1903 should intensify this desire to see whether Doyle repeated or excelled himself in his later publications. The reviewer for the *Athenaeum* had no doubt that Doyle's many admirers believed that the time was ripe for such a claim of permanence, though he (like Doyle himself, be it noted) believed that others—Dickens for a certainty, probably Kipling for another, and Stevenson as well—better deserved the imprimatur. Correctly measuring Holmes's importance as "an ineffaceable part of the English language," the critic compared novels one with another and confessed some puzzlement as to the path of Doyle's future development: "Sir A. Conan Doyle would appear to be deserting letters for affairs, so that it is difficult at present to judge of his true quality as a writer of fiction."

Andrew Lang, an authority on the writings of Poe and Scott, had useful things to say about Doyle's degree of indebtedness to these originators of very different literary traditions. But he believed that Doyle's genius was distinctive, and not dependent, in whole or even in large measure, on what had gone before. Lang argued that those who admired Holmes did not necessarily know (or care) about Doyle's literary antecedents; it was enough that Doyle pleased "a great number and variety of his fellow-citizens," and a critic's captiousness might be written off as irrelevant to their enjoyment. All of which did not prevent Lang from severely censuring Doyle's slandering of the Adamanese in *The Sign of Four* (Lang's credentials as an expert in the newly developing science of anthropology were formidable), as well as Holmes's ignorance of "the ordinary British system of titles."

Lang's enjoyment of Doyle's unaffectedness, as expressed in the lengthy essay reprinted herein, was shared by all his fellow critics. Lang had little patience with those who imitated Meredith's ornate style. His admiration of

Doyle's vigorous narratives recognized, and put to one side, Doyle's willingness to employ trite phrases, his inability to speculate philosophically in ways that might educe character (as Fielding and Thackeray had done), and his dull rendering of female psychology. Doyle dealt with stereotypes, with good people all too readily distinguishable from bad. But "Sir Arthur can tell a story so that you read it with ease and pleasure," and that singular art could not be taught. No "research, or study, or industry" could substitute for it.

It is astonishing how often this line of argument was repeated in contemporary reviews of Doyle's works. It was not advanced apologetically, as if enjoyment of a storyteller's art had fallen somewhere under suspicion. Nor was it presented with exaggerated claims for Doyle's respectability as an artist, complete with references to the recognized literary masters of the past. It made due allowance for Doyle's honest expression of personal feeling.

I have included several reviews of Doyle's plays, not only *A Story of Waterloo* and *Rodney Stone* but *Fires of Fate* and *The House of Temperley*, to indicate that Doyle's relations to theater at the turn of the century were more intense, longer sustained, and (all things considered) more successful than many readers appreciate. One anonymous reviewer, pleased by the melodramatic flourishes of Doyle's adaptation of *The Speckled Band*, applauded Lyn Harding's portrayal of the villain Dr. Rylott: "so striking and diabolical a figure . . . that Sherlock Holmes in this instance is outdone."[23] Though the play had no surprises ("when once Dr. Rylott has been seen with his serpent, the mystery is one no longer"), it remained "good popular drama." Indeed, the play has never been wholly forgotten by amateur theatrical companies.

For that matter, Doyle's interest in lucidity and his conviction that what interested him would in turn interest a large audience led to the publication of two minor works, collections of poems, that found their audience immediately. Doyle proved correct in his assumptions about the existence of a large and faithful public interested in more than simply his ability to fictionalize crime cases. This anthology is not the place to reprint assessments of his writings on real-life criminal investigations—those involving Roger Casement, George Edalji, and Oscar Slater, among others—for the intention of Doyle, in each of these celebrated cases, was not to exploit the injustice of various legal decisions for literary profit but to argue in behalf of human beings whose right to fair trial procedures had been abused.

Also, though it is easy to accumulate a large number of essays analyzing the merits and limitations of Doyle's treatment of two great conflicts, the Boer War and the Great War, I have assumed from the beginning that readers will be better served by critiques of Doyle's literary works. Even so, it seems necessary to record one constant in such essays: appreciation of Doyle's success in setting forth a clear picture of the chain of reasoning whereby he reached any given conclusion. The defense of British soldiers against the charges of inhumanity, made in *The War in South Africa: Its Cause and Conduct*, was painstakingly mounted and duly noted by reviewers. The "admirable detachment" of Doyle's *A History of the Great War* impressed fellow historians and contemporary critics. As one reviewer wrote, "Occasionally, as in descriptions of phases of the first battle of Ypres, there are flashes of dramatic quality in the writing of the book. But for the most part it is a 'straightaway' narrative, depending for its force not upon any charm or intensity in its presentation, but upon its quiet, lucid, well-poised record of events."[24]

The last essay in this part, George E. Slusser's tribute to Doyle's pioneering work in the field of science fiction (however that genre may be defined), supplies a corrective to the view that H. G. Wells must always be remembered as England's first and best response to the storytelling challenge posed by Jules Verne. Doyle's concern with the impact of scientific advances on the way human beings define their relationship to the universe was serious, well informed, and imaginatively dynamic. (Indeed, one of his enduring characterizations was of an aptly named Professor Challenger.) Doyle, Slusser reminds us, "not only asserts man's involvement in the process of making machines but raises the question of human responsibility as well." This stimulating reconsideration of Doyle's science fiction tales adds an important element to our understanding of Doyle's formidable narrative powers and the uses to which he put them.

III

We come, finally, to Doyle's writings on spiritualism. Literary critics have found themselves no less baffled by the content of these writings than most readers who hoped to find in Doyle's latest publication a new Holmes adventure, a Professor Challenger escapade, a Brigadier Gerard story, or a narrative about times past. To say that during the last quarter-century of his life Doyle became increasingly obsessed by spiritualism as a cause is only to state a truism. It does not seem excessive to add that Doyle understood well the inherent potential of that obsession to damage his literary reputation. His more skeptical contemporaries scarcely knew what to say about his lectures on the subject, his "conversion," his investigations, his troubled relationship with the Society for Psychical Research, his noisy arguments with Houdini, or his faith in the sincerity of any number of mediums who held séances he attended. What might one say about either fairies or spirit communication with the dead, two major concerns of much of Doyle's writing from the Great War onward?

No consideration would be complete without acknowledgment of the signal importance of spiritualism in Doyle's imagination, or of his passionate belief that he had discovered new insights into the truth. His hostile critics he denounced as "bumptious and ignorant" in the final pages of *Memories and*

Adventures.[25] His rejection of Christianity was bound to offend many of his most devoted readers. "Am I not far nearer to my son than if he were alive and serving in that Army Medical Service which would have taken him to the ends of the earth?" he asked. "There is never a month, often never a week, that I do not commune with him. Is it not evident that such facts as these change the whole aspect of life, and turn the grey mist of dissolution into a rosy dawn?"[26] But what he regarded as facts, others regarded as mistaken opinion, delusion, or worse.

E. T. Raymond, in his treatment of what he obviously considered to be an aberration from social norms, preferred the Holmes stories to the historical romances, and the historical romances to the "spiritualistic expositions." Something (and Raymond did not seem to be sure just what) had gone wrong with Doyle's respect for the truth: Doyle's notion of evidence was "a little different from that accepted in the King's Bench." Raymond's call for a "friendly remonstrance" was that of a common reader, personally aggrieved that Doyle had abandoned his formidable gifts of storytelling for "vagaries."

More savage in his articulating of a widespread anger against fraudulent practices among spiritualists, Joseph Jastrow used the occasion of the publication of *The Wanderings of a Spiritualist* to denounce what he considered to be Doyle's abuse of the scientific method. Jastrow would have willingly conceded to Doyle the right to believe in spiritualism as "a religious consolation," but he was baffled by Doyle's insistence that ectoplasm could be photographed, and by Doyle's attempt to "offer messages to the bereaved." Not only baffled but disgusted. Jastrow's examination of Doyle's increasingly embittered relationship with newspapers that refused to credit his discoveries or to publicize further the manifestations of apparitions that had already been proved false by other investigators is an important reminder that Doyle never shirked from offending disbelievers, and that he often did so with a zest that alienated many who had hoped to remain neutral.

Jastrow's involvement with literary controversies was wider than simply a disagreement with Doyle's beliefs; Jastrow, a professor of psychology at the University of Wisconsin, held strong convictions about the impropriety of almost any attempt by an author of fiction to cross the boundary lines of the scientific disciplines that he defended. Nor was he the most hostile of Doyle's adversaries. Others wrote more searingly about Doyle's abdication of "good sense," his repudiation of Holmes's methods of ratiocination, and his heavy-handed method for disposing of information that contradicted his set positions. Relatively rare was the kind of column that Heywood Broun, on one notable occasion, contributed to the *Nation*. Broun did not believe in spiritualism, at least as practiced by Doyle's mediums. But he admired Doyle's sincerity, and he thought that the "ease of mind" Doyle had gained for himself and for others through espousal of his doctrines was sufficient justification for continuation along the path he was following, despite "jibes from the side lines." Broun noted, in a flash of shrewd insight, that the very creation of Holmes in the 1880s should have been marked, by careful observers, as "the first stage of a longer pilgrimage." (Studying this connection might well become the subject of an extended analysis.) "Most logically," Broun wrote, "a belief in spiritism grows out of a faith and fondness for Sherlock Holmes."

A scholarly essay by Jeffrey L. Meikle usefully sets the larger scene by reminding readers that Doyle's interest in spiritualism grew inevitably from his hatred of a narrow-minded Roman Catholicism, his mother's "merely nominal faith," his interest in the great agnostic scientists of the late Victorian age, his deepening involvement with the journal *Light*, his attendance at séances, and—perhaps most important—his intensifying sense of anguish caused by the holocaust of the Great War. His brother-in-law, his son, and his brother lost their lives at the front. His wife's newfound gift of automatic writing led to one "revelation" after another, and Doyle's extraordinary career suddenly became absorbed by a series of speaking engagements that far eclipsed—in frequency, passion, and popularity—any lecture tours in which he had previously been involved. Meikle's study, based on a careful review of primary documents, is as sympathetic toward Doyle as the evidence will allow. It is particularly good in its summation of Houdini's behavior (a sore point with many Doyle admirers) and of the fascination with Atlantis that led Doyle to champion the Arabian spirit Pheneas during the early 1920s. Many readers will subscribe to Meikle's view that Doyle, despite a "few pathetic lapses from his customarily strict ethical code," maintained an overall record "as a selfless campaigner for the world's moral reformation through spiritualism."

IV

The status of Doyle's posthumous reputation is not fixed; nor are even the most sympathetic critics certain as to what, beyond the Holmes stories, will survive. Moreover, the major lines of interpretation of the Holmes stories seem to be shifting. Perhaps, as critics deepen their consideration of Doyle's contributions to imaginative literature, a fuller appreciation of Doyle's personal attitude toward his detective stories will take hold. The excesses of some of the Baker Street Irregulars have irritated many admirers of the stories in the canon and have distracted readers from seeing Doyle steadily and whole. A current vogue for semiotic studies may serve to document the assertion that critics with specialized interests tend to write for one another rather than for the general public. As one example, *The Sign of Three: Dupin, Holmes, Peirce*, edited by Umberto Eco and Thomas A. Sebeok,[27] poses more difficulties as a critical approach than it ever successfully solves.

The emphasis on Doyle's literary antecedents must give way to a more fruitful line of investigation, one that establishes links between Doyle and his literary descendants.

Surely, enough has been said by now about Doyle's grammatical lapses. Charges of bad writing seem odd when the critic who levies such charges goes on to concede, with an air of sheepishness, that Doyle's ability to tell a good story is hardly in question.

And perhaps more than enough has been said about Holmes as a "reptilian" character, or Watson as a "commonplace" individual whose only function is to set off Holmes's genius. Such debunking articles inspire wonder that their authors ever found attractive the task of writing about the Holmes stories in the first place.

Doyle once claimed that he had pioneered in creating a fictional hero whose adventures, in issue after issue of the same periodical, sustained his readers' interest. The assumption of that kind of originality was unwarranted; other authors had preceded him in stimulating readers to care about what happened next to a hero or heroine. But Doyle, because of the unusually long run of Holmes's adventures, supplied the audience that subscribed to, purchased, or read individual copies of The *Strand Magazine* with an extraordinary fund of information about Holmes and Watson. He thickened the outlines of his great detective by making his character far more than a catalog of idiosyncratic habits: the 7 percent solution of cocaine, the violin playing, the chemical experiments, the esoteric interests. Holmes and Watson were consistent despite relatively minor discrepancies between one story and the next. Readers became confident that they recognized the wholeness of Holmes and Watson as human beings, and knew them as well as they thought they knew members of their own families.

In the essays I have chosen for the first part of this anthology, Doyle's creation of a late Victorian world is stressed even more than his astonishing gifts for characterization. The direction of much Doyle criticism in the coming decades will probably concentrate on the extent to which the Holmes stories resemble and differ from the historical truth of what went on in the 1880s and 1890s. Doyle's London was so solid and three-dimensional that its images of Whitehall, dock areas, railway platforms, hotel lobbies, and fogbound streets have convinced Londoners (fully as much as overseas visitors) that they were, and always will be, definitive.

It is likely that future writers on the canon will want to explore the relationship between Holmes and the late Victorian concept of a scientist. The positiveness with which Holmes constructed his links of reasoning was not all that dissimilar from the certitude, held by many Victorian scientists, that answers to all questions about nature might be discovered if the questions were properly framed. As the twentieth century wanes, that conviction now seems unwarranted by the state of knowledge existing in almost any scientific discipline one might name. The more information we possess, the less likely we are to believe that we are close to drawing boundary lines around what remains unknown. But a little over 100 years ago, Doyle could indulge his fictional hero, who believed in the closeness of the correlations between his knowledge of discrete physical facts and the reality underlying the existence of those facts.

A study of the ways in which Holmes is like and unlike the detectives of his own times—the detective story of the late Victorian age was much more popular than most critics realize when they speak of Doyle's "originality"—would be similarly instructive. A large part of the appeal of the Holmes stories rested on the variety of puzzles solved; though written to order and bound by conventions Doyle willingly imposed on himself, these narratives were not restricted to crimes committed within locked rooms. Doyle obviously delighted in the ingenuity of problems he posed, problems no ordinary detective could be expected to solve.

The connections between Doyle's source materials (often newspaper clippings) and the finished Holmes stories deserve fuller treatment than they have received. Fully one-fourth of Holmes's adventures have nothing to do with a legally definable crime. Analyzing the kinds of information Doyle selected for construction of his stories would require the compilation of an ingeniously cross-filed dossier, and an investigator would have to evaluate the kinds of information Doyle omitted as well.

Holmes, like anyone of his time, knew a number of things that later research has invalidated. He believed that the influence of heredity on criminal psychology was greater than modern criminologists credit. He entertained a number of unworthy prejudices against entire classes of people. His views on the nature of memory, the workings of the mind, and women in general were occasionally ill-formed or ill-tempered. The study of Holmes as an essentially Victorian man of the middle classes, complete with prejudices that occasionally prevented him from understanding the data of a given crime, has surprisingly often been slighted in favor of a eulogistic treatment of all the ways in which Holmes's knowledge and intuition led directly to the solving of a crime, or anticipated future developments in criminology. (That favorite figure of nineteenth-century fiction, the boardinghouse bachelor who appears to defy social norms by not marrying, has scarcely been studied in relation to the most extraordinary bachelor of all.) A careful study of Holmes as a representative of his class will, however, have to take into account the fact—noted by Christopher Sykes, among others—that Holmes rises in class during the series: he first becomes known to us as a person from a commonplace background but eventually emerges transfigured as "a University man, with strong College loyalties," able to converse on an equal level with "the bloods in all spheres."[28]

All of which suggests that Holmes, as an individual and as a sociocultural phenomenon, will survive closer scrutiny, and remain a fascinating focus of interest.

Possible directions in future scholarship about the rest of Doyle's creative writings—more than 100 short stories, novels, plays, and poems—may be charted partly on the basis of what is reprinted here and partly on the basis of current trends in critical analysis for other Victorian authors. Not enough has been done with Doyle's self-conscious relationship to the Scott tradition of storytelling. *Micah Clarke His Statement as Made to His Three Grandchildren Joseph, Gervas, & Reuben During the Hard Winter of 1734* is, among other things, a novel that imagines Jeffreys and Monmouth interacting with vividly sketched personalities like Colonel Decimus Sexton and Sir Gervas Jerome as well as Micah Clarke himself; the extent to which Doyle drew on histories of Cromwell's era and the degree of Doyle's skill in authenticating character, setting, and event deserve renewed consideration. It is not particularly useful to say (as Doyle's contemporaries sometimes did) that the Scott tradition had played itself out. Historical romances very much like *Ivanhoe* are written to this day, and are widely read; the British statesman who exclaimed, "Bring me a novel to read. Bring me something that is *true*. Don't bring me history, for that, I *know*, is a lie," spoke for countless thousands who formed Doyle's audience at the turn of the century, and their hunger for a fiction they could believe in cannot easily be dismissed. Doyle's use of Scott went far beyond the mingling of historical figures like Cromwell, the Pretender, and Napoleon with fictional creations of his own. "There is a French chevalier," wrote one reviewer of *The Great Shadow*, "who is more real, more historical, than any French chevalier known to history."[29] Poetry, as the ancients knew, incorporates a higher truth than conventional history can ever hope to do.

Closely related to this concern is the question that Doyle's biographers often treat and sometimes fumble: how autobiographical are Doyle's stories? One critic complained that the hero of *The Stark Munro Letters* spoke too directly for the author: "It is his creator's fortune to be himself a medical man, and his misfortune to have views upon religion and upon various social problems. The book is full of the slang of the surgery, enlivened by interpolated disquisitions on subjects which are beyond the writer's reach."[30] He was attacking what he believed to be Doyle's views on religion before he addressed the substance of the hero's opinions, without analyzing the characterizing function of such views within the novel. Moreover, the possibility that Doyle was playing variations on the whole concept of authorial omniscience has not been seriously treated by critics. It deserves to be, if only because Doyle, well read in the novels of both Great Britain and of France, was duly aware of the controversy about the proper distance to be maintained between storytellers and the events they recounted.

Two intertwined problems exist here: the right of an author to speak in propria persona and the right of a critic to censure the interference of an author in the unfolding of a story. The anonymous poet of *Punch* who complained, *Whenever someone's going strong,/Sir A. dispatches several pages/To tell how codes of right and wrong/Have altered since the Middle Ages*[31] had a point: "speechifying" introduced an alien element to the story, a "booklore-laden atmosphere" that "knights don't really care for." But this too may turn out, on closer examination, to be still another convention of the Scott historical romance, and Scott, after all, did not invent the historical romance.

A full-scale treatment of Doyle's adventures in the Victorian and Edwardian theater would do much to inform readers of the ways in which he adapted stories originally written for another medium, the compromises that Doyle made to actor-managers to get his plays on the boards, and his relationships with actors and actresses in general.

It goes without saying—but perhaps should be said nevertheless—that the quality of Doyle's writings as a historian of two major wars should be reassessed. Are lucidity and vigor sufficient to redeem Doyle's overstatements about gallantry on the fighting front, his overconfident expressions of faith in the permanence of the British Empire (despite temporary setbacks), his unwillingness to criticize military tactics that turned out badly, and the incompleteness of his evidence (not always appreciated by Doyle himself)? How much of Doyle's *The War in South Africa: Its Cause and Conduct* is special pleading—for example, his defense of British soldiers against the charges of inhumanity? Were Boer mothers—with their "natural instinct" to cling to their children, thereby preventing them from being moved into quarantine— more responsible for the excessive mortality of minors than the British who created overcrowded conditions in the camps? Were the Boers *wholly* committed to a disregard of "the recognized rules of warfare"?[32]

As for the Great War, did Doyle concentrate too much on the British role in the fighting at the expense of the French (who, after all, lost 25 percent of their troops in the Battle of the Frontiers in the first six months and a half-million more at Verdun)? Did Doyle, like other war historians, accept too credulously the information supplied to him by generals and officers, who had vested interests to defend? For that matter, was his optimistic conclusion to *The British Campaign in France and Flanders* justified by the evidence that he himself had collected? Pierre Nordon, whose summary of Doyle's work as historian is more thoughtful and detailed than any other treatment in print, saw Doyle's restraint as the primary virtue of his account of the Great War: "The book is in fact a memorial to the fighting-men, in the form of a narrative which he tried to make as plain and unadorned as possible."[33]

Many of Doyle's miscellaneous writings—on divorce-law reform, home rule for Ireland, tariff questions relating particularly to the Scottish woolen industry, unjustly accused prisoners like Oscar Slater and George Edalji, Congo crimes, the civilian national reserve, polemical pamphlets supporting the Allied cause, and even the travel books reviewing his adventures on three continents—have served their day and will not attract much critical attention in the future.

Nevertheless, Doyle's prolific output on questions relating to paranormal phenomena requires consideration if we hope to appreciate the full dimensions of his career. Beginning with *The New Revelation* (1918), Doyle became swiftly and completely obsessed with the problem of how to make sense of that land from whose bourn no traveler returns. There followed *Life after Death* (1918), *The Vital Message* (1919), *Our Reply to the Cleric* (1920), *Spiritualism and Rationalism* (1920), *The Wanderings of a Spiritualist* (1921), *The Coming of the Fairies* (1922), *Spiritualism—Some Straight Questions and Direct Answers* (1922), *The Case for Spirit Photography* (1922), *The Early Christian Church and Modern Spiritualism* (1925), *Psychic Experiences* (1925), *The History of Spiritualism* (1926), *Pheneas Speaks* (1927), *Spiritualism* (1927), *What Does Spiritualism Actually Teach and Stand For?* (1928), *A Word of Warning* (1928), *An Open Letter to Those of My Generation* (1929), *The Roman Catholic Church—A Rejoinder* (1929), *A Form Letter* and *A Second Form Letter* (1930), and *The Edge of the Unknown* (1930). The intensity of feeling recorded in these publications suggests that biographers and critics who ignore a full one-third of Doyle's life do so at their peril.

At least three avenues of promise stretch before us. The first has to do with the fact that Doyle believed himself to be among the new intelligentsia in the early decades of this century. He aligned himself with Sir Oliver Lodge, Sir William Barrett, Sir William Crookes, General Sir Alfred Turner, Dr. Ellis T. Powell, and Lady Glenconner: men and women who had achieved distinction in widely disparate fields and who were united in their dissatisfaction with orthodox religion's answers to spiritual questions. The explanation of why Doyle so completely trusted his colleagues in the search for final answers must be sought in a fuller history of ideas, especially those relating to late Victorian attitudes toward science, than has thus far been written.

A second promising study would extend Doyle's interest in spiritualism to see whether it exists in his own creative works published before 1918. Some investigators have studied Holmes's disdain for supernatural explanations of wordly crimes as if that were the only note about spiritualism struck in the canon (which is not true). Biographical considerations must be taken into account (the nature and quality of the influence exerted by Mary Doyle, the importance of Michael Conan as godfather, Doyle's revulsion against his Jesuit-dominated education, and the conversations Doyle held with Dr. Bryan Waller, as well as Doyle's readings in Spencer, Darwin, and Huxley) if we are to assess fairly the rumblings about religion that are to be found in *The Stark Munro Letters, Micah Clarke, The Refugees*, and even *The White Company. The Poison Belt* (1913), second of the Professor Challenger novels, has been reexamined by Dana Martin Batory and found to signal Doyle's acceptance of a life after death: "Convinced by thirty years of Spiritualistic study that out conduct in this life quite possibly affects our understanding in the next, Doyle was trying to frighten his readers into moral reform— but instead of the usual foreign invasion to scare the English, Doyle warned all of humanity by summoning the Apocalypse."[34] This may overstate the case for a straight-and-steady line of development in Doyle's thinking about suprasensory possibilities, but the older line of thinking about a clear break between the "earlier materialistic Doyle" and the later Doyle who argued for the power of spiritual forces ("a vapor which used to be called animal magnetism, or odyllic force, but is now called ectoplasm, issues from certain specially endowed persons") are reductive. After all the debris of hostile criticism has been cleared away, Doyle's speculations about spiritualism as a new religion that might unite men and women of goodwill everywhere may be traced back to his childhood. They certainly lie imbedded in a surprisingly large number of his fictions.

A third interesting research possibility has to do with the way in which Doyle's ideas about spiritualism were received, contradicted or rejected, endlessly debated, and occasionally welcomed, even by those who had no patience with mediums and séances. A detailed reception study would be welcome. Doyle was one of the most visible literary figures of England, quoted as an authority on all kinds of topics almost as frequently as H. G. Wells or George Bernard Shaw; though not always believed, he was given credit for believing what he wrote, for writing in good faith. Some contemporary critics patronized his ideas as puerile, unworthy of the man who had created Sherlock Holmes. Others agreed with Doyle's basic proposition, that the evidence relating to the spiritualism movement had to be evaluated carefully because "the sources of all force" could be traced "rather to spiritual than to material causes."[35] Doyle would never have maintained that his involvement with spiritualism had much to do with the good health of literature, or even the nurturing of his own literary talents. But he was justified in saying, as he did in the concluding lines of *Memories and Adventures*, "For my part, I can only claim that I have been an instrument so fashioned that I have had some particular advantages in getting this teaching across to the people."[36]

We cannot and must not subdivide Doyle. From first to last he remained a fearless fighter for the truth as he believed it to be. He is worth getting to know—more so than we have known him in the past.

Notes

1. Ronald Burt De Waal, ed., *The World Bibliography of Sherlock Holmes and Doctor Watson* (New York: Bramhall House, 1974).

2. Ronald Burt De Waal, ed., *The International Sherlock Holmes* (Hamden, Conn.: Archon Books; London: Mansell, 1980).

3. The *New York Times*, 11 January 1991, C14.

4. Quoted by Cait Murphy, "The Game's Still Afoot," *The Atlantic*, Vol. 259, No. 3 (March 1987): 61. Hereafter cited as Murphy.

5. Murphy, 58.

6. Raymond Blathwayt, "A Talk with Dr. Conan Doyle," *Bookman* [London], Vol. II, No. 8 (May 1892): 50–51. Hereafter cited as Blathwayt.

7. Blathwayt, 51.

8. Blathwayt, 51.

9. Harry How, "A Day with Dr. Conan Doyle," The *Strand Magazine/An Illustrated Monthly*, Vol. IV (August 1892): 182–83.

10. Silas K. Hocking, *My Book of Memory/A String of Reminiscences and Reflections* (London: Cassell and Company, Ltd., 1923), 153. Hereafter cited as Hocking.

11. Hocking, 153.

12. Sir Arthur Conan Doyle, *Memories and Adventures* (Boston: Little, Brown and Company, 1924), 94. Hereafter cited as *Memories*.

13. Mortimer Menpes, *War Impressions: being a record in colour*, transcribed by Dorothy Menpes (London: Charles Black, 1901), 151. Doyle's comment, made to the famous artist Menpes in Bloemfontein, South Africa, during the Boer War, was repeated many times in various interviews over the next three decades.

14. Arthur Conan Doyle, "Sherlock Holmes on the Screen," *Arthur Conan Doyle on Sherlock Holmes: Speeches at the Stoll Convention Dinner, an Exchange of Rhymed Letters*, with an introduction by Roger Lancelyn Green (London: Favil Press, 1981), 5–6.

15. See, for example, Ian Ousby's *Bloodhounds of Heaven/The Detective in English Fiction from Godwin to Doyle* (Cambridge, Massachusetts: Harvard University Press, 1976), 171–75.

16. Keith Simpson, *Sherlock Holmes on Medicine and Science* (New York: *Magico Magazine*, 1983), 22. Hereafter cited as Simpson. Cf. A. E. Murch, *The Development of the Detective Novel* (London: Peter Owen, 1978), 182–85, for a gloomy assessment of Holmes's limited awareness of recent developments in criminological science.

17. Simpson, 23.

18. Simpson, 26.

19. *Memories*, 102.

20. The *New York Times*, 25 May 1924, Section 3, 17.

21. "The Lounger," *Critic* [New York], 20 July 1895.

22. *Literature*, 3 November 1900, 341.

23. *Athenaeum*, No. 4311 (11 June 1910): 716.

24. Anonymous, "Conan Doyle's History of the War," The *New York Times*, 21 January 1917, Section 6, 18.

25. *Memories*, 396.

26. *Memories*, 397.

27. *The Sign of the Three: Dupin, Holmes, Peirce*, Umberto Eco and Thomas A. Sebeok, eds., (Bloomington: Indiana University Press, 1983).

28. Christopher Sykes, "The Baker Street Case," *Books and Bookmen* [London] (August 1977): 34.

29. Laurence Hutton, "Literary Notes," *Harper's New Monthly Magazine* (March 1893): 348.

30. G. W. Smalley, *New York Herald*, 13 October 1895; reprinted in *Literary Digest* [New York], 26 October 1895, 761.

31. *Punch*, Vol. 131 (12 December 1906): 432.

32. Anonymous, "Dr. Conan Doyle on the Boer War," *Outlook* [New York], 1900, 128–29.

33. Pierre Nordon, *Conan Doyle* (London: Murray, 1966), 99.

34. Dana Martin Batory, "*The Poison Belt* as a Morality Tale," *Riverside Quarterly*, Vol. VII, No. 2 (March 1982): 100.

35. *Memories*, 398.

36. *Memories*, 399.

SHERLOCK HOLMES

◆

Dr. Watson's Christian Name

Dorothy L. Sayers

It has always been a matter of astonishment to Dr. Watson's friends, and perhaps of a little malicious amusement to his detractors, to observe that his wife[1] apparently did not know her own husband's name. There can be no possible doubt that Watson's first Christian name was John. The name "John H. Watson" appears, conspicuously and in capital letters, on the title-page of *A Study in Scarlet*,[2] and it is not for one moment to be supposed that Watson, proudly contemplating the proofs of his first literary venture, would have allowed it to go forth into the world under a name that was not his. Yet in 1891 we find Watson publishing the story of *The Man with the Twisted Lip*, in the course of which Mrs. Watson addresses him as "James."

Mr. H. W. Bell (*Sherlock Holmes and Dr. Watson*, p. 66, n. 2) has been unable to account for this, and despairingly suggests that it is a mere printer's error. "Watson," he remarks, with much truth, "was a very careless reader of proof." But if he had read the proofs *at all*, this particular error could not have failed to catch his eye. A man's own name is a subject on which he is sensitive; nothing is more exasperating than to be "called out of one's name." Moreover, in December, 1891, Mary Watson was still alive. Tenderly devoted as she was to her husband, she could not have failed to read his stories attentively on publication in the *Strand Magazine*, and she would have undoubtedly drawn his attention to an error so ridiculous and immediately reflecting on herself. In the month immediately preceding, the Doctor had made another trivial slip in connection with his wife's affairs; he said that during the period of the adventure of *The Five Orange Pips* Mrs. Watson was visiting her mother. Mrs. Watson, who was, of course, an orphan (*Sign of Four*), evidently took pains to point out this error and see that the careless author made a note of it; for on the publication of the collected *Adventures* in 1892 the word "mother" is duly corrected to "aunt."[3] On such dull matters as dates and historical facts the dear woman would offer no comment, but on any detail affecting her domestic life she would pounce like a tigress. Yet the name "James" was left unaltered in all succeeding editions of the story.

From *Unpopular Opinions* (London: Victor Gollancz Ltd., 1946), 148–51. Reprinted by permission of David Higham Associates Ltd.

How are we to explain this?

The solution is probably to be sought in a direction which has been too little explored by the commentators. In fact, the whole subject of Dr. Watson's second Christian name has been treated with a levity and carelessness which are a positive disgrace to scholarship.

Mr. S. C. Roberts (*Dr. Watson*, p. 9) suggests, without an atom of evidence, that Watson's mother was "a devout woman with Tractarian leanings," merely in order to presume that her son was named "John Henry" after the great Newman himself. If there were, in Dr. Watson's character, the slightest trace of Tractarian sympathies, or even of strong anti-Tractarian sympathies, the suggestion might carry some weight, for no one could be brought up in an atmosphere of Tractarian fervour without reacting to it in one way or another. But Watson's religious views remain completely colourless. Of Holmes' beliefs we know little, but of Dr. Watson's, nothing. The hypothesis is purely frivolous.

Mr. H. W. Bell, with his wonted scholarly caution, rejects the Newman theory. "It must be objected," he says (*Sherlock Holmes and Dr. Watson, loc. cit.*), "that Newman had become a Catholic in 1845, seven years before the date which Mr. Roberts proposes for Watson's birth. If Mrs. Watson had indeed had . . . Tractarian leanings . . . she would hardly have named her son after the illustrious convert." But Mr. Bell makes no effort to solve the problem himself, although this observation actually forms part of his note about the name "James." The true solution was staring him in the face, and if he had given the matter proper attention he must have seen it. But he dismissed "James" as a typographical error and went on his way, leaving the Watsons still enveloped in a cloud of ridicule.

Mr. T. S. Blakeney behaves still more absurdly. Postulating a composite James-John authorship, he calls for a J. M. Robertson to "sift the accretions of the pseudo-Watson from the core of matter deriving solely from the hand of the veritable John Henry"—forgetting that John *Henry* Watson is even more conjectural than *Jesus* Barabbas,[4] and thus making the fabulous name into a guarantee of the genuine identity. Illogicality could go no further.[5]

There is only one plain conclusion to be drawn from the facts. Only one name will reconcile the appellation James with the initial letter H. The doctor's full name was John Hamish Watson.

Hamish is, of course, the Scottish form of James. There is no reason to feel any surprise that Dr. Watson should bear a Scottish name. Sturdily and essentially English as he was, he may well, like most English people, have had a Scottish ancestor in his family tree. The English are probably the only people in the world who actually make a boast of mongrel ancestry. The words "hundred per cent. English" are never heard on true English lips, for the English know well enough that their cross-breeding is their strength. Scotsmen, Welshmen, Irishmen, Jews cling to the purity of their descent, realising that to blend their nationality is to lose it. But English blood is so strong that one drop of it will make the whole blend English. A hundred Scottish ancestors, nay, even a Scottish mother, would in no way affect the indomitable Englishry of Dr. Watson.

In fact, there is some slight evidence for a Scots strain in Watson. It may not be mere coincidence that led Holmes (a shrewd student of national character) to select the adjective "pawky" for the vein of humour which Watson displayed during the adventure of *The Valley of Fear* and which took his distinguished friend a little aback. Watson's mother may have been a Scot—not, I think, a Highland woman, but a native of Eastern Scotland[6]— and it may have pleased her to give a Scottish name to her son.

But there is no real need to assume Scottish descent to explain a Scottish name. The English, with their romantic love of the outlandish, their tendency to concoct a mixed genealogy for themselves, and their incurable disdain for other people's racial sensitiveness, are notorious for their habit of annexing foreign names, merely because they think them pretty or poetical. The suburbs of London swarm with Douglases and Donalds, Malcolms and Ians, whose ancestors never crossed the border, with Patricks and Brians and Sheilas who owe nothing to Erin, with Gwladyses whose names are spelled according to fancy and not to inheritance, and with other exotics still more remote. The combination John Hamish Watson has nothing about it that need disconcert us.

Nor is it at all unusual for a wife to call her husband by his second name, in preference to his first. It is a pretty thought that he should be known to her by a name which is not the common property of the outside world. Possibly Mrs. Watson did not care for the name John. It was painfully connected in her mind with Major John Sholto, who had helped to ruin her father and bring about his death. "Johnnie" would be open to the same objection; besides, no one with any sense of the fitting would call Dr. Watson "Johnnie." There seems to be nothing specially objectionable about "Jack," but it may have seemed to her too flippant and jaunty. The probability, however, is that she preferred to cut out all association with "John." There remained the choice between "Hamish" and a pet-name. "Hamish" seemed to her perhaps a little highfalutin. By playfully re-Englishing it to "James" she found for her husband a pet-name which was his own name as well; a name by which no one else would think of calling him, a name free from the tiresome skittishness of the ordinary pet-name, and a name eminently suitable to his solid and sober character.[7]

It would be natural enough that Dr. Watson, accustomed for over three years to being called "James" by his wife, should automatically incorporate the name into his story when reproducing the dialogue between his Mary and himself—forgetting that, to the uninstructed reader, it might present an odd appearance. Nor would Mrs. Watson correct it. To her, the doctor was "her James"; that she should be supposed to call him by any other name would seem to her unnatural, almost improper. Smilingly she perused the pages of the *Strand*, delighted to recognise herself and her home life accurately portrayed in all the glory of print.

Notes

1. His first wife, and only true love, Mary, *née* Morstan. There is a conspiracy afoot to provide Watson with as many wives as Henry VIII, but, however this may be, only one is ever mentioned by him and only one left any abiding memory in his heart.

2. It also appears, plainly marked in capitals, at the foot of the sketch-plan illustrating *The Priory School*.

3. It appears from this that Watson, with a shyness not uncommon in authors, did not show his wife either his manuscript or his proofs. After publication he would probably leave the *Strand* carelessly lying about the house to be dutifully perused by Mary, to his deprecatory astonishment.

4. For the complicated structure of deduction built by Drews and others upon this highly disputable reading, see Thorburn, *Mythical Interpretation of the Gospels*, pp. 264 *sqq*.

5. It is only justice to add that Mr. S. C. Roberts lost no time in pointing out this lamentable confusion between "objective data and legitimate surmise" and deprecating it with equal firmness and courtesy (*Observer*, October 30th, 1932).

6. The true Highlander is a Celt—quick-tempered, poetical, and humourless—everything that Watson was not. Dourness and pawkishness belong to the Aberdeen side of the country.

7. An interesting parallel case of the interchangeability of "James" and "Hamish" occurs in Mrs. Wood's novel, *The Channings*: "The eldest son of the family, James; or, as he was invariably styled, Hamish." This book was extremely popular in the 'nineties, achieving its hundred-and-fortieth thousand in 1895, and may actually have suggested the idea to Mrs. Watson.

"Ring for Our Boots"

Arthur Marshall

How often do we quote Doctor Watson, but how sadly few are the details about him that we can call to mind. We remember his indignant outbursts and his cry of "Good Heavens, Holmes! This is intolerable," on hearing that their rooms at 221 Baker Street have been set on fire by Professor Moriarty. We remember his tendency ("My head is in a whirl") to be somewhat easily baffled. We remember, of course, his firm grasp of the obvious:

> Sherlock Holmes had not come back yet. It was nearly ten o-clock before he entered, looking pale and worn. He walked up to the sideboard, and, tearing a piece from the loaf, he devoured it voraciously. . . .
>
> "You are hungry," I remarked.

But this cannot be all, and two questions immediately present themselves: Whatever became of Mrs. Watson (prominent in *The Sign of Four*), and what, if anything, was Doctor Watson's practice?

Indefatigable as he was in reporting at length over fifty of the cases, Doctor Watson inexcusably excites us by the mention of twenty-two of which we have nothing but the bare names. A little more assiduity and a little less harping on his leg (wounded in the Afghan Campaign and apt to throb in wet weather), and we should have at command such matters as Mrs. Farintosh and the Opal Tiara, Ricoletti of the Club Foot and his Abominable Wife, The Singular Affair of the Aluminium Crutch, and The Tragedy of the Atkinson Brothers at Trincomalee. He tantalises us further with The Vatican Cameos, The Sudden Death of Cardinal Tosca, The Card Scandal at the Nonpareil Club, and The Affair of the Bogus Laundry (the mangles, one supposes, were disguised counterfeiting apparatus). Watson could hardly claim, as you shall see, that marital or professional obligations encroached seriously upon his time. Nor will the plea that some of the cases were "complete failures" appeal to the amateurs among us. We know the correct methods, then let us apply them to the affair of "Isadore Persano, the well-known journalist and duellist, who was found stark staring mad with a

From *New Statesman and Nation* (25 September 1948): 256–57. Reprinted by permission of *New Statesman and Society*.

match-box in front of him which contained a remarkable worm, said to be unknown to science."

But to Watson's marriage. Despite "an experience of women which extends over many nations and three separate continents" it is to Lower Camberwell that Doctor Watson comes for his bride and to the house of a Mrs. Cecil Forrester. Within is a "needy governess" with blue eyes, Miss Mary Morstan, attired, for our first view, in "sombre, greyish beige . . . and a small turban of the same dull hue." The Doctor, badly smitten, has "never looked upon a face which gave a clearer promise of a refined and sensitive nature." The respectability of Lower Camberwell plays its part in the furthering of the romance:

> As we drove away, I stole a glance back, and I still seem to see that little group on the step—the two graceful, clinging figures, the half-opened door, the hall-light shining through stained glass, the barometer and the bright stair-rods. It was soothing to catch even that passing glimpse of a tranquil English home.

Miss Morstan is similarly enraptured with the Doctor, with his moustache and his square jaw and the Afghan tales which enliven his conversation. Her joy, poor girl, is brief. Her share of the Agra Treasure is dropped, bauble by bauble, into the Thames by Jonathan Small, and after a few months of married life in Paddington ("complete happiness" though it was) the Doctor, hot for Holmes, leaves her repeatedly. Occasionally, before departure, he "dashes upstairs" to inform her, but once in Baker Street she is totally forgotten. Small wonder that latterly she is often "away upon a visit" or "on a visit to her aunt's." We can but admire her demeanour: loving and dutiful to the end, she fades gradually from the picture, playing graciously into her selfish husband's hands ("Oh, Anstruther would do your work for you. You have been looking a little pale lately. I think the change would do you good. . . ."). And so into oblivion, in what manner we do not know, curtly dismissed in a passing reference to "my recent sad bereavement."

But, once in Baker Street, what chance would even an experienced charmer have had against the fascinator in the "mouse-coloured dressing-gown"? The world is well lost indeed when Holmes springs to his feet crying "Ring for our boots and tell them to order a cab." And off the hansom jingles to Stepney or Covent Garden or Bloomsbury or Holborn, or even to Saxe-Coburg Square. There are trips to Croydon, the Cornish Peninsula, Brixton Workhouse, and "the pretty Surrey village of Esher." There are thrilling peeps into private houses: The Myrtles, Beckenham, Laburnum Villa, Hammersmith, or Briarbrae, Woking. Every call was obediently answered: "Come at once if convenient," telegraphs Holmes, "if inconvenient come all the same," and off scuttles the Doctor, complete with jemmy and dark lantern and chisel, to Goldini's Restaurant, Gloucester Road. London, the outer suburbs and the Southern Counties are the most productive; there appears to have been little serious crime (*The Stockbroker's Clerk*) farther north than Birmingham. Back in Baker Street, with the Borgia jewel deftly prized from the last of the six Napoleon busts, there can be no thought of rest: "Put the pearl in the safe, Watson," orders Holmes, "and get out the papers of the Conk-Singleton forgery case."

A less-devoted slave might well have found some of Holmes' habits a little wearing to the nerves. The constant "ping" of the hypodermic and the frequent snatches upon the violin (a Stradivarius, picked up in the Tottenham Court Road for fifty-five shillings) would perhaps have been bearable if they had been the only idiosyncrasies. They were not. There were the "weird and often malodorous scientific experiments" and, more alarmingly, the "occasional revolver practice within doors." There were the "devouring of sandwiches at irregular hours" and the tendency to awaken Watson before dawn on frosty winter mornings (insupportable, even if it meant a trip to Chislehurst). There were the biting of the nails, the times when he "ran out and ran in," the refusal to make small-talk with the chatty Doctor, the clouds of the strongest shag tobacco. There was, horror of horrors, a recital at the St. James' Hall with Holmes "gently waving his long thin fingers in time to the music."

To offset these failings, Watson had, it must be allowed, much to intrigue him in Holmes' conversation. One's own reminiscences, even when about Afghanistan, are apt to pall and Holmes could hold forth on matters other than crime, passing lightly from severed thumbs to Warships of the Future, from clubbed skulls to the Bertillon System of Measurements, from suffocated peeresses to Miracle Plays. Watson had to learn about The Polyphonic Motets of Lassus and both Mediaeval and Chinese Pottery (including "the marks of the Hung-wu and the beauties of the Yung-lo and the writings of Tang-ying"). To what extent the good Doctor's education had been previously neglected we cannot say. He can bring out a Latin quotation of fourteen words but of his school days we know nothing except that he had been "intimately associated with a lad named Percy [or "Tadpole"] Phelps," nephew of Lord Holdhurst, and that it had been considered "piquant" to "chivy him about the playground and hit him over the shins with a wicket." We can, perhaps, safely assume that Holmes, with his instructive chatter, was not wasting his time. Phelps turns up again at the time of *The Naval Treaty* when "he was still weak after his long illness and his misfortunes made him querulous and nervous." Doctor Watson advances upon the invalid and endeavours ("in vain," alas) to distract him with tales of (can you guess?) Afghanistan.

One would, I think, hardly have cared to be one of Doctor Watson's patients. He was so seldom there. However, there was at first some pretence of being concerned with medicine, and he purchased "a connection in the Paddington district" from "Old Mr. Farquhar." The tottering practice (Old

Mr. Farquhar suffered from "an affliction of the nature of St. Vitus' Dance") had three advantages: it was better than the practice next door (Holmes observed that the step was worn three inches lower), there was a convenient substitute at hand, and it was near a station where "railway cases were seldom trivial." For three months he worked hard but the wretched man's heart was never in it ("My practice is never very absorbing") and after that it was simply fits and starts, cases "of great gravity" and "pressing professional business" alternating with absences of days at a time. How listless the bed-side manner must have been. Sometimes even Holmes points out the path of duty: "You want to go home, no doubt, Doctor?" "Yes, it would be as well," but of course he is shortly back, armed, in Baker Street, and sipping from "the spirit case and gasogene" until all hours. A Kensington practice follows (from which he is secretly bought out by Holmes) and after that there is no more pretence, though he does sometimes take down a volume from his "small medical shelf" and is always ready, should Holmes require it, with a diagnosis. Nor does his hand lose its cunning: asked by Holmes why Professor Presbury should move so mysteriously and on all fours down dark passages, Watson is not for a moment at a loss: "Lumbago" he replies. It is not one of Holmes' tetchy days: "We can hardly accept lumbago" is the only admonishment.

So it is back to Baker Street, in glorious permanence, with the fog swirling outside and cold partridge and Montrachet for supper, and the test tubes and the hydrochloric acid and "the newly framed picture of General Gordon" to feast the eyes on, and the visits to the Turkish Bath where Holmes is "less reticent and more human than anywhere else" and cases can be discussed "over a smoke in the pleasant lassitude of the drying-room." And there are the occasional visits to Holmes' brother, Mycroft, and the sight of the "beshawled and bediamonded" ladies outside the Lyceum. And there is the agreeable flutter of Holmes being offered a knighthood in 1902, and the solid comfort of knowing that one is John H. Watson, M.D. (why did his wife call him James?), late Indian Army, who played Rugger for Blackheath and was once thrown into the crowd at the Old Deer Park by "Big Bob Ferguson." There are, to be sure, occasional clouds. When in teasing mood, Holmes can reply to an oversimple deduction by the Doctor with "Excellent, Watson! You scintillate to-day." But the mood was not always so. Even though he is feigning delirium (in *The Dying Detective*) Holmes comes out with some unpleasant truths: "Facts are facts, Watson, and after all you are only a general practitioner with very limited experience and mediocre qualifications." It does not need the Doctor to tell us that he is "bitterly hurt."

But he has his reward at last. He finds that he is more than the useful errand-boy, the bottle-washer, the willing horse. He is wounded in a shooting affray and Holmes, thinking the wound more serious than it is, allows something to pierce the bleak façade:

My friend's wiry arms were round me and he was leading me to a chair. "You're not hurt, Watson? For God's sake, say that you are not hurt."

It was worth a wound—it was worth many wounds—to know the depth of loyalty and love which lay behind that cold mask. The clear, hard eyes were dimmed for a moment, and the firm lips were shaking. For the one and only time I caught a glimpse of a great heart as well as of a great brain. All my years of humble but single-minded service culminated in that moment of revelation.

Exactly. And what chance had poor Miss Mary Morstan against a moment such as that?

The Importance of Being Watson

Peter V. Conroy

One of the basic axioms in Sherlockian criticism is that Dr. Watson serves as a foil for Holmes himself. As Sir Sidney Roberts says, "Holmes found in Watson, as Johnson found in Boswell, the perfect foil." An "occasional" drug addict (he uses his seven-percent solution only when other mental stimulation is lacking), Holmes often falls prey to extreme and rapid changes in mood, sometimes sitting motionless and smoking for weeks on end, at other times so caught up in the exhilaration of the chase that he neither eats nor sleeps. His disorder is as monumental as it is incorrigible: the huge encyclopedia of crime which he keeps religiously is in fact a heterogeneous conglomeration of facts and artifacts whose arrangement and classification only Holmes himself comprehends. Those famous nocturnal chemistry experiments, often involving deadly poisons and filling the Baker Street flat with a pungent and nauseous odor, are still not as dangerous or disruptive as Holmes's target practices in his sitting room when he initials *VR* in bullet holes on the wall. Brilliantly perceptive and analytical, Holmes reasons so swiftly and flawlessly while maintaining such complete control over his emotions and so nonchalant an attitude towards everything around him that he is considered by some to be a heartless thinking machine, an indictment that his deep-seated misogyny only collaborates.

Needless to say, Watson is thoroughly appalled by such goings-on. Having loyally performed his military service, in the course of which he was wounded and honorably discharged, the good doctor calmly waits out his convalescence collecting his pension. After taking up his medical practice again, he finds himself a wife and aspires to bourgeois tranquillity. While competent as a medical man, Watson cannot lay claim to any great intelligence. Whatever deficiency that may be, he repairs with a warm heart and a deep affection for and loyalty to his friend Holmes, qualities which nonetheless expose him to the charge of being overly sentimental and romantic. Such a typical Britisher and stolid Victorian stands in marked contrast, then, with the bohemian detective whose strange habits place him on the nether side of respectability and even of legality.

Reprinted from "The Importance of Being Watson," by Peter V. Conroy, from *Texas Quarterly* Vol. XXI, No. 1 (Spring 1978): 84–103. Reprinted by permission of the author and the University of Texas Press.

Such fundamental differences in life-style do not, however, make the two incompatible. Although they come to share rooms only by the greatest of chances, they quickly become fast friends, forming one of the most famous friendships in literature, even to the point where Watson eventually "loses" his wife so as to be able to return to Baker Street and participate more easily in Holmes's adventures.

Yet in saying all this, we have taken into account only Watson's role as actor and participant in these stories, his function as a foil for the character and personality of Holmes. Watson is, however, also the narrator of Holmes's adventures. It is in fact Watson as narrator that we would like to examine here and thus present the case for the "importance of being Watson," since, in our opinion, as teller of the tale, directing and controlling the narrative line, he eclipses Holmes himself as the distinctive mark of these detective stories.

Watson is a visible narrator, clearly situated in time and space, modifying and correcting the "factual" material which he is recounting. Holmes himself criticizes Watson for his narrational interference in *A Study In Scarlet*, claiming that the latter added too much romanticism to the story and neglected the element of rational analysis.

"I glanced over it," said he. "Honestly, I cannot congratulate you upon it. Detection is, or ought to be, an exact science and should be treated in the same cold and unemotional manner. You have attempted to tinge it with romanticism, which produces much the same effect as if you worked a love-story or an elopement into the fifth proposition of Euclid."

"But the romance was there," I remonstrated. "I could not tamper with the facts."

"Some facts should be suppressed, or, at least, a just sense of proportion should be observed in treating them. The only point in the case which deserved mention was the curious analytical reasoning from effects to causes, by which I succeeded in unravelling it."

(p. 90)

Had Holmes narrated this same adventure, then, it would have been quite different in its emphasis and possibly even in some of its details from Watson's version. Watson's distinctive tone of voice as well as his simple presence, always in harmonious juxtaposition to Holmes, mark indelibly the stories he tells, as can easily be seen by contrasting them with the adventures Holmes recounts himself, epg., *The "Gloria Scott," The Adventure of The Lion's Mane*, and *The Adventure of The Blanched Soldier*.

Despite his claim of being faithful to the "facts," Watson on other occasions points out the changes or modifications he saw fit to make as narrator in retelling an adventure.

He shrugged his shoulders when I asked him what luck he had had in his interview. Then he told the story, which I would repeat in this way. His hard, dry statement needs some little editing to soften it into the terms of real life. (p. 991)

Half an hour later we were seated, all four, in the small sitting-room of Signora Lucca, listening to her remarkable narrative of those sinister events, the ending of which we had chanced to witness. She spoke in rapid and fluent but very unconventional English, which for the sake of clearness, I will make grammatical.

(p. 911)

Watson's rewriting or editing of other people's conversations also explains the remarkable stylistic similarity which characterizes the accounts of all those clients who come to Baker Street seeking Holmes's intervention in their little mysteries.

Given this evidence that Watson is an active narrator who emphasizes his presence by narrative interference, the case before us is to determine the character and function of Watson the narrator as distinguished from Watson the actor, whom we have already seen as a foil for Holmes.

Upon first reading Holmes's newspaper article detailing his method of observation, analysis, and deduction, Watson registers only disbelief and a certain amount of contempt for the unknown (he thinks) and presumptuous author.

"What ineffable twaddle!" I cried, slapping the magazine down on the table; "I never read such rubbish in my life."

"What is it?" asked Sherlock Holmes.

"Why, this article," I said, pointing at it with my eggspoon as I sat down to my breakfast. "I see that you have read it since you marked it. I don't deny that it is smartly written. It irritates me, though. It is evidently the theory of some armchair lounger who evolves these neat little paradoxes in the seclusion of his own study. It is not practical . . . I should like to see him clapped down in a third-class carriage on the Underground, and asked to give the trades of all his fellow-travellers. I would lay a thousand to one against him."

"You would lose your money," Holmes remarked calmly. "As for the article, I wrote it myself."

(p. 23)

After Holmes demonstrates his powers, however, Watson quickly changes his opinion:

Here was an opportunity of taking the conceit out of him. He little thought of this when he made that random shot.

"May I ask, my lad," I said, in the blandest voice, "what your trade may be?"

"Commissionaire, sir," he said, gruffly. "Uniform away for repairs."

"And you were?" I asked, with a slight malicious grin at my companion.

"A sergeant, sir, Royal Marine Light Infantry, sir. No answer? Right, sir."

He clicked his heels together, raised his hand in salute, and was gone. I confess that I was considerably startled by this fresh proof of the practical nature of my companion's theories. My respect for his powers of analysis increased wondrously.

(pp. 25–26)

While this particular scene is found only once in an early story, it does define a typical situation which, repeated and reworked in nearly all the other adventures, becomes a basic pattern for the Sherlockian adventure. In its most complete form, the pattern appears like this: Holmes and Watson are in conversation, usually in the Baker Street flat, when Holmes unexpectedly makes one of those penetratingly accurate statements which leaves Watson speechless in amazement. Holmes then backtracks and explains the logical chain of observations, inferences, and conclusions which led him to make his original statement. This preliminary demonstration ends just as a client arrives to seek Holmes's intervention in a mysterious matter which offers him a wider field in which to use those powers adumbrated in the preliminary.

This pattern admits a number of variations. At times, Holmes directs his demonstrations not to Watson, but to his client, who is either sitting before him in the Baker Street flat,

"We shall soon set matters right, I have no doubt. You have come in by a train this morning, I see."

"You know me, then?"

"No, but I observe the second half of a return ticket in the palm of your left glove. You must have started early and yet you had a good drive in a dog-cart, along heavy roads, before you reached the station."

The lady gave a violent start in bewilderment at my companion.

"There is no mystery, my dear madam," said he, smiling. "The left arm of your jacket is spattered with mud in no less than seven places. The marks are perfectly fresh. There is no vehicle save a dog-cart which throws up mud in that way, and then only when you sit on the left-hand side of the driver."

(pp. 258–59)

or else outside in Baker Street, prior to entering:

. . . on the pavement opposite there stood a large woman with a heavy fur boa round her neck, and a large curling red feather in a broad-brimmed hat which was tilted in a coquettish Duchess of Devonshire fashion over her ear. From under this great panoply she peeped up in a nervous, hesitating fashion at our windows, while her body oscillated backward and forward, and her fingers fidgeted with her glove buttons. Suddenly, with a plunge, as of the swimmer who leaves the bank, she hurried across the road, and we heard the sharp clang of the bell.

"I have seen those symptoms before," said Holmes, throwing his cigarette into the fire. "Oscillation upon the pavement always means an *affaire de coeur*. She would like advice, but is not sure that the matter is not too delicate for communication. And yet even here we may discriminate. When a woman has been seriously wronged by a man she no longer oscillates, and the usual symptom is a broken bell wire. Here we may take it that there is a love matter, but that the maiden is not so much angry as perplexed, or grieved. But here she comes in person to resolve our doubts."

(p. 192)

The demonstration can on occasion be very rapid and cursory, a brief comment that Holmes makes almost as an aside, but it always reveals his quick and incisive mind at work.

"Give me your coat and umbrella," said Holmes. "They may rest here on the hook and will be dry presently. You have come up from the southwest I see."

"Yes, from Horsham."

"That clay and chalk mixture which I see upon your toe caps is quite distinctive."

(p. 218–19)

These miniatures, in their own rapid manner, fully replicate the salient elements of one basic pattern.

"We are going well," he said, looking out of the window and glancing at his watch. "Our rate is fifty-three and a half miles an hour."

"I have not observed the quarter-mile posts," said I.

"Nor have I. But the telegraph posts upon this line are sixty yards apart, and the calculation is a simple one. I suppose . . ."

(p. 335)

At other times, the demonstration is implied, as in those stories when Watson depicts himself in the act of reviewing Holmes's most interesting adventures and selecting the one he will tell.

When I glance over my notes and records of the Sherlock Holmes cases between the years '82 and '90, I am faced by so many which present strange and interesting features that it is no easy matter to know which to choose and which to leave. Some, however, have already gained publicity through the papers, and others have not offered a field for those peculiar qualities which my friend possessed in so high a degree, and which it is the object of these papers to illustrate.

(p. 217)

Whether a reader

> From time to time I heard of some vague account of his doings: of his summons to Odessa in the case of the Trepoff murder, of his clearing up of the singular tragedy of the Atkinson brothers at Trincomalee, and finally of the mission which he had accomplished so delicately and successfully for the reigning family of Holland. Beyond these signs of his activity, however, which I merely shared with all the readers of the daily press, I knew little of my former friend and companion.
>
> (p. 161)

or a narrator

> Of all the problems which have been submitted to my friend, Mr. Sherlock Holmes, for solution during the years of our intimacy, there were only two which I was the means of introducing to his notice . . . that of Mr. Hatherley's thumb, and that of Colonel Warburton's madness. Of these the latter may have afforded a finer field for an acute and original observer, but the other was so strange in its inception and so dramatic in its details that it may be the more worthy of being placed upon record, even if it gave my friend fewer openings for those deductive methods of reasoning by which he achieved such remarkable results.
>
> (pp. 273–74)

Watson does not fail to emphasize the remarkable and singular nature of Holmes's powers as well as his success in exercising them. Such a historical perspective not only reminds the reader of past examples of Holmes's power (thus complementing the "demonstration" proper, which shows Holmes at work in the present), but it also clearly establishes Watson's narrative function and his wide influence over and shaping of these narratives.

The final form the pattern takes is when Holmes disguises himself and, after fooling Watson, finally reveals himself. Thus, in an opium den:

> I walked down the narrow passage between the double row of sleepers, holding my breath to keep out the vile, stupefying fumes of the drugs, and looking about for the manager. As I passed the tall man who sat by the brazier I felt a sudden pluck at my skirt, and a low voice whispered, "Walk past me, and then look back at me." The words fell quite distinctly upon my ear. I glanced down. They could only have come from the old man at my side, and yet he sat now as absorbed as ever, very thin, very wrinkled, bent with age, an opium pipe dangling down from between his knees, as though it had dropped in sheer lassitude from his fingers. I took two steps forward and looked back. It took all my self-control to prevent me from breaking out into a cry of astonishment. He had turned his back so that none could see him but I. His form filled out, his wrinkles were gone, the dull eyes regained their fire, and there, sitting by the fire and grinning at my surprise, was none other than Sherlock

Holmes. He made a slight motion to me to approach him, and instantly, as
he turned his face half round to the company once more, subsided into a
doddering, loose-lipped senility.

(pp. 231–32)

The purpose of all these variations is the same: to show or to remind the
reader of Holmes's extraordinary powers which will shortly be put to a more
demanding task.

A typical Holmes adventure, or more exactly Watson's narration of it,
presents a binary structure. In the first place, which we have called the
preliminary demonstration, a remark or action by Holmes provokes Watson's
incredulous reaction. Initial disbelief changes to comprehension and enthusiastic support, however, once Holmes explains how he proceeded in his
deductions. In the second part, or the case proper, Watson's incredulity
reappears and is even reinforced when he is (again) unable to interpret the
clues or to elucidate the circumstances of the crime. Only after resolving the
enigma and unmasking the culprit does Holmes share with Watson the
whole deductive process, the chain of reasoning which led to the solution,
and thereby restores Watson's faith in him. These "two parts" are identical
in their thrust, although the first part is a miniature version of the much
larger second. By having recourse to this pattern and to this binary, parallel
structure, Watson is implicitly telling his readers that the ultimate issue is
never in doubt, that Holmes will of course succeed in unmasking the guilty
party. In the absence of any real doubt as to whether Holmes will succeed
or not, reader interest shifts to *how* he will succeed.

Suspense now involves the deductive process itself. Suspense becomes
methodological: the question is not "who-dun-it" but rather how Holmes
can observe details and infer the truth from their mute testimony. The
public's reaction to Holmes's death in *The Final Problem* bears eloquent
testimony to their unshakable confidence in his necessary and ultimate triumph. For Holmes to plunge to his death in the arms of Moriarty at
Reichenbach Falls was correctly felt as a betrayal of all that the pattern
implied. In the opinion of Vincent Starrett, a prominent Holmesian critic,
"It was as if a god had been destroyed by treachery." Arthur Conan Doyle
had no choice but to resuscitate Holmes—with the rather lame excuse that
Holmes wanted to disappear and travel incognito in the Orient—and thereby
to recognize and revalidate Watson's narrative pattern.

The suspense peculiar to the Holmes adventures thus derives from the
tension between knowing that Holmes will (must) succeed and yet not
knowing how. Just as in the preliminary demonstration the reader, like
Watson, does not know how Holmes arrived at his original statement until
the latter reveals the logical chain of deductions leading from observation to
conclusion, so too in the case proper he is unable to interpret correctly the
clues attending the crime. As there is rarely any physical danger involved,

this suspense is entirely cerebral in nature. No calamity threatens, no catastrophe is imminent. Thus Holmes's crimes resemble drawing-room riddles which test the participant's wit and ingenuity. The rules governing such conundrums require that the reader, like Watson, have access to the same information, to the same clues as Holmes and yet at the same time be unable to deduce the same conclusion. To navigate in these troubled waters, Watson steers a difficult narrative course between the Scylla of telling too much and the Charybdis of not telling enough.

In his narrations, Watson always presents Holmes and his investigations from a rigidly external and present-tense point of view. At the scene of the crime, Holmes lies on the ground muttering and exclaiming to himself as he takes his careful but inexplicable measurements or else examines closely debris like ashes with his magnifying glass. Watson's astonishment, the most usual form that his incredulousness takes in the case proper, as well as the mockery of the others present (detective Lestrade is often among these), encourage [s] the reader to share such unfavorable impressions about Holmes's method, true to the pattern discussed above, especially since Watson, although a retrospective narrator, refuses to supply here the few words of explanation which would place Holmes's ostensibly ridiculous actions in their true context. Watson's silence at these points is illogical given the narrative framework he himself has constructed. Since these adventures are narrated retrospectively, with a heavy accent placed upon the process of remembering and retelling, it is obvious from the outset that Watson already knows the conclusions. His cross-references to other adventures, his promise to tell someday even more interesting stories,

> The first of these, however, deals with interests of such importance and implicates so many of the first families in the kingdom that for many years it will be impossible to make it public . . . I still retain an almost verbatim report of the interview in which he demonstrated the true facts of the case to Monsieur Dubuque of the Paris police and Fritz von Waldbaum, the well-known specialist of Dantzig, both of whom had wasted their energies upon what proved to be side-issues. The new century will have come, however before the story can be safely told.
>
> (p. 447)

all support this retrospective time frame. Nonetheless Watson does not budge in the actual telling from a strict present-tense point of view. Despite his subsequent knowledge of the situation as narrator, he retells it from the coign of vantage of his ignorance as participant.

This point is well worth making since it indicates a definite and unusual narrative choice on Watson's part. Although other first-person detective fiction appears similar on this point (i.e., the narrator hides his hand, so to speak, to maintain reader interest and to further the suspense of "who-dun-it"), it is in fact quite different. In most detective first-person fiction, a true retrospective point of view—the differentiation of one character into actor and narrator, and the impression of retelling a story—simply does not exist. The major technical incongruity and one of the prime characteristics of such fiction is that it is told in the past tense when in fact it is felt or understood to be happening in the present.

Expressed another way, this means that the first-person format is handled exactly like the third-person format, eliminating the play between the observer and the actor, the narrator and the participant, who are one person in two different states, which is the chief and unique quality (or possibility) of a first-person narrator. Perhaps this is due to an atavistic memory of some literary convention; perhaps it is a badly made connection between popular and sophisticated literature. In any case, Watson's silence stems from reasons and from a complex motivation which clearly separate him from the rather simple, straightforward, and possibly naive narrators like Philip Marlowe, Hammett's Continental Operative, San Antonio, or Mike Hammer.

Were Watson to abandon this illogical (in its own terms) present-tense point of view and accept the greater knowledge implicit in his own narrative stance, he would naturally destroy the suspense he is trying to create and ruin the whole effect of a story like *The Dying Detective* which depends for its climactic reversal on Watson's complete ignorance of Holmes's scheme and indeed upon Holmes's exploitation of his friend's good faith. The only way to obtain the desired suspense is for Watson to block off one of his options as narrator. More than his dullness as participant, the good doctor's voluntary blindness as narrator informs the Sherlockian adventures.

Beyond imposing limitations on himself as narrator, Watson also neglects (purposefully, we would argue) to elucidate sufficiently certain lacunae in his narrative. There are simple periods of time and even elements of the inquiry which he does not present adequately. Of course Holmes is close-lipped, and generally offers only the vaguest indications about his various activities, so Watson does have something of an excuse.

> There was a curious secretive streak in the man [i.e., Holmes] which led to many dramatic effects, but left even his closest friend guessing as to what his exact plans might be. He pushed to an extreme the axiom that the only safe plotter was he who plotted alone. I was nearer him than anyone else, and yet I was always conscious of the gap between.
>
> (p. 994)

Nonetheless some gaps in the narrative are exceptional. Often Holmes announces that he is going out alone, or else Watson, pretexting pressing business elsewhere, plans to join him later on. During such intervals Holmes typically puts his hands on the last piece of information he needs to close the case. Rising early and leaving while Watson is still asleep, Holmes will often return by lunchtime after having done basic "detective" work, the type of investigation that provides so much of the substance and the interest of a Maigret story. Shortly thereafter, the reply to his telegram arrives, containing the last link in the chain, the conclusive proof he needs before unraveling the riddle.

The motive behind such omissions is not hard to find. Were Watson to document the pedestrian minutiae of the investigation, Holmes's dramatic "solutions," his incisive conclusions drawn by sheer and seemingly unaided brain power, those climatic *coups de théâtre* which Watson prepares so carefully, sometimes gathering all the principals on the stage of the Baker Street flat where Holmes's monologue of deduction turns into a scene of recognition, unmasking the culprit as in *A Study in Scarlet*, all would necessarily be diminished. The pattern we have discovered in these stories is not a cumulative one; rather it is a suddenly reversible one. The reader, like Watson, arrives at a point of incredulousness which is suddenly reversed and transformed into comprehension when Holmes explains his procedure (preliminary demonstration); the reader, like Watson, is again baffled by the mystery until Holmes offers a seeming impossible explanation which he then shows to be the only possible one (the case proper). By passing over in silence elements which provide the bulk of other detective fiction, Watson's narrative *persona* emphasizes the basic pattern and the theatrical climaxes which characterize these stories.

This laconic Watson stands in marked contrast to an exceedingly garrulous Watson. For, while we are never quite sure how Holmes handles the details of his investigation, we are very well informed as to his personal idiosyncrasies. At one time or another, Watson refers to his friend's monograph on bees or to the one on the polyphonic motets of Lassus, which is supposed to be the last thing written on the subject. Holmes is also an expert in tobacco ash, having distinguished and classified one hundred and forty varieties (of bicycle tires he knows about two score), all of which he can identify on sight or smell. Watson prattles on about Holmes's violin playing as well as about himself. Watson is a well-defined narrator precisely because he does go into such detail about himself even if, when referring to his old war wound, he forgets if the Jezail bullet is still lodged in his shoulder or in his leg. The Baker Street flat becomes more precise and real as Watson continuously adds new details or repeats the old ones in a most casual and offhanded but effective manner: the tantalus glowing in the middle of the room, Holmes's persian slipper atop the mantelpiece filled with shag tobacco, the seventeen steps up to their flat, Mrs. Hudson's copious breakfasts. Such minor and personal details, as well as those with which we opened this paper, all possess an enormous evocative power. From them a special brand of Sherlockian criticism has sprung up which tries to weave the strands lying loose in Watson's narratives into a larger and more coherent chronology/ biography of Holmes and Watson. Although secretive at times, Watson nonetheless does describe the scene of several adventures with enough precision and accuracy that H. W. Bell, working some fifty years later, has been able to identify and locate the exact places. Other critics have noticed and commented upon his realism, his recording of the sights and sounds of late Victorian England, especially of London.

> But what a record of achievement they [i.e. these stories] reveal! What a picture they disclose of London at the century's end! Is it too much to claim that social historians in the years to come are more likely to return to Watson than to the dull McCarthy or the sardonic Strachey? Of all the annalists of that curious time one must prefer the humble Watson, with his chronicle of crime and detection and his swift, kaleidoscopic record of bowler hats and "kerridges," of bicycles and Turkish Baths, of green November fogs and baking August summers . . . The picture is unforgettable and unique.

Significantly, a foreigner also recognizes London thanks to Watson's accurate observation and attention to detail.

> Dans les récits proprement londoniens, la topographie est indiquée de façon habituellement si précise que le Londonien ou le lecteur ayant une connaissance assez nette de cette ville, éprouvera quelque chose d'analogue au plaisir d'une seconde découverte lorsqu'il en parcourt certains passages. Watson est un guide qui nous conduit . . .
>
> Point n'est besoin d'une longue description: une notation impressionniste suffit très bien à rappeler la présence si attachante et si personnelle de l'immense cité . . . Les Londoniens sont l'objet de descriptions également brèves, précises, vivantes. Leurs habitudes, les lieux qu'ils fréquentent, leurs costumes ne passent jamais inaperçus.

Watson as narrator is then something of a Janus figure. To compensate for the omissions regarding the investigative procedure or background of these adventures, he takes great pains to enrich the foreground, the personal and palpable dimension where he and Holmes seem literally to live and breathe.

But we must return now to our principal question of Watson's manipulation of his narrative in order to involve his reader in the very special suspense of the Holmes adventures. One of Watson's most important narrative tricks is having the victim of the mystery recount his own experience in his own words when he comes to seek Holmes's assistance. There is of course a fine economy at work here—logically, since these people are prospective clients trying to induce Holmes to take their case, and literally, since the short-story format does not provide the scope for involving Holmes in each adventure in a more complex or more sophisticated manner.

Still, there is much more to it. These secondary narrators present all the facts, all the clues (or nearly all) that Holmes will need to solve the case or at the very least to form a working hypothesis which his subsequent investigations will bear out conclusively. This is to say that often Holmes has solved the crime or mystery merely by listening to the oral statement of the situation. Indeed, Holmes is, in his own words, a *consulting* detective: he often helps out Scotland Yard by offering advice and suggesting new interpretations for old facts when regular police investigations lead nowhere. He does not turn up new facts, he merely sees new possibilities in the old and already known ones.

By simply recording these clients' words and letting them stand on their own without the benefit of his subsequent knowledge (the changes that Watson does permit himself to make are usually stylistic in nature, which explains why all of Holmes's clients speak Watsonese), the good doctor is following the same principle which, as we have already seen, limits his own presentation of Holmes's action to a present-tense point of view and which prevents him from elucidating ambiguous situations with the near-omniscient knowledge his retrospective narrative position implies. As narrator, Watson tells only what he knew then, as participant, before Holmes solved the mystery, and he wants to keep his reader in exactly the same position. The challenge the mystery poses to Holmes is the same one Watson offers to his readers. Of course the reader does, or is supposed to, fail. In this, the reader resembles Watson himself, whose attempts to apply Holmes's methodology are greeted by Holmes's ironic praise and by total failure.

"Well, Watson, what do you make of it?"

Holmes was sitting with his back to me, and I had given him no sign of my occupation.

"How did you know what I was doing? I believe you have eyes in the back of your head."

"I have, at least, a well-polished, silver-plated coffeepot in front of me," said he. "But, tell me, Watson, what do you make of our visitor's stick? Since we have been so unfortunate as to miss him and have no notion of his errand, this accidental souvenir becomes of importance. Let me hear you reconstruct the man by an examination of it."

"I think," said I, following as far as I could the method of my companion, "that Dr. Mortimer is a successful, elderly medical man, well-esteemed, since those who know him give him this mark of their appreciation."

"Good!" said Holmes. "Excellent!"

"I think also that the probability is in favour of his being a country practitioner who does a great deal of visiting on foot."

"Why so?"

"Because this stick, though originally a very handsome one, has been so knocked about that I can hardly imagine a town practitioner carrying it. The thick iron ferrule is worn down, so it is evident that he has done a great amount of walking with it."

"Perfectly sound!"

"And then again, there is the 'friends of the C.C.H.' I should guess that to be the Something Hunt, the local hunt to whose members he has possibly given some surgical assistance and which has made him a small presentation in return."

"Really, Watson, you excel yourself," said Holmes, pushing back his chair and lighting a cigarette. "I am bound to say that in all the accounts which you have been so good as to give of my own small achievements you have habitually underrated your own abilities. It may be that you are not yourself luminous, but you are a conductor of light. Some people without possessing genius have a remarkable power of stimulating it. I confess, my dear fellow, that I am very much in your debt. . . ."

"Has anything escaped me?" I asked with some self-importance. "I trust that there is nothing of consequence which I have overlooked?"

"I am afraid, my dear Watson, that most of your conclusions were erroneous."

(pp. 669–70)

Like Watson, the reader is unequal to the task. Were it otherwise, there would be no suspense, no story. Were the reader able to unravel the mystery like Holmes, the latter would automatically lose his reputation as the world's greatest detective and his exclusive privilege of being consulted on matters of importance by the principal crowned heads of Europe. Indeed, the purpose of Watson's narratives is precisely to glorify his friend, to prove that his genius is inimitable and unequaled.

Given this intention, Watson's narrative problem is simultaneously to give the reader access to all the information Holmes has and yet to ensure that he will fail to analyze it correctly. By referring to an elementary linguistic model, and adopting it to our discussion, I think we can explain how Watson brings off this *tour de force*.

In the example cited, and indeed throughout his Sherlockian narratives, Watson believes in a single and fixed relation between *signifiant* and *signifié*, in the unicity of the referent, and as narrator he subtly imposes this thinking upon his reader. Just as the reader follows Watson in the preliminary demonstration and later in the case proper in his moments of surprise, incredulousness, and finally renewed confidence in Holmes, so too does he accept this implicit attitude of Watson towards the "facts" of the case. Watson is convinced, and he brings the reader along to share this belief, that every action, every clue has one interpretation. Such evidence with its single referent is supposed to elucidate the crime—but it never does.

Holmes, however, is a more profound thinker and indeed "reader" of the text of crime. Significantly Watson often asks Holmes how he "reads" a situation. Again, the mystery is first presented to Holmes as a text, the oral statement of his new client from which he quickly draws a working hypothesis.

"It is certainly delicate," said my friend with an amused smile, "but I have not been struck up to now with its complexity. It has been a case for intellectual deduction, but when this original intellectual deduction is confirmed point by point by quite a number of independent incidents, then the subjective becomes objective and we can say confidently that we have reached our goal. I had, in fact, reached it before we left Baker Street, and the rest has merely been observation and confirmation."

(p. 1042)

Finally, Holmes reads newspapers avidly (and collects old cases in his scrapbook), always on the lookout for signs and traces of crime. Written newspaper accounts of crimes usually afford Holmes all the information he needs to solve them. When Scotland Yard consults with Holmes, he offers his solutions not after new investigations but only after his reading of the appropriate texts. Searching through the newspaper accounts of crime, Holmes has gradually become aware of the unity of all crime. Each newspaper account is merely a trace of some larger text whose author, Moriarty, remains hidden and invisible to those, unlike Holmes who cannot decipher the text.

As you are aware, Watson, there is no one who knows the higher criminal world of London so well as I do. For years past I have continually been conscious of some power behind the malefactor, some deep organizing power which forever stands in the way of the law, and throws its shield over the wrongdoer. Again and again in cases of the most varying sort—forgery cases, robberies, murders—I have felt the presence of this force, and I have deduced its action in many of those undiscovered crimes in which I have not been personally consulted. For years I have endeavoured to break through the veil which shrouded it, and at last the time came when I seized my thread and followed it, until it led me, after a thousand cunning windings, to ex-professor Moriarty, of mathematical celebrity.

He is the Napoleon of crime, Watson. He is the organizer of half that is evil and of nearly all that is undetected in this great city. He is a genius, a philosopher, an abstract thinker. He has a brain of the first order. He sits motionless, like a spider in the centre of its web, but that web has a thousand radiations, and he knows well every quiver of each of them. He does little himself. He only plans. . . . This was the organization which I deduced, Watson, and which I devoted my whole energy to exposing and breaking up.

(p. 471)

Whereas Watson and the reader are content to accept the clues as possessing only a readily apparent meaning, Holmes looks for additional nonapparent interpretations. To one clue Holmes can thus assign several *signifiés*. It is precisely in this manner that he *deduces* Moriarty's presence behind London crime: Watson stops at the surface, at each particular crime, while Holmes seeks the deep structure, the organizing principle which connects them all.

In this extra step, in this search for the nonapparent unity, lies Holmes's genius. To him, crime is a closed semiotic system in which every element is meaningful because it bears a relationship to all the other elements in the system. Individual facts are therefore less important than the structure which unites them and thus gives them meaning, as the young detective Stanley Hopkins so clearly understands: "I've got my facts pretty clear," said Stanley Hopkins. "All I want now is to know what they all mean" (p. 608). A client talking to Holmes repeats this statement almost verbatim:

> "I had got into the way of supposing that you knew everything without being told," said he. "But I will give you the facts, and I hope to God that you will be able to tell me what they mean."
>
> (p. 1001)

Clearly Holmes is seen as a reader, as one who deciphers a code or finds meaning in a text which remains incomprehensible to others.

In this closed system, nothing can be discounted, everything must be seen in function of everything else. Marshall McLuhan notes perceptively, "Every fact, every item of a situation, for Holmes, has total relevance. There are no irrelevant details for him." Thus Holmes always denies the possibility of coincidence in favor of some deep underlying connection.

> "Well, Watson, what do you think of this?" asked Holmes, after a long pause.
> "It is an amazing coincidence."
> "A coincidence! Here is one of the three men whom we had named as possible actors in this drama, and he meets a violent death during the very hours when we know that that drama was being enacted. The odds are enormous against its being coincidence. No figures could express them. No, my dear Watson, the two events are connected—*must* be connected. It is for us to find the connection."
>
> (p. 655)

Instead of seeing the various clues as separate, detached facts, each having an independent and fixed explanation, Holmes seeks out the deep structure or sequence that alone can connect them all and that determines which of the several possible *signifiés* is the correct one.

> Not so, Watson. It had struck me at my first perfunctory reading as very strange, and now that I am in closer touch with the case it is my own firm ground for hope. We must look for consistency. Where there is want of it we must suspect deception.
>
> (p. 1065)

The correct *signifié* for each *significant* alone fits into the logical sequence.

This must be serious, Watson. A death which has caused my brother to alter his habits can be no ordinary one. What in the world can he have to do with it? . . . There we have it at last, Watson! British government—Woolwich. Arsenal—technical papers—Brother Mycroft, the chain is complete. But here he comes.

(pp. 915–16)

Consequently Holmes verifies each clue and its various explanations to find how they fit into the chain, how they make the all-important connection.

"Now, let us calmly define our position, Watson," he continued as we skirted the cliffs together. "Let us get a firm grip of the very little which we do know, so that when fresh facts arise we may be ready to fit them into their places."

(p. 960)

With mathematical precision and infallible accuracy, Holmes can reconstruct the crime because in his semiotic system all the details are pertinent and only one solution can account for all the details. Like a puzzle, there are no leftover pieces, nor is it possible to substitute one piece for another. Although Holmes never formulates this semiotic element with as much precision or as often as he emphasizes the need for observing small details (which Watson, ironically, does quite well without being able to use them semiotically), he *does* turn round the point. What he calls "whim" here, for example, is the feeling one gets when all the parts of a puzzle fall into place, or rather when they don't fall into place as they should.

I am sorry to make you the victim of what may seem a mere whim, but on my life, Watson, I simply can't leave that case in this condition. Every instinct I possess cries out against it. It's wrong—it's all wrong—I'll swear that it's wrong. And yet the lady's story was complete, the maid's corroboration was sufficient, the detail was fairly exact. What have I to put up against that? Three wine glasses, that is all.

(p. 642)

Three wineglasses: one detail that does not fit into the sequence. And so Holmes will reconstruct a new situation that does take these three wine glasses into account and thus solve the mystery.

The client who recounts all the details, Watson who transcribes them and we who have read them all know the same *signifiants* as Holmes does. He alone sees each of them as susceptible of several interpretations and all of them together as explicable by one and only one theory. Watson, in a passage quoted above, attempted an analysis in Holmes's manner. Although he has grasped the importance of observing detail, he nonetheless is unable to interpret each part in function of the whole.

". . . I would suggest, for example, that a presentation to a doctor is more likely to come from a hospital than from a hunt, and that when the initials 'C.C.' are placed before that hospital the words 'Charing Cross' very naturally suggest themselves."

"You may be right."

"The probability lies in that direction. And if we take this as a working hypothesis we have a fresh basis from which to start our construction of this unknown visitor."

(p. 670)

To consider Holmes's method of detection as an exercise in semiotics rather than as a contribution to real police investigative techniques or as Doyle's elaboration upon the medical examination as taught by his professor, Dr. Joseph Bell, seems by far to be the most satisfactory and the most literary solution. Despite all the claims to the contrary, Watson and Holmes are fictional creations; their existence is purely a literary one. Rather than searching far afield in the "real world" for an explanation of Holmes's detective prowess, we should seek it in the same literary mode which has given both him and Watson life.

Considering the Sherlockian mysteries as conundrums, as puzzles worked out semiotically, helps explain the nature of the suspense we discussed above. This suspense is more curiosity, a bright and cheerful bewilderment which contrasts sharply with the pulse-quickening effect of the modern detective "thriller" and which presents, as Hesketh Pearson points out, the same healthful and relaxing tonic as do sports.

Few readers think of Holmes as a sportsman, but that is how he figures in the popular imagination: he is a tracker, a hunter-down, a combination of bloodhound, pointer, and bulldog, who runs people to earth as the foxhound does the fox.

On one occasion when Holmes turns down the offer of official governmental recognition for his collaboration on a case, he also uses a sporting metaphor: "I play the game for the game's own sake" (p. 917). Considering them as puzzles also helps to understand why these stories often involve no criminal, or, when one does exist, why he is often not brought to justice. Watson is not narrating stories concerned with the triumph of good over evil or with the eventual victory of justice over crime: witness Holmes's distant attitude towards policemen in general and the consistently hostile characterization of Inspector Lestrade. Holmes struggles against Moriarty more for the challenge he represents than for any commitment to law and order. In his exalted moments, Holmes can even imagine himself a criminal and his powers in the service of evil. Rather, Watson's interest lies in persuading his readers of the wonders, indeed the miracle, of Holmes's intellectual acumen.

Despite the shortcomings in Holmes's character, the reader instinctively recognizes the monument of friendship and admiration which Watson erects in his narratives to "him whom I shall ever regard as the best and the wisest man whom I have ever known" (p. 480).

What we have been attempting here is to prove that Watson is a much more complex and important character than we might think. Not only does he incarnate a very subtle handling of narrative point of view which permits the most effective recounting of his story, but he also impregnates these narrations with their warm human glow, with that overpowering sympathy which allows us to forgive Watson his dullness and Holmes his aloofness and polite disdain.

Perhaps the most important reason for the tremendous success of the Holmes adventures is precisely this human dimension which Watson has created for Holmes and himself. To the later and more sophisticated readers who have grown up reading an entire literature of detective fiction, Holmes's mysteries have paled somewhat. Nonetheless Watson's excellent retelling, his ability to manipulate his material, his exploitation of all the resources available to him—as well as his careful camouflaging of this astute narrator behind a mildly incompetent actor—continue to stand out as exceptional. In this clever and complex narrator, Arthur Conan Doyle's stroke of genius, we find the real importance of being Watson. And it was elementary, my dear Holmes, elementary.

Notes

All the citations here have been drawn from Christopher Morley's edition of Arthur Conan Doyle, *The Complete Sherlock Holmes* (New York: Doubleday and Company) which, while dating back to 1930, is currently being reprinted and is therefore readily available.

A great deal of humorous or "whimsical" criticism has grown up around Sherlock Holmes and Doctor Watson. The most prominent of the "Baker Street Irregulars" responsible for this fictional criticism of fiction include the following: S. C. Roberts, whose *Dr. Watson* (London: Faber and Faber, 1931) purports to be a biography of Watson including a discussion of his marriage to Miss Morstan, the female "lead" in *The Sign of Four*, and who also wrote *Holmes and Watson: A Miscellany* (London: Oxford University Press, 1953); Christopher Morley, who wrote under his own name and a number of pseudonyms; and Vincent Starrett, author of *The Private Life of Sherlock Holmes* (London: Ivor Nicholson and Watson, 1934). Starrett also edited a collection of essays, *221B: Studies in Sherlock Holmes* (New York: Biblio and Tanner, 1969 [a reprint of the 1940 edition]), which includes the house identification by H. W. Bell.

To realize fully the scope and detail of such imaginative writing around Holmes and Watson, one has only to peruse Ronald De Waal's *The World Bibliography of Sherlock Holmes and Doctor Watson* (Boston: New York Graphic Society, 1974), which is long (626 pp.) and very complete, at least for English contributions. There is also a smaller, earlier bibliography, clearly of the Baker Street Irregulars' stamp, Edgar Smith's *The Baker Street Inventory* (Summit, N.J.: The Pamphlet House, 1945).

Strangely enough, French critics have been quite seriously interested in Sherlock Holmes. Pierre Nordon's long *Sir Arthur Conan Doyle: L'Homme et l'oeuvre* (Paris: Didier, 1964) is a full-scale literary analysis of Doyle's work, and most prominently of the Sherlock Holmes stories, along the thorough lines of traditional French university scholarship. Holmes's contribution to police methodology had been carefully and most seriously evaluated long before that in Edmund Locard's *Policiers de Roman et de Laboratoire* (Paris: Payot, 1924). Josée Dupuy's *Le Roman policier* (Paris: Larousse, 1974) and Francis Lacassin's *Mythologie du roman policier* (Paris: 10/18, 1974) both devote chapters to an analysis of Holmes and discuss his role in the creation and development of a distinctive and significant sub-genre, the detective story. Marshall McLuhan's "Sherlock Holmes vs. the Bureaucrat" in *Explorations* (October 1957) and a most recent article by Charles Moorman in *The Southern Quarterly* entitled "The Appeal of Sherlock Holmes" (January 1976) are equally serious contributions in English.

The Case of the Great Detective

STEPHEN KNIGHT

Everyone knows the traditional image of Sherlock Holmes. An artist only needs to touch in a deerstalker hat, a checked Inverness cape, large curved pipe and a magnifying glass: then if you just add the words "Elementary, my dear Watson" the world famous icon is complete. It's an epitome of the figure which first seized public attention in 1891, when Arthur Conan Doyle began publishing short stories about Sherlock Holmes in the new London monthly magazine, *The Strand*. To become a best-seller like that a writer of crime stories has to embody in the detective a set of values which the audience finds convincing, forces which they can believe will work to contain the disorders of crime. What then were the values that gave power to the Holmes phenomenon—what does the great detective stand for?

In the first place he stands for science, that exciting new nineteenth-century force in the public mind. Doyle said in his memoirs that contemporary crime fiction disappointed him, because it depended so much on luck for a solution: the detective should be able to work it *all* out. So the overt techniques of science, the careful collection and rational analysis of information, were realised in Sherlock Holmes. He can explain the causes of material evidence either by "the science of deduction" as Doyle calls it, or through his knowledge of forensic facts and criminal history. That was a vividly contemporary and credible force against crime. But it also had its inherent drawbacks, as many people found facts and objective science potentially anti-humane: Charles Dickens' automaton teacher Mr. Gradgrind is a fictional realisation of that fear. Darwin's theory of evolution was a real scientific cause of alarm, insisting as it did that men and animals weren't truly different. Naked science could itself appear to be a disorderly force. Doyle avoided such a bad aura by making the second major value of his great detective that equally potent contemporary force—individualism: the essence of humanity as it seemed to many then, and now. Holmes isn't only a man of objective science: he's also aloof, arrogant, eccentric, even bohemian. His exotic character humanises his scientific skills: a lofty hero, but crucially a human one.

That extreme individualism itself had alarming possibilities: to be too

From *Meanjin*, Vol. 40, No. 2 (July 1981): 175–85. Reprinted by permission.

aloof was to be unacceptable. Doyle skilfully mollifies Holmes's individualism by a whole series of subtle shifts. Holmes does take some cocaine in the
early stories; like the romantic artists in legend and reality, he needs to
liberate his consciousness from the shared, everyday world. But he doesn't
isolate himself—it's only a little cocaine, "to relax him," as Watson says.
After all, Holmes *is* Watson's friend and fellow-lodger, Watson who represents so plainly the average respectable man, so often puzzled, so often in
need of heroic assistance to explain crime and disorder. And all Holmes's
eccentricities are qualified—his strange atonal violin playing, the accompani-
ment to his private thinking, is itself matched by visiting ordinary social
concerts in Watson's company. And similarly, Holmes fasts while on the
scent of a solution, but at other times there are stout English breakfasts,
with a house-keeper to match.

The shape of the stories itself acts in support of this dual characterisation:
Doyle's pace and tone don't let his detective become a passive, academic
figure like Poe's Chevalier C. Auguste Dupin. Holmes may think all night,
but he'll be bustling early in the morning. He may wave the wand of science,
but he and the narration have a crisp, ironic tone about them, all the sharper
if you read the stories beside the often sentimental and pompous material
that also appeared in *The Strand*. A vigorously modern quality enables Sherlock Holmes to fight disorder in a credible, audience-attracting way.

Those are reasons why the great detective is an effective figure. But what is
he effective at? One of the crucial features of crime fiction is that different
periods, different audiences, see different crimes as being disturbing. Just as
the detective's aura embodies values that the audience holds to be important,
so the crimes and criminals realise what the audience most fears. In the
Agatha Christie pattern, for example, the feared crime is treacherous murder
for gain by a relative or trusted friend. The view of the writer, the view of
the audience, can give remarkably different accounts of what is the basic
source of disorders in the surrounding world.

We are so used to crime novels dealing with murder, it's a real surprise
to many people to find that in the early Holmes stories murder is a rare
crime. Stranger still, crime itself is relatively rare, especially in the first
twelve stories which were reprinted in one volume as *The Adventures of Sherlock
Holmes*. These established the fascination of the great detective, and so they're
the ones discussed here. Doyle was well aware of the lack of crime as such
in the stories. At the beginning of the "The Blue Carbuncle," the seventh
story, the authority of Holmes is used to justify that pattern. Watson reports
that Holmes said, about his London cases:

> Amid the action and reaction of so dense a swarm of humanity, every possible
> combination of events will be presented which may be striking or bizarre
> without being criminal. We have already had experience of such. "So much

so," I remarked, "that of the last six cases which I have added to my notes, three have been entirely free of any legal crime."

There was plenty of real crime in late Victorian London, as you might expect, but Doyle didn't introduce professional crime and criminals in these early stories. Nor did he at first present a fantastic master criminal reaching in to disturb ordinary life, not until he created Professor Moriarty to dispose of Holmes at the end of his second dozen of stories. What then were the crimes, the problems in the early stories? Broadly speaking, they deal with disorders in the respectable bourgeois family. There are various threats to established middle-class order, but they come from within the family and the class, not from enemy criminals. One major force is a selfish greed which cuts across normal family responsibility. In "A Case of Identity" and "The Copper Beeches" a father interferes with his daughter's marriage prospects, to keep her money. In "The Speckled Band" the father has actually murdered one step-daughter and tries to kill the other to stop them marrying and taking their money with them. In "The Man with the Twisted Lip" money distorts a man away from his normal, open-faced respectable family life. In "The Beryl Coronet" the greed of an outsider disturbs the family order because of the daughter's love for him. In "The Boscombe Valley Mystery" and "The Five Orange Pips" the greedy crime is in the past and it comes back to haunt what seems a respectable family—but their peaceful prosperity was based on the past crime that is revenged in the present. In three other stories greed leads to a breach of trust just outside family relations. In "The Blue Carbuncle" and "The Red-Headed League" a living-in servant betrays his employer's trust for money and joins up with criminals. In "The Engineer's Thumb" the employers themselves are greedy and untrustworthy and betray the engineer they employ.

The remaining two stories of the first dozen are a little different. In them a prospective marriage and a past love affair are shown in ruins. In "The Noble Bachelor" Lord St. Simon's bride disappears because her first husband turns up again; in "A Scandal in Bohemia" the King of Bohemia has to extricate himself from the scandal that may follow a love-affair. Sherlock Holmes's distaste for both these noblemen shows that their arrogant insensitivity to respectable bourgeois values is the selfish disturbance here and they deserve their discomfort. The middle class distaste for noble arrogance is close to home; St. Simon represents those English peers who felt themselves above bourgeois values and the King of Bohemia is a fairly thin disguise for the Prince of Wales, that great antagonist of Victorian respectability.

In these twelve stories those who cause the disturbance act in a selfish way, and all but the two aristocrats are motivated by greed for money. There is another structure of motivation which acts behind and within this one, to be discussed in a while. But the quest for money is a manifest cause of an irresponsibility that leads to disgrace, crime, social breakdown. That path to disgrace and disaster is not just Doyle's concern; it is a major topic in the period. Tennyson called this process "reeling back into the beast." Others, including Doyle, talked about plunging into "the abyss," a measureless chasm where reason, self-control, respectability, the bonds that hold society together, are all loosened, even lost. This fear is so insistent because it is structurally related to the positive values of Victorian society: its evil is a reflex of Victorian good. Total self-indulgence, uncontrolled individualism, moral anarchy, they are no more than unfettered developments of the much praised Victorian, and modern, virtues of self-help, independence and the legitimate practices of acquiring money, pleasure, comfort. You've just gone too far, self-help has become helping yourself to everything.

The disorderly selfishness that Holmes unveils is the dark side of the acquisitive individualism which is basic to the economic world-view of the city workers, clerks and businessmen who patronised *The Strand*. The greed specifies an economic formation, and the individualism is also basic to the religious and personal dynamic of a world that was largely capitalist, protestant, and individualised. But not only the crimes in Doyle are structural to his society: so are the controls that fictionally operate against them. The detective's central values, rationalism and individualism, are themselves authentic to that world. The crimes and their controls realise the fears and the hopes integral to what was then, and still largely is, modern society. The ideological, rather than truly investigative, nature of the stories lies in this intimate relationship between the threats and the values that foreclose them: both have the same determining conditions. So the threats (covert in any case) are neither realised nor resolved in ways which unmask the contemporary conditions of life, but in ways which actually validate those creators of anxiety. The ideological circle is complete.

I hope this doesn't suggest that Doyle sat down with some graph paper and took one axis for detective methods and the other for the audience's central anxiety. It's conceivable to compose fiction like that, and it may well become a viable method in the future. But Doyle did it the old-fashioned way: his imagination created issues that were of importance in his period. One of the reasons he was able to imagine such effective fables of anxiety and comfort for his audience was that he was himself one of them. The fear that selfish greed could bring disorder is especially evident in the stories without Holmes. There Doyle's anxieties are often more evident, because Holmes was a comforting force for him as well as his audience. In fact the stories Doyle wrote just after he killed Holmes off in 1893 are the most revealing of all: he felt Holmes kept "his mind from better things," but the absence of that comforting figure also left him vulnerable to his anxieties.

The largely autobiographical book he started in 1893 lays out the fear of selfish greed very fully. In *The Stark Munro Letters* there is some concern with religion and politics, but both those areas of doubt are resolved by a mixture of science and optimism. Stark Munro declares himself a Deist, believing at least in a creating force behind the universe, a sort of divine super-scientist. And he also espouses Social Darwinism, the notion that social evils are steadily being evolved away, and that a better world waits for the poor and oppressed—for those who survive, at least. These large public problems are easily enough resolved. The real drama in the novel lies in the struggle between Munro, the image of the young Dr. Doyle, and James Cullingworth. Based on a man Doyle knew well, Cullingworth is vigorous, confident, manic. He's full of ideas to make money, a ruthless aggressive doctor-businessman. In fact he's a "worst case" hypothesis of an individual crazed by money and power, devoted to the quest for them. He and Munro are medical partners, but they fall out and Cullingworth tries to ruin Munro. The threat enacted by Cullingworth is not just a bullying and manipulative dominion. It's his attractiveness that's the key to the worry. Munro at least partly admires him. Vigour, confidence, success, self-help, making your own fortune—Cullingworth stands for these and Munro approves. It's the mad limits he goes to that are too much. Notice the character's name, Cullingworth. There's something there worth culling. But Munro is strong enough to resist him—"Stark" enough in the Scottish idiom both he and Doyle grew up with.

Finally, Cullingworth is contained and avoided, not defeated. He goes off to South America at the end, that land of mystery and high speculative profits. Munro himself, and his young wife, die in a rail crash, consumed by the technology of the modern Cullingworth-like world; but Munro is also put to silence gladly by the Doyle who had only just lived through a similar crisis. As he was writing that novel he was rich with money from the Sherlock Holmes stories, a series he felt to be a money-grubbing venture, an improper use of his own impressive powers. He felt he should be writing historical novels, making himself a new, English version of the ultra-respectable bourgeois hero Sir Walter Scott. Even before he had made his Holmes success Doyle had expressed his feelings about sudden wealth. This was in 1891, in a short novel called *The Doings of Raffles Haw*. It's a fable about a man who stumbled, by a scientific accident, on great wealth and found it caused nothing but trouble to him and to the world. But not only science is suggested. Raffles was the great entrepreneur of the eastern colonial and business empire, founder of Singapore. And the surname suggests what Doyle thought you were like morally if you just did things for money. He soon enough found himself a bit like Raffles.

Doyle's distaste for Sherlock Holmes is well known, and it caused him to kill his hero after the second series of a dozen stories. That extreme measure arose from Newnes's determination to buy more and more stories. During the first six Doyle was already tiring of Holmes; so he asked £50 a story for the second batch, hoping Newnes would refuse. Doyle was naive. That was only £15 a story more than the first, and they were strong sellers. Newnes jumped at it. Then, hoping for another stop, Doyle asked £1000 for the next dozen. Newnes accepted readily again, so Doyle put himself beyond purchase by killing Holmes; that story was hopefully entitled "The Final Problem." But writers don't just encounter their problems in business terms. Their anxieties are the material of their work, and Doyle's feelings intrude into at least two of the first dozen stories. As I have argued elsewhere (*Form and Ideology in Crime Fiction*, Macmillan, London, 1980, pp. 99–101), in "The Man with the Twisted Lip" and "The Engineer's Thumb" the heroes both encode the sense of shame, even of emasculation, that Doyle derived from his association with Newnes and his press.

In the narrative of those stories Holmes reveals the fictional causes of disorder; but in reality he was the medium of the real disorder, and he was interpreted by Doyle as its cause. A figure of such dialectic force was not easily disposed of, not even by death. In 1901 Doyle published a new Holmes story, *The Hound of the Baskervilles*—not a total surrender, as he carefully set it back in time, before Holmes had died. But this wasn't enough. In 1903 Newnes offered the stunning sum of £100 a thousand words, perhaps equivalent to as much as $20,000 a story now, and so Doyle resurrected Holmes in an adventure with the glum title "The Empty House." Doyle never did rid himself of the albatross he felt Holmes to be. In later life he was a busy public man—politics, patriotism, spiritualism, individual rights were all issues he spoke about a lot. But whenever he spoke, people always wanted to know about Sherlock Holmes. It irritated him: and so the figure was his private model of the selfish greed which his stories show as a manifest cause of disorder among respectable men.

It is only seen among men; that limitation, the exclusively masculine viewpoint of the stories, points towards another, more hidden, and perhaps ultimately more threatening source of disorder for Doyle and for his audience: the relations men have with women. The audience of *The Strand* was predominantly male; they bought the magazine, in shops, at bookstalls, especially on stations. They did take it home—there were sections for women and children, but they are just sections, they're kept in their place. Subordination has the structural reflex of insubordination: oppressors must fear the power of the oppressed. To keep women down and yet to need them as wives, mothers, housekeepers, lovers, means there is constant pressure, constant fear that the male dominance will crack. The stories show that pressure; it is certainly latent, and it often operates within the greed structure—it is the daughter's money that the aggressive father is after in several stories. Or is it? Perhaps the greed structure, being related to that acquisitiveness that is at least partly admirable, is itself a euphemism for the darker, less mentionable reasons why fathers desire daughters—which Freud worked out at just this period. Money may stand for the power women hold to attract, unbalance, even to destroy the controlled, organised Victorian male as he sees himself. This fear, like the fear of greed, is expressed most directly in a story written just after Doyle disposed of Holmes, when he had to cope alone with potential disorders.

The short novel *The Parasite* is little known and very hard to get hold of. Largely because Doyle suppressed it; it had only two early reprints, in quite small runs, and one U.S. edition. Doyle dropped it from the impressive list of publications that faces the title page of his books. Some have thought this was because its critique of mesmerism clashed with his later spiritual beliefs, but I suspect it may have been a bit too overt for comfort in the threats its hero discovers. He is a lecturer in medicine at Edinburgh . . . a plain enough projection of Doyle. He is happily engaged, respectable, settled—about to shape a family. He meets a Miss Penelosa, a mesmerist. She is fortyish, ugly, even crippled, from the West Indies; an exotic, foreign, grotesque figure, but she claims to have powers. He scoffs at mesmerism, offers himself as a subject. He becomes enslaved by her; he tries to fight it, locking himself in his bedroom so he can't get to her (or is it so she can't get to him?). But it's no good: he still gets out. Disgrace falls on him; he loses interest in his work; the university actually notices and he's suspended. Then he tries to rob a bank. Finally he goes off, under Miss Penelosa's control, to throw vitriol in his fiancée's face. But luck intervenes—or perhaps it's grace. The vicar calls while he's waiting to do the deed, the spell is broken, and the mesmerist herself dies, across the town, at that moment. There can be little doubt that mesmerism is really a displacement, a code, for sexual obsession. The disorderly and compulsive force of sexuality reeks and smokes through the writing: it's a brilliant piece of imaginative work, reaching into the dark underside of masculine confidence and domination. The woman who threatens masculine control is made foreign and ugly as a way of distancing and judging female power and sensuality together, a witch to remove guilt from her victim.

This fear of the seductive power by which women can bring men to the abyss is recurrent in Doyle's non-Holmes stories, outlasting and apparently deeper than the fear of greed. I'll give two very striking, even stunning examples. "The Terror of Blue John Gap," written in 1909, enacts the fear of being engulfed by feminine sexuality. The hero penetrates a cave and then senses a fearful, powerful shuddering presence. The phallic and vaginal imagery of the story is obvious. He finally escapes this debilitating experience and arranges for the mouth to be blocked up for ever; that gap that the title tells us is blue, from a male viewpoint obscene, is closed. If that seems a strained interpretation of the name, what other explanation can be given for Doyle's frequent use of versions of it, as in "The Gully of Bluemansdyke" and "The Parson of Jackman's Gulch"? The story does rationalise "Blue John" as a type of valuable stone—greed is brought in as a euphemism— but the barely latent forces of the story are at work even in the title.

Another even more neurotic and savage way of immobilising the sexual force of women is presented in a little known story "The Case of Lady Sannox." It was written in 1894, that revealing year after Doyle killed off Holmes and encoded his fears without the protecting hero to minimise them. Lady Sannox is the wife of a London physician—Doyle territory again. She is having an affair with a surgeon. Her lover is called out to do an emergency operation on the wife of a wealthy Turk. Lying drugged, shrouded by veils, in a darkened room, she appears to have an infected wound on her lower lip. The surgeon is reluctant to operate, but the husband assures him it is crucial, and presses a hundred sovereigns on him (greed for money is here too). So he acts. With a quick double slash he cuts a thick "broad V-shaped piece" from her bottom lip. Blood spurts. Pain cuts through the opium. As she jerks, the veils fall away. Yes, that's right, it *is* Lady Sannox all the time. This terrible story does not just present a sadistic disfigurement. It is a barely coded version of the cruel operation called female circumcision—itself a euphemism for the removal of the clitoris. It was recommended at times in Victorian England for women who were "restless," a codeword for improperly sensual. The husband makes this meaning of the story quite clear as he turns to the stunned lover: " 'It was really necessary for Marion, this operation' said he, 'not physically but morally, you know, morally.' "

Doyle wrote "The Case of Lady Sannox" while his wife was already ill with the tuberculosis that would kill her in 1906. He remarked at the time that their bedroom had become a sickroom. Sexual frustration and the associated guilt sat on him heavily, but only some of the stories tell the tale; he controlled himself otherwise. And before long he had more specific pressures to control. In 1897 he fell in love with Jean Leckie. They conducted a platonic and even courtly love affair till they married in 1907, the year after his wife's death. Doyle coped with this situation through a chivalrous moral structure more like that of his medieval historical novels than ordinary life, but the reflex of such containment strikes out in those stories which take fierce vengeance on the disturbing attractiveness of women. The circumstances of his wife's illness and the Leckie affair didn't create this hostile, fearful attitude to women; they only exacerbated it. The Holmes stories themselves, written before his wife was even ill, bear clearly the traces of the same fear that women tempt men to be disorderly, that they offer another path to the abyss. And just as that fear is realised, so there is a force to contain it—Sherlock Holmes himself. The importance of this structure to Doyle and to his audience is indicated by the fact that it's defined in the very first paragraph of the very first *Strand* story, "A Scandal in Bohemia." Watson states Holmes's position on women:

> He never spoke of the softer passions, save with a gibe and a sneer. They were admirable things for the observer—excellent for drawing the veil from men's motives and actions. But for the trained reasoner to admit such intrusions into

his own delicate and finely adjusted temperament was to introduce a distracting factor which might throw a doubt upon all his mental results.

Masculine, delicate, scientific . . . the ideas go together to state the male self-concept, the delicate frailty it perceives in itself, and the protection it finds in a scientific hero. And even for Holmes, woman is a threat; vigilance must be eternal. Irene Adler is the heroine of this story. She's the discarded mistress of the King of Bohemia. She outwits not only the King, but Holmes as well, and he recognises her power. Watson actually opens the story by saying "To Sherlock Holmes she is always *the* woman." And so she is, she throws out the archetypal challenge to men. She's clever, determined, a royal mistress, a match even for Sherlock Holmes, a concise statement of the power of those seen as the enemy. In the early stories there are two distinct, but related, patterns of masculine fear. One is the fear of castration, directly losing potency. The other is the fear of being supplanted, losing control over a daughter or a wife—a less direct but equally severe threat to the potency of the possessing man. Greed is still the dominant force in the two stories where a past crime disturbs a present family, and in the two where a servant betrays a family's trust. The past and the male servants are forces beyond sexual anxiety. But the other eight stories are rich with masculine neurosis, underlying and often energising the greed motifs.

In "A Case of Identity," "The Copper Beeches" and "The Speckled Band" a father refuses to let a daughter have her money and the independence to leave him. The most famous of the three stories, "The Speckled Band," indicates the primacy of the sexual force: Dr. Roylott attacks his stepdaughter by driving a snake through a hole he has pierced in her bedroom wall. In "The Beryl Coronet" the father loses a daughter and at the same time the precious circlet is wrenched out of shape, a piece broken off: a clear token of the disturbing deflowering. The threat of Irene Adler in "A Scandal in Bohemia" has been discussed, and it's noteworthy that her most private place (it's a safe in the overt plot) is where she locks away the instrument of power by which she can politically emasculate the King. "The Noble Bachelor" loses his promised wife to a man with a prior claim, and different types of masculine debilitation are suffered in "The Man with the Twisted Lip" and "The Engineer's Thumb."

Against these disturbed states, the happy married life of Watson is an ideal: but it's so because you never hear about the wife, he spends all his time with Holmes. Mrs. Watson is a good housekeeper who makes no claim on her husband. To create this passive relationship seems the main reason why Doyle made Watson leave the rooms he shared with Holmes. I doubt if Doyle was ever bothered by the fear of a trace of homosexuality between the room-mates. Watson and Holmes have the sort of British male relationship which excludes all sexuality, including anything as positive as homosexual feelings. The French and the Americans tend to see and depict Holmes as a foppish dandy, with a distinct effeminacy, but they're misled by the languid manners that among the English are held to reveal effortless superiority.

It seems clear enough that the early Holmes stories realised fears the respectable audience had about their own weaknesses. Selfishness, greed, sexual tensions might disrupt the carefully poised bourgeois nuclear family. But these forces are not explored fully, not brought out into an analytic, unmasking light. Rather they are appeased by a figure from the very socioeconomic matrix that generated the disturbance in the first place, a helping hero who enacts a faith in rational individualism. So the ideological trick is turned, in a way so neat and so transitory that the fears remain and need to be assuaged again, and again—as each monthly issue appears.

The well-remembered icon of Holmes catches strikingly well the essence of the myth and its functioning force. Yet this powerful image is not Doyle's work: it's a notable example of the part the audience plays in the constitution of cultural ideology. The essence of the icon is itself a myth. In the early stories and illustrations. Holmes smokes a straight pipe, and like any other respectable gentleman of the period would only wear a deerstalker hat and Inverness cape in the country—not in town. But once an illustrator gave him a big curved meerschaum pipe, it seemed so right that it stuck, though it's in none of the early illustrations. You have to support a big curved pipe as you smoke, it's too heavy just for the teeth: a passive, thinking man's pipe. And though Holmes rarely uses a magnifying glass, that's what he has in the other hand in the familiar picture, to show how his thinking is applied, investigative. The original Holmes dressed smartly, striped trousers and bowler for business, a trilby for informal occasions, a silk hat on formal outings, and on one relaxed occasion even a straw boater. So the original illustrations tell us. But in our memory he must wear the country outfit, wherever he is, to stress that he's a hunter, stalking the fugitive weaknesses of his readers. And he never does say "Elementary my dear Watson." He says "Elementary" and he says "My dear Watson" often enough, but the completion process of a live myth has run them together, because together they perfectly catch the aloof and the friendly sides of his relation with Watson and, by extension, with the reader.

So even if you don't read the stories, Sherlock Holmes is memorable and functional, he lives. He won't live in a functional way for ever. He'll become a historical curiosity, like other heroes of the past. Nicholas Meyer's novel *The Seven-Per-Cent Solution*, and the film made of it, indicate a stage in this process: insisting that Sigmund Freud was a greater detective than Holmes—in Meyer's culture the subjective consolations of bourgeois psychiatry play the role that rational individualism fulfilled for Holmes's initial audience. That is an authentic and intimate development: the two medical men lived in similar metropolitan conditions but Freud made overt the forces that Doyle only covertly realised in fiction. Further developments will no doubt be more distant from Doyle's patterns: new societies, new cultures; new anxieties, new consolations.

For his period, Doyle caught in the Holmes stories an ensemble of attitudes, of fears and hopes. For anyone interested in seeing how dominant social groups use their literature to state and control fears, the Holmes stories are a fascinating source. They provide a means of recreating the structure of feeling in a complex period, one which has both continuities and contrasts with our own period. To illuminate the continuities and contrasts will illuminate our own patterns of disturbance, among them our own urgent and individualist quest for money and our still uneasy relations between the sexes—and just what are our hopes? What contemporary figures embody our values, act now as the great detective did for Doyle and his audience? Media figures? Industrialists? Paperback gurus? Politicians? Whoever they are, is their protective aura not in fact just as fictional, just as illusory—just as ideological—as that of Sherlock Holmes himself?

Sherlock Holmes, Order, and the Late-Victorian Mind

CHRISTOPHER CLAUSEN

Few characters in all of literature are as widely known as Sherlock Holmes. From his first appearance in *A Study in Scarlet* (1887), the four novels and fifty-six short stories of which he is the protagonist have been among the most continuously popular works of fiction ever created. Even among those who have never read any of the stories or seen the film and television adaptations, there must be very few people over the age of ten in the English-speaking world who have never heard of Sherlock Holmes, or of his equally imaginary chronicler, Dr. Watson. As T. S. Eliot pointed out in the *Criterion* in 1929, Holmes is *real* in a way that only the greatest fictional characters ever achieve. Less sophisticated readers think so, too: letters of admiration and requests for help are still addressed to the mythical rooms of a man who, had he ever lived at all, would now [1986] be a hundred and thirty years old. No other Victorian literary character, not even Alice, has maintained so powerful a hold on so many twentieth-century readers' imaginations.

Holmes's continued popularity with all levels of readers is all the more striking when one reflects that he is probably the most cerebral protagonist of any importance in English fiction. His life is almost wholly intellectual. "I am a brain, Watson," he says in "The Mazarin Stone." "The rest of me is a mere appendix" (II, 1014).[1] When he has no case to occupy his mind, he often takes morphine or cocaine because he cannot bear the boredom of everyday life. He has no friends but Watson, he says in "The Five Orange Pips." He is jarringly egotistical. His contempt for the average mind—usually represented by poor Watson's—is displayed again and again. "There, Watson!" he announces after a successful series of deductions in *The Valley of Fear.* "What do you think of pure reason and its fruit?" (II, 773). To that commitment he is rarely unfaithful. He never once falls in love. "All emotions, and that one particularly," we learn in "A Scandal in Bohemia," the first of the short stories, "were abhorrent to his cold, precise but admirably balanced mind. He was, I take it, the most perfect reasoning and observing

Reprinted from Christopher Clausen, *The Moral Imagination: Essays on Literature and Ethics* (Iowa City: University of Iowa Press, 1986), 51–85. Copyright 1986 by University of Iowa Press.

machine that the world has seen. . . . He never spoke of the softer passions, save with a gibe and a sneer" (I, 161).

Although a gentleman by birth and education, he belongs to no club, unlike Watson. He is, in fact, the sort of isolated intellectual who today would be called alienated: introverted, frighteningly analytical, and often cynical. In at least one case, "The Yellow Face," his cynicism leads him to the wrong conclusion. Although patriotic, he has little use for the conventions, in some cases even the laws, of Victorian society that it is his profession to uphold. He entirely lacks the glamour of James Bond, the snob appeal of Lord Peter Wimsey, the ostentatious whimsicality of Nero Wolfe.

This is hardly a recipe for a hero of popular fiction. Yet Holmes, accompanied and interpreted by his more conventional friend, has been so much in demand for over ninety years that his creator reluctantly abandoned all thought of killing him off, and other authors continue to write nostalgic best-sellers about him today. He has also been the subject of the most tedious pseudoscholarship in the history of letters, most of it premised on the facetious assumption that Holmes was a historical character whose biography needs filling in. Meanwhile his most important fictional predecessors, Poe's Dupin and Gaboriau's Lecoq, have faded into relative obscurity.

Holmes's real status as an anomalously popular hero of fiction has rarely been examined by historians of literature or ideas. Whether because of its ambiguous standing somewhere in the no-man's-land between "popular culture" and serious literature, or because the people who write articles about what university Holmes attended and whether he was ever an actor have driven everyone else away, there has been remarkably little critical discussion of the Holmes canon. Yet it amply repays study. Conan Doyle published stories about Sherlock Holmes over a period of forty years, from 1887 to 1927; the range of life—of people, settings, ideas—that Holmes encounters or reflects upon in that time is extraordinarily wide. For reasons I will discuss presently, the stories written after 1914 (all but one of them set before the war) are inferior to the earlier ones, and any high literary claims must rest on *The Hound of the Baskervilles* and a dozen or so short stories. Nevertheless, the canon as a whole, with its observant, analytical hero who comes into professional contact with all strata of urban and rural society from kings (for example, in "A Scandal in Bohemia") to beggars (for example, in "The Man with the Twisted Lip"), offers an unrivalled and largely overlooked source for the study of ideas, attitudes, and culture in the period when British power and confidence were at their peak, from Queen Victoria's golden jubilee until the outbreak of the First World War.

As Thomas Love Peacock pointed out in "An Essay on Fashionable Literature," "The moral and political character of the age or nation may be read by an attentive observer even in its lightest literature, how remote soever *prima facie* from morals and politics."[2] The minds of authors and characters are revealed not only by what they assert but also by what they take for granted. When the author writes for and is popular with a wide audience, attentive readers at a later time may learn something about what views of itself and its world that audience was prepared to accept. Furthermore, of all forms of "light literature," the detective story is the most inescapably concerned with moral issues. A crime is committed; the criminal must be discovered and judged. The opportunities detective fiction offers for the study of changing ideas about the motives and consequences of human action will be obvious.

The pattern of intellect at war with mystery is set at the very beginning, in *A Study in Scarlet*, and although it is developed in subsequent works, it never changes in any essential way. In view of the notorious inconsistencies of biographical detail from one Holmes story to another, this coherence of purpose over a period of forty years needs to be stressed. Deduction, the elucidation of mysteries through scientific reason, is Holmes's ruling passion, and only by subordinating everything else to it can he serve as the guardian of a threatened society that his author means him to be. If as a result he seems somewhat one-dimensional as a character, that is an essential part of the stories' meaning.

Holmes is first described by Stamford, a medical friend of Watson's, in terms that would be equally apt at the end of Holmes's career:

> "It is not easy to express the inexpressible," he answered with a laugh. "Holmes is a little too scientific for my tastes—it approaches to cold-bloodedness. I could imagine his giving a friend a little pinch of the latest vegetable alkaloid, not out of malevolence, you understand, but simply out of a spirit of inquiry in order to have an accurate idea of the effects. To do him justice, I think that he would take it himself with the same readiness. He appears to have a passion for definite and exact knowledge."
>
> (I, 17)

Stamford's only purpose in the story is to introduce Holmes and Watson; having accomplished this momentous act, he disappears forever. At the moment of the introduction, Holmes—as vivid and fully realized as he will ever be—has just discovered an infallible test for distinguishing blood from all other stains. One of the two most famous lines in the whole cycle follows when, glancing at Watson, Holmes declares, "You have been in Afghanistan, I perceive" (I, 18). It is a powerful entrance, and although we learn about the darker side of his nature later on, it defines Holmes as a character forever.

Fittingly, the second chapter of *A Study in Scarlet* is entitled "The Science of Deduction." It is here that Watson, a slow learner but no fool, begins to grasp the dimensions of the man with whom he has so rashly committed himself to share rooms. At first he is baffled. In both qualities and habits, Holmes is unlike anyone Watson has ever met. He is alternately energetic and lethargic. He seems to have no profession, yet his activities appear to be guided by a purpose.

> He was not studying medicine. . . . Neither did he appear to have pursued any course of reading which might fit him for a degree in science or any other recognized portal which would give him an entrance into the learned world. Yet his zeal for certain studies was remarkable, and within eccentric limits his knowledge was so extraordinarily ample and minute that his observations have fairly astounded me. Surely no man would work so hard or attain such precise information unless he had some definite end in view.
>
> (I, 20)

A methodical observer himself, Watson makes up a list which he heads "Sherlock Holmes—his limits." It is not much help. Next to Knowledge of Literature, Philosophy, and Astronomy, Watson writes "Nil." Knowledge of Politics is "Feeble," of Botany "Variable": Holmes knows a great deal about poisons but nothing of gardening. Geology is "Practical, but limited"; Holmes can tell different soils at a glance and explain where each one came from. His knowledge of chemistry is "Profound"; anatomy, "Accurate, but unsystematic"; sensational literature, "Immense." He plays the violin well, is an expert in the arts of self-defense, and has "a good practical knowledge of British law" (I, 21–22). Having completed this odd list, Watson throws it into the fire in despair.

It is Watson's deprecation of Holmes's magazine article "The Book of Life" that leads to enlightenment of a sort, for in defending his article Holmes reveals his profession. The article falls into the nineteenth-century tradition of essays applying scientific canons of reason and evidence to everyday life. What is quoted of it suggests the influence of Thomas Henry Huxley, a writer whom Conan Doyle greatly admired:

> From a drop of water, a logician could infer the possibility of an Atlantic or a Niagara without having seen or heard of one or the other. So all life is a great chain, the nature of which is known whenever we are shown a single link of it. Like all other arts, the Science of Deduction and Analysis is one which can only be acquired by long and patient study. . . .

The man whose knowledge of philosophy was "Nil" proves to have a philo-sophical bent after all. (His knowledge of literature and politics will similarly expand in later stories.) It is, however, applied largely to the needs of Holmes's own profession. In a sentence that we will see illustrated time and again in this and later stories, the article declares, "By a man's finger-nails, by his coat-sleeve, by his boots, by his trouser-knees, by the callosities of his forefinger and thumb, by his expression, by his shirt-cuffs—by each of these things a man's calling is plainly revealed" (I, 23). Through proper observation and analysis, the scientific mind can make deductions in everyday life that will strike less acute witnesses as magical.

The particular pattern of scientific reasoning that Holmes finds most useful is akin to that of the archeologist or evolutionary biologist and involves working back from effects to causes. After demonstrating for the first time the success of his methods, he provides a further explanation of them at the end of *A Study in Scarlet*:

> Most people, if you describe a train of events to them, will tell you what the result would be. They can put those events together in their minds, and argue from them that something will come to pass. There are few people, however, who, if you told them a result, would be able to evolve from their own inner consciousness what the steps were which led up to that result. This power is what I mean when I talk of reasoning backward, or analytically.
>
> (I, 83–84)

He expands on this explanation in "The Five Orange Pips," when he declares, "As Cuvier could correctly describe a whole animal by the contemplation of a single bone, so the observer who has thoroughly understood one link in a series of incidents should be able to accurately state all the other ones, both before and after" (I, 225). It is this kind of anterior reconstruction that Holmes manages to accomplish in case after case.

Whether Holmes's methods and results in his detecting career really satisfy scientific standards of rigor is another question entirely. It has often been pointed out that many of his deductions are far from airtight. Although he frequently denounces guesswork, at times he seems alarmingly dependent on lucky intuitions. In one case, "The Musgrave Ritual," his solution depends on the assumption that an elm and an oak have not grown at all in two hundred and fifty years; but then, we have already been told that his knowledge of botany is variable. It would be possible to pick many holes in both his methods and his conclusions. The important point, however, is that he is conceived—and conceives of himself—as a man who applies scientific methods to the detection of crime, and that his success as a detective is due to those methods. He uses them more convincingly than most other fictional detectives, and he hews to them with a religious intensity. His reaction to Watson's first account of his exploits is not merely in character but deeply revealing: "Honestly, I cannot congratulate you upon it. Detection is, or ought to be, an exact science and should be treated in the same cold and unemotional manner. You have attempted to tinge it with romanticism, which produces much the same effect as if you worked a love-story or an elopement into the fifth proposition of Euclid" (I, 90). Like many other nineteenth-century enthusiasts, Holmes thinks of science as a purifying discipline whose chief goal is the clearing away of mysteries. The difference lies in the particular mysteries to which he applies it—and, perhaps, in the utter single-mindedness with which he devotes himself to his vocation. Tennyson's King Arthur was not the only kind of Victorian protagonist who represented "soul at war with sense."

Anyone who carries reason this far is bound to be rather solitary. In the second novel, *The Sign of Four* (1890), from which the above passage is quoted, we begin to see some of the sacrifices that Holmes has made in the pursuit of detachment, for it is in this story that Watson finds a wife. After what we have come to recognize as a typically brilliant series of deductions, Holmes is told of his collaborator's impending defection from Baker Street. "I feared as much," he responds. "I really cannot congratulate you." When Watson wishes to know whether he disapproves of the young woman, Holmes declares that, on the contrary, she is brilliant and charming. "But love is an emotional thing," he adds, "and whatever is emotional is opposed to that true cold reason which I place above all things. I should never marry myself, lest I bias my judgment" (I, 157). The price of his commitment is lifelong isolation and loneliness, and while these states are frequently mitigated by Watson himself (whose wife soon disappears) and by success and fame, they never cease to be the essential conditions of Holmes's existence. At the end of *The Sign of Four*, fame is in the future and Watson is about to disappear. Credit for the case having gone to the police, Watson wonders "what remains for you?" The answer, which ends the novel, is genuinely tragic: " 'For me,' said Sherlock Holmes, 'there still remains the cocaine-bottle.' And he stretched his long white hand up for it" (I, 158).

What was it all *for*, we might well ask at this point? Why such dedication, such an apparatus of self-conscious methodology, and above all such sacrifices, merely to be a private detective? The answer lies in some Victorian attitudes towards crime, mystery, and their detection. When we have explored these attitudes and Holmes's relation to them, we may be in a better position to understand his resonance as a literary character.

Much Victorian literature makes it clear that for the comfortable classes in nineteenth-century England, crime and revolution were related concepts. Both were threats to the social order, and many people did not distinguish closely between them. For a variety of reasons—the growth of poverty and social unrest that followed the industrial revolution, the example of repeated revolutions on the Continent (Tennyson's "red fool-fury of the Seine"), the rise of socialism and of labor unions, the dependence of affluent households on servants whose loyalty might be questionable—those whose interests lay in the existing social order felt threatened and vulnerable throughout virtually the whole nineteenth century. Naturally they demanded protection.

Speaking of the mid-Victorian police, Geoffrey Best maintains: "I cannot rid myself of the impression that its main function was the protection of the property, the amenities and the institutions of the propertied: their homes and business premises, their parks and promenades, their religion and their politics. These good things badly needed protection."[3] Although the middle and upper classes' sense of being a besieged minority eased somewhat in the second half of the century, it did not disappear either in country or in city. The country squire or West End gentleman who feels himself inadequately protected against reds, foreign agitators, unionized laborers, or simply vagrants is a figure of fun when he turns up in the plays of Shaw, but he had many real counterparts in the days when Sherlock Holmes began plying his trade. Any serious crime was a threat. An unsolved crime might be a mortal threat, for it left an unknown enemy at large, perhaps in one's own house. "The butler did it" was a revealing fear before it was a joke. The two nations' ominous predilection for masquerading as each other (for example, in "The Man with the Twisted Lip," one of the most satirical of the stories) made things even more ambiguous.

The crimes Holmes encounters include not only murder, the staple of later detective fiction, but blackmail of the rich and famous (for example, in "Charles Augustus Milverton"); theft on a grand scale, frequently from the aristocracy or from major institutions such as banks ("The Red-Headed League"); attempts to inherit property and position illicitly (*The Hound of the Baskervilles*); revenge for crimes committed in the conquest of the Empire (*The Sign of Four*); a reign of terror by a corrupt labor union (*The Valley of Fear*); crimes whose roots lie in radical political agitation ("The Red Circle"); and espionage that threatens the security of Britain itself ("The Naval Treaty," "The Second Stain," "The Bruce-Partington Plans," "His Last Bow"). Three of the four novels involve secret societies, a focus of much late-Victorian and Edwardian paranoia.[4] The importance of these crimes is greater than that of the individuals who commit them or are their immediate victims. In solving them, Holmes does more than simply satisfy his clients or uphold the abstractions of the law. He single-handedly defends an entire social order whose relatively fortunate members feel it to be deeply threatened by forces that only he is capable of overcoming. "I am," he says in *The Sign of Four*, "the last and highest court of appeal in detection" (I, 90). When all else has failed—and the police almost always fail in the earlier Holmes stories—the isolated, disclassed genius is the one who saves the day. No wonder that by the end of the cycle he has numbered among his clients Queen Victoria, King Edward VII, the pope, the king of Bohemia, the king of Scandinavia, the royal house of Holland, the sultan, and more than one British prime minister.

"The values put forward by the detective story from the time of Holmes to the beginning of World War II," Julian Symons observes in his excellent history of the form, ". . . are those of a class in society that felt it had everything to lose by social change."[5] This generalization applies most obviously to the detective fiction of the 1920s and 1930s, in which the detective is frequently an aristocrat and the whole effect is often deliberately snobbish and reactionary. Dorothy Sayers' Lord Peter Wimsey, Margery Allingham's Albert Campion, and Ngaio Marsh's Roderick Alleyn clearly fit this mold. The Holmes stories, on the contrary, subject the English class system to as penetrating a scrutiny as it ever received from Jane Austen or Charles Dickens, and Holmes himself frequently shows contempt for his aristocratic or royal clients. It would be most accurate to say, however, that the world of the Holmes stories is merely a more realistic one, in which aristocrats are comparatively rare and the majority of crimes do not take place on country-house weekends. The conventions of the detective story as Conan Doyle found and formed them in the 1880s and 1890s were far less rigid and escapist than they became in the hands of his successors. Perhaps one reason was that before 1914 there was less nostalgia (among both writers and readers) for a fading England where everyone knew his place and the upper class maintained its perquisites intact.

Whatever the reasons, the greater realism and more jaundiced view of wealth and power in the Holmes stories should not blind us to the fact that their essential conservatism is not altogether different from that of later detective fiction. Order, if not always law, is upheld, and in those cases where Holmes allows the criminal to escape, it is either because the victim represented a greater threat to society than the criminal (as in "Charles Augustus Milverton") or because the crime was a pardonable act of revenge for acts that the law is helpless to redress ("The Crooked Man"). The law, after all, is a weak reed in the Holmes stories; society needs more effective protection. As Symons continues:

On the social level, then, what crime literature offered to its readers for half a century from 1890 onward was a reassuring world in which those who tried to disturb the established order were always discovered and punished. Society's agent, the detective, was the single character allowed to have high intellectual attainments. He might be by ordinary standards (that is, those of his readers) eccentric, quaint, apparently a bit silly, but his knowledge was always great, and in practice he was omniscient. . . . Part of Holmes's attraction was that, far more than any of his later rivals, he was so evidently a Nietzschean superior man. It was comforting to have such a man on one's side.[6]

It is not quite accurate to say that the detective was the only character with "high intellectual attainments." There was also the master criminal, whose archetype in detective fiction is the brilliant Professor Moriarty, with whom Holmes grapples at the edge of the Reichenbach Falls. "He is the Napoleon of crime, Watson," Holmes explains in "The Final Problem." "He is the organizer of half that is evil and of nearly all that is undetected in this great city. He is a genius, a philosopher, an abstract thinker" (I, 471). It takes no great discernment to observe that Moriarty is Holmes's mirror opposite—fittingly, we are led to believe that they died grasped in each other's embrace, as though a single character had been divided and rejoined— and that in the face of such a dire threat to society, the police are wholly ineffectual.

Readers of the stories seldom ask themselves why the police should be such buffoons when confronted by an intelligent criminal. Such fumbling helplessness of course became one of the conventions of a rigidly conventional literary form, but a convention, at least while it is forming, generally reveals an attitude. I have already pointed out that the prestige of the police was low when Doyle began to write, and this historical fact has something to do with the popularity of an unofficial genius like Holmes. But we might also extend Symons' point about the detective's permitted eccentricity by saying that the detective's success is in considerable measure dependent on that eccentricity. The police are conventional not merely in the literary but also in the social sense of the word; they think and operate by conventions. As a result, they are often the victims of their own orthodoxy, of their social roles as respectable, practical, untheoretical men, whenever they encounter an especially bright or unorthodox criminal. They become blinded by their own unimaginative assumptions about how people act, which are those of the classes they are sworn to protect. No policeman is likely to deduce that a long-lost heir to a baronetcy will set himself up in the neighborhood under an assumed identity and train a gigantic hound to frighten the superstitious baronet to death, or that a butler will make use of a seemingly meaningless family ritual to steal the ancient crown of England; or that the supposed victim of a murder, a former detective himself, will in reality turn out to be the killer. It would not occur to respectable men like Watson or Lestrade that a talented, educated man could earn more by begging than by working hard at a middle-class occupation, still less that having done so he would take a country house like any successful professional man ("The Man with the Twisted Lip"). All of these discoveries require a mind free from the assumptions of comfortable, law-abiding people. In extreme cases, society can be protected only by someone who does not share its orthodoxies, who sees through the disciplines of respectability, who despite his patriotism has little reverence for popular superstitions, who stands outside the normal system of rewards and punishments, who cares nothing for status and depends only on himself—someone, in short, who has more in common with many of the criminals he discovers than with many of his clients. The paradox of Holmes's eccentricity and isolation is one of the most important things that the stories seem to assert: in order to protect the social order effectively, one must separate oneself from it. The only person we ever see defeating Holmes hands down, Irene Adler in "A Scandal in Bohemia," is also a noncriminal who lives outside the system of conventional values and behavior; she is the only woman, besides the queen, whom Holmes unreservedly admires.

A figure who is at once so able and so detached could easily seem threatening to his readers instead of comforting. Holmes is rarely or never threatening, however, because his potentially corrosive intellect never questions the basic assumptions of his society. Crime and disorder result from a failure of individual responsibility, not of institutions. Generally speaking, Holmes finds aristocrats and industrialists unappealing, but he never says a word against either aristocracy or industrialism. Unattractive noblemen, even if they seem to form a remarkably large proportion of their caste, are not to be generalized into a condemnation of the nobility as an institution; they are merely individuals. The stories are consistently hostile to war, but the thought that England's preparations and policies (the subject of several stories) might contribute to the danger of war is never voiced. This is not to say that either Holmes or his author avoids contradicting all the prejudices of the time. Sometimes opinions are approvingly expressed that much of Doyle's original audience might have found excessively tolerant. Holmes is outspokenly pro-American, for example, and in "The Yellow Face," one of the many stories that have American backgrounds, a case of interracial marriage during Reconstruction is treated as a perfectly acceptable match. In matters of the first importance to his English audience, however, Doyle on the whole kept his character from stating unorthodox views. The interracial marriage is after all set in a remote time and place, not in England.

Holmes's social philosophy, if one may so describe such a random set of attitudes, is that while the existing order of things may be unattractive in many ways, his duty and vocation is nevertheless to protect it. One has the sense that both character and author feel any general remedy would be far worse than the disease. The total effect is somewhat similar to that in such Victorian novels of reform as *Hard Times*, where a vivid, detailed description of social and economic evils is followed by a vague, pious, and unconvincing conclusion. While Doyle's purpose, unlike Dickens's, was not to encourage social change—quite the contrary—Doyle dealt with the potentially threatening implications of his stories in ways that are reminiscent of other Victorian writers who found themselves frightened by the undertones of their own realism. As Holmes's critical observations apply only to individuals, so his vocation, the solution of individual crimes, merely restores the social balance that each crime had upset. It never brings that balance into question, for the causes of disorder, where they involve more than individual motives, are not his concern.

And yet, despite the attitudes that are so often expressed in them, the Sherlock Holmes stories are not as conservative as all that. The detective, to be sure, is by definition an upholder of the social order. But what kind of social order is presupposed by his very existence as a free-lance "highest court of appeal"—a court to whom his clients frequently appeal against the mistaken judgments of officialdom? How conservative, at bottom, is a series of books whose protagonist so often flouts both the police and the law in his determination to see that justice—the defining of which he takes to be his own individual prerogative—is finally done?

For after all, justice, not the defense of the existing order, is Holmes's ostensible aim in nearly all the stories. An exception might be made for the stories about espionage, although even here his purpose usually is not just to protect the safety of the nation but also to defend individuals who have been wrongly suspected or disgraced. More often than not, justice means not only robbing the police of their prey but showing them up as dunces. Yet doing so seems not to imperil either social stability or Holmes's own freedom of action. We have already seen that neither Holmes nor his creator shows any wish to change the workings of society in significant ways. That conservatism is a paradoxical tribute to a relatively free society, in which Holmes is free to function without interference from any official entity. No matter how many times he rescues innocent men from the police or allows guilty ones to go free, his own very wide freedom of action is never threatened. (Compare him with Nero Wolfe, whose comparable needling of the New York police leads to frequent threats that his license will be suspended, and more than once even to his arrest.) The society in which Holmes functions sets a high value on justice to individuals and has an astonishing tolerance for independent behavior. It rarely, in the stories, feels itself threatened by Holmes's treatment of the police, nor does it show any signs of ambivalence when forced to choose between upholding the prestige of Scotland Yard and doing justice to an obscure individual suspected of a crime. There are no bumper-stickers, mental or otherwise, advising the people of London to support their local police. On the contrary, it is an unquestioned axiom in the stories that individuals are the locus of value, and that it *cannot* be in the interests of society for an innocent suspect, of whatever class, status, or personal character, to be punished. No matter how often Holmes shows up the police, they still call on him for help. "We're not jealous of you at Scotland Yard," Lestrade announces after Holmes has solved "The Six Napoleons." "No, sir, we are very proud of you, and if you come down tomorrow, there's not a man, from the oldest inspector to the youngest constable, who wouldn't be glad to shake you by the hand" (II, 595). Institutions are fallible; demonstrating their fallibility does not undermine them.

There is no conflict in the stories between upholding the social order and defending the rights of individuals against the power of the state, because the social order is itself a liberal one in the strict sense: the rights and liberties of individuals are among its central values. If it were not liberal, Holmes could function neither as a detective nor as a popular literary figure. What George Watson calls "the English ideology"—the belief in liberty, expressed through parliamentary institutions, as the highest political goal—is central to the stories and their popularity, whatever qualifications one might wish to make about its actual effects in English society during the age of Holmes.[7]

To describe the stories as embodying "bourgeois ideology," as Stephen Knight does, is overly simple if one equates that ideology with retribution and the defense of property.[8] The contrast with British and American detective fiction after the First World War is striking.

Many kinds of justice and injustice are at issue in the stories. Not all injustices are susceptible of legal remedies. The first story of the whole series, *A Study in Scarlet*, is filled with ambiguities about crime, punishment, and the law. Its protagonist—for I doubt that either Holmes or Watson, who are present in only about two-thirds of the story, can be so described—is the murderer himself, Jefferson Hope, a romantic hero of the American frontier whose fiancée and intended father-in-law have been persecuted to their deaths by Mormons twenty years before the story proper begins. After his own escape from Utah, Hope devotes the rest of his life to avenging them, and it is the consummation of his revenge that Holmes is called in to investigate. Throughout the novel, Hope's two victims are presented as cowardly villains. Hope himself, on the contrary, is shown as courageous and resourceful both in committing his crimes and in outwitting pursuit. (His capture occurs only through an inconsistency in the plot, when he is inexplicably lured to an address that he had previously recognized as a trap.) Once he tells his own story, his implacable resistance to religious tyranny makes him the evident hero of the novel. "So thrilling had the man's narrative been," Watson declares, "and his manner was so impressive that we had sat silent and absorbed" (I, 82). Because legally constituted authority was powerless either to prevent or to avenge Hope's injuries, we are clearly intended to see his crimes as justified. As they will later be on Dartmoor, civilization and its institutions are weak forces; where their sway is lessened, or has never penetrated in the first place, superstition rules. Even London itself in this first story is a rough, chaotic place where authority is either ridiculous (the police, the press) or odious (the slumlords of south London).

In London, however, what to do with the captured Hope is a real dilemma. Doyle solves it by having him die of an aortic aneurism before he can make his appearance in court: "he was found in the morning stretched upon the floor of the cell, with a placid smile upon his face, as though he had been able in his dying moments to look back upon a useful life, and on work well done" (I, 83). Having him die in this fashion may evade the question of justice, but if one grants the initial premises of the story it becomes hard to see what else Doyle could have done. Vigilantism is intolerable in England; on the other hand, without it the crimes of twenty years ago would never have been redressed. The plot is a tale of three manhunts in which only the fittest survive and the law plays no part. *A Study in Scarlet* embodies two themes that will recur again and again in subsequent stories: the intrusion of primitivism and disorder (in this case, a medieval style of bigotry practiced in the wilderness) into the heart of civilization, and the long shadow cast upon the present by seemingly forgotten crimes committed far in the past. Contrived as it is, Jefferson Hope's natural death represents an appropriate form of justice and closure. The forces of law have been helpless bystanders throughout his career; his death enables them (and us) at least to be sympathetic bystanders at the end. A final injustice awaits us on the last page, however: Lestrade and Gregson of Scotland Yard receive credit for Hope's capture, and Holmes is described in press accounts merely as "an amateur." Newspapers, no matter how free or enterprising, are not among the forces of reason and justice that Doyle holds up to our respect.

Although Jefferson Hope manages to elude the hangman, he does not escape capture, and the device of having a sympathetic murderer die naturally before he can be tried is not one that Doyle uses again. Instead, the usual pattern in such cases is for Holmes to let the criminal go free. His habit of doing so certainly mitigates his commitment to the institutions of his society. "After all, Watson," he says after releasing a (working-class) jewel-thief in "The Blue Carbuncle," "I am not retained by the police to supply their deficiencies. . . . I suppose that I am committing a felony, but it is just possible that I am saving a soul. This fellow will not go wrong again; he is too terribly frightened. Send him to jail now, and you make him a jail-bird for life" (I, 257). In this instance, Holmes takes an enlightened view of crime, punishment, and his own duties despite the fact that the criminal in question is far from admirable. The more common pattern, however, is for him to withhold his evidence on behalf of killers in the mold of Jefferson Hope. Never again in his entire career does he turn an attractive murderer over to the police.

Doyle need not have created attractive murderers in the first place; his doing so dramatizes both the limitations of the law and the independence of his detective. In "The Abbey Grange" Holmes goes to Scotland Yard with the intention of identifying a young captain in the merchant marine who has battered in the skull of a rich, titled landowner; but he changes his mind and returns to Baker Street. "Once that warrant was made out," he explains, "nothing on earth would save him. Once or twice in my career I feel that I have done more real harm by my discovery of the criminal than ever he had done by his crime. I have learned caution now, and I had rather play tricks with the law of England than with my own conscience" (II, 646). The murderer had, it transpires, acted to protect the woman he loved from the brutality of her aristocratic husband. Holmes defends his decision a second time by contrasting his own position with that of the policeman in charge of the case: "I have the right to private judgment, but he has none. He must disclose all, or he is a traitor to his service." The implication is clear that Holmes is *not* a traitor to the cause he serves if, with some frequency, he makes his own judgment prevail over that of the authorities. Upholding the social order is not the same thing as making human sacrifices to it, still less abandoning one's own private judgment. In this story, uniquely, Holmes and Watson even go through the motions of a mock trial, in which Holmes represents the judge and Watson "a British jury, and I never met a man who was more eminently fitted to represent one" (I, 650). Responsible opinion, represented by the upright narrator, finds the killer not guilty, a judgment which Holmes sanctifies with the proverb *"Vox populi, vox Dei."*

Respect of a sort has been paid to the forms, but in the frequent cases where they prove inadequate, justice takes priority. The same situation is repeated in "The Crooked Man," where another wife-beater meets his end at the hands of a man he had wronged decades earlier. In "The Devil's Foot," the law is doubly limited, for the killer has acted to avenge an earlier murder, undetectable by the police, of a woman whom he wished to marry but could not because of the "deplorable" divorce laws of England. In "Charles Augustus Milverton," Holmes actually witnesses the murder of a blackmailer without either preventing or reporting it. (Throughout the canon, blackmail seems to be the one unforgivable crime.) His response when Lestrade asks him to help investigate perhaps sums up one important reason that his creator made him a private rather than an official detective: "I think there are certain crimes which the law cannot touch, and which therefore, to some extent, justify private revenge. . . . My sympathies are with the criminals rather than with the victim, and I will not handle this case" (II, 582). Despite what this attitude might suggest, there is not a single case in which Holmes himself takes justice into his own hands to punish a criminal whom constituted authority cannot touch. He flouts the law only in the interests of mercy. Only in "The Speckled Band" is he even inadvertently responsible for the extralegal death of a criminal, unless we count his shooting the Hound of the Baskervilles.

Although the nature of judicial punishments is never raised as an issue in the stories, it may not be irrelevant that during Holmes's career the death penalty was the normal (although far from invariable) punishment for murder and was never, except for a few cases of treason during the First World War, invoked for any other crime. The widespread belief today that Victorian public opinion approved of execution for a wide range of offenses has no basis, for although in 1795 there had been as many as two hundred crimes which were in theory punishable by hanging, by 1837 there was in practice only one. This rapid reform came about both for humanitarian reasons and because it came to be widely recognized that the death penalty was not an effective deterrent to crime. Whatever the laws might say, in practice only a small proportion of offenders had been executed even under the older system. "Moreover," as a recent book on English crime during the eighteenth and nineteenth centuries points out.

there is considerable evidence that the harshness of the code of laws resulted in fewer offenders being prosecuted than would otherwise have been the case. . . . Everybody in the long chain from detection of crime to final sentence, including the magistrates and judges themselves, was anxious to take every opportunity to avoid the possibility of causing one of their fellow-creatures to be executed for a mere offence against property. The victim of the crime would refrain from prosecuting. Witnesses would refuse to give evidence.

Magistrates would sometimes refuse to commit people for trial despite clear-cut evidence. Juries would often bring in a perverse verdict against the facts. And the judges were ready to take advantage of every legal loophole to save the accused.[9]

Holmes's laxness in enforcing the law, particularly against people who had committed murder under mitigating circumstances, was therefore backed by a long tradition in real life. Restricting the death penalty to murder did not end the objections; strong opposition to capital punishment for any crime was voiced throughout the Victorian period, although it achieved only the limited success of abolishing public hangings in 1867.

Throughout the reign, as today, the normal punishment for serious crimes was imprisonment. We have already seen Sherlock Holmes's theory that imprisonment could turn an amateur jewel-thief into a hardened professional. The belief that most crimes were committed by members of a criminal class, and that prisons were that class's universities, coexisted uneasily (as it does today) with the desire to reform rather than merely punish. If there really was such a thing as a criminal class or subculture—and modern research suggests that Victorian opinion was not altogether mistaken in believing that there was—then prison was hardly the most effective place to combat it.[10] In fact, the belief that such a class was at the root of most crime could logically be an argument for execution and for another form of punishment that has become extinct in the Western world, transportation.

So far as Sherlock Holmes is concerned, however, the criminal-class theory might never have existed. The vast majority of the crimes he investigates are committed by middle-class people who could by no stretch of the imagination be described as professional criminals, and while he occasionally suggests that a Moriarty or a Rodger Baskerville has a "criminal streak . . . in his blood" (I, 471), he describes crime more often as random and undirected than as a predictable pattern of occurrences. Far from being a conspiracy to undermine the social order, criminal behavior is usually petty and isolated. Most of the people who engage in it do so partly because of circumstances over which they have little control. Such conventional scapegoats as gipsies are sometimes suspected of serious crimes (for example, in "Silver Blaze" and "The Priory School"), but they always turn out to be innocent. The secret political societies that pop up so often in the stories are colorful, but not even the police ever regard them as a serious threat to English society; mostly they work ineffectually to overthrow various Continental despotisms. The Mafia appears once ("The Six Napoleons") as an exotic curiosity. Moriarty as a Napoleon of crime is not merely rare but unique in the stories, and after his death Holmes laments the fact that "London has become a singularly uninteresting city" (II, 496). It was widely, and apparently correctly, believed in the late nineteenth century that crime was a less serious problem than it had been a hundred years earlier.[11] Sherlock Holmes frequently complains that "audacity and romance seem to have passed forever from the criminal world" (II, 870), and that "the London criminal is certainly a dull fellow" (II, 913). Under these circumstances, protecting the social order does not require very draconian measures, at least in the pursuit of crime. The detective and society alike can afford to be magnanimous much of the time.

Earlier criminals were not so fortunate, and we are meant to see English society in the stories as more enlightened and humane than it had been even as recently as the 1850s. Not only public hanging, but transportation—the removal of convicts to forced labor in the Australian colonies—was part of the repertoire of punishments three decades before *A Study in Scarlet*.[12] James Trevor, in "The Gloria Scott," supposedly Holmes's very first case, was transported for committing an embezzlement which, like so many crimes in the stories, was a consequence more of weakness and ill luck than of malicious intentions. "The case might have been dealt leniently with," he aptly explains, "but the laws were more harshly administered thirty years ago than now, and on my twenty-third birthday I found myself chained as a felon with thirty-seven other convicts in the 'tween-decks of the bark *Gloria Scott*, bound for Australia" (I, 381).

As is so often the case in the stories, injustice leads to consequences far worse than the original crime, and secrets in the remote past bring disaster in the present. Subjected to inhuman conditions, the prisoners of the *Gloria Scott* mutiny, massacre the crew, and (with a few exceptions) accidentally blow themselves up. The survivors make their way to Australia, predictably strike it rich in the gold fields, and return to England under assumed names. But secrets will out, and many years later—while Holmes is supposed to be an undergraduate—a villainous seaman named Hudson, whom the surviving mutineers had saved, returns to blackmail Trevor. Thus over a period of twenty-five years or so, roles are reversed: the embezzler, mutineer, and escaped convict becomes a sympathetic figure (not to mention a wealthy and respected one), while an innocent young sailor proves to be thoroughly odious. We are even encouraged (by Holmes) to believe at the end of the story that Hudson has blessedly been murdered by another of the surviving mutineers. Law and order become wholly unattractive when they produce injustice; they even, Doyle seems to suggest, become dangerous to the very stability they represent.

Although "The Gloria Scott" dates from 1893 and is therefore an early story, Doyle had already begun to repeat himself, for the same plot had appeared with minor variations in "The Boscombe Valley Mystery" (1891). Evidently it represented a pattern that Doyle found compelling. Once again we have a wealthy, aging man, this time named McCarthy, who made his money long ago in the Australian gold fields and returned to England to live out his life as a country squire. It is not clear whether McCarthy had originally been transported, but his way of life in Australia was that of a criminal: having failed to strike it rich as a miner, he took up highway robbery and murder. Again the blackmailer is a formerly law-abiding man whom he had spared, this time in the robbery of a "gold convoy." As in "The Gloria Scott," our sympathy for the former criminal is firmly established before we ever learn the history of his relations with the blackmailer, Turner. In this case, the crime that Holmes has been called in to investigate is the brutal murder of Turner ("The head had been beaten in by repeated blows of some heavy and blunt weapon"), which proves in the end to have been committed by McCarthy. As in other cases that involve blackmail or reach far into the past, Holmes' notion of justice owes little to the law and less to the Old Testament. "God help us!" he exclaims after letting the murderer go free. "Why does fate play such tricks with poor, helpless worms? I never hear of such a case as this that I do not think of Baxter's words, and say, 'There, but for the grace of God, goes Sherlock Holmes' " (I, 217).

A character who behaves this way can hardly be described as a symbol of social conservatism and the sanctity of property. His concern is justice, and if by and large he takes the institutions of late-Victorian England as given, he reserves to his own judgment the complicated questions of what constitutes justice in a given set of circumstances and how far it involves bringing people who have committed crimes to the notice of those institutions. Both his detection and his magnanimity derive in part from egotism and from pleasure in the exercise of his powers; they are also, as we see in this last quotation, an expression of humaneness and humility that accords well with the period's prevailing notions.

Victorian writers from Disraeli to Dickens, from Tennyson to Arnold to Huxley, were almost obsessively aware of chaos lurking below the surface of civilized life, waiting for the opportunity to reassert itself. Not only the order of society but civilization itself was a precarious creation, maintained with immense effort against continuous threats. The theory of evolution gave to this pervasive fear a form that was at once scientific and iconographic, for the anarchic and bestial appetites that were so inimical to order could now be seen as survivals of primitive life, of the time when man was half an ape. Reason, morality, law, love, art—all the qualities that made civilization possible were late developments in the evolution of the species, and their hold on humankind was as yet so tenuous that the slightest emergency might reestablish the control of older, darker forces. "Move upward, working out the beast, / And let the ape and tiger die," Tennyson had counseled in *In Memoriam*. Much Victorian opinion cried "Amen!" to the sentiment; only an optimistic few were at all confident that the ape and tiger had yet died out of human nature. "The highest type of man may revert to the animal if he leaves the straight road of destiny," as Sherlock Holmes puts it in "The Creeping Man" (II, 1082).

Among the literary expressions of this set of attitudes, *The Hound of the Baskervilles* (1902) is one of the masterpieces. It is the most highly symbolic of all the Sherlock Holmes stories and the most carefully constructed of the novels. The phosphorescent hound itself, hurtling inexorably across the foggy wastes of Dartmoor after its victim, is the most powerful figure of horror in all the literature of crime, an apparition worthy to threaten not just the existing order of society but the order of the rational mind itself. It is fitting that the threat should manifest itself not in Holmes's own London, the capital of the civilized world, but in a remote rural area among the ruined dwellings of prehistoric man.

Holmes's predilection for London and anti-romantic mistrust of the countryside are made clear from the start of his career and never change. London is the locus of all those aspects of civilization and intellectual progess that he values most highly. Rural England, on the other hand, has never altogether evolved out of barbarism. The ape and tiger retain a stronger hold there; law and reason are correspondingly frailer. Holmes makes his feelings clear in the early story "The Copper Beeches": "It is my belief, Watson, founded upon my experience, that the lowest and vilest alleys in London do not present a more dreadful record of sin than does the smiling and beautiful countryside" (I, 323). He might have added that in the country, as this story and others illustrate, the squire is a nearly absolute power and may be an absolute tyrant; neither law nor public opinion is strong enough to bridle him, and geographic isolation sometimes permits him to get away with murder. In *The Hound of the Baskervilles* we are never allowed to forget the contrasts between London and Dartmoor, and it is only by submitting to live for a time in a prehistoric stone hut on the moor that Holmes's London mind can defeat and partially exorcise the primitive forces arrayed against his client.

The early chapters of the book are heavy with references to nightmare, madness, the diabolical, and reversions to the primitive. Dr. Mortimer, who brings the case to Holmes's attention, is an archeologist and a specialist in atavistic diseases. His two published papers are significantly entitled "Some Freaks of Atavism" and "Do We Progress?" A man of scientific habits, and London-trained, he finds himself wholly at a loss to understand the story he tells Holmes of the mysterious death of Sir Charles Baskerville. A "spectral hound," a "hound of hell" in the England of 1889?[13] Yet he has seen the footprints in the yew alley beside the body of his friend. Having read Holmes the centuries-old legend of the nemesis hound, he does not know whether the tools of science will have any power to explain the horror on the moor. At the same time, he has won Holmes's respect by calculating the length of time Sir Charles had waited at the moor gate from the number of times ash had dropped from his cigar. "It is evidently a case of extraordinary interest,"

Holmes declares, "and one which presented immense opportunities to the scientific expert." Dr. Mortimer is more doubtful.

> "There is a realm in which the most acute and most experienced of detectives is helpless."
> "You mean that the thing is supernatural?"
> "I did not positively say so."
> "No, but you evidently think it."

Holmes's reaction is comfortingly skeptical:

> "I have hitherto confined my investigations to this world," said he. "In a modest way I have combated evil, but to take on the Father of Evil himself would, perhaps, be too ambitious a task. Yet you must admit that the footmark is material."
>
> (II, 680–81)

Soon Holmes prepares himself for the investigation of the case and the protection of the new baronet, Sir Henry Baskerville, who has just come back from the wide, empty spaces of western Canada to take up residence at Baskerville Hall. Needless to say, Sir Henry has no conception of what awaits him in the corrupt old world of his ancestors. A conversation with Watson foreshadows what is to come but hardly prepares us adequately for it. Watson comments:

> "It must be a wild place."
> "Yes, the setting is a worthy one. If the devil did desire to have a hand in the affairs of men—"
> "Then you are yourself inclining to the supernatural explanation."
> "The devil's agents may be of flesh and blood, may they not? . . . Of course, if Dr. Mortimer's surmise should be correct, and we are dealing with forces outside the ordinary laws of Nature, there is an end of our investigation. But we are bound to exhaust all other hypotheses before falling back upon this one. . . ."
>
> (II, 684)

The sense of foreboding, of menacing forces that transcend the ordinary powers of crime, increases markedly once the focus of the story shifts to Dartmoor. Holmes has already remarked, "I am not sure that of all the five hundred cases of capital importance which I have handled there is one which cuts so deep" (II, 693). When Watson approaches Baskerville Hall, we begin to wonder whether Holmes may this time be out of his depth. The very landscape conspires against rationality. "Over the green squares of the fields and the low curve of a wood," the normally unimaginative Watson describes gothically, "there rose in the distance a gray, melancholy hill, with a strange jagged summit, dim and vague in the distance, like some fantastic landscape in a dream." It is autumn. "The rattle of our wheels died away as we drove through drifts of rotting vegetation . . ." (II, 700–701). The nightmare landscape is not altogether uninhabited. Amid the bleakness stand the houses of Sir Henry's few neighbors and, farther away, the great prison of Princetown. There are soldiers on the road because a prisoner has escaped—a savage murderer, perhaps insane, with "beetling forehead . . . sunken animal eyes," "half animal and half demon" (II, 745, 748). A throwback to the primitive who might have stepped from one of Dr. Mortimer's papers, he is an appropriate inhabitant of this landscape, and it is fitting as well as chilling that after living for a time on the moor, he breaks his neck while trying to escape from the Hound.

At the center of this haunted wasteland, reducing even the Princetown prison to insignificance, is the great Grimpen Mire. "A false step yonder means death to man or beast," declares Stapleton, the naturalist, and Watson witnesses at a distance the death of a pony that has been caught in its grip. The pathways to the islands at the center of the bog are mysterious and dangerous; Stapleton warns Watson against trying to find his way there, adding, "That is where the rare plants and the butterflies are, if you have the wit to reach them" (II, 707–8). As we learn eventually, the Hound of the Baskervilles is there too, awaiting the night when his master will have need of him. Meanwhile, the moor has become a place of horror to the local peasants, haunted by the sound of his baying, and even steadier observers find that the mire has taken hold of their minds. "Life has become like that great Grimpen Mire," Watson says soon after his arrival, "with little green patches everywhere into which one may sink and with no guide to point the track" (II, 711).

By the end of the story, the rational mind is back on its throne, and the spectral hound is only a dead dog. But the outcome does not erase the impression of horror and unreason that has been so powerfully built up. Nor is it easily reached. Before it comes, Holmes must undergo an initiation by living on the moor, actually sleeping on the stone bed of vanished prehistoric inhabitants, and Sir Henry must confront the Hound alone, an experience that costs him a nervous breakdown. The forces of order and civilization are pitifully weak. The soldiers never come close to capturing the convict; indeed, they never appear again in the story. The police are never in evidence until Holmes summons them at the end. The local embodiment of the law is ridiculous: an eccentric landowner who indulges in petty lawsuits as a sport. No clergyman ever calls at Baskerville Hall. Dr. Mortimer is amiable but perennially baffled. Sir Henry, the local squire and symbol of order, is surrounded by malevolence. Even servants betray him, both in London and at Baskerville Hall. And Stapleton, the man of science, proves to be the trainer of the Hound, the murderer of Sir Charles, the disguised next heir to the baronetcy, and a throwback to the most evil of all the Baskervilles.

The Hound of the Baskervilles is in fact a story of throwbacks from beginning to end. Civilization is not merely fragile; its representatives are paralyzed. Stapleton nearly wins, for he is masterful, imaginative, wholly unscrupulous, and more purposeful than any other character in the story except Holmes. Since Holmes is absent from nearly half the story—living out on the moor when Watson believes him to be in London—Watson and the reader alike have a frustrating sense of being at war with forces that are menacing, unerringly directed, and impossible to identify. Only when Holmes reappears, discovered by Watson in his stone hut on the moor, does the situation begin to clarify. When Watson notes that Holmes's chin was "as smooth and his linen as perfect as if he were in Baker Street" (II, 740), we know that civilization will win, though thanks only to a single champion.

Even at that, the moor almost defeats Holmes. When he orders Sir Henry to walk home at night as bait for the Hound and its master, a dense fog drifts across the path. Holmes, Watson, and Lestrade are forced to retreat to higher ground, and when they finally see the Hound, it is nearly upon its victim. Once again, everyone is paralyzed except the detective himself. Watson describes the spectacle:

> A hound it was, an enormous coal-black hound, but not such a hound as mortal eyes have ever seen. Fire burst from its open mouth, its eyes glowed with a smouldering glare, its muzzle and hackles and dewlap were outlined in flickering flame. Never in the delirious dream of a disordered brain could anything more savage, more appalling, more hellish be conceived than that dark form and savage face which broke upon us out of the wall of fog.
>
> (II, 757)

Holmes manages, just barely, to shoot the Hound and save his client's life. Stapleton escapes from Holmes and the law but apparently falls victim to the mire. Primitive nature, not the forces of order, reclaims him in the end.

Holmes ultimately defeats Stapleton through what he calls "the scientific use of the imagination" (II, 687), and it is an impressive victory. Stapleton is the most powerful antagonist Holmes ever faces—"never yet have we helped to hunt down a more dangerous man than he who is lying yonder" (II, 760), he tells Watson near the end. Like Moriarty, who in the somewhat murky chronology of the stories is supposed not to have appeared on the scene yet, Stapleton is dangerous partly because he too represents the scientific intellect married to a Holmesian degree of determination. (He is, however, a much more realized and less abstract character than Moriarty.) He has become a dedicated student of the moor, and Holmes must do the same in order to defeat him. All the other characters appear puny and powerless in the setting of Dartmoor. One has the feeling that Holmes and Stapleton are equals who understand each other all along. On one occasion,

Stapleton even impersonates Holmes. As Stapleton, his plans, and his hound are repeatedly described as diabolical, so Holmes is once half-consciously referred to by Watson as "our guardian angel" (II, 739). Their combat is inevitable and without quarter. Each is immensely resourceful but lonely, aided only by smaller figures who do not understand what they are doing. Each, in fact, deceives his closest associate.

The victory is won, the demons are exorcised; Holmes's solution to the mystery vindicates science and civilization. "We've laid the family ghost once and forever," he announces at the moment of triumph (II, 757). But it is only a partial triumph, for the bleakness of Dartmoor and the mire remains as impenetrable and unconquerable as any Wessex landscape in the novels of Thomas Hardy. Stapleton is apparently dead, but his legacy of malice survives him, for we have learned that he used to run a school. As he told it himself soon after meeting Watson, "The privilege of living with youth, of helping to mould those young minds, and of impressing them with one's own character and ideals was very dear to me" (II, 710). Seldom is Conan Doyle quite so ironic as this, but then seldom in the Holmes stories are the issues as large as they are here. Sir Henry, instead of entering into the enjoyment of his inheritance, has had to leave the country for a year's convalescent travel with Dr. Mortimer. Holmes, needless to say, is back in London, center of the world he represents. As the story ends, he is about to celebrate his commitment to civilization in an entirely appropriate and symbolic fashion— by taking Watson to the opera.

After *The Hound of the Baskervilles*, Conan Doyle published only one more Sherlock Holmes novel—*The Valley of Fear* (1914), a second-rate thriller in which Holmes appears only at the beginning and end—and three collections of short stories. In two late stories, "The Devil's Foot" and "The Sussex Vampire," he tried to recapture the resonance and conviction of *The Hound of the Baskervilles*, but both stories are relative failures. The short-story form did not permit sufficient development to make the exorcism of the irrational fully persuasive. Furthermore, Doyle had by now grown tired of Holmes and Watson. Few of the stories in *His Last Bow* (1917) and almost none in *The Case Book of Sherlock Holmes* (1927), the last two collections, have anything like the depth or richness of even the less ambitious stories in the earlier volumes.

Perhaps Doyle's waning interest is sufficient to explain the decline, but there is another reason with effects that reached beyond Doyle. I have already pointed out that the seriousness and impact of the Holmes canon depended on the belief, shared by author and readers, that crime represented a potentially mortal threat to civilization and that the isolated but loyal detective was the only figure equipped to meet it. Early in the twentieth century, both halves of this belief became less plausible. The police (in England, at least) came to be more highly respected than before, and crime came to seem less pervasive and threatening.[14] By the time of the late stories, the police have improved to the point that in "The Red Circle" and "Wisteria Lodge," they figure things out more thoroughly than the now superfluous Holmes. But I offer the speculation that the First World War was the crucial event that made the detective story a less serious form of entertainment than it had been at Holmes's peak. After 1918, it was no longer easy for a serious writer to believe that domestic crime was among the most important threats to the stability of civilization. War, revolution, and foreign enemies had permanently replaced it. Who could regard a solitary murderer, or even a Napoleon of crime, with the same gravity in an age of world wars and political upheavals?[15]

From the 1870s until 1914, there had been a flourishing genre of popular fiction that dealt with the probable course of a future great war between Britain and Germany, or sometimes between Britain and France. Conan Doyle even contributed to this kind of fiction with a story called "Danger," which warned that German submarine warfare could imperil British supply routes in the event of a European war. Instead of preparing their readers for the realities of modern world war, however, most of the books and stories of this kind had the opposite effect, for they assumed that the wars of the future would be much like the brief wars of the mid-nineteenth century. I. F. Clarke, who has studied this genre exhaustively, declares:

> It became standard practice for writers in the major European countries to describe the shape of the war-to-come in order to demonstrate the need for bigger armies or better warships. . . . Almost all of them took it for granted that the next war would be fought more or less after the style of the last, and that war would continue to be conducted in a relatively restrained and humane manner. . . . The slaughter of the trenches, the use of poison gas, the immense damage caused by submarines, the very scale of a world-wide industrialized war were mercifully hidden from the admirals, generals, politicians, and popular novelists who joined in the great enterprise of predicting what was going to happen.[16]

When the *real* war came, its horror took everyone by surprise. Among the many things it swept away was the set of beliefs about civilization, and the threats to civilization, that underlay the creation of a hero like Sherlock Holmes.

One has the sense, in reading the late Holmes stories, of watching a play near the end of its run that has transferred to a smaller theatre. The wooden repetition of earlier plots in late stories like "The Mazarin Stone" and "Shoscombe Old Place" leads one to think that Doyle had not only tired of his characters but no longer felt that crime was very important. As Doyle became more and more devoted to spiritualism during and after the war, so Holmes in the late stories grows increasingly frustrated, as if conscious of the small scope in which his powers are effectual. "The ways of fate are indeed hard to understand," he exclaims in "The Veiled Lodger." "If there is not some compensation hereafter, then the world is a cruel jest" (II, 1101). In "The Retired Colourman," the final story in the last collection, he is even more wistful: "But is not all life pathetic and futile? . . . We reach. We grasp. And what is left in our hands at the end? A shadow. Or worse than a shadow—misery" (II, 1113). The Holmes who makes these statements is still a genius who solves crimes that baffle the police, but he has come a long way from the eager crusader who had just discovered a test for bloodstains.

In the preface to the last collection, where he bade farewell to Holmes and Watson, Doyle conjured up "some fantastic limbo for the children of imagination" and expressed the hope that "perhaps in some humble corner of such a Valhalla, Sherlock and his Watson may for a time find a place, while some more astute sleuth with some even less astute comrade may fill the stage which they have vacated" (II, 983). The successors duly made their entrances—indeed, Hercule Poirot was already before the footlights—but the stage proved to be a smaller one than before, with sets that were more obviously artificial. Agatha Christie, Margery Allingham, Dorothy Sayers, Cyril Hare, and their contemporaries all wrote superlatively well at times, but often it is hard not to feel that they regarded murder as a joke and an opportunity for clever twists of plot. Perhaps it had become too rare in real English life to be treated any other way. There are exceptions in the work of all these writers, but rarely do they take crime, its social context, or its implications as seriously as Doyle did in the stories that made Sherlock Holmes one of the most famous characters in the world's literature.[17] Their detectives remain guardians of conservative values in whom irony, eccentricity for its own sake, and upper-class affectations replace the earnestness of the Holmes stories. This problem of seriousness is sometimes dealt with by involving them in counterespionage, but as several of the Holmes stories had already demonstrated, the solitary detective's talents were incongruent with the scale of international relations. Much of the detective fiction written since 1945 is superior in character development to all that went before, but it lacks the social and moral resonance of Doyle at his best. A character like Sherlock Holmes could grow to full stature only in a time when crime could plausibly be seen as the greatest threat to order and its detection the greatest of services, when the police were widely believed to be ineffectual, when science was viewed by its enthusiasts as a new force crusading for progress against ignorance and unreason—above all, when the prospect of a devastating war could seem less menacing than an unsolved robbery or murder.

Notes

1. Sir Arthur Conan Doyle, *The Complete Sherlock Holmes*, 2 vols. (New York: Doubleday, n.d.). All quotations from the Holmes stories are from this, the standard American edition, and are identified by volume and page in parentheses. In citing the titles of stories, I have consistently omitted "The Adventure of" for the sake of conciseness.

2. Thomas Love Peacock, "An Essay on Fashionable Literature" (1818), in H. F. B. Brett-Smith and C. E. Jones, eds., *The Works of Thomas Love Peacock* (rpt., New York: AMS Press, 1967), vol. 8, p. 265.

3. Geoffrey Best, *Mid-Victorian Britain 1851–1875* (New York: Schocken Books, 1972), p. 270. One of Best's illustrations (fig. 5) shows "one of the guarded gates which protected so many superior-class residential streets and squares."

4. That is, if one accepts Doyle's view of the Mormons as a secret society. The preoccupation with secret societies had a long history, as Marilyn Butler points out:

After the French Revolution . . . the conservative imagination . . . becomes possessed by the idea of an evil conspiracy. The secret societies of the period become less clearly defined and perhaps even more terrifying a band of dedicated fanatics bent on drawing the innocent into their clutches as a step toward augmenting their power and influence. The fascination felt by writers of all opinions for secret societies, identified or not identified, contemporary or historical, is a symptom of the instability and political hysteria felt throughout Europe in the 1790's. (*Jane Austen and the War of Ideas* [Oxford: Clarendon Press, 1975], p. 115)

The revived literary interest in such societies a century later had something to do with the rise of anarchism; perhaps the chief literary monument to that interest is G. K. Chesterton's *The Man Who Was Thursday* (1908). See James Joll, *The Anarchists* (Cambridge, Mass.: Harvard University Press, 1979).

5. Julian Symons, *Mortal Consequences* (New York: Schocken Books, 1973), p. 10.

6. Ibid., pp. 10–11, 65. Pierre Nordon makes a similar series of points in *Conan Doyle* (New York: Holt, Rinehart, 1967), especially chapter 14. Like Nordon, Erik Routley, in *The Puritan Pleasures of the Detective Story* (London: Gollancz, 1972), sees Holmes as a figure of chivalric romance updated for the late nineteenth century. As Routley puts it, "Holmes is what he is because of the counterpoint between the character of the cold logical reasoner and the romantic remoteness of this character from the ordinary run of fictional heroes" (42). The word *romantic* in this formulation strikes me as lacking precision.

7. George Watson, *The English Ideology: Studies in the Language of Victorian Politics* (London: Allen Lane, 1973).

8. Stephen Knight, *Form and Ideology in Crime Fiction* (London: Macmillan, 1980), p. 87.

9. J. J. Tobias, *Crime and Police in England 1700–1900* (Dublin: Gill and Macmillan, 1979), pp. 145, 146.

10. Ibid., pp. 57ff.

11. Ibid., p. 73; cf. Best, *Mid-Victorian Britain*, p. 271.

12. Tobias, *Crime and Police*, pp. 159–70. Transportation to the American colonies began soon after the settlement at Jamestown; the Virginia General Assembly protested the practice as early as 1670, but it continued until the colonies rebelled in 1775. Tobias estimates that some fifty thousand convicts were eventually sent to America (162). From 1785 until the early 1850s Australia was used. Convict colonies were about as popular as nuclear-waste dumps today, and when the Australians declared their country off limits, the British government finally called it quits and built more prisons at home.

13.   Francis Thompson's poem "The Hound of Heaven," in which the canine pursuer represented a very different supernatural intrusion into civilized life, had appeared in 1893.

14.   G. M. Trevelyan, in his *English Social History* (New York: David McKay, 1942), optimistically dates this process back to the 1850s (530–31). But as Geoffrey Best makes clear (*Mid-Victorian Britain*, p. 271), it took a long time to become a reality. Furthermore, in 1877 the Detective Department of Scotland Yard "lost all its credibility in the eyes of both police and public" when three of its four chief detective inspectors were involved in a bribery scandal; in the following year, the modern Criminal Investigation Department was created (Tobias, *Crime and Police*, p. 112).

15.   As I discovered after finishing this essay, Ian Ousby speculates along similar lines in *Bloodhounds of Heaven: The Detective in English Fiction from Godwin to Doyle* (Cambridge, Mass.: Harvard University Press, 1976), pp. 173–75.

16.   I. F. Clarke, *Voices Prophesying War* (London: Oxford University Press, 1966), pp. 3, 68–69.

17.   Edmund Wilson put the same distinction another way in 1945: "My contention is that Sherlock Holmes *is* literature on a humble but not ignoble level, whereas the mystery writers most in vogue now are not" (*Classics and Commercials* [New York: Farrar, Straus, 1950], p. 267). Wilson is one of the few well-known critics to have discussed the Holmes stories as literature; unfortunately he did so very briefly.

The Case of the Domesticated Aesthete

Paul Barolsky

What one man invents another can discover.
—Sherlock Holmes

Sherlock Holmes, though of recent invention, is one of the most popular characters in English literature. After Hamlet, some would say, he is the most famous of them all. He has been called a version of the epic hero, a sort of Socrates, Sir Galahad, Hamlet, and even Superman. Sherlockphiliacs, and they are legion, have written about every facet of his life—his schooling, his medical education, his studies of chemistry, his literary taste, his love of music, his athletic skills, his religious beliefs, his philosophy, and his attitude toward women. They have traced his every step; in fact or fancy they have revisited every place that he went. 221B Baker Street has become a shrine, all the objects in it relics, Holmes himself a cult figure.

Curiously enough, however, Holmes stands outside the history of literature. Scholars and biographers have written extensively about the impact romantic fiction had on Conan Doyle's imagination, but students of Victorian and Edwardian literature have not placed Holmes squarely in a literary context. This is probably the case because, although he is indisputably a great character, the stories in which he appears are not what we consider to be major fiction. These writings thus remain marginal to the history of literature as it is currently written.

Holmes is nonetheless a typical figure of the *fin de siècle*. Flourishing in the 1890's, he has much in common with the aesthetes and decadents of his day, both real and fictional. In recent years critics have occasionally made this point in passing, but, perhaps because it runs counter to the conventional view of Holmes, its implications have not been fully explored. Granted, Holmes is neither so precious as Walter Pater nor so artificial as Oscar Wilde; but in many ways he is like them, like Wilde's Dorian Gray, Huysmans' Symbolist aesthete Des Esseintes, and the exquisite young connoisseur of art Bernard Berenson as well. A central figure in the history of aestheticism— that current of modern art and literature concerned with aesthetic experience and pleasure, with the cultivation of art for its own sake—Holmes is a closet

From *Virginia Quarterly Review* Vol. 60, No. 3 (Summer 1984): 438–52. Reprinted by permission.

aesthete. If he is never mentioned in the histories of aestheticism that treat both actual and fictional aesthetes, this is because his creator disguised or domesticated the detective's aesthetic propensities, making them palatable to a vast, popular audience. Although Holmes flouts conventions, he is never scandalous in the manner of a Dorian Gray; rather, his aestheticism is tempered and mitigated. His *domus* or domicile is 221B Baker Street, his major-domo, the sympathetic and legendary Watson, who plays the bourgeois fool, so to speak, to the refined and redoubtable "amateur" of crime.

Let us briefly consider the evidence for the theory linking Holmes to the notorious aestheticism of his day. Such data are amply furnished to us by Dr. Watson—"Good, old Watson," as Holmes calls him with affectionate condescension. Whereas Watson is conventional in his manner of thinking, Holmes is an eccentric, a "Bohemian," as Watson describes him; and Watson should know, for he has read Murger's *Scènes de la vie de Bohème*. Watson often pictures for us the "languid, lounging figure" of Holmes, ensconced in his "snug" quarters, seeking like all the distinguished aesthetes of his century— like Des Esseintes and Dorian Gray, like Poe, Baudelaire, Swinburne, and Pater—to escape from the "commonplace," to free himself from what Baude-laire denominates *"les noirs ennuis."* Holmes's existence is spent primarily in "impassioned contemplation," as Pater would call it, or in "reverie" à la Gautier. A recluse, like Des Esseintes and Dorian Gray in his essentially Esseintian ascendancy, he does not, for the most part, receive visitors other than his clients or his Boswellian companion. True, Holmes often ventures out and can be extremely active; but this activity is limited to the solution of mysteries, which depend, *au fond*, on "meditation."

As an aesthete, Holmes is obsessive, consumed by his "art" in the manner of a Flaubert. Just as the great French writer, whom Holmes quotes on one occasion, reads prodigiously in the service of his art, absorbing hundreds of books necessary to the plausibility of his own writing, Holmes reads extensively to achieve an impressive technical knowledge essential to his work of detection. If Flaubert's Bouvard and Pécuchet comically echo their author's own encyclopedic aspirations in their quest for knowledge, Holmes, in his technical studies, becomes a sort of Bouvard or Pécuchet, writing or planning treatises on cigar ashes, typewriters, handwriting, foot-prints, and tattoos—thus eliciting a smile of pleasure and bemusement from the reader at such singular compulsion. Flaubert once remarked that in writing *Madame Bovary* he steered a precarious course between the vulgar and the lyrical. The same can be said of Holmes, who finds a sort of poetry in crime. Newspaper reporters and the police see only the vulgarity of crime, as Holmes remarks, because they fail to be selective in their analysis of the facts; such selectivity depends on aesthetic sensibility.

For Holmes, brilliant crime is "art." Great crimes he considers "master-pieces," great criminals "artists." His point of view descends from that of Thomas De Quincey, who regarded murder among the "fine arts," who belonged to the society known as the "Connoisseurs of Murder." Holmes indeed speaks of himself as a "connoisseur of crime," and just as cognoscenti lament the decline of art in their own times, Holmes deplores the decline of the art of crime in his day, the lack of criminal "audacity" and "romance." An exception is the notorious criminal Professor Moriarty, the greatest "master" of Holmes's epoch and thus his greatest rival; Holmes respects him more than any of his contemporaries. This admiration can be likened to Wilde's celebration in "Pen, Pencil, and Poison" of Thomas Griffiths Wainwright— "a subtle and secret poisoner without rival in this or any age." Holmes would have agreed with Swinburne, who deplored the unaesthetic murders committed by Henry Wainwright: "Having chanced on a grim subject I must express to you the deep grief with which I see the honoured name of Wainwright associated with a vulgar and clumsy murder utterly inartistic and discreditable to the merest amateur. It is as though William Shakespeare were charged with the authorship (*pace Laureati*) of 'Queen Mary.' " Holmes would also have understood the Baudelairean aesthetic of Degas' remark that "one has to commit a painting the way one commits a crime." It is not surprising that an illicitly acquired painting by Greuze hangs behind the desk of Moriarty, for he is himself a connoisseur; nor is it unexpected that Holmes knows all about this work, its provenance, and the painter's place in the history of art.

The comparison of Holmes to the other aesthetes of his day, both real and invented, might appear strained were it not sound. For all his posturing, Wilde has a moral sense no less than does Holmes; and although he is never so preposterous as Wilde, Holmes himself, in his quiet way, rejects contemporary mores, as when he deems it necessary to commit burglary or withhold information from the police. Holmes' sense of justice also barely conceals the fact that the principal interest of his work is aesthetic. He refers to a murder as "charming" for the clues it affords, and he gives the impression that his love of crime even exceeds his commitment to justice. After all, as Holmes frequently asserts in the manner of Gautier, he practices his art "for its own sake." With his romantic forebears, from De Quincey to Pater, he is also attracted by what he calls the "bizarre." Holmes is an amateur of "caprice," "whimsy," the "queer," and what Pater describes in the wake of Baudelaire and Swinburne as "a life of brilliant sins." Blood bespattered corpses and perverse instruments of crime are what arouse or excite him. He is, one might almost say, intoxicated or drugged by crime, carried to a feverish pitch of excitement by a challenging mystery, just as Des Esseintes is transported by perfumes or Symbolist pictures or as Dorian Gray is uplifted by the sight of embroideries, tapestries, and jewels. When Holmes is not stimulated by his work, he succumbs to boredom and ultimately depression. He escapes from this tedium through the use of cocaine, and in this respect he belongs to the long and distinguished line of aesthetic users of drugs, including De Quincey and Coleridge, Poe and Baudelaire. When Watson finally cures Holmes of his habit, the detective becomes less of an outsider to the bourgeois world of Victorian England but only somewhat less so.

As if reacting to the idea of Holmes as aesthete, the author of a recent monograph on Conan Doyle began a chapter by contrasting the virile author with the effete Oscar Wilde. Yet Sherlock Holmes is never described in words as purple or flowery as those used by Huysmans and Wilde to portray Des Esseintes and Dorian Gray, and Holmes appears to be very different from the arch-aesthete Thaddeus Sholto whom he encounters in his London home, a sumptuous "shrine," an "oasis of art," filled with orientalia. Recalling the description of the entranced Holmes seated "like some strange Buddha" or of Holmes employing a piece of "real eggshell pottery of the Ming Dynasty" to entrap an aesthetic adversary, we realize, however, that there is more than a little of Sholto in Holmes himself. Indeed, like Sholto, Holmes is something of a dandy, for Watson remarks on his "primness of dress," "debonair manner," "suavity," and "nonchalance." He may not, like Des Esseintes, possess a gold turtle or, like Dorian Gray, a collection of precious *objets*, but he does display exquisite objects—his bejeweled turquoise snuffbox and emerald tiepin. Like Wilde, but not to the same degree, his speech is graced by witticisms and epigrams: "There is nothing more deceptive than an obvious fact," or ". . . there is nothing so unnatural as the commonplace." When he receives an invitation, he remarks to Watson that he can attend and be "bored or lie," recalling Wilde's more ironic telegram of regret: "I cannot come. Lie follows." Holmes even sends a message to Watson in the manner of Wilde: "Come at once if convenient—if not convenient come all the same." At times the tone of Holmes' speech approaches Wilde's sharp patronizing tone, as when he mocks his plodding companion, "Watson! you scintillate today." Indeed, his air of superiority is strikingly like that of Gilbert toward his naïve interlocutor Ernest, in Wilde's "The Critic as Artist." Holmes also sounds like Wilde or Wilde's Lord Henry Wotton in *The Picture of Dorian Gray*, objecting to the philistine or "popular taste" which Watson appeals to in the "meretricious finales" of his accounts of Holmes's exploits. Watson is a kind of foil to Holmes' more "finely adjusted temperament," and the good doctor's literal-mindedness throws into relief the very "delicacy" and "finesse" of the detective, which are described in terms reminiscent of Walter Pater's critical vocabulary.

No less than Wilde and his literary heroes is Holmes a man of broad culture. A scintillating conversationalist, he discourses on Buddhism, violins, and warships. His speech is ornamented with choice phrases or words in German, French, and Latin, conveying an air of culture. He compares Horace to Hafiz, carries a copy of Petrarch with him on a case, quotes from Shakespeare, Goethe, Richter, and refers to De Quincey (not surprisingly!), Meredith, and Flaubert. His taste for the latter two writers especially reflects his highly developed aesthetic sensibility. Holmes is also an amateur of music, a violinist, a connoisseur of violins, and the author of a treatise on the motets of Orlando De Lassus. Sometimes, while pondering a crime, he plays strange melodies—on his violin—suggesting that his very meditations, like all art, as Pater says, aspire to the condition of music. Working on a case, he plays Mendelssohn for Watson; and, with marvelous aplomb, indeed *sprezzatura*, he interrupts his investigations to visit Prince Albert Hall or other concert houses to hear Chopin or German lieder. These breaks are like those disarming pauses when Holmes invites Watson to partake of the "epicurean" delights of fine food and wines. There is ample evidence that Holmes has a refined palate and is something of a gourmet; for example, he orders "a couple of brace of cold woodcock, a pheasant, a *pâté de foie gras* with a group of ancient cobwebby bottles." These "luxuries" were delivered by two visitors who "vanished away, like the genii of the Arabian Nights."

In like fashion, despite Watson's claims to the contrary, Holmes is also something of a connoisseur of paintings. As such, he attributes paintings in the Baskerville collection: "I know what is good when I see it, and I see it now. That's a Kneller, I'll swear, that lady in the blue silk over yonder; and the stout gentleman with the wig ought to be a Reynolds." While working on the Baskerville case, Holmes stops off to see an exhibition of modern Belgian paintings in a gallery on Bond Street. Not inconceivably he saw works by the Belgian Symbolist Ferdinand Khnopff, who, much admired by Oscar Wilde, exhibited in London toward the end of the century. Holmes might very well have enjoyed the fantasy and morbidity of Khnopff, just as Des Esseintes admired the macabre Baudelairean works of the symbolist Gustave Moreau. Even the language of art criticism tinges Holmes's description of a case. He suggests to Watson, adapting "art jargon," that they refer to a bloody murder as a "Study in Scarlet." Scarlet is the color par excellence of the 1890's, and his adaptation of Whistler's symbolist titles of paintings (as studies in various colors) appositely aestheticizes murder in the very *mots justes* of the day. Calling one of his *Intentions*, "Pen, Poison, and Pencil," a "study in green," Oscar Wilde adapted a similar description, and it is suggestive to observe that Holmes' Whistlerian usage predates Wilde's use of the similar subtitle and Conan Doyle's first encounter with Wilde. "A curious conjunction in the history of English letters," as it has been called, Doyle's meeting with Wilde occurred in 1889 at a dinner party to which they had been invited by an agent of *Lippincott's Magazine*. The creators of Sherlock Holmes and Dorian Gray had much to talk about, and they both offered works to the magazine: Doyle's *The Sign of Four* and Wilde's *The Picture of Dorian Gray*, both published the following year.

II

Holmes, it is well known, insists that the investigator must be attentive to "details." He should go beyond mere "impressions" by careful observation to analyze the important data of a case. This is precisely what Pater says of the "aesthetic critic," who having experienced impressions strongly, "drives directly at the discrimination and analysis of them." Just as Pater delves into the "mystery" of Leonardo's personality, for example, analyzing its expression in art, Holmes carefully analyzes the "mind" of the criminal. Holmes's studies of criminal personality are, in fact, akin to Pater's investigations of artistic temperament. The Paterian critic has a finely developed sense of temperament, enabling him to extract the essence of artistic personality from a poem or painting; and in a similar way Sherlock Holmes intuits the "master" behind a crime. Insisting that the detective relies on "imagination" and "intuition," Holmes refers to qualities essential to aesthetic criticism; and when Watson mentions Holmes's "acute set of senses," he marks attributes fundamental to the aesthetic critic. Holmes repeatedly insists to Watson that it is not simply knowledge of facts that enables him to solve mysteries but his understanding of their significance. He has what Pater calls a "sense of fact;" and it is this intuitive power that makes of him, as Pater would say, "an artist, his work *fine art*." Holmes' attitude toward his art is also decidedly like Pater's. When Watson calls him "a benefactor of the race," Holmes modestly quotes Flaubert's letter to George Sand: "*L'homme c'est rien—l'oeuvre c'est tout*." In his *Miscellaneous Studies* Pater had also quoted Flaubert, implicitly voicing a similar ideal of impersonality: "It has always been a rule to put nothing of myself into my works."

There is one other curious way in which Holmes resembles Pater. The detective claims to be descended from the sister of the French painter Emile Jean Horace Vernet, insisting, therefore, that art is in his blood. In this respect he recalls Pater, who more than half-believed that he was a descendant of the French 18th-century painter and follower of Watteau, Jean Baptiste Pater. Holmes was a master of disguises (more about which below), and in this regard we might say that Pater disguised himself as Jean Baptiste Pater's sister, whose fictitious journal, "A Prince of Court Painters" in *Imaginary Portraits*, gives voice to some of Pater's own beliefs and desires.

Even to a greater degree than he resembles Pater does Holmes have affinities with Bernard Berenson, who was a follower of Pater. The American art critic never met Pater, but in his youth he regarded him as one of his "gods," and Pater's writings had a profound impact on his own. Like Pater and Holmes, Berenson had a fine sensitivity to artistic temperament; he objected, however, to the lack of precision, of exact science, in Pater's work, faulting him for his acceptance of countless inaccurate attributions. Relying on the more "scientific" methods of morphology, of the new connoisseurship developed by Giovanni Morelli, Berenson reattributed pictures by scrutinizing their precise structures—the ways in which draperies and anatomical forms were rendered in each. Not satisfied merely to discern the Giorgionesque or the Leonardesque, for example, Berenson, with magnifying glass in hand, examined paintings with the attention to details of a sleuth.

Determining attributions on the basis of how ears, noses, fingers were painted, he more exactly identified the hands of Giorgione's and Leonardo's followers. Berenson thus became a detective of art, just as Holmes had become a "connoisseur of crime."

In numerous respects, Holmes's professional procedures are akin to Berenson's. Both of them, the detective and the connoisseur, rely on anatomical classification in their work. Invoking the example of the great zoologist Cuvier, Holmes remarks that from the smallest detail the entire case can be reconstructed: "As Cuvier could correctly describe a whole animal by the contemplation of a single bone, so the observer who has thoroughly understood one link in a series of incidents should be able to accurately state all the other ones, both before and after." In the case of the cardboard box, Holmes recognizes, as Watson and Lestrade of Scotland Yard do not, the significance of two severed ears received in the box—that they are the result of murder. Berenson also closely attends to anatomical details in pictures, even earlobes, insisting that the way in which they are painted affords clues to the artists who painted them. The connoisseur and the detective also both apply a system of typology or classification to their investigations. Holmes is often able to attribute crimes to their perpetrators because he immediately recognizes the pattern of the crime through its relation to previous cases of which he has a prodigious knowledge. Similarly, Berenson can detect the author of a painting by referring to his comparably vast knowledge of related works of art. Berenson maintained a vast file of notes and photographs from his work of detection, similar in purpose to Holmes' extensive "collection" of cases necessary to his connoisseurship. Both of them sought to publish their observations on method for future detective work and connoisseurship. Berenson published lists of attributions and essays exhibiting the results of his connoisseurship, much in the way that Holmes wrote treatises on cigar ashes, handwriting, and footprints, useful in detective work. Holmes' studies of handwriting especially recall the work of the connoisseur, for as Holmes observes, the criminal will betray himself in the very "mannerism" of his script; Berenson might well have added that, similarly, the artist reveals himself through his characteristic stroke of the brush or pen.

Like Holmes, Berenson was a dandy and epicurean, a man of broad cultural interests, exquisite taste, and refined sensibility. Were Holmes to have come to life, he would surely have found his way to Berenson's famous salon of writers, scholars, artists, and politicians at his villa outside Florence, I Tatti, where they would have discoursed on art, music, language, and, not in the least, connoisseurship. Each would have admired the accomplished detective work of the other, bemused at the similarities between their apparently disparate professions. Berenson would eagerly have shown his collection to such a keen observer as Holmes, and they would have discussed Buddhism while standing before Berenson's splendid collection of oriental works. Holmes' sharpness of observation would have charmed Berenson, as Berenson's inquiring mind and sharp wit would have delighted his guest. Would that one might find among the countless letters to Berenson from distinguished correspondents still preserved at I Tatti just a few from Baker Street!

Holmes's "method" also has affinities with the critical principles espoused by Oscar Wilde—protégé of Pater and friend of Berenson. Exaggerating the principles of Pater's criticism, stiffening them into caricature, as Pater might have said, Wilde focuses on the "critic as artist." He finds such "art" in the criticism of Ruskin and Pater, and he recognizes the critical virtues of Rossetti's poems about painting. In Wilde's terms, Holmes is a type of critic as artist. If the work of art is, as Wilde observes, a "starting-point for a new creation," so too is a crime a point of departure for the creative detective, who must, in a sense, "re-create" it in order to penetrate its mystery. Just as the great criminal is a "master," so too is the detective-critic. No less than great crimes are Holmes' solutions "masterpieces," and what we admire in them is the "delicacy" and "refinement" of their art. For Watson, and for us as well, Holmes, the critic-detective, is one of "the greatest artists."

We have postponed to the very last consideration of perhaps the single most significant likeness between Holmes and Wilde—that is, their shared theatrical gifts. Yeats and George Bernard Shaw pointed out that, above all, Wilde was an "actor." As a *fin de siècle* Pierrot, he made his entire life into a stage performance, highlighted by brilliant theatrical soliloquies. Holmes, who regarded cases as "tragic" or "comic," was also a great performer. As Watson remarks, the stage lost a "great actor" when Holmes decided to become a detective; and throughout his career he exploited these dramatic gifts, adapting numerous brilliant disguises or feigning illness to achieve his ends—sometimes fooling and stunning Watson and the reader, both, with such splendid performances. "Encore," his audience cried, and Conan Doyle brought his great actor back for performance after performance, decade after decade. Even though Watson detects and hints at Holmes's feelings and sympathies, we never come to know the Holmes behind the mask. Forever "play-acting," Holmes suggestively asserts: "The best way of successfully acting a part is to be it." He could be speaking as well for Wilde, whose ironic identity is similarly inseparable from the part he played upon the stage of Victorian life.

III

T.S. Eliot once remarked that "every writer owes something to Holmes." Although exaggerated, this claim nevertheless reminds us that one of the greatest writers of our century, Vladimir Nabokov, owed more than a little to the great detective. The connection is significant in light of our present theme because, after Proust and Joyce, to whom he was much indebted,

Nabokov is one of the most distinguished writers of our time in the direct line of descent from 19th-century aestheticism. As one of his finest scholars has observed, allusions to Sherlock Holmes abound in Nabokov's novels. In *The Defense*, Luzhin loves the book about Holmes, "who endows logic with the glamour of a daydream"; in *Despair*, Hermann imagines the perfect ending of the Holmes stories—Watson committing a murder. The narrator of *The Real Life of Sebastian Knight* employs a "Holmes stratagem" in his own investigation, and the narrator of *Pnin*, speaking for Nabokov himself, finds by his bedside in a furnished room an omnibus edition of Sherlock Holmes which had "pursued" him for years. Nabokov plays on the detective's name in *Lolita*, speaking of Shirley Holmes, and in *Pale Fire* Holmes is mentioned in Canto I of John Shade's poem, a reference glossed by Charles Kinbote in his commentary.

The influence of the Holmes stories is evident in the very structure of Nabokov's novels as detective stories or mysteries—notably in *The Real Life of Sebastian Knight, Lolita*, and *Pale Fire*. For Watson, Holmes is a conjuror, a "magician"; and Nabokov, himself an amateur magician when he began to read Doyle as a child, aspired to Holmesian enchantments. Doyle spoke of his tales as belonging to "the fairy kingdom of romance," and in this way Nabokov understood all fiction, including his own, to be "fairy tales." Holmes could have been speaking for Nabokov when he commented on the strangeness of the commonplace, for *Lolita* is the sublime example of how the magical is found in the quotidian world. Speaking of himself as a "chess player," Holmes regards his profession as a "game" that he plays "for the game's sake," and in this way Nabokov creates gamelike fictions, filled with allusions to chess. The protagonist of *The Defense* is, in fact, a chess player who turns his entire life into a chess game—the exaggeration, we might almost say, of a Holmesian obsession. It may even be no coincidence that just as the Holmes stories seem to have ended with the image of the detective hanging over the Reichenbach Fall, stalemated as it were in the grasp of Moriarty, *The Defense* concludes with Luzhin last described suspended above the chessboard-like "chasm" divided into "dark and pale squares."

On account of the very playfulness of his art, Nabokov has been called a type of *homo ludens*. The reference is to Johan Huizinga's classic study, *Homo Ludens: A Study of the Play-Element in Culture*. Like Doyle's stories before him and Nabokov's fiction in his own time, Huizinga's study was influenced by the playfulness of 19th-century aestheticism. The affinities between the highly playful aestheticism in court rituals, described by Huizinga, and the modern aesthetic rituals of Huysmans and Wilde, for example, are especially striking. Nabokov's childhood hero, Holmes, is also decidedly a sort of *homo ludens*, as we have observed already. Always smiling, jesting, laughing, and performing "practical jokes," with a "mischievous twinkle" in his eyes, as Watson observes, Holmes "plays" out each case, inspired by the quality of the competition or the degree of mystery involved. Among his greatest assets are his above-mentioned "disguises," playfully employed to deceive his adversaries and admirers alike. Indeed, the uses he and his adversary Irene Adler make of disguises in the case of the scandal in Bohemia carry the story into the realm of farce. Such Holmesian disguises are the staple of Nabokov's fictions as well. Disguised as the narrator V. in *The Real Life of Sebastian Knight*, Nabokov is also, in a sense, Sebastian Knight himself, creating a fiction which dissolves the apparent reality of the narrative into a more vertiginous realm of fiction. In other words, if it had appeared throughout that Sebastian Knight was the subject of Nabokov's book, at the end it almost seems that, having posed as the narrator, Sebastian Knight could have actually written it.

In their deceptions, the Holmes stories ultimately raise the very questions about identity and reality which were to be embellished with far more nuance by Nabokov. Watson is always accusing Holmes of holding back pertinent facts as a case unfolds, and Holmes in turn perpetually complains of Watson's misleading, overly dramatic recounting of his cases. Whom do we believe? Or are they accusing each other of the same artistic vice? Playing on this ambiguity in the final volume of tales, *The Case Book of Sherlock Holmes*, Doyle has Holmes tell two of the stories—as if to correct the false impressions given by Watson. And, as if Holmes himself were not to be trusted either, one of these tales is told by an impersonal narrator. The situation here is almost Nabokovian, approaching that in *The Real Life of Sebastian Knight* in which Nabokov is writing about the narrator correcting the account of the critic Goodman, who is writing an account of Sebastian Knight and his writings.

Holmes once observed that "it is the first quality of a criminal investigator that he should see through a disguise." Nabokov's fictions are filled with such disguises which we, as playful readers or investigators of his fictions, are asked to see through, though as master-deceiver Nabokov is always one step ahead of us, beyond our Watson-like grasp. Nabokov implicitly suggested how we should read his own work when he called his course in European literature at Cornell a "detective investigation of the mysteries of literary structure." The numerous ground plans of the settings of novels that he drew on the blackboard for his students and his close attention to "details"—for example, his famous, scrupulous "anatomy" of Gregor Samsa— bespeak the Holmesian approach to criticism that informs his own fictions as well. In an age of prodigious literary theories, Nabokov's criticism is the supreme, possibly unique example of the subtle and clearheaded Holmesian kind of literary criticism, just as his fictions, elaborate criminal investigations, are the perfection of Sherlockian methods. Of all Nabokov's contrived, aestheticized literary games, perhaps *Despair* stands most clearly in the tradition of "murder considered as one of the fine arts" that we have sketched from De Quincey and Swinburne to Wilde and Holmes. Here the narrator, Hermann, having committed a murder, transforms his crime into art in his very narration—an artistic reenactment of the murder of his doppelgänger Felix. If Holmes's doppelgänger Moriarty was the "Napoleon of crime" in his own day, Nabokov is both the Moriarty and the Holmes of art of our own time. Through Nabokov's craft, we come to see more clearly than before the aesthetic implications of Sherlock Holmes; and, following his clues, we discover in a way what Holmes, or Doyle if you like, invented.

Inside and Outside Sherlock Holmes:
A Rhapsody

Kim Herzinger

Since *Sherlock Holmes Baffled* in 1900, there have been over 150 films about Holmes, around 120 television productions, 55 stage plays (not including three by Arthur Conan Doyle himself), 162 radio plays, 37 records, two musicals, and one ballet. There have also been something like 3,000 books and articles about Holmes and the Holmes Saga, many of which first appeared in the 28 periodicals solely devoted to Sherlockian studies. There have been well over 700 parodies and pastiches of Holmes written since Conan Doyle did his work. Some, like Schlock Holmes, Hemlock Shomes, Picklock Holes, Sherlock Bones (tracer of lost pets), and so on, have been interested in mocking the mock seriousness of Sherlockians. Others, like Nicholas Meyers' *The 7% Solution* and Michael Dibdin's *The Last Sherlock Holmes Story*, which is a better novel than it is a prediction, are interesting attempts to situate Holmes outside his fictional context, while at the same time retaining all of Holmes' fictional characteristics. Meyers' and Dibdin's books are just two of the 45 full-length novels featuring Holmes which have been published since 1970.

The existence of so many literary, cinematic, and musical recreations of Holmes attests to our unquenchable fascination with him. Perhaps an even more telling kind of testimony, however, comes from those major writers in and out of the language who have so often been avid readers and assimilators of the Saga. James Joyce, for instance, constantly alludes to Holmes in his work, including his use in *Ulysses* of a distinct, and no doubt conscious, similarity between Holmes-Watson and Dedalus-Bloom. T.S. Eliot, in a 1929 review called "Sherlock Holmes and His Times," insisted that Conan Doyle applied his dramatic ability "with great cunning and concentration; it is not split about. The content of the story may be poor; but the form is nearly always perfect."[1] Although the Old Possum later forgot having ever written on the subject, his admiration for the Holmes Saga is further suggested by his "deliberate and wholly conscious"[2] use of a healthy section of "The Musgrave Ritual" almost *verbatim* in *Murder in the Cathedral*, and by modeling the character of Macavity, one of his more important practical cats,

From *Shenandoah*, Vol. XXXVI, No. 3 (1986): 91–109. Reprinted by permission.

on Holmes' arch-enemy, Moriarty. As Trevor Hall has pointed out, Eliot's description of Macavity "gives the impression that if we could see Macavity and Moriarty together we would hardly be able to distinguish one from the other, apart from the fact, perhaps, that Moriarty was clean-shaven and Macavity, like most cats, was not."[3]

Simply put, then, Sherlock Holmes is probably the most famous fictional character ever created, and one of the few who possesses a separate and unmistakable identity to millions who may not have read any of the works in which he originally appeared. In 1891, when Conan Doyle confessed to his mother that he was tired of Holmes and wished to get rid of him, she was understandably appalled. "You won't! You can't! You mustn't!" she stormed in reply. When he did it anyway, in 1892, he was deluged with letters of protest from grief-stricken readers, and sober London businessmen openly wept and wore black mourning bands in the streets. Like Eliot and Joyce and Conan Doyle's mother, we are all complicit in creating the imaginative figure that Holmes has become. We are all complicit in the largeness and persistence of his appeal.

Why Holmes has such appeal, why we love him so much and have for so long a time is, however, perhaps the greatest of the Holmes mysteries, as well as the most insoluble. Most of the traditional literary solutions just don't seem to apply in the curious case of Sherlock Holmes. Holmes, after all, is cheap. We all know that, but we love Holmes for it. It is the kind of cheapness that lasts. As Bertolt Brecht once said of life in Weimar Berlin, "It's trash, but of what a quality." There have, of course been a good number of Sherlockians, as well as others who know better, who have made reasonably serious claims about the literary quality of the Holmes stories. Conan Doyle's attention to detail has often been remarked, as have his frequent splashes of wit, his handling of Victorian atmospherics, and his rather sophisticated use of narrative structures and points of view. Still, I am compelled to say that, for the most part, the Holmes stories are made from materials bought at a kind of nineteenth-century K-Mart, and that without the wondrous appeal of the character of Holmes our estimation of Conan Doyle's talent as a writer would be that he was a sort of *Boy's Life* Marie Corelli, who combined the moral insight of Queen Victoria with the historical precision of Sir Walter Scott.

Even in the best of the stories, Conan Doyle's writing achieves a kind of laughable mediocrity. One well-known passage from *The Sign of Four*, for instance, is frequently offered by Sherlockians as evidence of Holmes' feeling for nature. "How sweet the morning air is!" says Holmes. "See how that one little cloud floats like a pink feather from some gigantic flamingo." If there is feeling here it is that of Oscar Wilde on a bad day, or Gladstone in yellow lace; it's florid and exotic but without the ironic self-consciousness that might have saved it from being merely silly.

In "The Speckled Band," which has been the favorite of Sherlockians almost from the moment of its publication, as well as the favorite of Conan Doyle himself, Watson reports on the horrible death of Dr. Grimesby Roylott, who has, as you will no doubt recall, just been bitten on the head by his own swamp adder—"the deadliest snake in India," as Holmes tells Watson. "In an instant his strange headgear began to move, and there reared from among his hair the squat diamond-shaped head and puffed neck of a loathsome serpent." "Strange headgear"? "From among his hair"? "A loathsome serpent"? In the interests of literary time-traveling we are perhaps used to ignoring some of our modern aesthetic strictures with regard to flagrant and unshaded boy's story writing like this, but the case for the quality of Conan Doyle's prose generally suffers whenever we pay too much attention to the text.

What is interesting, of course, is that we usually don't give Conan Doyle's prose a close reading; more interesting yet is that we don't *want* to give it a close reading. To do so would be to have our pleasure checked by the awful claims of aesthetic principle, and to disallow the kind of indulgence Holmes deserves. So, with regard to "The Speckled Band," for instance, Sherlockians must bypass the language of the text, and concentrate on the swamp adder itself. They regret, after much discussion, to have to say that no known species of snake, including the actual Indian swamp adder, fully satisfies all the requirements of the "speckled band" as it is described by Watson. Since Holmes could hardly have been in error, they speculate that Watson must have misunderstood Holmes altogether, or that some error was committed by the compositor—caught up, perhaps, in the excitement of the tale. But Sherlockians, like Holmes himself, do not leave such problems unresolved. One, a Mr. Klauber, has publicly surmised that the creature in question was in fact a terrible hybrid raised by Dr. Roylott himself—"a sinister combination of the Mexican Gila Monster (Heloderma horridum) and the Indian cobra, now known as Naja naja naja."[4] Perhaps, then, Watson, Victorian gentleman that he was, was merely protecting us from such awful knowledge—that such things could exist and that such men could create them. In any case, Mr. Klauber has indulged himself fully, and if we are to read Holmes we had better prepare to do the same.

As Mr. Klauber's efforts suggest, studies of Sherlock Holmes are often, like the stories themselves, a kind of inspired imbecility. They are, more than anything, fields of play. And the basic ground rules for such play begin with one simple assertion: that Sherlock Holmes did, of course, exist, and that this man Conan Doyle was, at best, a fictional character, and, at worst, a failed eye doctor who managed somehow, probably in some sinister way, to get his hands on Watson's manuscripts. T.S. Eliot, in that forgotten review of 1929, noticed that "when we talk of [Holmes] we invariably fall into the fancy of his existence. Collins, after all is more real to his readers than Cuff; Poe is more real than Dupin; but Sir Arthur Conan Doyle, the eminent spiritualist, the author of a number of exciting stories which we read years ago and have forgotten, what has he to do with Holmes?" It should be obvious from this that never has a created character so completely gotten away from his creator as Holmes has gotten away from Conan Doyle. Not only did the irrepressible detective spring back to life after Conan Doyle tried to throw him off the Reichenbach Falls, but he has since—as I noted earlier—participated in a vast number of stories, novels, and movies which are as much a part of what we think we know about Holmes as anything in the Sacred Canon. It is surely not the literary value of Conan Doyle's stories which commands our attention; what we admire is the figure Holmes cuts in the world of the imagination. And that figure far transcends the value of the texts themselves.

In fact, there simply is no longer a purely literary Holmes, and even if we could recover such a one, we could not fully succeed in establishing what fascinates us about him. Holmes has long since stepped beyond his literary origins; he is no longer bound by them. Sherlock Holmes walks up and down in the world like a god, and, as so commonly happens with gods, he has evoked a vast industry of believers who keep busy tidying up the inconsistencies in his career. In the case of Holmes and Conan Doyle, then, the creation has so transcended the creator that it is almost appropriate that Sherlockians have removed Conan Doyle to a shadowy corner during their critical deliberations. Anyway, their simple notion—that Holmes existed and Conan Doyle is, well, expendable—sustains at least 95% of all Sherlockology.

This notion, among others central to the study of Sherlock Holmes, is, of course, quite loony, and it drives almost all professional critics to distraction. Clive James, for instance, in an article notable for its shocking disdain for whimsy, declares: "This is a field in which all credentials, and especially impeccable ones, are suspect. To give your life, or any significant part of it, to the study of Sherlock Holmes is to defy reason."[5] The high critical seriousness which James would be likely to applaud has, thankfully, never burdened the study of Sherlock Holmes. He simply could not stand the pressure. Instead, the studies of the Sacred Canon (or, as Sherlockians call it, the Sacred Conan) are by dilettantes for dilettantes. "Never," said Christopher Morley once, "has so much been written by so many for so few." With that, let me digress for a moment to defend the dilettante—for in doing so I have the sneaking suspicion that I might be defending Holmes himself.

The British love the dilettante—his playfulness, his amateurishness, his insouciance—just as Americans love the professional. Americans are in the habit of loving and trusting the professional because he does not mistake the claims of his aesthetics for the claims of his duty. The British love the dilettante—especially the dilettante aesthete—precisely because his duty is to enact the claims of his aesthetics. The classic English detectives are almost all dilettantes, or, as American newspapers might say, "self-proclaimed." I might merely mention that pornographer of class, Dorothy Sayers, and her insufferable Lord Peter Wimsey as one example; G. K. Chesterson's Father

Brown, whose job is not so much solving crimes as saving souls, as another. In any case, Americans love the professional because he cultivates expertise in a homemade world; he forms a basis for order in a world of excessive energy which always teeters on the edge of disorder. The British, conversely, love the amateur, the dilettante, because he goes his own eccentric way, he creates his expertise in an already structured world, and forms a basis for energy in a world which always teeters on the edge of dullness.

Sherlock Holmes is such a figure: by official standards a dilettante, an aesthete of detection, the world's first consulting detective—self-announced—who is a professional only by virtue of there never having been one before. He creates his own rules and methods, indulges in singular quirks and idiosyncracies, and thus creates a kind of detection which cannot be duplicated. Inspectors Lestrade, Gregson, and Athelney Jones, however adequate they might be found to be, are official and therefore restricted—stamped as such by the organization they work for. They are "Scotland Yarders," quick and energetic, but deficient in imagination and technique. As Holmes tells Watson in *The Sign of Four*, "When Gregson, or Lestrade, or Athelney Jones are out of their depths—which, by the way, is their normal state—the matter is laid before me."

The roles the Scotland Yarders are allowed to play are, inevitably, limited. They are mere husks of the detectives they might otherwise have become. Their official roles disallow them the advantages of Holmes the dilettante: full concentration on one case alone; hours working single-mindedly in their homemade chemistry labs; good breakfasts served promptly by Mrs. Hudson, 7% solutions of cocaine; hours of melodic musing with their Stradivarii; assistance on their cases by whomever they choose—especially if their choice consists of a gaggle of street Arabs, or a decent English doctor with an unaccomplished mind but an accomplished heart, and a Jezail bullet embedded in his shoulder.

Only the dilettante, albeit a dilettante of recognizable genius, can possibly hope to succeed in the resolution of cases beyond the mere commonplace. Holmes creates his world entirely, and it depends on nothing other than his own talents and energies, enough time to allow those talents to operate, and a "faithful Boswell" to record them when they do. Detection for Holmes is an art—it has little to do with the inflexibility of mere law. Legal justice—the actual fate of the criminal—often plays a minor role or is bypassed altogether in the resolution of Holmes' cases. Justice for Holmes is usually Saturday matinee justice, the justice of our adolescence, more assured and final than the mire and complexity of the courts, and made so by our being so certain of Holmes' absolute sincerity and straightness, the authority of his moral vision. It is not enough, not nearly enough, for Holmes to have trapped and captured his quarry; for the truly successful completion of a case, Holmes' aesthetic sense—as well as ours—must be fulfilled. The whole art of detection is the only thing that can rouse him from the lethargy of contemplating a dull and fog-bound world. "I cannot live without brain-work," says Holmes to Watson in *The Sign of Four*:

> What else is there to live for? Stand at the window here. Was there ever such a dreary, dismal, unprofitable world? See how the yellow fog swirls down the street and drifts across the dun-coloured houses. What could be more hopelessly prosaic and material? What is the use of having powers, doctor, when one has no field upon which to exert them?

Holmes is aroused by one thing, not by any thing, and it marks him as a dilettante, just as the kinds of cases he chooses mark him as an aesthete, an aesthete of detection. To quote Watson again, "Working as he did rather for the love of his art than for the acquirement of wealth, he refused to associate himself with any investigation which did not tend toward the unusual, and even the fantastic."

In *The Victorian Temper*, Jerome Buckley defined the Nineties aesthete as one "committed in principle to a scorn of the commonplace and a defense of a calculated artistic eccentricity." So when Holmes announces, "I play the game for the game's own sake," and damns the public for not comprehending his art, he is functioning well within the role of the aesthete.

Talking of Holmes as an aesthete leads me semi-directly into the matter of his appeal. A few Sherlockians have noticed the extent to which Sherlock Holmes is one of the aesthetic, "world rejecting heroes of the 1880s and 1890s."[6] No less a critic than Hugh Kenner has noticed the way the Holmes stories exploit the tension between the aesthete and the citizen. And if, as we probably should, we immediately object to the notion of Holmes as "world rejecting"—since it is precisely in his active relationship with the world that he does his work—we might at least note what David Cecil calls the "stronger side" of aestheticism. Lord Cecil claims that it needed "self-discipline, strict and strenuous, if it was to be carried out according to its precepts. Intelligence and sensibility must be kept continuously at work in detecting and discriminating what is not exquisite in experience. And then a rigid self-control must be exercised: the attention must be wholly concentrated on these things, rejecting any temptation of ease or ambition that might lead to living at a lower level."[7] This is Holmes exactly, and it is this "stronger side" of aestheticism which keeps the figure of Holmes from a full-fledged Nineties decadence, and which steers him away from the "cul-de-sac of despair and defeat that destroyed so many of the best minds," actual and fictional, of the period.[8]

The dilettante-aesthete Holmes with the stronger "Bohemian soul" constitutes, I imagine, at least part of what fascinates us about him. And that fascination is heightened because these qualities still manage to mesh with the larger culture, and Holmes is revealed as a "nonconformist in a conformist age," who nevertheless "wins all the conformist rewards."[9] Holmes has his scone and eats it, too. There is a kind of cozy reassurance about such a figure, because he appears to be getting away with so much. The effect of this gets us, I think, closer to the center of Holmes' continued appeal.

Holmes can be seen this way—and I want to argue that this is precisely the way that he is seen—only if we take him as an unvarying fictional character, made out of Doylean whole cloth. A rereading of the stories in the order of their publication reveals, however, that Holmes changes somewhat radically during the 40 years of his published career. The aesthete Holmes appears mainly in the early tales, those written before the turn of the century, and is already being backgrounded by the time of the *Strand Magazine* stories of 1891 and 1892. By 1901 and 1902, with *The Hound of the Baskervilles,* Holmes has acquired a certain moral zeal and a passion for justice which suggests an assimilation of the standards of gentility. He has become much more the gentleman hero, "the embodiment of the values and aspirations of the contemporary middle-class public."[10] His success depends more often than not on his power to assuage the anxieties of that audience. "Whereas the early Holmes was wont to retreat into narcotic fantasy at the end of a case," notes one Sherlockian, "the middle period Holmes is more likely to propose that he and Watson dine at a fashionable restaurant or spend an evening together at the opera."[11] It is during this, the middle period, that Conan Doyle most blatantly offers fables which examine the dangers that arise when respectable, middle-class English people are untrue to respectable middle-class codes.

In the later stories, especially those published during and after World War I, the world has darkened so completely that we find in Holmes an almost neurotically urgent pressure to resolve the cases he takes up. The crude optimism of the early stories has vanished; the aesthete has given over completely to the bloodhound of heaven. There is a growing stress on the "cruel, the gruesome, and the physically repulsive"[12] in these stories. Mutilations and psychoses are revealed in the old country houses and suburban villas. As Gavin Lambert, among others, has noted, characters become deformed: a dwarf with a bulbous head; a man with a curved back and convulsively twitching hands; a suburban spinster who received two freshly severed human ears in the post; a middle-aged professor who tries a rejuvenation drug and turns into a kind of chattering missing link, clambering up the walls of his house and attacking his dog. Retribution for criminals becomes more direct and more violent. The fiendish Charles Augustus Milverton, for instance, is shot between the eyes by an elegant and aristocratic lady who has been the subject of his blackmail. Holmes, who might have stopped the killing, stands aloof when, before she leaves, she grinds "her heel into his upturned face." We do not feel that Holmes' conscience is much disturbed.

The world of the late stories suggests that even Holmes has begun to accept the inevitability of violence around him. The comparative calm of the late nineteenth century has been supplanted by an underlying sense of chaos and unresolvable despair. Even Holmes begins to lose his composure in a world threatened by forces beyond his grasp, and he becomes the brooding "flawed superman," as Colin Wilson calls him, who is almost "as helpless and defeated as the rest of us." "What is the meaning of it, Watson?" asks Holmes at the end of "The Cardboard Box":

> What object is served by this circle of misery and violence and fear? It must tend to some end, or else our universe is ruled by chance, which is unthinkable. But what end? There is a great and standing perennial problem to which human reason is as far from an answer as ever.

And, at the end of "His Last Bow," Holmes seems to realize his mortality, his inability to cope with a world grown too complex and terrifying even for him.

> "There's an east wind coming, Watson."
> "I think not, Holmes. It is very warm."
> "Good old Watson! You are the one fixed point in a changing age. There's an east wind coming all the same, such a wind as never blew on England yet. It will be cold and bitter, Watson, and a good many of us may wither before its blast."

Not to take into account these three differing phases of Holmes' career is a mistake, I suppose, but finally it is only a technical mistake. The glory of Holmes as a character in the imagination is precisely that these different Holmeses insist on congealing back into one. Instead of being fragmented or protean, the Holmes of our imagination resolves back into a single figure of extraordinarily rich fullness. He becomes simultaneously an aesthete, the protector of respectability, and a flawless—but not infallible—human being in the world. He is better than us, no doubt, but he is like us, too. It is this, our imaginative response to the Holmes Saga as a whole, which allows us to see him as very human indeed, but one who somehow manages to secure the rewards of the official culture while at the same time rejecting the very culture which bestows them. And, too, such flexibility allows Holmes to transcend his original time, his original place, and his original medium.

So, here we have this extraordinary Holmes, as curious and wonderful a hybrid as the Indian swamp adder concocted by our Mr. Klauber. Although this accounts for some of our fascination with Holmes, and perhaps accounts partially for his ability to emerge anew for each generation, it does not account for everything—our response to the Victorian London he traditionally inhabits, for instance. In some recent books and movies, Holmes has helped to resolve the Kennedy assassination in Dallas, delivered the mind of Ludwig Wittgenstein back into the hands of Bertrand Russell at Cambridge, aided the United States during World War II, helped Professor Challenger deal with an invasion from Mars, and chased Jack the Ripper through the corridors of time. But we almost invariably want to locate the essential Holmes "in a romantic chamber of the heart, in a nostalgic country of the mind, where it is always 1895."[13] There is something stirring about that gaslit, late-Victorian London; its very fog seems to render misery into nostalgic yearning. One suspects that it was precisely the technological collision of the old world with the new, the violent rapidity of cultural change, which evoked the figures which dominate our imaginative version of London at the end of the last century: Holmes and Watson, of course, but also Dr. Jekyll and Mr. Hyde, Dracula, Jack the Ripper, the Elephant Man, the occult societies, Liza Doolittle, members of gentlemen's clubs who go ballooning around the world in eighty days. The real and the fictional are here gathered into a conspiracy of possibility, of unlimited and astonishing potential, still available to the dedicated amateur solely through the exercise of his energies and talents. The London we love in the Holmes Saga is not, of course, a London which ever existed. Still, it seems to me very likely that untold numbers of tourists go in search of that London each year, and come home disappointed when they do not find it. Holmes' London is a fairy tale London; it is bounded by a magic circle; it is a field of play which cannot and, more importantly, should not, be tested against truth. To insist that such a world be true, as tourists and critics (the tourists of literature) sometimes do, is to fracture that fragile world altogether. It is simply not playing the game fair; it is being a spoil sport; it is like blowing fish out of the water with dynamite and calling it "fishing." For the fairy tale world to exist, it must be kept safe from tampering, and we all know it.

In some ways Holmes' London is like a joke; we can say almost anything about it except that it's not true. And Conan Doyle, who knew something about fantasy, never leads us into a position where we might be tempted to say that. Crime in Holmes' world is clinical, not social. He hardly glances at the horrifying social conditions which produced his band of street Arabs, The Baker Street Irregulars, for example. Sherlock's adventures cannot be understood, and his appeal cannot depend, upon his participation in a kind of Victorian social therapy. He is interested only in disorder which is primarily individual, and he protects his world and confirms our innocence by throwing the rascals out. "Singularity" is the crucial aspect of Holmes' cases, and the word is used in the Holmes stories more frequently than almost any other, including "fog" or—certainly—"elementary."

Here again we feel the presence of the dilettante-aesthete Holmes, still capable of loving his cases and his clues, scouring rugs and gardens in his passionate search for them. The superior sensibility must always look for the "singular," that peculiar beauty which shines out of the fog of the everyday, and especially when the "singular" has been mistaken by everyone else for the commonplace. One tendency of Holmes' famous demonstrations of logic is to reduce the amazing to the commonplace, and at the same time, since in the framework of the Saga the commonplace is seized upon and illuminated by genius, to suggest how the commonplace is really amazing.

Holmes continually instructs us to "look upon the ordinary trivia of the physical world with renewed vision."[14] In this he reminds us of Carlyle's "natural supernaturalism," T. H. Huxley's piece of chalk, James Joyce in *Ulysses*, or, as Nicholas Meyer has shown us, Sigmund Freud and his clues to the psyche. "It has long been an axiom of mine that the little things are infinitely the most important," says Holmes in "A Case of Identity." "I can never bring you to realize the importance of sleeves, the suggestiveness of thumb-nails, or the great issues that may hang from a bootlace."

Now, in many of the stories the "singular" simply means un-English. One of the delights of Holmes' fairy tale England is that it is so peculiarly homogeneous; it is a world with a thoroughly integrated pattern of behavior, values, and common assumptions. One of my favorite moments in the Saga occurs in "The Copper Beeches," when Miss Violet Hunter, an unemployed governess, accepts a job in which she must sit where she is told, wear any dress required, and cut short her beautiful chestnut hair. Shaken by such extraordinary stipulations, she seeks Holmes' advice. He says: "I think, Watson, that it would be as well for you to have your pistol ready." Such stipulations are evidently so un-English that Holmes notices at once that there is something singularly sinister about her situation. What we should perhaps notice is how familiar her situation is to us, and the extent to which we are removed from the kind of world she lives in.

Like Miss Hunter, Holmes' clients are almost always presented as the epitomes of characteristic English virtues. His clients may sometimes be in particular need of Holmes in his role of rationalist hero—one who "explodes superstitions and frees people from their influence"[15]—but they are usually quite sane and always absolutely, unbelievably, honest. This last feature is especially amazing when we think, for instance, of the clients of Sam Spade, or Philip Marlowe. "Singularity" is almost invariably a clue for Holmes because it usually represents the intrusion of something alien into the otherwise seamless fabric of English life as it is evoked in the Saga. More often than not, especially in the early stories, the peculiarity which catches Holmes' shining eye is literally un-English—the Continental boot, the Indian cigar ash, the American cipher—and the criminal who has left the clue behind is either not English at all, or has been away from England for so long that he has forgotten how to behave.

One major exception to this English/un-English dynamic is, naturally, Moriarty. But Moriarty—Holmes' equal—must be English. Vigorous English heroism can be matched only by equally vigorous English villainy. Conan Doyle took great care to establish a commonality between Holmes and the Napoleon of crime. Moriarty is in some ways more than Holmes' equal; he is his double, his dark mirror. Holmes tells Watson in "The Final Problem" that Moriarty is a "genius, a philosopher, an abstract thinker. He has a brain of the first order. He sits motionless, like a spider in the center of its web, but that web has a thousand radiations, and he knows well every quiver of each of them." And here is Watson, in "The Cardboard Box," telling us about Holmes: "He loved to lie in the very centre of five millions of people, with his filaments stretching out and running through them, responsive to every little rumour or suspicion of unsolved crime." Their methods are as similar as their powers, and the final emblem of their similarity is the one given us by Sidney Paget: Holmes and Moriarty become one figure, locked forever in each other's arms, about to reel over into the Reichenbach Falls, to disappear together.

Moriarty is to be understood as being particularly sinister precisely because he fits so easily into the homogeneous, commonplace world which it is Holmes' interest to protect. It is because Moriarty is so thoroughly English, because he knows fully the values and the assumptions of his culture, and because he appears not to deviate from those values and assumptions, that he is so difficult to discover and identify. "Aye, there's the genius and the wonder of the thing!" Holmes tells Watson. "The man pervades London, and no one has heard of him." He is all the more sinister for seeming to be fully integrated into the very culture he endangers. Just as Holmes "understands the social codes of the world he investigates,"[16] so Moriarty understands the social codes of the world he corrupts. It is precisely for this reason that Holmes' urgency to rid the culture of its greatest malefactor is raised to its highest pitch. "I tell you, Watson, in all seriousness that if I could beat that man, if I could free society of him, I should feel that my own career had reached a summit, and I should be prepared to turn to some more placid line in life."[17]

It is in his confrontation with Moriarty that we are best able to see what Holmes' main function is: it is to protect his comparatively cozy, homogenous world from disorder. His urgent drive to retain this cultural homogeneity is deeply embedded in his famous method of reasoning. As Peter V. Conroy has pointed out, for Holmes "all the details of a case are pertinent, and only one solution can account for all the details."[18] Holmes is a kind of reader of crime "who deciphers a code or finds meaning in a text which remains incomprehensible to others." There are no irrelevant details for Holmes, nothing can be discounted, because everything is seen as part of everything else. Holmes is in search of a deeper structure, a homogeneity of detail and event: "We must look for consistency," Holmes tells Watson. "Where there is want of it we must suspect deception."[19] Holmes' world can only make sense when it can be fitted back into a logical, coherent sequence.

Holmes, then, protects his world from forces which would shatter its connectedness. As the story of Miss Violet Hunter suggests, the late-Victorian reader may well have understood, as a matter of course, just what kind of world Holmes was protecting. We don't. But it was Conan Doyle's good fortune to have hit upon an objective correlative for that whole set of values and assumptions and emotions which animated that homogeneous world, one that we still yearn for and still respond to—and that objective correlative is 221B Baker Street.

It is the job of all fictional detectives, perhaps, to protect us from what threatens to fragment our universe. George Grella has convincingly maintained that the detective (at least the detective of the Formal Detective Novel) functions much as the hero in the comedy of manners tradition: "He is an engineer of destiny, with power to recreate a new society from the ruins of the old." But only Holmes lives in an imaginative space which is the very image of what he protects. Sherlock Holmes allows us to participate in a drama of intimate geometry; he involves us in a dialectic of inside and outside, where inside—his rooms at 221B Baker Street—suggests security, warmth, friendship, propriety without rigidity, order without constraint, the opportunity to daydream, a location for bliss. Outside is cold, foggy, rainy, dark, and chaotic.

Holmes' job is to recreate the outside in the image of the inside, to put a sure lock on our homes. The image of home in the Holmes Saga is, of course, 221B Baker Street. The home, after all, is the environment in which protective beings live. It is the inhabited space *par excellence*; it is the one space which defends intimacy and well-being. 221B Baker is a highly-charged space because it is so fully inhabited by Holmes and the suggestion of what Holmes lives to protect. 221B Baker is full of clues which lead us back to Holmes: tobacco in the toe of a Persian slipper, V R pockmarked in bulletholes on the wall, files in a terrible snarl, chemicals bubbling, the props of detection standing alert in every corner. At the center of things is the fire—the hearth. In the imagination, as in many of the stories themselves, a case begins with Holmes and Watson sitting intimately by the fireside. This is where we begin and where we desire to return. Outside, as in "The Five Orange Pips," "gales . . . set in with exceptional violence."

All day the wind had screamed and the rain had beaten against the windows, so that even here in the heart of great, handmade London we were forced to raise our minds for an instant from the routine of life, and to recognize the presence of those great elemental forces, which shriek at mankind through the bars of his civilisation, like untamed beasts in a cage. As evening drew in, the storm grew higher and louder, and the wind cried and sobbed like a child in the chimney.

Almost all of the Holmes movies begin shrouded in fog and cold. Of the 56 original stories, and the four longer pieces, 40 take place in cold weather, when the dynamic rivalry between inside and outside is operating at its fullest potential. The reminder of bad weather always increases the house's value as a place to live in. In stories which take place during the warmer months, there is usually no description of the weather at all, unless, as in "The Cardboard Box," it is "like an oven," so blazing hot that the sunlight is "painful to the eye."

But the outside always intrudes, in the form of a visitor who brings bad news from that world, and who will inevitably cause Holmes to step outside his rooms and bring things back into balance. Usually, the intruder is a client, and an embodiment of those virtues for which 221B Baker is itself an emblem. When, however, the outside intrudes in the form of a malefactor, we are immediately struck by the extent to which this is a perversion of particularly horrifying proportions. In "The Final Problem," Moriarty first attempts to eliminate Holmes by setting fire to his rooms. Watson's response to such perversity is our own: "Good heavens, Holmes! This is intolerable." Ordinarily though, Holmes is able to redress such an imbalance immediately and dramatically. When, for instance, Moriarty himself intrudes, Holmes coldly faces him off. The image of his visit is Holmes' own revolver—cocked and lying on a table midway between them. When Grimesby Roylott intrudes, though he is an altogether more controllable outside element, Holmes redresses that imbalance quite literally, by straightening out the poker (that symbol of the hearth) which Roylott, in his rage, had bent.

Naturally, when Holmes finally does go outside he takes the inside out with him—his pipe, his deerstalker, his Inverness cape, his magnifying glass, his mind, his Watson. We love Holmes because, like the dilettante, the amateur, he is capable of loving something enough to go out into the cold to protect it. He goes because of love, not duty. And at the end of his efforts in our behalf—in behalf, that is, of security, warmth, friendship, and order—he returns. It is important that Holmes comes back to his rooms, the way a bird does to its nest. Holmes does not always come back to 221B Baker Street in the stories and movies, but he always does in our imagination. Once there, he settles again by the fire, absently watching the ember glow flicker on the test tubes heaped dolefully in the corner. A fine rain pats the window pane. Watson—good old Watson—gently tamps his English briar, the smoke curls pungently above his head, Mrs. Hudson's footsteps sound on the carpeted stair, Holmes turns slightly as she unlatches the door, bringing a warm breakfast of white eggs and cream tea. And once again he is—as we are—home.

Notes

1. T. S. Eliot, "Sherlock Holmes and His Times," *Criterion* 8 (1929), p. 554.

2. Eliot, quoted by Trevor Hall, in *Sherlock Holmes and His Creator* (London: Duckworth, 1978), p. 54.

3. Hall, p. 48.

4. William S. Baring-Gould, ed. *The Annotated Sherlock Holmes*, vol. I (N.Y.: Clarkson N. Potter, 1974), p. 266.

5. Clive James, *First Reactions* (N.Y.: Knopf, 1980), p. 189.

6. Colin Wilson, "The Flawed Superman," in Michael Harrison, Ed., *Beyond Baker Street* (Indianapolis: Bobbs-Merrill, 1976), p. 322.

7. David Cecil, "Fin de Siecle," in *Ideas and Beliefs of the Victorians* (N.Y.: Dutton, 1966), p. 369.

8. Wilson, p. 323.

9. James, p. 194.

10. Ian Ousby, *Bloodhounds of Heaven* (Cambridge, Mass.: Harvard Univ. Press, 1976), p. 158.

11. Ousby, p. 158.

12. Ousby, p. 171.

13. Vincent Starrett, *The Private Life of Sherlock Holmes* (N.Y.: Pinnacle, 1975), p. 73.

14. Ousby, p. 155.

15. Ousby, p. 155.

16. George Grella, "Murder and Manners," *Novel* 4, i (1970), p. 37.

17. "The Final Problem," in Baring-Gould, vol. I, p. 302.

18. Peter V. Conroy, "The Importance of Being Watson," *Texas Quarterly* 21, i (1978), p. 100.

19. "The Problem of Thor Bridge," in Baring-Gould, vol. II, p. 600.

The Medical Model

PASQUALE ACCARDO, M.D.

When a doctor goes wrong he is the first of criminals.

—Doyle

He played his part without knowledge of his predecessors and successors in it, as though he were its first and only actor—for each of us must consider himself that in every part he plays, as though he had made it all up himself, yet with a sureness and dignity which comes to him, when he plays it, so to speak, in daylight for the first time, not from his supposed invention of the role, but on the contrary from the well-grounded consciousness that he is once more presenting something legitimate and traditional, and must perform it, however repellent, to the best of his ability according to the pattern.

—Thomas Mann, *Joseph in Egypt*

ARTHUR CONAN DOYLE

You are yourself Sherlock Holmes!

—Joseph Bell to Arthur C. Doyle

Holmes was to a large extent Conan Doyle himself.

—Adrian Conan Doyle

That untidy boy with his strange power of observation.

—Marquis of Villavieja on his classmate A. C. Doyle

What is once well done is done forever.

—Thoreau

Anybody, almost, can make a beginning: the difficulty is to make an end—to do what cannot be bettered.

—Shaw on Music

Arthur Conan Doyle was a Scottish physician-writer born in 1859. His

From *Diagnosis and Detection: The Medical Iconography of Sherlock Holmes* (Rutherford, N.J.: Fairleigh Dickinson University Press, 1987), 22–47. Excerpted and reprinted by permission. Footnotes have been renumbered.

early schooling was at the hands of the Jesuits of Stonyhurst. He then studied medicine at the University of Edinburgh under such brilliant clinicians as Dr. Joseph Bell and took his Bachelor of Medicine and Master of Surgery in 1881 and his M.D. degree in 1885. He worked as a ship's doctor on Arctic whalers, voyaged to the West African coast, went into medical partnership with a psychopathic quack, and came close to starving in a solo practice. In 1891 he spent several months in Vienna in a futile attempt to subspecialize in ophthalmology, joined the Ophthalmological Society of the United Kingdom, opened an oculist's office close to prestigious Harley Street, and then, to the salvation of many a patient, gave up the practice of medicine to pursue a full-time literary career.[1]

Although he achieved phenomenal success as a writer, especially as the creator of Sherlock Holmes, Doyle came to regard his fictional detective as some kind of Frankenstein monster who detracted from the public's appreciation of his true literary worth: "All things find their level, but I believe that if I had never touched Holmes, who tended to obscure my higher work, my position in literature would at the present moment be a more commanding one."[2]

Doyle's growing distaste for the popularity of his detective cannot be attributed merely to the fact that this hero returned (even from the grave) in more than sixty sequels; all his better characters did the same. The Gascon adventurer Etienne Gerard (*l'audace, et encore de l'audace, et toujours de l'audace*) brought Napoleonic France alive in the Brigadier Gerard series;[3] Professor George Edward Challenger personified muscular Victorian scientism in several science fiction classics; and Sir Nigel Loring's gesta were recorded in the tediously accurate historical novels that Doyle considered his highest literary achievement—*The White Company* and *Sir Nigel*—if only Holmes hadn't interfered. If Holmes, Gerard, Challenger, and Sir Nigel represented different aspects of Doyle's personality, how could one of them overwhelm his creator? How could the part be greater than the whole?

Doyle disclaimed any significant contribution from earlier English fictional detectives to his portrayal of Holmes, and certainly the traces of William Godwin's Caleb Williams, Charles Dickens's Inspector Bucket, and Wilkie Collins' Sergeant Cuff are slight. It somehow seemed more fitting for Holmes to have real-life medical-scientific prototypes rather than literary ones. The bookish Doyle could not bring himself to accept Huxley's dictum that the proper study of mankind is books. While Dr. Oliver Wendell Holmes provided a name with both literary and scientific associations, the main inspiration that Doyle acknowledged was his old medical school teacher, Dr. Joseph Bell.

The diagnostic skill and personality traits of Sir William Arbuthnot Lane (1856–1943) made him another medical model for Holmes. An active and innovative professional, Lane was senior surgeon at both Guys Hospital and the Hospital for Sick Children, Great Ormond Street. This address perhaps inspired the name of Ormond Sacker, who was the narrator in Conan Doyle's manuscript, *A Tangled Skein*. (When published in 1887, the narrator's name and the title of the novel were changed to John H. Watson and *A Study in Scarlet*, respectively.) Lane was also rumored to be the original Doctor Cutler Walpole in Shaw's *Doctor's Dilemma*. Unfortunately, "Lane's disease" was a very unscientific amalgamation of the older myth of Glénard's disease (visceroptosis) with the newer myth of autointoxication (self-poisoning) and resulted in many unfortunate patients being subjected to unnecessary ileosigmoidostomies and colectomies. Dr. Lane was one of the prophets of the twentieth-century religion of (bowel) regularity.[4]

Doyle is supposed to have left numerous clues to his own (partially) unconscious identification with his most famous creation. Both Sherlock Holmes and Arthur Conan Doyle had Irish names and were descended from a family of squires with prominent artists (Antoine, Claude, Carle, and Horace Vernet/John Doyle) and French blood. Both men had gray eyes, one brother, a friend named Dr. J. Watson, a secondary reputation for nonfictional writing (monographs on detective and other subjects/military propaganda and spiritualist tracts), an encyclopedic if often superficial range of interests (highlighted by an almost morbid curiosity in murder and mayhem), and a passion for dressing gowns and pipe tobacco stored in slippers. Both were sportsmen (boxing and fencing), were chivalrous to a fault, were manic depressive, were monist (materialist/spiritualist), had a horror of destroying documents (and, therefore, large cumbrous files), perused the popular press, irritatingly played a musical instrument (violin/brass horn), and (almost, in Doyle's case) declined a knighthood.

According to his son Adrian, Doyle had the same power of keen observation that characterized Holmes: a glance at clothes and physical habitus enabled him to (accurately?) deduce a stranger's life history. Dostoyevsky's *Diary of a Writer* (1873) records his preoccupation with closely observing strangers, guessing at who they were, how they lived, what kind of work they did, what presently interested them, and then inventing episodes in their lives to coincide with his fabricated portraits.[5] These were exercises in creative imagination rather than logical deduction but they certainly required the latter.

Several of the real-life criminal cases in which Doyle was successfully engaged testify to his concern for the victims of bureaucratic injustice. But they also bear witness to the wide gulf separating the two detectives: the most striking quality of Doyle's solutions to the cases of horse mutilation (George Edalji) and murder (Oscar Slater) is their total lack of adventure, insight, and anything approaching brilliant deduction. They represent instead shining examples of plodding investigation, problems that any rural constable of middling intelligence could have solved if he had set his mind to it. The level of interest of the cases is such that Holmes would have declined to undertake them even when afflicted with the severest boredom.

Doyle's own detective work is the strongest proof that he was not Sherlock Holmes.

Doyle's concept of a great author was someone in complete conscious control of his characters; he once referred to Holmes and Watson as "my puppets." He retreated like Hemingway into the assumption that public praise was always misdirected to the worst aspects of one's work. "Literature" could not be clumsily and hastily written, with bourgeois themes, and for crass, financial motives—except, of course, by Balzac, Cervantes, Dostoyevsky, Dickens, Poe, Shakespeare, and a host of other hacks. If Holmes's oversimplification of scientific method can appropriately be described as "high school," so can Doyle's misconception of great literature. It was not that the public misunderstood which were Doyle's more important works; they understood better than he did, because they actively participated in the immortalization of his characters. As he had rejected the Catholicism of his childhood, so he balked at the promised literary immortality of a writer of detective fiction. He chose, instead, to follow in the footsteps of the chemist, William Crookes, and the codiscoverer of evolution, Alfred Russel Wallace, and was converted to spiritualism. To a Catholic (capital and/or lower case "c") sensibility the popularity of Holmes was easily intelligible; to the more pompous and smug spiritualist aesthetic, it could represent only a blasphemous parody of an all too serious truth.

The remaining details of Doyle's life are, in Martin Gardner's phrase, irrelevant to the understanding of Sherlock Holmes.[6]

A Tintinnabulary Bell

> "And yet you say he is not a medical student?"
> —A. C. Doyle

> Doctors are trained by other doctors. Each physician, then, is not only himself but is made up of other men, and each teacher becomes a part of his students.
> —Eric Cassell, *The Healer's Art*

> *Ars medica tota in observationibus*
> —Osler

> Spot diagnosis you should hate
> Until you are a surgeon great.
> —Zeta

Joseph Bell was professor of surgery at the University of Edinburgh when Arthur Doyle lackadaisically matriculated there. Bell was an imposing and memorable character both as a physician and as a teacher. "Thin, wiry, dark with a high nosed acute face, penetrating grey eyes, angular shoulders, and a jerky way of walking"—Doyle would remember "his sharp piercing eyes, eagle nose, and striking features"[7] years later when the young author consciously set about to add a new dimension to the detective genre: "I thought of my old teacher, Joe Bell, of his eagle face, of his curious way, of his eerie trick of spotting details. If he were a detective, he would surely reduce this fascinating, but unorganized, business into something nearer to an exact science. It was surely possible in real life, so why should I not make it plausible in fiction. It is all very well to say that a man is clever, but the reader wants to see examples of it . . . such examples as Bell gave us every day in the wards."[8]

Bell was "a very skillful surgeon, but his strong point was diagnosis, not only of disease, but of occupation and character"; before examining patients, "he would tell them their symptoms, and even the details of their past life, and would hardly ever make a mistake."[9] On the dull side of normal, like Watson, the impressionable Doyle was easily awed by Bell's parlor tricks: he "would tell us where all the other passengers in the carriage were from, where they were going, and something of their occupation and habits. All this without having spoken to them. When he verified his observations, we though him a magician."[10] Bell sensed that the athletic "60% for effort" medical student would make a perfect foil and appointed Doyle his out-patient clerk: "I had ample chance of studying his methods and in noticing that he often learned more of the patient by a few quick glances than I had done by my questions."[11]

As a teacher, Bell stressed the careful observation of details: "I always impressed over and over again upon my students the vast importance of little distinctions, the endless significance of the trifles. . . . Eyes and ears which can see and hear, memory to record at once . . . precise and intelligent recognition and appreciation of minor differences as the essential factor in all successful medical diagnosis." He was aided a great deal in his diagnostic coups by the fact that Victorian society was heavily stratified; clothes, body habitus, and other markings could quickly locate individuals in their place in the hierarchy: "Nearly every handicraft writes its sign-manual on the hands. The scars of the miner differ from those of the quarryman. The carpenter's callosities are not those of the mason. . . . The soldier and sailor differ in gait. Accent helps you to district and, to an educated ear, almost to county."[12] (Shades of Professor Henry Higgins!)

This skill in deducing occupation and life history from trifling details had its more famous practitioners: Jean Nicolas Corvisart (1755–1821) was a military surgeon and personal physician to Napoleon I. He performed "miracles" of diagnosis; with him observation replaced examination. Other Holmesian mind readers included Corvisart's pupil Baron Guillaume Dupuytren (1777–1835), Armand Trousseau (1801–67), and the pioneer dermatologist of sarcastic wit, Ferdinand von Hebra (1816–80). Even Sir Arbuthnot

Lane published a number of papers on the marks of occupation on the human frame. But it was Joe Bell who incarnated this medical fine art for the young Doyle. Bell later recollected that young Arthur

> was amused once when a patient walked in and sat down. "Good morning, Pat," I said for it was impossible not to see that he was an Irishman. "Good morning, your honour," replied the patient. "Did you like your walk over the links to-day as you came in from the south side of the town?" I asked. "Yes," said Pat. "Did your honour see me?"
>
> Well, Conan Doyle could not see how I knew that, absurdly simple as it was.
>
> On a showery day, such as that had been, the reddish clay at bare parts of the links adheres to the boot and a tiny part is bound to remain. There is no such clay anywhere else round the town for miles. That and one or two similar instances excited Doyle's keenest interest and set him experimenting in the same directions, which, of course, was just what I wanted with all my other students.[13]

In these days of rapid, automated transit, the Holmesian diagnostician would probably need to take his clay samples from automobile tires.

Another example of Bell's art:

> "This man is a left-handed cobbler."
> "You'll obsairve, gentlemen, the worn places on the corduroy breeks where a cobbler rests his lapstone? The right-hand side, you'll note, is far-r more worn than the left. He uses his left for hammering the leather."

Again:

> "This man is a French-polisher."
> "Come, now. Can't you smel-l-l him?"[14]

Again:

> A woman with a small child was shown in. Joe Bell said good morning to her and she said good morning in reply.
> "What sort of crossing di' ye have fra' Burntisland?"
> "It was guid."
> "And had ye a guid walk up Inverleith Row?"
> "Yes."
> "And what did ye do with th' other wain?"
> "I left him with my sister in Leith."
> "And would ye still be working at the linoleum factory?"
> "Yes, I am."
> "You see, gentlemen, when she said good morning to me I noted her Fife accent, and, as you know, the nearest town in Fife is Burntisland. You notice

the red clay on the edges of the sole of her shoes, and the only such clay within twenty miles of Edinburgh is the Botanical Gardens. Inverleith Row borders the gardens and is her nearest way here from Leith. You observed that the coat she carried over her arm is too big for the child who is with her, and therefore she set out from home with two children. Finally she has dermatitis on the fingers of the right hand which is peculiar to workers in the linoleum factory at Burntisland."

And, probably the most famous:

> "Well, my man, you've served in the Army?"
> "Aye, sir."
> "Not long discharged?"
> "No sir."
> "A Highland Regiment?"
> "Aye, sir."
> "A non-commissioned officer?"
> "Aye, sir."
> "Stationed at Barbadoes?"
> "Aye, sir."
> "You see, gentlemen, the man was a respectful man, but he did not remove his hat. They do not in the army, but he would have learned civilian ways had he been long discharged. He has an air of authority and he is obviously Scottish. As to Barbadoes, his complaint is elephantiasis, which is West Indian and not British, and the Scottish regiments are at present in that particular island."[15]

This was mind reading or white magic; in the next generation, it would be replaced by the interpretation of dreams. It recalls the age-old unity of Aesculapian medicine, which originally was a mantic art.

"Try to learn the features of a disease or injury as precisely as you know the features, the gait, the tricks of manner of your most intimate friend. Him, even in a crowd, you can recognize at once. It may be a crowd of men dressed alike, and each having his full complement of eyes, nose, hair, and limbs. In every essential they resemble one another; only in trifles do they differ and yet, by knowing these trifles well, you make your recognition or your diagnosis with ease"[16] Trifles, signs and symptoms, clues—all were grist for Bell's diagnostic mill.

The emphasis on meticulous observation is traditional in medicine and has been repeated in many forms: "More is missed by not looking than by not knowing" (Thomas McCrae); "For one mistake made for not knowing, ten mistakes are made for not looking" (J. A. Lindsay);

> More harm is done because you do not look
> Than from not knowing what is in the book.[17]

This observational imperative requires, however, a long apprenticeship. "In the last analysis," said Charcot, "we see only what we are ready to see, what we have been taught to see. We eliminate and ignore everything that is not a part of our prejudices."[18] In this case, prejudice is not necessarily bad; the number of facts to be observed in a single still-life approaches infinity. Through the categories of experience and prejudice, meaning and intelligibility are imposed on the chaos of phenomena.

Bell's bravura performances were only elementary lessons for beginners. Time and experience were necessary to transform these novice physcians into practitioners of mature judgement. The possibility of error was always near at hand to humble the most brilliant diagnostician.

> "You are a bandsman?"
> "Aye," replied the sick man.
> Dr. Bell cockily turned to his students, "You see, gentlemen, I am right. This man has a paralysis of his cheek muscles, the result of too much blowing at band instruments."
> And turning again to the patient, "What instrument do you play, my man?"
> "The big drum," came the reply.[19]

The impression that Joseph Bell made on Doyle was unique in the annals of medical education. Bedside teaching skills usually live on only in the clinical practice of students. Rarely has such a teaching style been so transformed—and immortalized. When Doyle wrote to Bell—"It is most certainly to you that I owe Sherlock Holmes, and although in the stories I have the advantage of being able to place him in all sorts of dramatic positions, I do not think that his analytical work is in the least an exaggeration of some effects which I have seen you produce in the out-patient ward"— Bell's response to Holmes as an alter ego included such descriptives as "cataract of drivel" and "heap of rubbish."[20] Doyle was not entirely unsympathetic to his old mentor's opinion, but Bell reportedly later grew reconciled to his fate and possibly was even secretly pleased.

THE AUTOCRATIC HOLMES

> "Good morning, Holmes—what's your name?"
> —Josiah Quincy

> For high and dangerous action teaches us to believe as right beyond dispute things for which our doubting minds are slow to find words of proof.
> —O. W. Holmes, Jr.

One of the most notable figures of the nineteenth century earned his professional reputation by the scientific application of deduction to the solution of a long series of mysterious deaths, although he rarely appeared in court to give evidence at criminal trials. His personal adventures, slightly disguised and appearing under a physician's byline, almost singlehandedly made the reputation of one of the most popular periodicals of the day. He had annoying passions for chemistry and the violin, a strong interest in boxing, a fondness for lenses (the magnifying glass and the microscope), and an inclination to the meerschaum. His library contained innumerable works of reference, and he was himself more solitary than social but took great care to engineer his own public image.

The magazine whose reputation he established was *The Atlantic Monthly* and not *The Strand*, for this list of Sherlockian traits is actually a capsule biography of Oliver Wendell Holmes.[21] A pioneer of American medicine and letters, Holmes studied in Paris and returned with three principles: not to take authority when he could have facts, not to guess when he could know, and not to think a man must take physic because he is sick. His analytical approach to clinical problems produced the classic paper "The Contagiousness of Puerperal Fever" (1843), in which he anticipated Semmelweis by two decades in identifying the cause of childbed fever. Holmes was dean of the Harvard Medical School when Professor John Webster murdered Dr. George Parkman; in one of his rare courtroom appearances, his forensic evidence helped identify the victim's remains. A writer of occasional verse that has long survived its original stimulus, Holmes also had a conversational style that bordered on mind reading: "Holmes talks very nearly all the time but the secret of the charm of the monopoly is the fact that he is, all this time, *broidering on your woof*—apparently dwelling only on what you have suggested, and reading your mind very truly to yourself, only that he makes it seem a good deal clearer than you thought it!"[22] A very private individual, he fashioned his literary persona with careful deliberation: "I have come before the public like an actor who returns to fold his robes and make his bow to the audience."[23]

Holmes recognized that confidence is both appropriate to the professional and helpful to the patient: "Keep your doubts to yourself, and give the patient the benefit of your decision."[24] While a certain amount of bluff may be necessary—"Audacious self-esteem . . . is always imposing";[25] "The specialist is much like other people engaged in lucrative business. He is apt to magnify his calling, to make much of any symptom which will bring a patient within range of his battery of remedies"[26]—it can lead to both overdiagnosis and unnecessary treatment, if not outright charlatanism. The fifth physician to examine an infant with a simple cold may discover a pneumonia undetected by the previous four pediatricians. The anxious parents will be awed by this brilliant (mis)diagnostic coup, and the impression is reinforced that their baby's life has been saved only by the timely (albeit unnecessary) penicillin injection. Patients receiving dietotherapy for imaginary complaints will present a physician with their previous glucose tolerance test curves. When, after careful perusal, the practitioner informs them that all these laboratory results are normal, they respond, "Doctor Fiscalin D. Pendence warned us that other (namely, less competent) doctors would misinterpret it as normal."

As a professional medical educator, Holmes was committed to the scientific method and was a harsh critic of the many forms of imposture prevalent in the medicine of his day. As a man of letters, however, he understood that scientific facts did not begin to encompass the human domain with which medicine dealt. "All generous minds have a horror of what are commonly called 'facts.' They are the brute beasts of the intellectual domain. . . . Scientific knowledge . . . has mingled with it a something which partakes of insolence. Absolute, peremptory facts are bullies, and those who keep company with them are apt to get a bullying habit of mind. There is no elasticity in a mathematical fact."[27]

Medicine needs a scientific base and method but can never become a pure science. Science can study the disease process but physicians treat patients not diseases. The humanist, Holmes, combined a belief in the necessity of a scientific approach with a certain skepticism with regard to the physician's ability to consistently distinguish science fact from personal opinion:

> Science is the topography of ignorance. From a few elevated points we triangulate vast spaces, inclosing infinite unknown details. We cast the lead, and draw up a little sand from abysses we may never reach with our dredges.
> The best part of our knowledge is that which teaches us where knowledge leaves off and ignorance begins. Nothing more clearly separates a vulgar from a superior mind, than the confusion in the first between the little that it truly knows, on the one hand, and what it half knows and what it thinks it knows on the other.[28]

Like Doyle and his detective hero, Dr. Holmes has a penchant for embedding subtle literary references in his occasional verse on mundane topics. Both doctors were in rebellion against the religion of their failed fathers (the Reverend Abiel Holmes had been dismissed by his congregation).[29] Faith in a materialistic determinism and rejection of a paternalistic providence are themes that pervade their writings (at least that part of Doyle's opera presently under consideration). They outlived the popularity of their doctrines and suffered a certain ingratitude on the part of their callous offspring (Sherlock Holmes/Justice Oliver Wendell Holmes, Jr.). Over time their essentially middle-class popularity with the common man became obscured; later generations would view these bourgeois writers as aristocrats and Brahmins.

William Osler recommended Holmes's Breakfast Table series as one of the ten works to be included in the physician's bedside library; that advice remains good today.

Chelm: The Place of Error in Medical Education

> A mythology reflects its region.
> —Wallace Stevens

> The politics of emotion must appear
> To be an intellectual structure. The cause
> Creates a logic not to be distinguished
> From lunacy.
> —Wallace Stevens

> This is a case of my reasoning being, with one partial exception, perfectly correct. Everything I had deduced would no doubt have fitted the real owner of the clothes.
> —Maurice Baring, "From the Diary of Sherlock Holmes"

At the very time that medical student Doyle was falling under the influence of the brilliant Dr. Joseph Bell, there were stories current of less reputable practitioners utilizing a similar observation-and-deduction methodology. One example from the *Lancet* of 1892 has been reprinted in three medical journals as narrated by Dr. Lauder Brunton:

> An admirable example of the application to medicine of this method of tracking used to be told with great gusto by my late friend, Dr. Milner Fothergill, and I regret greatly that I cannot tell it with the same power and vividness that he did. In the town of Leeds there once lived a quack who had received no professional instruction whatever, but was known far and wide for his wonderful cures, and especially for his power of diagnosing the diseases of patients whom he had never seen, by simply examining their urine. A celebrated surgeon, Mr. X—, wishing to see his method of working, desired to be presented one day, and the quack readily acceded to his request, feeling much flattered that so great a man should patronize him. Shortly after Mr. X—had taken his seat, a woman came in with a bottle of urine, which she handed to the quack. He looked at her, then at the bottle, held it up between him and the light, shook it, and said:
> "Your husband's?"
> "Yes, sir."
> "He is a good deal older than you?"

"Yes, sir."

"He is a tailor?"

"Yes, sir."

"He lives at Scarcroft?"

"Yes, sir."

"His bowels are obstinate?"

"Yes, sir."

"Here," he said, handing her a box of pills, "tell him to take one of these pills every night for a week, and a big drink of cold water every morning, and he will soon be all right."

No sooner had the woman gone out than Mr. X—turned to the quack, curious to know how he had made out all this.

"Well, you see," said the quack, "she was a young woman, and looked well and strong, and I guessed the water was not hers. As I saw she had a wedding ring on her finger, I knew she was married and I thought the chances were it was her husband's water. If he had been about the same age as she was it was hardly likely that he was going to be ill either, so I guessed he was older. I knew he was a tailor because the bottle was not stopped with a cork, but with a bit of paper rolled up and tied around with a thread in the way that no one but a tailor could have done it. Tailors get no exercise, and consequently are all very apt to be constipated. I was quite sure that he would be no exception to the rule, and so I gave him opening pills."

"But how did you know she came from Scarcroft?"

"Oh, Mr. X—, have you lived so long in Leeds and you don't know the color of Scarcroft clay? It was the first thing I saw on her boots the moment she came in."

Now, of late years we have got so many new methods of investigation that we are sometimes apt to forget the old habits of close observation by which this quack made out so much, and proved himself, although without any diploma, a worthy descendant of the water doctor whose picture by Gerard Dow occupies such a distinguished place in the gallery of the Louvre.[30]

These brilliant deductions impress medical students and lay people but, as in the case reported here, are totally independent of the practitioner's honesty or true medical ability.[31]

Holmesian deduction from meticulous observation has been criticized directly and indirectly from a number of perspectives. The best anticipatory criticism came from the mythical shtetl of Chelm, a town whose inhabitants were legendary for their stupidity. Their anti-intellectual transvaluation of all values is not as literarily refined as in the antirational tales of Nahman of Bratslav, but the moral of virtue and goodness residing in innocence and simplicity is just as clearly expressed. Dr. Magnesia of Chelm visits the doctor of a neighboring town for some postgraduate study. Since he persistently misdiagnoses cases, he goes to learn Dr. Smartest's method of diagnosis by observation: a man with a stomachache has been eating too much canned food (many empty tin cans were observed outside the house), a small boy with a stomachache has eaten green apples (the apple cores were observed in the orchard), a woman with a backache has been rearranging furniture (new furniture was observed in the house). He then proceeds to misapply his lesson by interpreting a horse's harness under the bed of a man with a stomachache as proof that the patient has eaten a horse![32]

Another Chelmite employs age, dress, and time to successfully (?) solve a case of identity:

A young man from Chelm was traveling to Pinsk to see his fiancee.

No sooner was he seated in the train than the stranger next to him said:

"So you are Mottle, the son of my good friend, Zalmen, and you're going to see Rifke." The stranger scrutinized him carefully and said: "Ah, Zalman has a fine-looking son. I'm glad for Zalmen. And Rifke will have a good husband."

The Young man was mystified. "Yes, I am Zalmen's son and I'm going to Pinsk to see my fiancee, and I plan to propose to her. But how did you know all this? I have never seen you."

"Neither have I seen you, Mottle," said the stranger, "but what I told you is as plain as the nose on your face. You see that brief case you carry—the one you are holding on your lap."

"Yes, yes," said Mottle, impatiently.

"Well," said the stranger.

"Well," said Mottle.

"It's simple."

"Well, go on," said Mottle.

"Only a lawyer would carry a brief case. And I know you're from Chelm. And I think—I know Chelm a little—who in all Chelm has a son who is a lawyer? It doesn't take much thinking, for how many lawyers are there in all Chelm but one. And I know my friend, Zalmen, has a son who is a lawyer.

"And what would a young man be doing away from his work and traveling from his home on a weekday? The only such person would be a man in love. So I think. I know Pinsk much better than I do Chelm. Who would be a proper match? You could not be marrying Bebble. She is too old. Nor Sarah, her family would not be right for you; she is too low in class. So the only proper one left is Rifke. She is the right age and she is the doctor's daughter. It equals. It comes our perfectly."

"How remarkable!" said Mottle, Zalmen's son. "Unbelievable!"

The stranger shrugged his shoulders. "It's nothing. Nothing at all. It's simple, as plain as day—like the nose on your face. If one carries a brief case like you, to what other figure can one come?"[33]

In the *Boston Medical and Surgical Journal* for 26 May 1904, Dr. Courtney published an interesting parody of Sherlockian deduction, "Dr. Watson and Mr. Holmes; or the worm that turned." The Chelmite Watson takes Holmes on medical rounds and demonstrates the fallaciousness of the apparently obvious in clinical diagnosis. Watson first asks the externe to show in the musician:

"I'm sorry, sir," said the externe, "but I haven't had time to take any histories, and I don't know who you mean."

Watson walked to the door, threw it open, and beckoned to a man sitting on the front seat. The patient entered and sat before Watson's table.

"Musician, did you say?" asked Holmes apathetically.

"Yes, musician, and I should add, a player on a wind instrument."

Holmes examined the man's buccinators in their normal condition, and then got him to puff out his cheeks. He appeared satisfied with his examination, and when Watson asked him if he had made up his mind as to how he, Watson, had arrived at his conclusion as to the man's occupation, he answered in a tired way, "Why, certainly, you have only to look at the muscles of his lips and cheeks; they tell the story."

"Wrong," said Watson; "it's much simpler than that. Just observe the little goatee he wears. I venture to say he believes the loss of that would prevent his playing for a week. Am I right?" he asked, turning to the man.

"Oh, yes, sir. I wouldn't cut that off for the world; it's strengthening to the lip, and I shouldn't be able to play till it grew again."

Watson soon got at the facts of the case, examined and disposed of it.

During this time Holmes looked absently out of the window.

The next patient was ushered in, and without speaking, presented a note to Watson. The latter, without looking at the note, exclaimed, "Ah, a teamster, I see."

"That observation was superfluous," broke in Holmes superciliously. "I knew he was a teamster the moment I saw him. He has the complexion of a man much exposed to the weather and wears the sort of clothes common to people of that class."

"That may all be true, but it would apply equally well to a cabman; and it is dangerous to draw conclusions on such general grounds. Perhaps you did not notice that this man took the note he brought me out of his hat—a typical teamster trick."

Holmes made no reply, but bit his lips furiously while Watson read the note. Watson turned the case over to his assistant and called for the next patient. It proved to be a man with a marked tremor of the right hand. Without a word, Watson took hold of the trembling hand and observed it closely for a few moments. Then he said quietly, "Here, my dear Holmes, is an interesting tremor in a left-handed plasterer, who has done no work for some time. Am I right, my man?"

"Quite right, sir," was the answer. "I'm left-handed and I'm a plasterer by trade, but this cursed shaking has laid me up for nearly six months now."

At this point Holmes was about to say something, but hesitated and looked the man over carefully in silence. Watson sat quietly back in his chair and observed his friend's scrutiny of the patient with an amused twinkle in his eye.

Holmes' face was a study. It had grown several shades yellower than usual, and again made Watson think of pernicious anemia. The powerful magnifying lens was now brought into play and the man's nails, ears and eyebrows thoroughly examined by its aid. Obviously Holmes was stumped. By this time he was breathing hard and mopping his brow.

After a time Watson broke in with: "Well, my dear Holmes, what do you say?"

"Nothing, except that it's beastly stuffy in this room," growled Sherlock, the peerless.

"Well, let's have a window open, and then, perhaps, I can show you a thing or two of interest about this man that you may have overlooked with your glass. You will first observe that the tremor involves the right hand. On looking at this hand closely, you will see a half-softened callus over each joint of the thumb, and similar ones over the root joint and the one next to it of the forefinger. You see none over any other joints. This shows that these particular joints mentioned must habitually come in contact with some hard surface. Now, from my study of artisans' hands, I know that this condition is peculiar to the plasterer, and that it is brought about by the contact of the mortar board. In this case it is the right hand that shows the condition, so the man must do the actual plastering with the left. I hardly need mention that the somewhat softened condition of the calluses indicates this man's abstinence from work for some time."

While Watson was engaged in demonstrating the reasons for his conclusions, Holmes paced rapidly up and down the room, apparently paying not the slightest attention. Finally he whipped out his watch, looked at it, and said, "By Jove, Watson, I must go. I've got an important engagement that I had almost forgotten."

"Oh, don't be in such an infernal rush," replied the doctor. "I've got to get away early myself. I'll tell you what I'll do. I'll just turn this man over to my assistant, see the next case or two hurriedly, and then go along with you."

At Watson's order the next case was led in. "This man," said the externe, "is a rubbercutter, and his complaint is of headache and dizziness."

"Now, Holmes," said the doctor, "won't you just look at this fellow's gums with your glass and see if you don't see a dark line at the junction of the gums and teeth. You do—thank you. It's a clear case of lead poisoning, just as I thought. Now, my man, let me look at your tongue."

A sudden exclamation from Holmes caused Watson to look at him. As he did so he noticed that his friend's face had suddenly taken on an expression very like what one might expect to see in a mummy that had been spoiled in the making. "Did you speak?" he asked, somewhat maliciously.

"No," growled Holmes between his clenched teeth, "but the diagnosis in this case is too absurdly clear. This man has either been doing some painting at home, or else he uses a hair wash containing lead. Isn't that so, my good fellow?" asked Sherlock, addressing the patient.

"Aw, I never washes me hair," was the reply; "and I have enough to do in the shop without bothering with no painting at home. It ain't in my line."

Holmes collapsed in his chair.

"Perhaps if he will tell us just what his functions as a rubber-cutter are, it will help you to arrive at a correct solution of the problem," put in the doctor, dryly. "Exactly what is your work, my man?"

"I just puts the patterns down on the sheet rubber and cuts around them with a knife," was the answer.

"Does that help you, Holmes?" asked Watson.

The great detective sat dejectedly and made no reply.

"Well, we won't waste any more time on it," rattled on Watson, "but the situation is just this. From your extensive reading and observations, you must know that in the preparation of rubber there is used a considerable amount of litharge, or the red oxide of lead. Now you don't have to examine this fellow's hands very closely to conclude that soap is not a large factor in his items of expenditure. My glance at his tongue showed me that he is an habitual tobacco chewer. On the basis of these two observations, I concluded that the transference of really considerable amounts of the lead from fingers to mouth was a daily occurrence.[34]

With experience to bolster his limited powers of observation and deduction, Watson does to Holmes what Holmes typically does to the Metropolitan Police; the lessons are not different, the shoe is merely on the other foot. Apart from the fact that in Doyle's stories Watson never exhibited any hint of the most basic skills of observation and deduction, what this role reversal really demonstrates is the preeminence of clinical experience over the required (but minimal) superficium of abstract deductive logic that is frequently confused with science.

Individuals are unique and react differently to the same disease process. Commenting on the appropriateness to medicine of Butler's axiom "Probability is the guide of life," William Osler offered the following example of a detailed (but erroneous) sequence of observations and conclusion:

Surrounded by people who demand certainty, and not philosopher enough to agree with Locke that "Probability supplies the defect of our knowledge and guides us when that fails and is always conversant about things of which we have no certainty," the practitioner too often gets into a habit of mind which resents the thought that opinion, not full knowledge, must be his stay and prop. There is no discredit, though there is at times much discomfort, in this everlasting *perhaps* with which we have to preface so much connected with the practice of our art. It is, as I said, inherent in the subject. Take in illustration an experience of last week. I saw a patient with Dr. Bolgiano who presented marked pulsation to the left of the sternum in the second, third and fourth interspaces, visible even before the night-dress was removed, a palpable impulse over the area of pulsation, flatness on percussion, accentuated heart sounds and a soft systolic bruit. When to this were added paralysis of the left recurrent laryngeal nerve, smallness of the radial pulse on the left side, and tracheal tugging, there is not one of you who would not make, under such circumstances, the diagnosis of aneurism of the aorta. Few of us, indeed, would put in the *perhaps*, or think of it as a probability with such a combination of physical signs, and yet the associate conditions which had been present—a small primary tumour of the left lobe of the thyroid, with secondary nodules in the lymph glands of the neck and involvement of the mediastinum and tumour causing the remarkable intrathoracic combination was not aneurismal but malignant. Listen to the appropriate comment of the Father of Medicine, who twenty-five centuries ago had not only grasped the fundamental conception of our art as one based on observation, but had laboured also through a long life to give to the profession which he loved the saving health of science—listen, I say to words of his famous aphorism: "Experience is fallacious and judgment difficult!" [italics deleted][35]

The exaggeration of Holmes's deductive powers frequently borders on absurdity. Doyle corrects this impression by documenting many false trails followed, missed clues, premature hypotheses, and erroneous conclusions. Although an occasional client is buried, a fair number of mismanaged cases are solved in spite of these logical errors, which are more often due to "the overrefinement of his logic—his preference for a subtle and bizarre explanation when a plainer and more commonplace one lay ready at hand" (*The Sign of Four*). It is a medical maxim that common diseases cause uncommon symptoms more often than uncommon diseases cause common symptoms.

The status of "The Yellow Face" as the great detective's most clear-cut failure needs to be reassessed. Holmes's preliminary hypothesis of blackmail is quite valid, despite Watson's reservations:

"What do you think of my theory?"
"It is all surmise."
"But at least it covers all the facts. When new facts come to our knowledge which cannot be covered by it, it will be time enough to reconsider it."

But it is entirely the product of history taking; there is no physical examination; when firsthand data are later sought, they are obtained directly by the client and yield an immediate denouement to the case (see Figure 1). Many details are left unresolved and have led to much speculation with regard to other possible solutions—"one can always conceive alternative explanations" ("The Problem of Thor Bridge"). However, this relatively superficial reading of "The Yellow Face" does not do it justice, and a more detailed investigation of its structure may prove rewarding. A careful review of the opening framing sequence at 221 B Baker Street allows a somewhat different interpretation of this tangled tale. Aristotle noted that in dramatic prologues and in epic poetry, a foretaste of the theme should be given in advance instead of keeping the audience in complete suspense. Just as Holmes's apparent failure to solve the case hinges on his lack of any firsthand physical evidence, so his initial analysis of his client's character is completed before he ever sets eyes on Mr. Grant Munro. From an inspection of Mr.

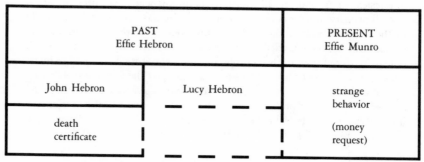

Figure 1. "The Yellow Face"

Holmes correctly traces the cause of Mrs. Munro's strange behavior to something from out of her past. The unusual request for a large sum of money suggests the possibility of blackmail, so Holmes quite legitimately hypothesizes that the late Mr. Hebron's death certificate may be false: a live ex-husband would threaten Effie's current marital status. The detective blunders by not applying the lesson of "Silver Blaze": the failure of the dog to bark is quite analogous to the absence of little Lucy's death certificate. It is not her first husband's survival that Effie wants concealed from her second husband but rather his race, a fact quite clearly revealed by Lucy's skin pigmentation. The crime in this most peculiar narrative would appear to be one of self-blackmail.

Munro's pipe alone, it may be concluded that its owner is a creature of habit who prefers to keep old used things rather than replace them with new ones. The pipe has two silver rings and is charred down one side from its previous mode of being lit, which also identifies its owner as, in some way, sinister. These deductions from the pipe have all but summarized the entire plot of the tale that follows; all that remains is to clarify the client's identity, which Holmes proceeds to do by the not very subtle trick of reading his name from an exposed hat lining.

Holmes's description of the pipe and its owner matches the story line in the same way that a (?pipe) dream distorts the reality on which it is based. All the elements are there; it merely remains to see them in the right perspective. Although Holmes is not instrumental in solving the case (as more often than not a patient's recovery is independent of any medical intervention), he maintains a professionally supportive role throughout. With the goal of bringing "peace to many troubled souls," he reassures—"and above all things do not fret until you know that you really have a cause for it"—and counsels pursuing a definitive diagnosis—"Any truth is better than indefinite doubt." Doyle's handling of deductive errors and the limitations of science may be a more accurate reflection of his medical models than his finest examples of detective skills.

Holmes stresses observation as the basis of his new science of detection; Gargantua placed the faculty of observation at the foundation of his new scheme of pedagogy for the young Pantagruel. The roots of puzzle literature might be traced to the kennings of the ancient skalds, but there are stronger influences from the *Halsrätsel*, or "capital riddle," in which the detective— a Gawain or an Oedipus—must solve the riddle or forfeit his head. Sherlock Holmes is not an ivory-tower academic researcher; he risks action in a world of intense physical danger. Often such decisive action redeems otherwise inexcusable logical failures.

Notes

1. The most comprehensive recent biography of Conan Doyle is Charles Higham, *The Adventures of Conan Doyle: The Life of the Creator of Sherlock Holmes* (New York: Pocket Books, 1978).

2. Quoted in Charles Snyder, "There's Money in Ears, But the Eye Is a Gold Mine," *Archives of Ophthalmology* 85 (March 1971): 365.

3. A recent reprinting of the Brigadier Gerard stories has had the Sherlockian passion for chronology applied to the text with dates and ages rectified to convert fiction to pseudohistory. The reductio ad absurdum of this misguided methodology is easily imagined (if it has not already been reached) when one considers the possible result of amending literary classics to conform to such a corrected chronology. Temporal sequences play an exceedingly important role in such works as Dante's *Comedia* and Joyce's *Ulysses*, but the frames of reference are as much internal as external.

4. The mythical Lane's disease is described in Edward C. Lambert, *Modern Medical Mistakes* (Bloomington: Indiana University Press, 1978), pp. 15–22.

5. W. W. Rowe, *Dostoevsky: Child and Man in His Works* (New York: New York University Press, 1968), p. 144.

6. Martin Gardner, "The Irrelevance of Conan Doyle," in Michael Harrison, ed., *Beyond Baker Street* (Indianapolis, Ind.: Bobbs-Merrill, 1976), pp. 123–35.

7. Quoted in H. Douglas Thomson, *Masters of Mystery: A Study of the Detective Story* (New York: Dover, 1978), p. 125.

8. Quoted in Edward E. Harnagel, "Joseph Bell, M.D.—the Real Sherlock Holmes," *The New England Journal of Medicine* 258 (5 June 1958): 1158.

9. Conan Doyle, *Memories and Adventures* (1924), quoted in E. P. Scarlett, "The Method of Zadig," *Archives of Internal Medicine* 117 (June 1966): 833.

10. C. C. Stisted, quoted in Irving Wallace, "The Incredible Dr. Bell," *Saturday Review of Literature* 31 (1948): 7–8.

11. Conan Doyle, quoted in Thomson, *Masters of Mystery*, p. 126.

12. Joseph Bell, quoted in Joseph V. Klauder, "Sherlock Holmes as a Dermatologist," *A.M.A. Archives of Dermatology and Syphilology* 68 (October 1953): 363. A compendium of modern occupational signs and diagnoses is E. R. Plunkett, *Folk Name & Trade Diseases* (Stamford, Conn.: Barrett Book Co., 1978). A selection from this work appears in Paul Trachtman, "Monday Head to Tango Foot (and Worse), It's Sick, Sick, Sick," *Smithsonian*, April 1979), pp. 123–34.

13. Quoted in Thompson, *Masters of Mystery*, p. 125.

14. Quoted in John Dickson Carr, *The Life of Sir Arthur Conan Doyle* (New York: Vintage, 1975), p. 35.

15. Arthur Conan Doyle, preface to *A Study in Scarlet* (London: Ward Lock and Bowden, 1894).

16. Joseph Bell, quoted in Vincent Starrett, *The Private Life of Sherlock Holmes* (New York: Pinnacle Books, 1975), p. 21.

17. Zeta (Z.C.), *The Diagnosis of the Acute Abdomen in Rhyme* (London: H. K. Lewis & Co. Ltd., 1962), p. 5.

18. A. R. G. Owen, *Hysteria, Hypnosis and Healing: The Work of Jean-Martin Charcot* (New York: Garrett, 1971), p. 36.

19. Quoted in Harnagel, "Joseph Bell, M.D.–the Real Sherlock Holmes," p. 1159.

20. Quoted in ibid., p. 1159.

21. The major primary source of biographical data on Dr. Holmes is John T. Morse, Jr., *Life and Letters of Oliver Wendell Holmes*, 2 vols. (Boston: Houghton, Mifflin and Company, 1897).

22. N. P. Willis, quoted in M. A. DeWolfe Howe, *Holmes of the Breakfast Table* (New York: Oxford University Press, 1939), p. 95.

23. O. W. Holmes, quoted in Eleanor M. Tilton, *Amiable Autocrat: A Biography of Dr. Oliver Wendell Holmes* (New York: Henry Schuman, 1947), p. 138.

24. Oliver Wendell Holmes, *Medical Essays 1842–1882* (Boston: Houghton Mifflin Co., 1911), p. 389.

25. Oliver Wendell Holmes, *The Autocrat of the Breakfast Table* (Boston: Houghton Mifflin and Company, 1889), 1:13.

26. Oliver Wendell Holmes, *Over the Teacups* (Boston: Houghton Mifflin Co., 1918), p. 129.

27. Holmes, *The Autocrat of the Breakfast Table*, vol. 1, p. 6.

28. Holmes, *Medical Essays 1842–1882*, p. 211.

29. That the American doctor had a clergyman father and that much of his philosophy of life was in direct opposition to his father's faith were facts whose significance could not have been lost on Doyle. The name Holmes may also reflect some dim association with Sterne's clergyman, Dr. Homenas in *Tristram Shandy*, or even Rabelais's Homenas, the bishop of the Papimanes.

30. Dr. Milner Fothergill's story is quoted in Sir Lauder Brunton's retelling by Scarlett, "The Method of Zadig," pp. 832–35.

31. The association between the trick of observing and deducing details of a client's life and the fine art of medical quackery is of great antiquity. In the Arabic tale of "The Weaver Who Became a Leach," a henpecked husband takes up as a physician and is observed by the great healer Jalinus (Galen):

Presently, up came a woman, and when the Weaver saw her afar off, he said to her, "Is not your husband a Jew and is not his ailment flatulence?" "Yes," replied the woman, and the folk marveled at this; wherefore the man was magnified in the eyes of Jalinus, for that *he heard speech such as was not of the usage of doctors.* Then the woman asked, "What is the remedy?" and the Weaver answered, "Bring the honorarium." So she paid him a dirham and he gave her medicines contrary to that ailment and such as would only aggravate the complaint. [italics added]

Challenged by Jalinus to explain his performance, the Weaver replies,

"We people of Persia are skilled in physiognomy, and I saw the woman to be rosy-cheeked, blue-eyed, and tall-statured. These qualities belong not to the women of Roum; moreover, I saw her burning with anxiety; so I knew that the patient was her husband. As for his strangerhood, I noted that the dress of the woman differed from that of the townsfolk, wherefore I knew that she was a foreigner; and in her hand I saw a yellow rag, which garred me wot that the sick man was a Jew and she a Jewess. Moreover, she came to me on First Day; and 'tis the Jew's custom to take meat-puddings and food that hath passed the night and eat them on the Saturday their Sabbath, hot and cold, and they exceed in eating; wherefore flatulence and indigestion betide them. Thus I was directed and guessed that which thou hast heard."

A similar tale from the Turkish of Ahmed Ibn Hemdem She Ketk-Hoda (called Sohailee) relates the encounter between "Avicenna and the Observant Young Man." The greatest of Arabic physicians observes a young man distributing remedies in the marketplace. The latter again diagnoses a Jewess but also uncovers the identity of the incognito court healer. The Weaver story is found in Julian Hawthorne, ed., *Library of the World's Best Mystery and Detective Stories* (New York: Review of Reviews, 1908), 6: 45–49.

32. Samuel Tenenbaum, "Chelm's Doctor," *The Wise Men of Chelm* (New York: Collier, 1969), pp. 38–45.

33. Samuel Tenenbaum, "It Figures," *The Wise Men of Chelm*, pp. 153–54.

34. J. W. Courtney, "Dr. Watson and Mr. Holmes; or the Worm That Turned," *Boston Medical and Surgical Journal* 150 (26 May 1904): 553–55.

35. William Osler, *Aequanimitas with Other Addresses* (Philadelphia: P. Blakiston's Son and Company, 1928), pp. 348–49.

The Comic in the Canon: What's Funny about Sherlock Holmes?

BARRIE HAYNE

"I have a theory that the individual represents in his development the whole procession of his ancestors, and that such a sudden turn to good or evil stands for some strong influence which came into the line of his pedigree. The person becomes, as it were, the epitome of the history of his own family."

"It is surely rather fanciful."

"Well, I don't insist upon it."

—"The Empty House," 491[1]

"A dog reflects the family life. Whoever saw a frisky dog in a gloomy family, or a sad dog in a happy one? Snarling people have snarling dogs, dangerous people have dangerous ones. And their passing moods may reflect the moods of others." I shook my head. "Surely, Holmes, this is a little farfetched," said I.

—"The Creeping Man," 1071

Sherlock Holmes and Dr. Watson. Don Quixote and Sancho Panza. The intuitive genius, half-mad, and his down-to-earth squire. Two great characters reprised or refracted from the greatest comic novel ever written.

Yet Watson's literal-mindedness is not always a corrective to Holmes's intuitive flights. When Watson's old friend Bob Ferguson puts his own case before the detective as that of someone else, Watson is struck by Ferguson's altruism. Holmes remarks, "I never get your limits, Watson. . . . There are unexplored possibilities about you. . . . We must not let him think that this agency is a home for the weak-minded." ("The Sussex Vampire," 1036). Perhaps most notably—and comically—of all, there is that moment when Professor Presley, subsequently found to be taking the monkey-gland treatment, is seen crawling along a corridor. When Watson diagnoses the man's peculiar gait as lumbago, Holmes rejoins, "Good, Watson! You always keep us flat-footed on the ground." ("The Creeping Man," 1074).

And at the end of what, in the lives of the two characters, is their very last case, when Watson takes literally Holmes's metaphor, "There's an east

From *Comic Crime*, edited by Earl F. Bargainnier (Bowling Green, Ohio: Bowling Green State University Popular Press, 1987), 145–67. Reprinted by permission.

wind coming," Holmes remarks, "Good old Watson. You are the one fixed point in a changing age." ("His Last Bow," 980).

Fixedness, rigidity, the predictably mechanical—these, as Bergson and others[2] have observed, are of the essence of comedy. Someone who remains mechanically unaltered while circumstances change around him is essentially comic. Yet the fixedness is sometimes Holmes's rather than Watson's, if fixedness suggests feet firmly planted on the ground. There are times when the literal-mindedness is all the detective's, and Holmes, the supreme rationalist, keeps a realistic rein on Watson. Forever after *A Study in Scarlet*, Holmes chides Watson for his introduction of the sensational into the chronicles ("but," says Watson, "the romance was there." *The Sign of Four*, 90). As the saga continues, Holmes complains of Watson's "meretricious," or "sensational," treatment of his cases, which Watson has "degraded," and "embellish[ed]," "tinge[d] with romanticism" what ought to be an exact science. Yet Holmes himself shrugs off his cases in a more literal, realistic way, as "little," "trifling," "simple." When he sits down to tell the tale himself, however, he discovers the necessity of embellishment, romance, concealment, recognizing that Watson "could elevate my simple art, which is but systematized common sense, into a prodigy. When I tell my own story, I have no such aid." ("The Blanched Soldier," 1011)

This disparity of viewpoint when looking at Holmes's deductions, Holmes himself viewing them as commonsense reared into a system, and Watson, unable to see the system, bedazzled by their brilliance, makes for a series of stichomythic exchanges which echo throughout the canon and strike a continuing comic note. Three, beginning with the very first one, will suffice as representative:

"Wonderful!" I ejaculated.
"Commonplace," said Holmes, though I thought from his expression that he was pleased at my evident surprise and admiration.

(*A Study in Scarlet*, 26)

"It is wonderful!" I exclaimed.
"It is obvious."

("The Boscombe Valley Mystery," 214)

"Excellent!" I cried.
"Elementary," said he.

("The Crooked Man," 412)

Here is the essence of the comedy of repetition, which Bergson sees as a major device of verbal comedy.[3] Surely "Elementary, my dear Watson," which in that precise form Holmes never actually says, any more than Rick Blaine ever says "Play it again, Sam," takes its place, with all its synonyms, as a comic repetition, alongside Moliere's "Et Tartuffe? . . . Le pauvre homme!" Of course there are also those other moments, comic in a different way, showing the fragility and inflation of Holmes's pride, when the detective's explanation elicits a "how absurdly simple" from Watson. Holmes remarks on the first such occasion, and the simile he uses reminds us that his deductions are infused with his egotism, and inextricable from his showmanship (as Watson, with a usually uncredited shrewdness, had noticed in the very first exchange quoted above): "I'm not going to tell you much more of the case, Doctor. You know a conjurer gets no credit when once he has explained his trick" (A *Study in Scarlet*, 33).

The fanciful knight and the literal-minded squire may be less of an apt model than a still more archetypal partnership in which complementary qualities match and sometimes interchange. Watson's fanciful side, his tendency to romanticize in order to interest the reader, is a necessary corrective to Holmes's belief that his cases "should have been a course of lectures" ("The Copper Beeches," 317), something along the lines of "the Fifth proposition of the Book of Euclid" (*The Sign of Four*, 90). But Holmes's fanciful side, the inheritance of the Bi-Part Soul which devolved from Dupin and which is passed on to all the great detectives of fiction, the essential mixture in all of them of the Reason and the Understanding, the intuition and the merely rational powers—this fanciful or intuitive side is held in check by, or more properly tested against, Watson's common-sense. This is perhaps best expressed in Watson's own understanding of his role in the saga:

> I was a whetstone for his mind. I stimulated him. He liked to think aloud in my presence. His remarks could hardly be said to be made to me—many of them would have been as appropriately addressed to his bedstead—but none the less, having formed the habit, it had become in some way helpful that I should register and interject. If I irritated him by a certain methodical slowness in my mentality, that irritation served only to make his own flame-like intuitions and impressions flash up the more vividly and swiftly. Such was my humble role in our alliance.
>
> ("The Creeping Man," 1071)

Expressed, significantly, in one of the last stories Doyle wrote in the canon, this opinion is clearly endorsed by Doyle; in it there is nothing of Watsonian obtuseness.

That the "alliance" of Holmes and Watson is psychically a marriage needs no insistence here, since it has been taken so long for granted, and reared into the kind of comedy that passes for Baker Street Irregularity by no less a personage than Rex Stout, in the famous "Watson was a Woman," nearly fifty years ago.[4] But it is worth noting that from the marital nature of their alliance arises much of the comedy of the Sherlock Holmes stories, and especially the badinage that goes on between two people who clearly care about one another, but who sometimes feel the irritations of familiarity.

Watson's more-than-medical concern about Holmes's use of cocaine, and especially about his apparent fatal illness in "The Dying Detective," or his once-in-a-lifetime faint when Holmes returns from Reichenbach, are matched by Holmes's horror when he has almost killed Watson in "The Devil's Foot" ("I had never seen so much of Holmes's heart before," 965), or when he has caused him to be shot, in "The Three Garridebs" ("For the one and only time I caught a glimpse of a great heart," 1053)—these moments clearly delineate the affection between the couple. The irritation is seen in the many many times Holmes, easily the more testy of the two, derides Watson's abilities, and the occasional crucial thrust, more telling for its rarity, which Watson delivers to Holmes.

One surely does not need to verify the comic qualities of marital tension. Except where such tension extends into tragedy, as in *Othello*, wife-husband bickering has been the stuff of comedy from *Lysistrata* through *A Midsummer Night's Dream* to *Private Lives* and *Who's Afraid of Virginia Woolf*. (In *The Odd Couple*, oddly, it takes the pseudo-marital form it has in the Sherlock Holmes stories; emphatically so, and pointing to the universality of Holmes's constitutional untidiness, and Watson's attempts to reform him.) One of the most striking passages illustrating this bickering opens *The Valley of Fear*, the last of the long stories:

> "I am inclined to think—" said I.
> "I should do so," Sherlock Holmes remarked impatiently.
> I believe that I am one of the most long-suffering of mortals, but I'll admit that I was annoyed at the sardonic interruption. "Really, Holmes," said I severely, "you are a little trying at times."
>
> (769)

Here is the "impatient" husband, self-absorbed, "trying," and the "long-suffering" wife, who is usually content to let the gibes pass. But a few lines later, the repressed returning, Watson makes one of his rare put-downs of Holmes, and an effectively heavy one it is:

> "You have heard me speak of Professor Moriarty?"
> "The famous scientific criminal, as famous among crooks as—"
> "My blushes, Watson!" Holmes murmured in a deprecating voice.
> "I was about to say, as he is unknown to the public."
> "A touch! A distinct touch!" cried Holmes. "You are developing a certain unexpected vein of pawky humour, Watson, against which I must learn to guard myself."
>
> (769)

The word that Holmes uses, "pawky," is of Scottish origin, and may well be a passing fling at J. M. Barrie, who twenty years before had written a parody of Doyle, which Doyle later acknowledged in his autobiography as the best of many,[5] but the word ignites rather than defuses the bickering between Holmes and Watson, for it connotes an unintentional humour, and in using it Holmes is relegating Watson to the usual uncomprehending role; three times more in the same chapter, with Watson ignoring the gibes, Holmes tries to confirm his partner in that role. As the two discuss the key to the cipher Porlock has sent, and in particular which reference book he has used, Holmes rallies Watson for "that innate cunning which is the delight of your friends," points out that "perhaps there are points which have escaped your Machiavellian intellect," and even, when Watson reaches a correct solution, [says] "you are scintillating this morning," urging him to "one more coruscation."

This exchange, marked by Holmes's ironical depreciation of Watson's reasoning powers, is typical, though lengthier than any other in the canon. Even when Watson is giving Holmes information he does not himself have, the detective either rejects it as not germane to his concerns, as he does with the Solar System ("I shall do my best to forget it," *A Study in Scarlet*, 21; though of course he has made a sophisticated use of it in the case later recorded as "The Musgrave Ritual") or else patronizes it as being on an insignificant topic, as he does with Watson's flow of information about the race track at Shoscombe Old Place ("I seem to have struck a rich vein," 1103; is this double use of the word "vein" a geological metaphor, or yet another gibe—at Watson's profession?). When Holmes examines the Baskerville portraits, he remarks, "Watson won't allow that I know anything of art, but that is mere jealousy because our views upon the subject differ" (749); and this is distinctly an intimate, carping comment of a kind often used by spouses to score off one another, gratuitously. Holmes's famous reaction to Watson's announcement of his engagement to Mary Morstan ("I feared as much, . . . I really cannot congratulate you," *The Sign of Four*, 157) is scarcely justified by his following statement that "love is an emotional thing . . . opposed to that true cold reason which I place above all things," for he has hardly demonstrated, even thus far in the canon, much faith in Watson's dedication to cold reason, so that he cannot claim that love is losing him a partner in the rational detection of crime. He sounds much more like a spurned and jealous spouse; and Watson's more sane reply ("laughing,"— "I trust . . . that my judgment may survive the ordeal,") is both free of jealousy, and self-aware. Holmes's is neither. In one of the very late stories, after some praise of Watson, which is characteristically faint, being more praise of his intellectual failings than of his strengths, Holmes begins his narration with the statement that "the good Watson [itself a patronizing expression] had at that time deserted me for a wife, the only selfish action which I can recall in our association. I was alone" ("The Blanched Soldier," 1000). Any irony here is surely Doyle's, with Holmes the butt; the petulance of the statement again bespeaks the jealous spouse.

Indeed, from the very beginning of the acquaintanceship, Holmes and

Watson have looked at each other as prospective mates might do. Surely the scene in *A Study in Scarlet* in which they lay bare their respective failings, and stipulate their demands, calls to mind the "contract" scene in *The Way of the World*, in which Mirabel and Millamant, with obvious affection behind the badinage, rationally lay down the rules for their forthcoming union. Holmes sometimes smokes tobacco, as does Watson. Holmes keeps chemicals about, which Watson will tolerate. Watson has a bull-pup (which we hear nothing more about); Holmes makes no comment, though he might have been remembering his only college chum, Victor Trevor, and how he had used that earlier friendship to lay the foundation of his career, after Trevor's bull terrier had bitten him on the leg. Holmes is given to moods of depression; this suits Watson, who in his present state of nerves wants to avoid noise, from which category Holmes confidently excludes his own violin-playing. The whole basis of the relationship thus entered into—and one need not dwell, so often has it been remarked, on the alacrity with which Watson ups and leaves his various wives at a moment's notice when Holmes signals that the game is afoot—is keynoted in Holmes's remark, "It's just as well for two fellows to know the worst of one another" (19). As Millamant says, "I'll never marry, unless I am first made sure of my will and pleasure." To which Mirabel [replies] "Would you have 'em both before marriage? Or will you be contented with the first now, and stay for the other till after grace?"[6]

In, therefore, the central relationship in the canon, the Holmes-Watson relationship, is recognizably a comic marriage, usually harmonious, but subject to some tensions and jealousies (at least on one side). The long-suffering Watson, as we have seen, largely suffers Holmes's ironies, but responds quite emotionally to gestures of affection. When Holmes shows that unwonted glimpse of his heart in "The Devil's Foot," Watson's loving reaction is followed immediately by Holmes's ironical one. Both reactions are absolutely typical: "You know," Watson says, "that it is my greatest joy and privilege to help you"; whereas Holmes "relapsed at once into that half-humorous, half-cynical vein which was his habitual attitude to those about him" (966). The whole relationship is in conception comic, and, like all elements of comedy, recognizably human.

One reason for its comic quality is indeed that rigid, mechanical element already mentioned that Bergson saw as eliciting our laughter. Again, Watson is not the only fixed point in a changing world and neither even is Holmes. The partnership itself is predictable, as the badinages and tensions of marriage are predictable. In "The Retired Colourman," which, though not written last, Doyle chose to place last, we have a case which deals tragically with marriage; Holmes describes the facts as "the old story . . . a treacherous friend and a fickle wife." Holmes's view of marriage is always a mordant one ("He never spoke of the softer passions, save with a gibe or a sneer," as we are told in the very first paragraph of the very first short story, "A Scandal in Bohemia," 161). His doubts about the marital relation therefore continue to the end. But this characterization by the detective of one of his last recorded cases follows an extraordinary effusion of emotion by Holmes, from which he is quickly brought back to earth by "the good doctor": "But is not all life pathetic and futile? Is not his story a microcosm of the whole? We reach, we grasp. And what is left in our hands at the end? A Shadow. Or worse than a shadow—misery" (1113). The depression that Holmes admitted to in his opening "contract" with Watson continues to the end as well, and it is linked with his marital status, or lack of it. The "marriage" of Holmes and Watson may be one of the essential comic elements in the saga, but the rigidity of Holmes the marital sceptic, the misogynist, is no less surely one of the ruling comic qualities in his character. We must take Watson's word for Holmes's idolization of Irene Adler, and his interest in Violet Hunter is primarily Watson's wishful thinking. It is when he reports directly to us of Maud Bellamy in "The Lion's Mane" that we glimpse what he may have missed, being now in his retirement, with the Queen safely segregated: "Women have seldom been an attraction to me, for my brain has always governed my heart, but I could not look upon her perfect clear-cut face, with all the soft freshness of the downlands in her delicate colouring, without realizing that no young man would cross her path unscathed" (1088). This is no country for *old* men, but the danger is still inherent in the sex-relation ("unscathed"). In Watson is a much safer, more long-suffering spouse. The canon certainly bespeaks no "Come back to Baker Street again, John (or James?) honey," for any homo-eroticism is buried in the badinage, but to see two grown men behaving within all the comic conventions of a marriage is to see the centre of the comedy. Neil Simon knew that this was a sure comic recipe for *his* play, and Billy Wilder, who dealt from his first film (*The Major and The Minor*) with disguised and therefore comic sexuality, bringing the theme to its climax in *Some Like It Hot*, gave one more turn to the screw in a later film, *The Private Life of Sherlock Holmes*.[7] The film does not question the sexual normality of the two, any more than the canon raises the question, but Holmes in his dressing gown, Watson always at his beck and call, is an abiding stereotype of comic domesticity.

If we now look at the two characters separately rather than as a pair, it is on the face of things Watson who is the comic character and Holmes the hero of the saga. As Ronald Knox has noted, with his tongue not quite fully in his cheek, "Watson provides what the Holmes drama needs—a chorus . . . his drabness is accentuated by contrast with the limelight which beats upon the central figure."[8] Watson's comic qualities reside in his obtuseness rather than in his occasional deflations of Holmes. "I saw in the gas-light that Holmes wore an amused smile at this brilliant departure of mine" ("The Resident Patient," 430) sums up his function as obtuse narrator, as well as Holmes's attitude towards him. "There is a delightful freshness about you, Watson, which makes it a pleasure to exercise any small powers which I possess at your expense" (*The Hound of the Baskervilles*, 683) sums up again Holmes's attitude towards Watson, but emphasizes as well his own vanity. As Watson had fixed him for all time at the earliest stage of their acquaintance, "I had already observed that he was as sensitive to flattery on the score of his art as any girl could be of her beauty" (*A Study in Scarlet*, 34).

Dr. Watson and Mr. Holmes, with its no doubt fortuitous recollection of Stevenson's famous novel of dual personality the year before, might well have been Sherrinford Holmes and Ormond Sackler.[9] "Sherrinford" Holmes would have altered little of Sherlock's character, still suggesting his origins in a line of country squires, though perhaps "Sherlock," with its Coleridegean echoes of the person from Porlock (more directly alluded to in *The Valley of Fear*) and the consequent entry into a Xanadu of the Imagination, carries better the suggestions of the Vernet artistic strain. But Ormond Sackler certainly suggests a degree of pomposity and comic rigidity that reminds us again that the ostensible comedy of the stories resides in Watson, and that "John H. Watson, M.D." domesticates, anglicizes and even conceals that comic quality much better than "Ormond Sackler" could have done.

But it is only the *ostensible* comedy that resides in Watson. Sherlock Holmes is above all a character of humours. As Raymond Chandler, with some hyperbole, has said, "Sherlock Holmes after all is mostly an attitude and a few dozen lines of unforgettable dialogue."[10] While Holmes's particular humour, vanity, comes to us more forcibly through the eyes of the eminently ordinary observer who records it, we ought to remember that Watson is not as obtuse as he is often given discredit for being; he is usually apace with his reader rather than several steps behind; and in "The Three Students" his acumen compares favorably with that of a Camford Don's. And as we have just seen, Watson's penetrating gaze sometimes sees through Holmes's veil.

Holmes's vanity appears especially in those *coups de theatre* with which he closes a handful of his cases, an intrinsically comic device, with Holmes appearing as a more or less mock-heroic, practical-joking *Deus ex machina*. Watson several times notes that Holmes "loves to dominate and surprise those who were around him" (*The Hound of the Baskervilles*, 754). In *The Valley of Fear*, the announcement of the murder is "one of those dramatic moments for which my friend existed" (774). In the same novel, Holmes observes: "Watson insists that I am a dramatist in real life" (809). Holmes's *coups* usually serve his vanity as well as dramatizing it, since they score off those who have presumed to doubt his great powers: Colonel Ross, to whom he dramatically introduces Silver Blaze as the murderer of his trainer; the Prime Minister in "The Second Stain," to whom he reveals the dispatch safely in its box; or, especially, Lord Cantlemere, into whose pocket he actually puts the Mazarin Stone. In each of these cases, especially the last, Holmes is in an almost comic-Christly, again mock-heroic, role, staging a miracle which is at once a put-down and a proof for the Doubting Thomas. Poor Percy Phelps has almost given up hope of recovering his Naval Treaty when Holmes reveals it to him under the breakfast cover. When Phelps's shock occasions Watson's customary production of the brandy, which one might be forgiven for thinking is the only prescription he knows, Holmes apologizes: "Watson here will tell you that I never can resist a touch of the dramatic" (466). But no doubt the detective's greatest *coup de theatre* is reserved, appropriately, for Watson, when he throws off the garb of the old bookseller (in context, there is absurd comedy in *The Origin of Tree Worship*, a subject too outre for the hardheaded Watson) and returns to his friend after a two-year absence. It is no less appropriate that Watson submits to Holmes's mastery by fainting for the one time in his life ("The Empty House").

Aside from these grand theatrical gestures, Holmes remains fairly poker-faced. A. G. Cooper has counted 292 occasions on which the Great Detective either laughs, chuckles, or smiles.[11] But more than once Watson notes the rarity of risibility in his partner: "Holmes seldom laughed, but he got as near to it as his old friend Watson could remember" ("The Mazarin Stone," 1022; this laughter, at the expense of the sceptical Lord Cantlemere, is oddly omitted from Cooper's canvass).

Still, if Holmes rarely laughs, he has a verbal wit which reflects, throughout the chronicles, comedy at the level of the word. Often that wit is sharpened at the expense of Watson and the public officials, the Chorus and the Sophists, in Knox's whimsical terms, characters of fixity. When Watson explains Professor Presley's behaviour in commonsensical terms which do not explain why his dog has attacked him, Holmes comments: "and the wolfhound no doubt disapproved of the financial bargain" ("The Creeping Man," 1075). Just so he had demolished Athelney Jones's reading of the Sholto murder, in a locked room: "on which the dead man very considerately got up and locked the door on the inside" (*The Sign of Four*, 113).

The guying of the police is a game Holmes engages in throughout the stories, beginning with his acceptance of the murder investigation in *A Study in Scarlet* along with Gregson and Lestrade ("However, we may as well go and have a look. I shall work it out on my own hook. I may have a laugh at them, if I have nothing else," 27). Holmes mellows towards his principal police antagonist-coadjutor over the years, and Lestrade towards him, so that in "The Six Napoleons" they become a mutual admiration society for a few moments in which Holmes, by Lestrade's praise (vanity remains his comic sore point), is "more nearly moved by the softer human emotions that I had ever seen him" (595). There is even indulgence in his first remarks to Lestrade after his return from Reichenbach: "you handled the Molesey Mystery with less than your usual—that's to say, you handled it fairly well" (492).

The higher form of comedy in relation to the police, however, draws attention to their failings and professional vanities by distinguishing them directly from Holmes, whose vanity is rarely brought face to face with failure: the method used is dramatic irony, as it is Holmes who solves the case, a fact which we, Watson and the detective know—as do Lestrade and his cohorts, who actually get the credit. This happens so often that quotation is scarcely necessary; it will be enough to note that such an incident occurs for the first time in *A Study in Scarlet* ("The man was apprehended, it appears, in the rooms of a certain Mr. Sherlock Holmes, who has himself, as an amateur, shown some talent in the detective line, and who, with such instructors, may hope in time to attain to a degree of their skill," 86), and for the last time in the story placed last in *The Case-Book*, "The Retired Colourman" ("The remarkable acumen by which Inspector MacKinnon deduced, . . . the bold deduction, . . . and the subsequent inquiry . . . should live in the history of crime as a standing example of the intelligence of our professional detectives," 1122). And so ends the Saga.

Holmes's awareness of his mastery of the rational and intuitive, like Dupin's, is what makes him ultimately superior to the police, who are merely rational, with no spark of genius. The denigration of the official police, however, which began with Dupin's Prefect, and comes to apotheosis with Holmes and the Lestrades and Gregsons, is in the 1890s by no means the commonplace of detective fiction it became over the next fifty or so years. Aside from Dupin, all Holmes's major predecessors *are* official policemen, from Inspector Bucket to the retired Sergeant Cuff to Lecoq. Holmes's famous disparagement of both Dupin and Lecoq (*A Study in Scarlet*, 24–25) plays no favorites between unofficial and official police. But that same awareness on Holmes's part of his mastery of the rational world through means both intellectual and imaginative bears with it the realization that he cannot deal with the powers "devilish," which suggest both their evil qualities (from the villain's point of view) and their preternatural power, Holmes frequently accepts such characterizations as complimentary: "I believe you are the devil himself." "Not far from him, at any rate" ("The Mazarin Stone, 1021) is both a wry acceptance of those preternatural powers, and a subtle dig at his interlocutor. But in the truly devilish world even Holmes's deductions cannot be valid; and his recognition of his limitation is comic. "In a modest way I have combatted evil," he says in *The Hound of the Baskervilles*, when he seems to be confronted with the very powers of darkness, "but to take on the Father of Evil himself would, perhaps, be too ambitious a task" (681) (We note the "perhaps," as we note the "even" of the Retired Colourman's consulting, as an act of bravado, "not only the police but even Sherlock Holmes" [1122]). And in "The Sussex Vampire" he looks for the rational explanation of "a Grimm's fairy tale," and reports deadpan his solution of the case in the same dry prose the lawyers used to draw it to his attention: "Referring to your letter of the 19th . . . the matter has been brought to a satisfactory conclusion. With thanks for your recommendation, I am, sir, faithfully yours." (1044)

Holmes's wit is rarely self-directed, though the guying of the police, and the dramatic irony associated with their having the glory and he the satisfaction ("Populus me sibilat, at mihi plaudo / Ipse domi simul ac nummos contemplar in arca," 86) echoes in those moments when he is in error, and wryly concedes as much, both to Watson and the official police:

> "Watson," said he, "if it should ever strike you that I am getting a little overconfident in my powers, or giving less pains to a case than it deserves, kindly whisper 'Norbury' in my ear, and I shall be infinitely obliged to you."
> —"The Yellow Face," 362

> "Well, well, Inspector, I often ventured to chaff you gentlemen of the police force, but *Cyanea capillata* very nearly avenged Scotland Yard."
> —"The Lion's Mane," 1095

Here he has the glory—the second case is very nearly his last—established by fame; but his two principal butts in so many earlier cases have the satisfaction, which he accepts with a gracious wit, of seeing him bested.

There are other times when Holmes's wit approaches self-parody. When he first dazzles a skeptical Watson in *A Study in Scarlet* with his "You mean the retired Sergeant of Marines" (25) on the other side of Baker Street, we are fairly in the realm of pure deduction. But there is both showing-off and self-parody in Holmes's assessment of the red-headed Jabez Wilson: "Beyond the obvious facts that he has at some time done manual labour, that he takes snuff, that he is a Freemason, that he has been in China, and that he has done a considerable amount of writing lately. I can deduce nothing else" (177). Still, we can imagine how Holmes reached each conclusion in the chain. There is even deeper satire of Holmes's methods in his very similar appraisal of the unhappy John Hector McFarlane: "beyond the obvious facts that you are a bachelor, a solicitor, a Freemason, and an asthmatic, I know nothing whatever about you" ("The Norwood Builder," 497). The joke of such statements lies in the fact that most observers (though here Watson follows for us the chain of reasoning, rather than have Holmes explain it) would indeed know nothing about him. The wit is self-aggrandizing as well as, mainly from Doyle's viewpoint, self-satirical.

"Holmes could talk exceedingly well when he chose," Watson says early in their relationship (*The Sign of Four*, 134), and while the foregoing remarks have no doubt borne out Watson's statement, Holmes's wit is reactive and dry rather than epigrammatic. Aphorisms are relatively few, and indeed his observations upon life or the larger topics tend to be fairly prolix, like the famous comparison of crime in the city to that in the country, on the train en route to the Copper Beeches (322–323), or the remarks about unattached women prompted by the disappearance of Lady Frances Carfax (942–943). In the exchange between Holmes and Moriarty in their only meeting before the Reichenbach, there is certainly epigrammatic wit, but Holmes, however witty, is still reacting to Moriarty's verbal agility: it is a fencing with words we are watching; and Moriarty makes the last play:

"If you are clever enough to bring destruction upon me, rest assured that I shall do as much to you."

"You have paid me several compliments, Mr. Moriarty . . . Let me pay you one in return when I say that if I were assured of the former eventuality I would, in the interests of the public, cheerfully accept the latter."

"I can promise you the one, but not the other," he snarled . . .

—"The Final Problem," 473

Another characteristic feature of Holmes's wit is insouciance; the exchange I have just quoted follows closely Holmes's remark that "in the pleasure of this conversation I am neglecting business of importance which awaits me elsewhere." The violin or the syringe are tangible examples of Holmes's own brand of sprezzatura, or, more widely, his quality of turning casually away from what is in fact of the utmost importance to him. Once the case is solved, there is always Patti at Covent Garden, a good dinner at Simpson's, or even the pleasures of the cocaine bottle. This is sometimes expressed as verbal witticism: after solving the problem of the Blue Carbuncle by discovering the precious gem in the goose's crop, Holmes ends the story with "If you will have the goodness to touch the bell, Doctor, we will begin another investigation, in which also a bird will be the chief feature" (257).

The particular kind of epigram, however, delphic, often concealing a dramatic irony, which is especially Holmesian is the one Ronald Knox called the Sherlockismus, of which the chief example is the exchange in "Silver Blaze" touching "the curious incident of the dog in the night-time" (347).[12] Another is certainly the closing paragraph of "Charles Augustus Milverton" in which Lestrade, ever the dupe, asks Holmes to investigate the murder of the black-mailer at which Holmes and Watson have been present, and from which they have only just got away from the police. "That's rather vague," says Holmes of the Inspector's description of the less agile of the two escapees. "Why, it might almost be a description of Watson!" Which piece of dramatic irony amuses Lestrade no end.

To the extent, however, that Holmes is a wit at all, his literary context and kinship are inevitably invoked. Critics of detective fiction are a self-regarding lot, as self-regarding as the genre they study, and are much more apt to treat their subjects in isolated relation to that genre. So they find the principal intimations of Holmes in the Dupin and Lecoq he professed to deplore, or even in Sergeant Cuff.[13] There is perhaps here an additional reminder that Holmes may be more profitably placed in the larger context of his immediate time. While all this has been done before, and even in the earlier parts of this paper, here it is once more, with succinctness. Fifty years after Dupin, Holmes is still a romantic, still bringing his intuition to bear on the problem, supplemented by his powers of logic; Watson admires, in "The Speckled Band," "the rapid deductions, as swift as intuitions and yet always founded on a logical basis" (258). He is as much that Bi-part soul, "creative and resolvent," as Poe's detective was. Though Poe deplored Emersonian Transcendentalism and all that Kant (*cant*, or *can't*, as Melville called it), Dupin did bequeath to Holmes that amalgam of Reason and Understanding, imagination and rational thinking. And Holmes, before Thorndyke, was also bringing the ultimate weapons of logic, the scientific tools of the laboratory, to prove his intuitions—we and Watson meet him, as he rushes from the lab full of his latest finding, a scientific test for blood stains. And this meeting takes place the year after Stevenson's strange case of dual personality: in Holmes's spurts of energy alternating with cocaine depressions is yet another reminder of his Bi-part soul. Fully born, at Christmas 1887, is Holmes the dual man, using the methods of the approaching twentieth century to deal with a romantic and mysterious intractability, with which he is at the same time fully in tune.

None of which is especially comic, though there is certainly comedy in the conception overall of a man born out of time who is nonetheless well able to adapt and cope with an alien world. Not the tragic conception of a Matthew Arnold trapped in the monastery of the Grand Chartreuse, but the more comic one of a Hank Morgan who is triumphant in both worlds between which he wanders.

But if Holmes appeared two years before *A Connecticut Yankee*, he also appeared in the same decade as *Patience*, and there is a happy conjunction (and a reminder) in the simultaneous solicitation by Lippincott's of both *The Sign of Four* and *The Picture of Dorian Gray*:[14] though it is odd to find Watson whiling away the time over *La Vie de Boheme*, Holmes certainly is a recognizable bohemian, and belongs to the same aesthetic movement as Wilde. The qualities that Ian Ousby points to in his discussion of this question owe, as he himself admits, as much to Dupin as to the Decadents.[15] But with the title of *A Study in Scarlet* making direct reference to the world of art, and with Holmes himself more insistent than later on his profession as an art, this early Holmes is a figure to be associated with Bunthorne and Grosvenor, or still more Wilde himself. One could certainly imagine Holmes, entering the United States, having nothing to declare but his genius, and his life illustrates Wilde's epigram, that to love oneself is the beginning of a lifelong romance: Holmes and the Wildean persona (or poseur) share a common overwhelming egotism with a touch of disarmingly boyish I-don't-really-mean-it-you-know. Holmes's chief quality of decadence, of course, is his addiction to cocaine, and even of this there is a broad hint in Dupin. While this addiction is eventually phased out of the canon, and is of course deeply tragic in reality, it is presented, despite Watson's air of reproval, and perhaps because of the very pomposity of that reproval, as a touch comic. "Why should you, for a mere passing pleasure, risk the loss of those great powers with which you have been endowed?" sounds rather like a father uneasily cautioning his son against the evils of masturbation. And in the treatments of Holmes in legend and parody, the cocaine addiction has frequently been seized upon as essentially funny. Mr. Dooley, adopting the persona of the Great Detective, says to friend Hennessy, "Pass th' dope, Watson."[16] The phrase "Quick, Watson, the needle!" seems to have acquired an early, jokey currency in newspaper cartoons and elsewhere, though used nowhere in the stories. It encapsulates the comic nature of the addiction and is used as late as 1940 as the last line of the most famous film version of *The Hound of the Baskervilles*. Doyle, however, had already expressed the comedy of the situation, without foregoing altogether its poignancy, in the last line of *The Sign of Four*, the novel which both gives greatest emphasis to the addiction and is closest in spirit to the Decadent movement: " 'For me,' " said Sherlock Holmes, " 'there still remains the cocaine-bottle.' And he stretched his long white hand up for it" (158).

There is one final element in Sherlock Holmes himself which links him with Decadence and Wilde (the long white hand almost suggests Aubrey Beardsley!) and this is his aversion to women. Again, it is a trait so familiar as to need no documentation here; Watson discusses it at greatest length at the beginning of "A Scandal in Bohemia," within the context of the detective's great respect for Irene Adler: women are the irrational element which stands in the way of reason, the grit in the sensitive instrument. And the canon rings with Holmes's depreciation and distrust of that sex which he allows in Watson's department. "Women are never to be entirely trusted— not the best of them," he says to a Watson in love in *The Sign of Four*, a sentiment which Watson finds "atrocious" (129), but which he characteristically does not try to rebut; again we see the comic fixity of the two characters, with Holmes's instinctive and unbending misogyny set against Watson's no less stereotypical conventional reaction.

Inevitably, over the forty years that Doyle (or Watson) annalised Holmes's activities, changes occurred in the character of the detective. The anecdote in Doyle's autobiography concerning Holmes's never being "quite the same man" after the Reichenbach Falls is a familiar one. One insistent note after the return is certainly that of self-parody. "The remarkable narrative" of the previous two years with which Holmes regales Watson is full of Holmesian comic self-aggrandizement, reflecting (no doubt) both Doyle's exasperation with this enforced resurrection and the increasingly comic presentation of Holmes; the tone is very different, obviously, from the one of reverence with which "The Final Problem" ends—"the best and wisest man whom I have ever known." In his own account, Holmes has "passed through Persia," communicating the results of "a short but interesting visit" with the Khalifa at Khartoum to the Foreign Office (There are intimations here of Mycroft, many of whose traits are comic underlinings of Sherlock's). He has spent some months "in a research into the coal-tar derivatives" in a laboratory in Montpelier; and he has "amused" himself with a visit to Lhassa and the head lama (The Sherlockians have spilt ink in querying the spelling: was this a man or an animal?).[17]

But the greatest note of self-parody lies in the references to cases unre-counted. Of some fifteen such references, only four occur before Reichenbach, and these are cited in the service of mystification and the aggrandizement of Holmes rather than of parody: "The new century will have come, however, before the story can safely be told." (447). The one pre-Reichenbach allusion which gives the details of an unreported case does so to highlight the formal problem—"Sherlock Holmes was able, by winding up the dead man's watch, to prove that it had been wound up two hours before, and that therefore the deceased had gone to bed before that time" (218). The later references, to the Giant Rat of Sumatra, "the repulsive story of the red leech" (607), "Wilson, the notorious canary-trainer" (559), and the two Coptic Patriarchs, are on a level of sensationalism and even absurdity which takes them into the realm of the comic. "I have Mr. Holmes's authority for saying," Watson begins "The Veiled Lodger," "that the whole story concerning the politician, the lighthouse, and the trained cormorant will be given to the public" (1095). Another case "worthy of note" begins "Thor Bridge:" "that of Isadora Persano, the well-known journalist and duellist, who was found stark staring mad with a match-box in front of him which contained a remarkable worm said to be unknown to science" (1055). This allusion, indeed, amplifies upon the self-parodic nature of such citations: the victim is, like Holmes himself as well as most of his great antagonists, a double man, leading a life of normality along with one of violence (Moriarty the professor and the Napo-leon of crime): he is also well-known, invoking a world of privilege and high politics to which the reader and Watson are only partly privy; the irrational has invaded the everyday world in a seemingly banal way (madness in a match-box); and, once again, as in "The Speckled Band," or later in "The Lion's Mane," nature itself has given us a glimpse of its secrets before which the ultimate twentieth-century defence, science, is powerless. The case of Isadora Persano was one of Holmes's failures, though it is little wonder that these parodic sketches for stories never written have provided points of departure for later pastiches, in *The Exploits of Sherlock Holmes* and elsewhere.[18]

While these untold stories present us with tantalizing and potentially comic situations, in the canon itself there are relatively few cases which actually deliver comedy of situation, and then only momentarily: Holmes is enlisted as a witness at Irene Adler's wedding, Toby the bloodhound loses the creosote trail and returns to his starting point, Watson is caught out while posing as an expert in Chinese pottery. Of the sixty cases recorded, fewer than half—twenty-seven—deal with murder, and Holmes himself points out in "The Copper Beeches," the last story in the first collection, that four of the cases already recorded contained no crime at all (317). "A Case of Identity" and "The Noble Bachelor" are both comic in their conception and form, leading to the discomfiture rather than defeat of the clients, whose short sight or aristocratic hauteur makes them comic butts—the poor girl is defeated of her marital expectations, as the pompous lordling is of his. No murder is present to import a note of tragic seriousness; Holmes all but lays a whip across the shoulders of the wrongdoer in the first case, and lays a quite epicurean little supper for those who wronged Lord St. Simon in the second. In the only two cases in which Holmes loses a client to murder, "The Five Orange Pips" and "The Dancing Men," the elements of comedy and play are there, as both cases, especially the latter, begin with the semblance of a child's game, but are entirely superseded by the seriousness of the unfolding events.

If after Reichenbach, Holmes becomes more self-quizzical, Watson may become more philosophical, and he raises more than once the question of the intrusion of the comic into his records. In the earlier review which begins "The Speckled Band," he surveys the material before him—"many tragic, some comic, a large number merely strange, but none commonplace" (257). He begins the much later case of "The Three Garridebs" with a more sophisticated formulation: "It may have been a comedy, or it may have been a tragedy. It cost one man his reason, it cost me a blood-letting, and it cost yet another man the penalties of the law. Yet there was certainly an element of comedy. Well, you shall judge for yourselves" (1044). This story is a reworking of both "The Red-Headed League" and "The Stockbroker's Clerk:" a man is lured away from a particular place so that crime may be done there. In the first two cases the criminal activity is merely the robbing of a financial institution. In "The Three Garridebs" it is the recovery of a counterfeiter's printing press. While the criminal in the third case is the most formidable of the three (he almost kills Watson), the situation he sets up as the basis of his crime is the most comic. Hall Pycroft is lured by career advancement, Jabez Wilson by the lucrative task—testifying comically to his stupidity—of copying out the *Encyclopedia Britannica*. But Nathan Garrideb is a much more absurd butt than either of these, goat-bearded, peering, cadaverous, an indiscriminate but relentless collector—"Syracusan—of the best pe-riod. . . . They degenerated greatly towards the end" (1048). His attention to minutiae makes him comic, and we feel little sympathy even when the loss of the fortune he was foolish enough to believe in sends him mad at the end. The comic structure of the case—someone looking for a person with the impossible name of Garrideb—insulates us from any feeling of tragic apprehension and gives us a comic detachment which is more marked than in "The Red-Headed League," where the robbery of "one of the principal London banks" strikes at the heart of the established order, or "The Stockbro-ker's clerk," where murder is actually done. Comedy is anarchic, but the order premised in the canon cannot be endangered; in "The Three Garridebs," it is not.

On the other hand, one notable story with all the elements of com-edy about it, in which murder does not loom, is given a serious turn by its raising of the question so often raised in the canon of the irrationality underlying a precariously stable civilization, the very duality which the dualities of a Dupin or a Holmes hold in check. "The Creeping Man" is "one of the very last cases handled by Holmes before his retirement from practice" (1070–71), and concerns a middle-aged professor's taking of a monkey gland treatment on the eve of his marriage to a much younger woman. Pantaloon and Columbine are at least as old as the *commedia dell'arte*. But Holmes "the dreamer" points the tale in the direction of a moral: "When one tries to rise above Nature one is liable to fall below it. . . . There is danger there—a real danger to humanity. . . . It would be the survival of the least fit. What sort of cesspool may not our poor world become?" (1082–83). But the moment passes, Holmes "the man of action" springs from his chair, and he and Watson, with the note of comedy on which so many of the stories end, and which is a study in itself, confirming the continuity and the security associated with the pair, are off to tea at the Chequers. "Cosy peril," the phrase Edmund Wilson attributes to Christopher Morley,[19] aptly sums up this essentially comic feel of the whole canon.

There are, of the sixty cases, four not narrated by Watson: "His Last Bow" and "The Mazarin Stone" are told in the third person, and "The Blanched Soldier" and "The Lion's Mane" are told by Holmes. One of the minor sources of comedy in the canon arises on those occasions when Watson is charged by Holmes as his deputy—in "The Solitary Cyclist," *The Hound of the Baskervilles*, "Lady Frances Carfax," and "The Retired Colourman," and is either allowed to remain unaware that Holmes is also working on the case (as in *The Hound of the Baskervilles*), or is shown to have failed in his mission (as in "The Solitary Cyclist"). The comedy arises, as we have seen, from Holmes's caustic superiority and Watson's hurt, Holmes's acumen and Watson's obtuseness. But there is another element as well. When Watson disappears as narrator, or even as helper (and he mostly sits "long-suffering" in the chauffeur's seat in "His Last Bow," and plays the part of a messenger in "The Mazarin Stone"), Holmes is seen in the third person as a still more triumphant figure than Watson's customary surprise at this brilliance makes him, or in the first person as a rather less triumphant one. In the two third person stories he brings off *coups de theatre* which confound Von Bork and Count Sylvius; in his own narratives he is defeated by the deadly seaweed or a disease which appears to be leprosy. In either person, however—and none of these four cases gives us a murder, though "The Lion's Mane" gives us death without human agency—the structure of the tale is comic. The least comic of the four is no doubt "The Blanched Soldier," which is at basis about the contest between a man seeking information about his missing friend and the friend's father, who is bent on withholding it; though it raises the spectre of leprosy, it confirms its comic status by bestowing a lesser skin disease on the missing man. "His Last Bow" has the most serious of backdrops ("the most terrible August in the history of the world," 970), but is really concerned, as its somewhat diminishing title-metaphor suggests, with one last performance by these two fixed points in a changing age.

There is also, in these four stories, in the greater aggrandizement and diminution of Holmes, a further dimension to the comedy of his character, either dressed to look like Uncle Sam, or living in retirement with his bees. Lost without his Boswell and his meretricious finales, Holmes comes to be seen in perspective, comically, as both superhumanly powerful and humanly impotent. The one tendency is illustrated in "His Last Bow," as he enumerates the ways in which, since the episode of the King of Bohemia, he has thwarted a series of German designs ("It was I. . . . It was I. . . . It was I. . . ."): "Von Bork sat up in amazement. 'There is only one man,' he cried. 'Exactly,' said Holmes." (979). The other tendency is illustrated in "The Lion's Mane," in his plaint for the missing Watson: "Ah! had he but been with me, how much he might have made of so wonderful a happening and of my eventual triumph against every difficulty!" (1083). In fact, Holmes is "culpably slow" in "The Lion's Mane," and the case is one of his failures, nearly avenging, as he says, Scotland Yard. But these four stories, almost standing outside the canon, and certainly ranking low in any reader's qualitative judgment of the sixty, give us the real Holmes, not triumphing against every difficulty, and not free of a certain amount of posturing ("The Mazarin Stone," as we have seen, ends with one of his theatrical gestures), and in this double view of Holmes is a comedy which, epitomized here, is evident throughout the canon.

Finally, it may be illuminating to look at the stories as representing certain archetypal characteristics of comedy. Northrop Frye has pointed to the game-playing which is intrinsic to detective fiction,[20] which is what saves it, he asserts, from being a *practical* blueprint, as it is already a theoretical one, for the police state. Though Frye is talking of later detective fiction, it seems clear that Holmes, representing established British Victorian order, which Edmund Wilson seems to have seen as his especial value,[21] represents as well, despite his bohemianism and his frequent taking of the law into his own hands, conservative, even conventional, social values. To extend Frye's terms,[22] Holmes is the *eiron* who in most cases is fully aware, fully in control and who puts matters right at the end. But he is also, in some sense, since I have insisted on seeing him as a dual figure, the *alazon*, the pretender: he does know most of what is to be known, he does, not always with total sincerity, deprecate his own performance, and he does aggrandize himself. And no less is Watson a dual figure. He is plainly an *alazon* (coming into our ken from Afghanistan, he might even be seen as a *miles gloriosus*, for a time!), so often the dupe of Holmes and the facts, though not an *alazon* in the sense that Holmes the posturer is. Watson is even an *eiron* in his knowledge of his own limitations, if not in an ultimate Holmesian potency of knowledge. The *eiron* and *alazon*, of course, are inhabitants of ironic comedy, which is where Frye places detective fiction, and where, too, he places the third character type of the *pharmakos*, or scapegoat. It seems clear that, besides the two central, dual figures, there is a whole succession, within the chronicles, of *alazons* and, more importantly, of *pharmikos*.

The succession of *alazons* is represented in the very first short story by the King of Bohemia, who is indeed (in Holmes's estimation, in a different sense from his own) "on a very different level" from Irene Adler, and whose extended hand Holmes ignores at the end of the story. For Holmes, a classless figure, the King is the first of many in high place whom the detective puts in their proper place, making them the butt of either his wit or his censoriousness. When Lord St. Simon condescends to him by assuming that his clients are rarely of his class, Holmes rejoins, "No, I am descending" (291): when the Duke of Holdernesse is found to be implicated in the kidnapping of his heir from the Priory School, Holmes lectures the proud nobleman in his own hall. It is curious that several of these characters, whose fall from dignity is satisfying to the reader as well as confirmatory of Holmes's power as *eiron* over the *alazons*, show their family likeness in their names: Hohenzollern, Holdernesse, Holdhurst, Holder.

But the villains whom Holmes must face, the Napoleons of crime, are altogether more formidable. As Ronald Knox has said, "they do the cleverest thing a criminal could probably do in the given circumstances," but Holmes is still too clever for them. These villains are not viewed with unequivocal lack of sympathy: like Holmes himself, who says frequently that he could have been a great criminal, they could have turned their great powers to good. Moriarty and Moran, again with the kinship suggested by the similarity of name, are clearly *pharmikos* in the sense of *scoundrel*, but also in the sense of being scapegoats for the society. Yet again we have a point that need hardly be labored: these villains are all doubles, alter egos, of Holmes, the great upholder of the law who might have been a criminal, and his purging of society of these villains is premised on his projection of his dark side on to them. There is, after all, an absolute rightness about the chronicles coming to their appointed end with Holmes and Moriarty, locked in each other's arms, perishing at Reichenbach. And while Von Bork, Charles Augustus Milverton, Baron Gruner and Count Sylvius are, in rough descending order of greatness, lesser beings, they belong to the same family, representing the guilt of a society which Holmes, in purging them, purges of that guilt. In five of the six cases, (Moran being the exception), Holmes levies his own justice on the villain, or else watches while, with pistol or with vitriol bottle, it is done.

If all this sounds less then comic, still less actually funny, it is all part of a corpus of sixty stories which scrutinize ironically, with a good deal of wit, a pervasive sense of the game being afoot, and a large sense of fun, a society reared upon reason but not always proof against the attacks of the irrational. As Edmund Wilson says, "no matter what those queer Greeks do in London, there will always be a British porter and he will always help you to get your train." There are the parameters, and much of the comedy of the chronicles lies in the wry recognition that life goes on, reason prevails, despite strange whistles in the night, or dogs who do not bark, or professors who climb vine-wreathed walls, or mysterious powders which drive sanity from those who inhale them. We may laugh that we have escaped such horrors. But always our guide in escaping them is himself both queer Greek and British railway porter, both dreamer ("We reach. We grasp") and man of action and reason ("Come, Watson, come! . . . The game is afoot").

A FINAL NOTE

At the risk of myself becoming like one of those popular tenors still tempted to make repeated farewell bows before their indulgent audiences, I cannot end this essay without some reference to the remarkable number of parodies, pastiches and homages which the Sherlock Holmes stories have engendered over the years, and which show few signs of diminishing. As I have noted, many of Watson's passing, wry, even "pawky" (the word Christopher Morley aptly applies) allusions to the unreported cases have been used as hints for fuller treatments. And while Holmes has encountered in these treatments almost all his contemporaries, from Freud through Jack the Ripper to Theodore Roosevelt, he himself, from Robert Barr's Sherlaw Kombs to Robert L. Fish's Schlock Homes, has been the direct object of the parody. Writers as diverse as Mark Twain and Agatha Christie[23] have ridiculed the great detective, with varying degrees of affection, but even in one of the least sympathetic of his parodists, Mark Twain, there is a glimpse of the sincerest form of flattery, for *Tom Sawyer, Detective* and, most notably, *Pudd'nhead Wilson* belong to the genre which Doyle made one of the most popular of all time.

Why this flurry of parody and extrapolation? Generally parody seeks out the serious subject, especially the pompous, and magnifies what it sees as absurd or self-important, inflates what it sees as trivial. Chaucer's *Sir Thopas*, Max Beerbohm's impaling of Henry James in "The Mote in the Middle Distance," John Fowles's guying of the Victorian novel in *The French Lieutenant's Woman*, all have serious butts. At first sight, comedy is not the obvious object of parody; and I have written in vain if by now my reader has not accepted the presence of at least some comedy in the canon.

John Fowles's explanation, coming from a distinguished toyer with genres, is an enticing one:

> The danger of Conan Doyle's method is caricature, which is properly a weapon of humour or satire. That is why Holmes and Watson have been endlessly parodied, have been sent up in both senses—into the Pantheon of national archetypes as well as by countless teams of professional comedians . . . it is not just that he Holmes is too clever to be true, but rather that he is too true

to pure caricature to be "clever" by the highest literary standards. . . . In the Sherlock Holmes stories caricature becomes the end; it is not related to any significant truth or human folly.[24]

If Holmes and Watson do not belong in the highest literary circles, we might ask Leslie Fiedler's question, "What Was Literature?"[25] to discover why. The Sherlock Holmes chronicles have something of the quality, something of the life of their own, of *Uncle Tom's Cabin*, a book Fiedler has sought to redeem from the strictures of those dons who dismiss it as written for an imperfectly educated mass audience and lacking in the "tragic ambiguity" of the acknowledged great works of literature. As we have seen here, however, the Holmes Saga is fundamentally comic rather than tragic, and the solutions that Holmes imposes dispel, as far as can be, the ambiguities. But the parodies and the sequels, the sense that Holmes and Watson were real people, who still receive notes from correspondents seeking advice, testify, as similar considerations testify to Uncle Tom's, to their humanity. As Fowles noted, and he might have stopped short at this point, they are both revered and affectionately rallied. And as Doyle had hoped, they have their less than humble corner in the same Valhalla where Fielding's beaux, Scott's heroes, and Dickens's delightful cockneys exist. *That* was Literature.

Notes

1. The 56 short and four long stories in which Sherlock Holmes and Doctor Watson appear are so well known by title that I do not list them here. But because of that very familiarity, I have also refrained from abbreviating those sacrosanct titles in the text of the essay. All references to the Saga, the Chronicles, the Sacred Writings, the Canon, the Conan, are to *The Penguin Complete Sherlock Holmes* (reprint of Christopher Morley's edition for Doubleday in 1930), Penguin Books, 1981.
2. While my formulations in this essay are indebted to a wide variety of commentators on the comic, from Aristotle on, I would cite especially Henri Bergson, *Laughter* (edited by Wylie Sypher for Doubleday Anchor Books, 1956, and bound in with George Meredith's *An Essay on Comedy*); Northrop Frye, *Anatomy of Criticism* (Princeton University Press, 1957); and Elder Olson, *The Theory of Comedy* (Bloomington: Indiana University Press, 1968).
3. *Laughter*, especially Chapter Two.
4. This essay is most readily accessible in *Profile by Gaslight* (New York: Simon and Schuster, 1944), ed. Edgar W. Smith, pp. 156–165.
5. See Arthur Conan Doyle, *Memories and Adventures* (London: Hodder and Stoughton, 1924), pp. 102–106. See also Dorothy Sayers' remarks, quoted in *The Annotated Sherlock Holmes*, 2 vols (New York: Potter, 1967), I, 68.
6. Act IV, Scene v.
7. I have heard by reliable word of mouth that this film was originally much longer, and did indeed present Holmes and Watson as a homoerotic couple.
8. "Studies in Sherlock Holmes," *Essays in Satire* (New York: Dutton, 1930), p. 163.
9. See *Memories and Adventures*, pp. 74–75, where the first name is given as "*Sherringford* Holmes." The best discussion of the naming of *Sherlock Holmes* is contained in *The Annotated Sherlock Holmes*, I, 9–10.

10. "The Simple Art of Murder," in *The Simple Art of Murder* (London: Hamish Hamilton, 1950), p. 321.

11. "Holmesian Humour," *The Sherlock Holmes Journal*, 6, 4 (Spring, 1964), 109–113.

12. "Studies in Sherlock Holmes," p. 175.

13. It was the same Lecoq and Dupin who are cited by Doyle himself as the principal fictional models for Holmes (*Memories and Adventures*, p. 74).

14. *Memories and Adventures*, p. 79.

15. *The Bloodhounds of Heaven* (Cambridge: Harvard University Press, 1976), p. 142.

16. See Edward Lauterbach, "Our Heroes in Motley," *The Armchair Detective*, 9.3 (June, 1976), 178–179; also George F. McCleary M.D., "Was Sherlock Holmes a Drug Addict?," in *Profile by Gaslight*, pp. 40–46.

17. *The Annotated Sherlock Holmes*, II, 320–321. In the words of Ogden Nash: "The one-l lama He's a priest. / The two-l llama. He's a beast."

18. *The Exploits*, by John Dickson Carr and Doyle's son Adrian, remains amongst the very best of the pastiches (London: John Murray, 1954).

19. "Mr. Holmes, They Were the Footprints of a Gigantic Hound!," in *Classics and Commercials* (New York: Farrar, Straus, 1950), p. 273.

20. *Anatomy of Criticism*, pp. 46–47.

21. *Classics and Commercials*, p. 273.

22. *Anatomy of Criticism*, pp. 39–42, and *passim*.

23. Mark Twain's parody is *A Double-Barrelled Detective Story* (New York: Harper's, 1902). Agatha Christie's parody is Chapter 9, "The Case of the Missing Lady," of *Partners in Crime* (London: Collins, 1929), in which novel Tommy and Tuppence Beresford act out the adventures of most of the prominent detectives of her day and before.

24. "Afterword," *The Hound of the Baskervilles* (London: Murray and Cape, 1974), pp. 190–191.

25. *What Was Literature?* (New York: Simon and Schuster, 1982).

"The Colorless Skein of Life": Threats to the Private Sphere in Conan Doyle's *A Study in Scarlet*

Lydia Alix Fillingham

There's the scarlet thread of murder running through the colorless skein of life, and our duty is to unravel it, and isolate it, and expose every inch of it.[1]

So Sherlock Holmes describes his fascination with crime in Conan Doyle's *A Study in Scarlet*, the novella that introduced Holmes in 1887. For Holmes, life without violence is contentless. As the cocaine-addict aesthete whose psyche is constantly threatened with dissolution by the ordinariness of existence, he needs the stimulus of the blood-spattered room, and the "malignant and terrible contortion" of the dead (32). And a murder is necessary, not simply to allow him to delve into the dark and colorful secrets of the private realm, but to sanction the thought that such secrets exist. The skein of life is not colorless, but the gaze focused on it is governed by a willful colorblindness that blocks out all colors but red.

When, however, the sight of blood gives Holmes a motive for viewing the rest of the spectrum, his scrutiny is unparalleled in its intensity. Holmes becomes the exemplary reader of the scene of the crime. In *A Study in Scarlet*, faced with a corpse in an empty room in an abandoned house, he proceeds by first expanding the definition of the text to be read. The police have looked at the body, its clothes, and its belongings, and have given a glance around the room. Holmes begins his reading while still outside on the road, and includes the front yard and steps and the hall. Then Holmes redefines what will be blank page and what writing, or, as he calls it, data. As Watson puts it,

> For twenty minutes or more he continued his researches, measuring with the most exact care the distance between marks which were entirely invisible to me, and occasionally applying his tape to the walls in an equally incomprehensible manner.

(36)

Reprinted from *ELH* Vol. 56, No. 3 (Fall 1989): 667–688. Reprinted by permission of The Johns Hopkins University Press.

What is a blank wall to others is covered with signifiers to Holmes—and even as he examines them, they remain invisible to Watson. To the police, Holmes is frenetically reading a blank page, his running chain of "exclamations, groans, whistles, and little cries" (36) indicating that he is in fact reading aloud, and so they question his sanity. Watson, however, has a little more faith, and believes that "Holmes's smallest actions were all directed towards some definite and practical end" (36), that while the mood is on him, Holmes is as saturated with significance as he proves the room to be.

The question then oddly becomes, with all this significance floating around, why doesn't Holmes solve the murder at once? Why does the trace left in the room serve to go so far and no farther? In fact, when Holmes is done examining this room, he seems to have amazingly detailed information about the murderer. He announces, while the police still have only a single false clue:

> There has been murder done, and the murderer was a man. He was more than six feet high, was in the prime of life, had small feet for his height, wore coarse, square-toed boots and smoked a Trichinopoly cigar. He came here with his victim in a four-wheeled cab, which was drawn by a horse with three old shoes and one new one on his off foreleg. In all probability the murderer had a florid face, and the finger-nails of his right hand were remarkably long.
>
> (37)

He also knows, though he does not say so, that the murderer was a cabdriver, who forced the dead man to take poison in revenge for some earlier event involving a woman. And yet all this information avails him nothing without outside help. He cannot start looking for the murderer, Jefferson Hope, until he has cabled to the U.S. and gotten his name.

What forestalls Holmes here is precisely what Walter Benjamin has identified as essential to the detective novel:

> "It is almost impossible," wrote a Parisian secret agent in 1798, "to maintain good behaviour in a thickly populated area where an individual is, so to speak, unknown to all others and thus does not have to blush in front of anyone." Here the masses appear as the asylum that shields an asocial person from his persecutors. Of all the menacing aspects of the masses, this one became apparent first. It is at the origin of the detective story.[2]

The question of identity is crucial for the detective story—not solely for the criminal, since it is as often the corpse that cannot be identified. The city provides a location where the masses mask the individual, and industrial capitalism provides a society in which individuals are interchangeable. London's peculiar position in the economic structure of the country made it a particular site for the "residuum." As Gareth Stedman Jones argues in *Outcast*

London, London's largely preindustrial situation relied on and produced a massive casual labor force, drifting in and out of work and in and out of the sight of the middle classes.[3]

This situation created a gap within representation such that society could no longer be mapped out completely. In the fantasy of a feudal golden age, the social hierarchy could theoretically be charted from the king down to the lowliest serf. This is a particularly powerful fantasy for Conan Doyle: what he considers his serious works are historical novels of the Middle Ages, such as *The White Company*; and he begins his autobiography, he tells us, with a genealogy before him which his mother had worked out with Sir Arthur Vicars, Ulster King of Arms, tracing their family back more than five hundred years, establishing the family's stability back into the chartable golden age.[4]

But in nineteenth-century Britain, only the royal family and the titled aristocracy can be nailed down as firmly as in Debrett's and Burke's—even the collateral branches of the Doyle family fade off into the darkness. The working classes can only be represented in the statistical aggregate or as "types," and the residuum is barely visible: "numerically very large, though the population returns do not number them among the inhabitants of the kingdom."[5] Charles Booth and Beatrice Potter were starting their frantic collection of statistics on the East End and their elaborate categorizations of its inhabitants just as Conan Doyle was tossing off *A Study in Scarlet* in March and April of 1886. Like the sociologist, Sherlock Holmes is an expert at assigning the individual to his category; he can spot a "retired sergeant of Marines" from across the street (26). Indeed, his main activity at the scene of the crime is refining the category of the murderer. He starts from the general and continually adds detail until he has the fairly precise description quoted above. Unlike the feudal village, however, capitalist London yields no individual from the category. Until Holmes has the name, he has nothing: and once he has the name, his precise description serves only to show his own cleverness and has no role in catching the murderer.

In fact, it is Jefferson Hope's own knowledge of the anonymity of the city that leads to his ultimate capture. Coming to London specifically to kill two men, he goes about always under his own name (as do the two men who are trying to escape from him), and having driven Enoch Drebber in his cab to a deserted house and killed him, he keeps on at the same job. As Holmes assumes, and later explains, Hope does so because he has no reason to believe that anyone in England, other than two men now dead, has any idea that he exists. Holmes relies utterly on Hope's presumption of his own invisibility— "if he had the slightest suspicion, he would change his name, and vanish in an instant among the four million inhabitants of this great city" (69).

From the murder room Holmes derives the category to which Hope belongs: to bridge the gap between the category and the individual, he turns to the individual who is known—the corpse. He cables to Cleveland for information on Enoch Drebber, the murdered man, and charts the intersection of the murderer's category and Drebber's private life story. The detective novel thus opens the private realm suddenly to narration, an indiscreet narration that would not exist but for the crime.

The body, as violated corpse, has left the private realm for good and is now the subject of public inquiry, to be put on display like the bodies in the French morgue. The murdered man and those who have surrounded him become the objects of intense scrutiny until the murderer is discovered and surrendered to the public sphere, perhaps to the unending gaze of the panopticon prison. For the reader, the purpose of the investigation is to restore the public world, to explain the murder in a way that reestablishes faith in the *status quo ante*, to restore the social balance that the murder has upset.[6]

The detective is a distasteful voyeur—the more distasteful if he is of a lower class than those subject to his gaze. Holmes and the other private gentlemen detectives, therefore, are infinitely preferable to the police—while they may violate the secrets of the family, at least they are already privy to the secrets of class. So there is a distinct limit to Holmes's curiosity; he resists the exposing of private life to the public that is essential to the detective story.

In the nature of things, detective stories contain two intersecting stories—the story of the murder, and the story of detection. The former logically ends with the crime, which is the motive force of the beginning of the latter. *A Study in Scarlet* makes the separation between its two stories far more complete than usual. The story behind the crime, its anchoring to a motive that witnesses to its stance within the rational, is utterly divorced from the story of detection—Holmes does not know it, and the murderer dies without revealing it. Having solved the crime, Holmes preserves a gentlemanly reticence: once public order has been restored, the excuse for voyeurism is at an end, whether the story is complete or not. The reader, however, is never a gentleman, and no limit to her curiosity is expected.

Holmes's reticence incarnates and justifies the minimalist impulse of the Liberal state. The state's duty is to stay out of the private lives of its citizens, or, more fundamentally, the state's duty is to preserve private life inviolate. The Metropolitan Police were created specifically to preserve the greater social order, and the enforcement of individual property rights was indeed secondary. The Liberal ideology was challenged on all sides in 1886, but murder still provided its justification: a murderer on the loose is an outrage against private life, a potentially political protest (since it is a socially levelling act) that takes the most personal form, and until the murderer is caught, no freeborn Englishman really has his God-given rights.

But while the police are a body formed to preserve the private lives of those who can afford to have them, they are an essentially intrusive body. In their insistent tendency towards investigation and invasion, they partake more of a bureaucratic ideology than of a Liberal one. And by 1886 investigation was becoming a crucial focus of the police force. Although detective work had been going on, in somewhat desultory fashion, since the police were formed, it was not regularized and brought under a unified control, that is to say rationalized, until the formation of the Criminal Investigations Department in 1878.

A more centralized and hierarchical bureaucratic structure developed in response to the Scotland Yard scandal of 1877, in which an Inspector and two Chief Inspectors were found to be investigating the police force itself, to help a criminal avoid detection. Sir Howard Vincent became head of the new CID after presenting himself as an authority on the French police system, renowned for its intrusions on individual rights. He increased the number of detectives from 207 to about 800, centralized criminal records, increased supervision, tightened regulations, and compiled the *Police Code and Manual of the Criminal Law*; the centralizing and hierarchical quality of his changes, as well as the emphasis on rules and the written document, all indicate their bureaucratic nature.[7] Later still, in response to Fenian bombings in London in 1883, the Special Branch of the CID was formed. Originally the Special Irish Branch, it was soon expanded to include surveillance of all of the politically suspect: German, Russian, Italian and French political refugees, as well as home-grown anarchists and socialists.[8]

The police were not alone in their invasion of the private sphere: its violation pervaded the bureaucracy in the form of the never-ending collection of information. Josephine Butler's 1879 pamphlet, *Government by Police*, speaks of "the hydra-head of a vast bureaucracy whose thousand eyes and hands are in every place at every moment," and notes that "private life is not secure against their prying observation."[9] Bureaucratic tax-collection gave the state ever-increasing information on every detail of the citizen's economic life. Election records registered the citizen's status and vote. The Census counted everyone and where they slept, and in 1851 had tried to force all citizens to reveal their religious affiliation, until Parliament heard of this intention and was outraged. And, since its authority is based upon the written document, what a bureaucracy once writes down, it never throws away.

But in the 1880s the British bureaucracy had not yet developed the means of dealing with the flood of information it had unloosed upon itself. What the bureaucracy needed was to develop an efficient means of sorting and collating information. Once it had done that, it had invented the computer. (To overcome the enormous difficulties of manually compiling the census, Herman Hollerith invented the punched card sorting machine in the U.S. in 1889, and the company he formed eventually became IBM.) But as yet different parts of the bureaucracy could not communicate with each other and had great difficulty sharing information. The individual tended to slip through the cracks.

The picture of the police that Conan Doyle gives is not one of all-knowledgeable, penetrating surveillance—the bumbling incompetence of the police helps the freeborn Englishman sleep at night. At the same time, of course, the threat of murder keeps him awake.

Conan Doyle's solution is to plug up the holes in the bureaucracy with an extragovernmental agent. In *A Study in Scarlet*, Holmes's crucial function is to ask the right question to extract information already held by the bureaucracy. Although the police have already cabled to Cleveland to ask for any information that might relate to Drebber's death, it is not until Holmes knows to ask about Drebber's marriage that the bureaucracy immediately kicks out Hope's name. Without this hint, the authorities apparently were unable to make the rather simple connection between a man arrested for threatening Drebber's life in connection with a woman, and Drebber's murder a short time later. Implausible as this lapse is, it points precisely to the bureaucracy's weakness—its inability to make connections between the myriad pieces of information it holds. Holmes, the exemplary reader, both of the traces of the individual and of the bureaucracy's archives, becomes the key figure in this bureaucracy when unresolved crime disturbs the social balance.

This solution, whereby the bureaucratic adjunct makes the connections that the bureaucracy cannot, is epitomized in a much later story, in a description of Holmes's brother Mycroft's role within the government. In the 1913 story "The Adventure of the Bruce-Partington Plans," Holmes tell Watson:

> [Mycroft's] position is unique. He has made it for himself. . . . He has the tidiest and most orderly brain, with the greatest capacity for storing facts, of any man living. The same great powers which I have turned to the detection of crime he has used for this particular business. The conclusions of every department are passed to him, and he is the central exchange, the clearing-house, which makes out the balance. All other men are specialists, but his specialism is omniscience. We will suppose that a minister needs information as to a point which involves the Navy, India, Canada and the bimetallic question: he could get his separate advices from various departments upon each, but only Mycroft can focus them all, and say offhand how each factor would affect the other. They began by using him as a short-cut, a convenience; now he has made himself an essential. In that great brain of his everything is pigeon-holed and can be handed out in an instant. Again and again his word has decided the national policy.[10]

Certainly this picture of Mycroft is a recognition of the necessity of collating and connecting information. It is also the picture of a man quickly transforming himself into the computer the government needs.

In *A Study in Scarlet* the detective, as bureaucratic adjunct, and the murders, as violence that cuts through the public/private dichotomy, help reconcile bureaucracy and the Liberal ideology. Murder justifies bureaucratic intrusion as necessary for the protection of the private realm from destruction, and the gentleman detective shows reassuringly that when real intrusion is necessary, it is not carried out by the lower-class bumblers of the bureaucracy itself, but only by those with true discretion.

The author and the reader, however, display no such reticence. Although not heard by Holmes and not told by Watson, the second section of the novel reveals the story of love and violence that lies behind the crime. As so often in the Sherlock Holmes stories, the origin of the crime is a former crime that has gone unpunished. Here again, as in other stories, only the later crime takes place in England.[11] "Part 2: The Country of the Saints" is a tale of love and death in Mormon Utah.

Mormonism is crucial to A *Study in Scarlet* both for its utter foreignness and for its familiarity to the English. Polygamy represented the furthest reaches of taboo exoticism, but many of those polygamous wives and husbands had emigrated from England. The religion seemed bizarre and perhaps heathen, but it could not with certainty be classified as non-Christian. At times reports came of barbaric acts of violence, at others of the pioneering spirit of Anglo-Saxon virtue.

The ambiguous position of Mormonism and the ambivalent English reaction to it center, in A *Study in Scarlet*, on two key anxieties threatening both private and public spheres: while tensions about marriage and the position of women challenge the closure and stability of the private realm, the public social structure feels endangered by both the concept and the physical presence of a state within the state. The English did not need to look to Utah to encounter these anxieties, but for Conan Doyle they are more comfortably discussed when projected onto a Mormon background. And yet it is more than a mere matter of comfort. The Mormons do not represent only a distanced Other: the liminal position of Mormonism means that their otherness always contains much sameness, that the horror directed against them would eventually be brought home.

The Mormon plot focuses on Lucy Ferrier, who as a child, along with her father, had been rescued by the Mormons from death in the desert, on the condition that they convert.[12] She grows up and becomes secretly engaged to Jefferson Hope, our murderer-to-be. Hope, a passing miner, is a non-Mormon and a rugged individualist. In Hope's absence, Brigham Young declares that the girl must wed, offers her a choice between the sons of two of the most prosperous Mormon families, and gives her thirty days to decide. Each morning, despite her father's most constant and wakeful nightly vigils, the number of days Lucy has left is displayed prominently in the house— the first day, the number appears pinned to the blanket above the father's chest. Naturally enough, the young polygamists carry the day, killing the father and dragging the unwilling Lucy into a wedding that brings her, more willingly, to an early grave. These evil polygamists, then, are the corpses that Sherlock Holmes meets some twenty years later. Jefferson Hope has sought revenge steadily for twenty years and has at last achieved it.

If Holmes does not know all of this story, he does know that it involves love. He describes his analysis of the motive of Drebber's murder:

> And now came the great question as to the reason why. Robbery had not been the object of the murder, for nothing was taken. Was it politics, then, or was it a woman? That was the question which confronted me. I was inclined from the first to the latter supposition. Political assassins are only too glad to do their work and to fly. This murder had, on the contrary, been done most deliberately, and the perpetrator had left his tracks all over the room, showing that he had been there all the time. It must have been a private wrong, and not a political one, which called for such a methodical revenge. . . . When the ring [a wedding ring] was found, however, it settled the question. Clearly the murderer had used it to remind his victim of some dead or absent woman.
>
> (132–33)

The question is ended precisely because a woman has entered it. A murder that involves a woman must be a "private wrong." That it centered on a conflict with the Mormon Church and was based on an earlier essentially economic crime could not change matters for Holmes in the least.

While the presence of a woman anchors matters firmly in the private, the plurality of polygamy renders the family an unstable social grouping that threatens to devour young girls. Although English conversion to Mormonism and emigration to Utah had somewhat died down by this time, the idea of servant girls being abducted to form the new blood in the Mormon harems, in a form of barely legalized white slavery, was undoubtedly still causing alarm, especially in the wake of the *Pall Mall* scandals of 1885—the sensational investigation of white slave traffic in young girls, and the subsequent trial and conviction of the editor, W. T. Stead, and others for abduction. [13]

Conan Doyle's one undoubted source on Mormonism, the autobiography of Mrs. T. B. H. Stenhouse, an Englishwoman who converted to Mormonism and lived in Utah for twenty years before leaving the Church, freely mixes moral indignation and hints of titillating secrets. Her assessment of polygamy would fully agree with John Ferrier's in *A Study in Scarlet*: "Such a marriage he regarded as no marriage at all, but as a shame and a disgrace" (92). Unwilling herself to write on the sexual secrets of polygamy, she repeatedly insists on their existence:

> In this book I have endeavored to be true to my title and to "*tell all*," as far as such a thing was possible. But there are thousands of horrible incidents, too degrading for mention, which form part and parcel of the system of Polygamy, but which no woman who had any respect for herself would think of putting upon paper. [14]

But Stenhouse recognizes polygamy, and attacks it, as contributing to patriarchal power and oppression.

Polygamy appears as exotic behavior, but, in the face of the extreme difficulty of getting a divorce, bigamy in England was an undoubted domestic reality. The public-private split hinges on an idea of monogamous marriage as the natural moment of constitution of the private. As Tony Tanner writes in *Adultery in the Novel*, "The most important mediation procedure that attempts to harmonize the natural, the familial, the social, and even the transcendental is, of course, marriage. . . . Ideally, then, marriage offers the perfect and total mediation between the patterns within which men and women live."[15] Polygamy, emerging as a kind of institutionalization of adultery, reveals radical instability in the private realm, the family, and the relations of men and women.

Mormon polygamy also reveals marriage as exchange and women as possessions in a startling way. In *A Study in Scarlet*, Brigham Young calls wives "heifers" (95), and Conan Doyle feels called upon to footnote the authenticity of the term. Women lose any pretense of individual identity, and become simply animals and objects of exchange. When the novel's prior crime, the basis of the London murders, stands exposed, it shows itself to have had very little to do with love indeed. The two young Mormons want Lucy Ferrier not because of any personal attractions she may have, but solely for her father's property. The motive for their crime is purely an economic one, demonstrating the evils of Mormon marriage in a way that hardly limits them to Mormons or to Utah. Indeed, this crime could easily have taken place in England, as various similar plots among the later Holmes stories show.[16]

But unlike in England, here the crime is not actionable: the invasion of private life by violence based on economic principles, a crime against both privacy and property, is fully sanctioned by the church state. The difference does not stem from any ideological difference between England and the United States: it resides instead specifically in the local Mormon government, which is opposed to the overall federal government. (Utah did not become a state of the Union until 1896). The Mormon church state, self-sufficient as it seemed and may have been, was not the ultimate power in the land: it was a smaller structure of authority competing for power with the larger entity—it was a state (if not yet united among the states) within the state.

A state within a state must always seem a threat to the larger entity when the internal group establishes relations of the individual to the group that are significantly different from those the larger group considers natural. When the Mormons allow the state to intrude into the Liberal taboo space of the private, then the private world of non-Mormons is immediately threatened by the idea that a legitimate state might act in this way, and their interest therefore lies in denying the legitimacy of such a state. At the same time, the Liberal state must realize that the smaller, intrusive state has much more control over its members, and thus implicitly might use them against the larger state. The fear of a state within the state is also a fear of violent revolution.

The picture of a community in which all power and knowledge resides in and is made manifest through the church necessarily raises the question of the role of church and state in England. The Mormon church state completely denies any separation of public and private, a consequence of uniting religion and politics when neither participates in the Liberal ideology. In contrast, the Church of England, despite its connections with the state, violates no one's rights—except those of Dissenters and the Irish; in fact, it demands so little in the way of belief that it rarely sets foot in the private domain of the soul.

Conan Doyle's accusations of the Mormon Church serve to exonerate the Church of England from any wrongdoing, but they deeply implicate the Catholic Church. Although an Irish Catholic on both sides, and educated in a Jesuit school, Conan Doyle renounced Catholicism in 1882, thus breaking with many powerful relatives. By 1891 his daughter was christened in, and his mother had entered, the Church of England.[17] In 1886 he was just beginning his lifelong involvement with spiritualism (*MA*, 82–92). It was a period of religious crisis, and there was real anger and resentment in his rejection of his relatives and their church.

In his autobiography, he says of the Jesuits who schooled him:

> In all ways save in their theology, they were admirable, though this same theology made them hard and inhuman upon the surface, which is indeed the general effect of Catholicism in its more extreme forms. The Convert is lost to the family. Their hard, narrow outlook gives the Jesuits driving power, as is noticeable in the Puritans and all hard, narrow creeds.
>
> (*MA*, 20)

Conan Doyle's Mormons are just such a hard, narrow creed. Their driving power is what he can, at moments, find to admire about them: "The savage man, and the savage beast, hunger, thirst, fatigue, and disease—every impediment which Nature could place in the way—had all been overcome with Anglo-Saxon tenacity" (85). When extremism leads to courageous imperialism, he can admire it in the Jesuits as well: "They are devoted and fearless and have again and again, both in Canada, in South America and in China, been the vanguard of civilization to their own grievous hurt" (*MA*, 20). What he cannot accept is the church's inability to allow for the individual among the civilized. But for others than the savage man—who only exists to be subjugated—it is intolerable that a hierarchical elite ("The inner Italian directorate," or Brigham Young and "The Council of Four") should dictate beliefs that must be accepted in their totality by all.

In *A Study in Scarlet*, the power-saturated Mormon Church can display its force within the furthest reaches of the privacy of the home. The church invades John Ferrier's very bedroom and bed to deliver to him the message of its power, showing itself the invincible master of signification. The church is revealed as no more than a means of forcing unanimity and submission on its members. When Brigham Young must decide the fate of the man and young girl found by the Mormons in the great alkali desert Conan Doyle believed to have stretched across the Midwest, the religious tyrant makes his position clear:

> If we take you with us . . . it can only be as believers in our own creed. We shall have no wolves in our fold. Better far that your bones should bleach in this wilderness than that you should prove to be that little speck of decay which in time corrupts the whole fruit.
>
> (84)

No diversity of voice can be tolerated, not even that of blond-haired pretty little girls. It is this unanimity of voice which makes the ideology of a state within a state so powerful, and so apparently threatening to the larger society. But the threat is not primarily represented in terms of working within the political structure of the greater state. It its representation, threat is taken to its most violent extreme and here ignites the fear of violent revolution.

In the first section of the novel, in the room where Drebber was killed, the murderer has scrawled "RACHE" on the wall, the German word for revenge. This is a ruse by the murderer, a false clue, but is taken up with alacrity by the newspapers. The *Daily Telegraph*, for instance, believes the crime to be perpetrated by "political refugees and revolutionists," assumes it to be a matter of socialists killing one of their own, and alludes to the Vehmgericht and the Carbonari (52).

The Carbonari and the early German socialist societies are, in their origins, typical primitive social movements like those discussed in E. J. Hobsbawm's *Primitive Rebels*—movements in which the socially and economically marginal mobilize in anger, but without any clearly defined political program. Mormons were, in the popular conception, similar to these groups in their emphases on ritual, initiation ceremonies, oaths of loyalty, and a pervasive use of symbolism.[18] The Mormons in *A Study in Scarlet* feel justified in killing apostates partly because these people, like John Ferrier, have taken oaths that bind them to the church for life. Conan Doyle calls up similar elements in his references to German secret societies. The fictional newspaper accounts speak of the Socialists' "unwritten laws" (52), and their "stringent code of honor, any infringement of which was punished by death" (53). These groups also share a totalizing revolutionary view, a desire to rebuild society from scratch.

Hobsbawm emphasizes the hierarchical or pyramidal structure of such groups, and speaks of "self-selected elite groups, imposing the revolution on an inert, but grateful mass" (171). When Conan Doyle's Mormons arrive in Utah, the church immediately sets about defining each member's exact relative position:

> Young speedily proved himself to be a skilful administrator as well as a resolute chief. Maps were drawn and charts prepared, in which the future city was sketched out. All around farms were apportioned and allotted in proportion to the standing of each individual. The tradesman was put to his trade and the artisan to his calling.
>
> (85)

In such a place Holmes's six-foot florid cabdriver could surely be located within minutes. The dominance of hierarchy creates a society once again fully known, chartable and representable.

The folklore of anti-Mormonism focused the fear of Mormon violence on a smaller group within the Mormon community, the "Danite Band" or "Avenging Angels." A *Study in Scarlet* describes the group:

> Its invisibility, and the mystery which was attached to it, made this organization doubly terrible. It appeared to be omniscient and omnipotent, and yet was neither seen nor heard. The man who held out against the Church vanished away, and none knew whither he had gone or what had befallen him.
>
> (92)

When Conan Doyle first mentions the Danite Band, he says that "not the Inquisition of Seville, nor the German Vehmgericht, nor the Secret Societies of Italy" (92) were ever more violent or more effective.

The Danite Band figures the worst dangers of a secret police. As Stenhouse puts it,

> It is beyond a doubt that, notwithstanding all the social changes and improvements of late years, the secret police of Salt Lake City are in matters of crime, as well as *in fact* . . . the successors of the original "death society";—many of its members are known to have committed grievous crimes and to have repeatedly dyed their hands in blood.
>
> (304–5)

And to emphasize the implications of such a situation, she later insists, "it is the police who there commit murders and other inhuman outrages" (579). Not that the police are among those who commit murders, but that when the physical force which lies behind political power is fully revealed, as in state death squads, murder no longer exists as a private matter. Not that some police murder, but that murder becomes a police, and thus a state, function.

Fear of violence and of revolution are strong, immediate fears, obscuring and perhaps used to obscure the political issues involved. A number of contemporary crises made the issues of a state within a state particularly resonant and problematic in the eighties, and worked to destabilize a social structure founded on separation of public and private spheres. Conan Doyle can refer obliquely to some of these crises, but the main force of the novel is to render the issues less problematic—to show the Liberal ideology triumphant even as he himself was splitting off from the Liberal party. The Mormon state within a state is in this novel specifically associated with German and Italian secret societies, socialist societies seeking revolutionary change. The larger question of socialist thought, in England and out of it, seemed to threaten the private sphere with annihilation by the state, as is pictured in the Mormon political structure. But the most immediate and violent threat to the English state, the Irish separatists, and specifically the Fenians, goes unmentioned in the novel.

German secret societies like the groups mentioned by the newspapers in *A Study in Scarlet* aroused much ambivalence. German refugees came to London largely after the German Anti-Socialist Laws of 1878. Many of them belonged to the kind of superstition-ridden secret brotherhoods that Marx particularly disapproved of. In fact, according to Hobsbawm, the League of Communists had grown out of just such a brotherhood, the League of Outlaws (169). But certainly by the time of the Second International, in 1881, these leagues could not be described as prepolitical: all of them were developing explicit political agendas amid vigorous debate. The mention of secret societies in *A Study in Scarlet*, in stressing the primitive, prepolitical side of these organizations, makes them perhaps more violent, but ultimately less disruptive and threatening. The fear is ignited only to be immediately defused.

An ambivalent attitude towards German and other refugees was inherent in British policy concerning them. England's controversial policy was to admit freely all political refugees, and not to prevent them from planning revolutions for their own countries while they stayed in London. As Phillip Thurmond Smith explains,

> Paradoxically, England's open-arms policy to refugees was built on a heavy degree of xenophobia, stemming from middle-class liberalism. . . . If liberalism was taken as the shedding of archaic restrictions and the unfolding of various "freedoms," then liberty in all forms was the result. . . . Would not political liberalism and free speech encourage an open healthy government capable of holding its own in an otherwise hostile world? . . . The English middle-class liberal was convinced of the manifest superiority of British institutions, so that a few wild-talking foreigners were little worse than nuisances even when they hatched conspiracies against their own countries. They could not be a real threat to Britain.[19]

Nevertheless the policy was constantly under attack. The Liberal desire to promote the freedom of private opinion was occasionally counteracted by the difficulty of separating private political views from public political action.

In *A Study in Scarlet*, the *Daily News* report on the murder displays the Liberal attitude when secret societies are suspected: "The despotism and hatred of Liberalism which animated the Continental Governments had had the effect of driving to our shores a number of men who might have made excellent citizens were they not soured by the recollection of all that they had undergone" (53). The novel's *Daily Telegraph* article, which ends by "admonishing the Government and advocating a closer watch over foreigners in England" (52), exhibits the countervailing tendency.

While Conan Doyle was writing, socialism in general and English socialists in particular were widely disapproved of. Socialists were seen as menacing the key points of the Liberal ideology. Socialism represented as full an intervention into private life as the Mormon Church possibly could. Charles Booth, for instance, opposed socialism to individualism, and disapproved of any but the most limited state socialism, where the state would interfere only in the lives of those unable to take care of themselves.

> In taking charge of the lives of the incapable, State Socialism finds its proper work, and by doing it completely, would relieve us of a serious danger. The Individualist system breaks down as things are, and is invaded on every side by Socialistic innovations, but its hardy doctrines would have a far better chance in a society purged of those who cannot stand alone.[20]

Booth's category of the "incapable" was clearly synonymous with the residuum, who are once again outside the control and the information of the bureaucracy. The invisibility of the residuum referred specifically to their lack of existence in the public sphere. They had no legitimate role in the political world, and only the most marginal in the economic. Only those with an acknowledged place in the public sphere had the right to a place in the private. Booth wished his State Socialism radically to disempower the residuum by placing them in huge work camps—thus rendering them thoroughly visible and removing the threat of their liminality. The residuum represents a space that neither Booth nor Holmes hesitates to invade and to expose to the public eye.

At the same time, English socialists were seen as empowering the residuum, creating it as a revolutionary threat. The socialist invasion of the middle-class private sphere and the danger of the residuum seemed to many suddenly and explosively to meet in the West End riots of February 8, 1886, just before Conan Doyle set pen to paper. Some were for the suspension of Liberal freedoms in the face of such violence. Indeed, free speech and assembly were effectively banned from Trafalgar Square just as *A Study in Scarlet* was appearing in *Beeton's Christmas Annual* for 1887, a ban that continued for five years.[21]

Much of the blame for the riots was assigned to the Metropolitan Police and focused specifically on issues of the bureaucratic flow of information: the police never notified the Home Secretary of the riot—he first received word of it from his wife; different divisions of the police had no idea what others were doing; the District Superintendent in charge of police action was lost in the crowd through most of the demonstration (and had his pockets picked); and the police system of telegraphic communication was found to be seriously flawed.[22]

The threat of violence against the British state which the English, and especially Londoners, would have feared most immediately in the eighties came from secret societies that are not mentioned in *A Study in Scarlet*—indeed, they are conspicuous in their absence. The mention of violent secret societies at this time must have brought to mind the various Irish secret societies—the Irish Republican Brotherhood, the Irish Invincibles, and the Fenians, American in origin.

The 1882 Phoenix Park assassinations, and the London bombing campaign by the Fenians and the Brotherhood that lasted from 1883 through 1885, were fresh in the public mind. A bombing of Scotland Yard was particularly embarrassing, although it hurt no one. There were no injuries precisely because there was absolutely no one in the building at the time, which certainly did not speak for the vigilance of the police. In 1886, Conan Doyle himself could hardly have forgotten the Fenians. While he wrote, Gladstone's 1886 government was tottering through its brief life, and Conan Doyle was making his first move into active politics. He joined the Liberal Unionist party, in opposition to Gladstone's Home Rule bill, and in June gave his first political speech. According to his own account, he found himself pouring out impassioned, overblown rhetoric against Irish Home Rule (*MA*, 92).

Although both Conan Doyle and his biographer John Dickson Carr maintain that it was the author's love for Ireland that made him want to keep Ireland part of Britain, he clearly felt as much anger and resentment towards his Irish as towards his Catholic background. A single sentence in his notebook sufficiently indicates the state of his feelings: "Ireland is a huge suppuration which will go on suppurating until it bursts."[23]

In July he would write a letter to the *Portsmouth Evening News*, laying out the Unionist platform. As the very first item in this platform he puts: "That since the year 1881 the agitation in Ireland has been characterised by a long succession of crimes against life and property."[24] While deeply concerned about the violence of secret groups within Ireland (in which he clearly feels implicated by his own origins), and feeling that he must oppose his own party on the issue of Ireland's becoming a separate, self-governing state within Britain, he writes a story of the dangers of a state within a state, and of the secret violent groups that tend to spring up within them, as well as of the violence of similar secret societies in London.

If Conan Doyle could not write of the Mormons and the Fenians in the same work, still he found them juxtaposed in one of his main sources, Robert Louis Stevenson's *The Dynamiter*.[25] Stevenson's novel is dedicated to two police officers, "Messrs. Cole and Cox," who attempted to remove the bomb found in the crypt of the House of Commons on January 24, 1885, and, when the bomb went off, were severely injured and buried in the debris. Cole was later given the Albert Medal.[26] In the dedication, Stevenson criticizes the policy towards political refugees, saying that England has "so long coquetted with political crime" (5), and yet is shocked by it when it appears at home.

Part of what horrifies Stevenson and others about the Fenian bombings is that they are aimed not at specific public figures, but at places. The people injured and killed in a successful bombing have no applicable public role, and thus are being attacked, "senselessly," as private individuals. Cole and Cox are praised specifically for protecting those prototypical private figures, the child and the "breeding woman" (5).

The Dynamiter concerns a group of dynamiting fanatics, but the work is structured far less around active adventures than around a series of stories told by members of the dynamiting group, and by others. The first long, involved, colorful tale is of a young woman's upbringing in Mormon Utah, and her subsequent escape after her father is killed by the Destroying Angels.

Although a desire for justice for oppressed groups is occasionally mentioned by those who talk of having joined the dynamiting group, this group is given no hint of any definite, particular political ends, which would lead the modern reader to look on it as a group of anarchists. Stevenson intends the dynamiters to be Fenians but can only indicate their affiliation by the dedication, by the Irish last names of several members, and by their paying for lodging in American money. Such discreet hints at Irish terrorism are typical of detective novels of the period. In H. F. Wood's 1888 *The Passenger from Scotland Yard*, an organization in Paris is reasoned to be a dangerous political one based solely on the arrival of a box from Boston and "the Irish dialect of the English language as spoken in America" used by one of its members.[27]

A conflict is clearly at work between the desire to speak and the desire to deny. Even Stevenson's dedication, although it brings up Parnell's name and thus leaves no doubt of the subject matter, still does not actually mention Ireland, and is overwhelmingly cryptic in a way that suggests not wishing to stir up the fears of women and children. Conan Doyle can coyly bring up foreign secret societies existing in London, and even the idea of their causing violence, but England must remain free from this violence, and from secret societies involved in domestic issues. The fear of violence from the Fenians and other groups is easiest to deal with when displayed in all its danger, but stripped of its political content—a fear simply of irrational violence directed by a small group at all outsiders, preferably far away from England. The projection of this fear onto the Mormons was practically inevitable given several violent conflicts between Mormon and other settlers, and the great wealth of anti-Mormon folklore.

In Stevenson's Mormon tale, the family tries to make the same escape from Salt Lake City as the family in A *Study in Scarlet*, but they are soon stopped:

> Judge of our dismay, when turning suddenly an angle of the cliffs, we found a bright bonfire blazing by itself under an impending rock; and on the face of the rock, drawn very rudely with charred wood, the great Open Eye which is the emblem of the Mormon faith. . . . The mules were turned about; and leaving that great eye to guard the lonely canyon, we retraced our steps in silence. Day had not yet broken ere we were once more at home, condemned beyond reprieve.
>
> (42)

Once they know they are under surveillance, they simply give up. The young woman feels the same helplessness on her trip to England, when she realizes she is being watched every step of the way. "Thus I crossed the States, thus passed the ocean, the Mormon Eye still following my movements; and when at length a cab had set me down before that London lodging-house from which you saw me fleeing this morning, I had already ceased to struggle, and ceased to hope" (60–61). This inability to escape is here specifically connected to the secret societies: "To the child born on Mormon soil, as to the man who accepts the engagements of a secret order, no escape is possible" (61). And indeed, one of the dynamiters later tells a story of his attempt to escape from the group which is strangely similar to the Mormon story. As soon as he determines that he is being followed he too gives in immediately, thinking that "timely submission might yet preserve a life which otherwise was forfeited and dishonored" (124).

Conan Doyle's Mormons also give their signs of the inescapableness of the power of a state within a state, in numbering the days of freedom for Ferrier and daughter, and they are fully as vicious in backing up their signs with the violent fact. But Jefferson Hope, whose very name has echoes of individual rights and of deferment, resists the power of these Mormons. In Utah he can do nothing against them, but in England, the true land of the free, he can reassert the importance of private life by wreaking private vengeance for private wrongs. In doing so he in turn upsets the balance of public and private in England, where vengeance is a function of the bureaucratic state, and thus becomes subject to the state's vengeance himself. His prompt death from a heart attack absolves the state from the necessity of punishing one of the few defenders of the Liberal ideology.

Notes

I would like to thank the Stanford Humanities Center for providing the environment in which this essay originated.

1. Arthur Conan Doyle, *A Study in Scarlet* (Harmondsworth, Middlesex: Penguin Books, 1981), 44. Further references will appear in the text.

2. Walter Benjamin, *Charles Baudelaire: A Lyric Poet in the Era of High Capitalism*, trans. Harry Zohn (London: New Left Books, 1973), 40.

3. Gareth Stedman Jones, *Outcast London: A Study in the Relationship between Classes in Victorian Society* (Harmondsworth: Penguin Books, 1971), part 1.

4. Conan Doyle, *Memories and Adventures* (London: Hodder and Stoughton, 1924), 9. Further references are cited in the text as *MA*.

5. Anonymous, "The Charities of London," *Quarterly Review*, no. 194 (1855), 411.

6. See D. A. Miller, "The Novel and the Police," in *The Poetics of Murder: Detective Fiction and Literary Theory*, ed. Glenn W. Most and William W. Stowe (San Diego: Harcourt Brace Jovanovich, 1983), 299–326.

7. Margaret Prothero, *The History of the Criminal Investigation Department at Scotland Yard from Earliest Times until To-day* (London: Herbert Jenkins, 1931), 74–85, 98.

8. Prothero, 99–115, and Richard Hawkins, "Government versus Secret Societies: The Parnell Era," in *Secret Societies in Ireland*, ed. T. Desmond Williams (Dublin and New York: Gill and Macmillan, and Barnes and Noble Books, 1973), 110.

9. Josephine E. Butler, *Government by Police* (London: Dyer Brothers, 1879), 19, 21.

10. Conan Doyle, *The Complete Sherlock Holmes* (Garden City, N.Y.: Doubleday, 1930), 914. Although Mycroft is described as an employee of the government, I describe him as an adjunct to the bureaucracy because his position is too anomalous to be essentially a bureaucratic one. The essence of the bureaucratic office holder is that he is *not* unique and has *not* made his position for himself.

11. *The Sign of Four*, "The Five Orange Pips," "The 'Gloria Scott,' " "The Crooked Man," "The Resident Patient," "The Adventure of the Dancing Men," "The Adventure of Black Peter," "The Adventure of the Golden Pince-Nez," *The Valley of Fear*, "The Adventure of Wisteria Lodge," "The Adventure of the Red Circle," and "The Adventure of the Veiled Lodger" all concern prior crimes; only in "The Resident Patient" and "The Adventure of the Veiled Lodger" do the prior crimes take place in England.

12. John Ferrier is, oddly, not her real father. He is the only other survivor of a group heading west, and claims her for his own.

13. Michael Harrison, *In the Footsteps of Sherlock Holmes* (New York: Frederick Fell, 1960), 114–15.

14. Mrs. T. B. H. Stenhouse, *"Tell It All": The Story of a Life's Experience in Mormonism* (Hartford, Conn.: A. D. Worthington & Co., 1874), 507. Further references appear in the text. For Conan Doyle's ownership of this book, as well as information on a number of other sources, I am indebted to Jack Tracy's *Conan Doyle and the Latter-Day Saints* (Bloomington, Ind.: Gaslight Publications, 1979).

15. Tony Tanner, *Adultery in the Novel: Contract and Transgression* (Baltimore and London: Johns Hopkins Univ. Press, 1979), 16.

16. "The Adventure of the Solitary Cyclist" is closest, with a young woman being kidnapped and forced into marriage after her father's death. "The Greek Interpreter" also has

a kidnapped fatherless woman, whose brother, come to save her, is tortured and killed. There is apparently no actual marriage here, but that does not improve matters. "A Case of Identity," "The Adventure of the Speckled Band," and "The Adventure of the Copper Beeches" all concern young women whose relatives use various evil means to prevent their marriage and the loss of their income to the family. These indeed represent the perversion of natural, private relations into unnatural (as the young woman who is courted by her own stepfather in disguise), and even deadly ones, by the presence of the economic within the private.

17.   John Dickson Carr, *The Life of Sir Arthur Conan Doyle* (Garden City, N.Y.: Doubleday, 1949), 44–46, 80.

18.   See E. J. Hobsbawm, *Primitive Rebels: Studies in Archaic Forms of Social Movement in the 19th and 20th Centuries* (New York: W. W. Norton, 1959), 151–52. Further references will appear in the text.

19.   Phillip Thurmond Smith, *Policing Victorian London: Political Policing, Public Order, and the London Metropolitan Police* (Westport, Conn.: Greenwood Press, 1985), 83.

20.   Charles Booth, *Life and Labour of the People*, 1st ed. (London and Edinburgh: Williams and Norgate, 1889), 1:27.

21.   Donald C. Richter, *Riotous Victorians* (Athens, Oh.: Ohio Univ. Press, 1981), 141.

22.   Richter, 103–32, and Victor Bailey, "The Metropolitan Police, the Home Office and the Threat of Outcast London," in *Policing and Punishment in Nineteenth Century Britain*, ed. Bailey (New Brunswick: Rutgers Univ. Press, 1981), 100–104.

23.   Carr (note 17), 66.

24.   Conan Doyle, *Letters to the Press*, ed. John Michael Gibson and Richard Lancelyn Green (Iowa City: Univ. of Iowa Press, 1986), 23.

25.   Robert Louis Stevenson. *Kidnapped and The Dynamiter* (New York: P. F. Collier and Son, 1902). Page references are cited in the text; note that the two novels in this volume are paginated separately.

26.   *Times*, (London) January 25, 1885, 10–11. Prothero, 209.

27.   H. F. Wood, *The Passenger from Scotland Yard*, 2nd ed. (London: Chatto and Windus, 1888; rpt. New York: Dover Publications, 1977), 87, 90.

OTHER WRITINGS

◆

[Review of *Micah Clarke*]

R. E. PROTHERO

It is not unreasonable that a prejudice should exist against historical novels. Their composition resembles the acrobatic accomplishment of riding two horses at once, and the evident difficulty of the author's feat renders the task of the reader equally difficult. But there are exceptions to every rule, and *Micah Clarke* is the exception which proves the general truth. Throw aside prejudice, and read *Micah Clarke*. To class the book "among the most popular productions of the day" would be no distinction; does not this category admit of 365 "popular productions" every twelve months and one extra in leap-year? To say that it is 'above the ordinary run' is a vague eulogy which is scarcely less indefinite than the "general reader," and implies the same degraded standard. But *Micah Clarke* is a noticeable book, because it carries the reader out of the beaten track; it makes him now and then hold his breath with excitement; it presents a series of vivid pictures and paints two capital portraits; and it leaves upon the mind the impression of well-rounded symmetry and completeness.

The scene of *Micah Clarke* is laid during Monmouth's rebellion. The subject is artistically chosen. The episode admits of detached and isolated treatment; it is concentrated within a brief space of time, surrounded by the romantic halo of a lost cause, rich in the elements of dignity and of pathos which belong to a warlike ebullition of religious zeal, and leading rapidly through stirring incidents to an inevitable and tragic catastrophe. And the treatment is as successful as the choice of the subject. The story exists for its own sake, and not for the sake of the accessories. Mr. Doyle waives his opportunity to be tiresome by following Boileau's advice—"Soyez vif et pressé." Pedantic in detail and ambitious of display, historical novelists, when astride of their antiquarian Pegasus, generally embarrass the reader much as the sporting-tailor on a hard-mouthed brute encumbers the hunting-field. Each bit of learning is so precious, that it must be brought in by hook or by crook. But Mr. Doyle scarcely ever introduces irrelevant touches of historic detail, or invites admiration of the antiquity of his furniture. Almost always he writes of the past as unconsciously as he would of contemporary life, and the appropriate colouring seems to suggest itself so spontaneously

Reprinted from *Nineteenth Century* (August 1889): 330–32.

that his mind is never distracted from the rapid progress of his narrative. There is nothing excessive or obtrusive in the sixteenth-century accessories; they are so disposed that there is no appearance of crowding or of design in the arrangement; they are met with, as it were, incidentally. The period is quite sufficiently indicated to produce that suspension of the critical faculties which constitutes imaginative belief. The facts are not too solid to arouse incredulity of the fiction, nor the fiction so wild that it fosters suspicion of the facts. Thus Mr. Doyle escapes the great peril of the historical novelist. Science, history, and theology generally look as awkward in fiction as policemen in plain clothes. But the first and strongest impression which *Micah Clarke* creates is that it is an excellent story excellently told. Subsequent reflection shows that it is also an admirable piece of imitative art, a *tour de force* of correctness and vigour, a faithful yet dramatic picture of an historical episode.

Micah Clarke is full of incident. In subject it may be called sensational, if we remember that whatever depreciatory meaning attaches to that epithet belongs only to the treatment. Mr. Doyle never strains after impressions beyond his power. He does not stud his pages with volcanic phrases; he is not feverishly intent upon extracting from his incidents the maximum of horror; he revels in no nightmare effects. His villains are not moral Calibans. He interpolates quiet intervals of repose, employs sober tints for his backgrounds instead of splashing on lurid colours by the pailful, avoids the spasmodic style or the gorgeous treatment of simple incident, and never mistakes exaggeration for force. His method is that of Scott rather than of Bulwer. The latter centers his interest on the well-known historical figures of Rienzi, Harold, or the King-maker. But Mr. Doyle, like Scott, seeks his chief actors in subordinate and imaginary characters. Monmouth, Ferguson, Jeffreys move across the stage at intervals, but the true heroes are Micah Clarke, the Hampshire yeoman, Decimus Saxon, the soldier of fortune, Sir Gervas Jervoise, the broken-down but imperturbably courageous baronet. The portraits of the two last personages could hardly be better painted; Saxon is an English Dugald Dalgetty, and Sir Gervas is true to the life. Besides these leading figures, there are a crowd of minor actors distinguished from one another by strongly marked individualities, not merely assembled on the principle on which Falstaff filled his company—"Mortal men, mortal men— they'll fill a pit as well as better."

The novel with which *Micah Clarke* challenges comparison is *Lorna Doone*; and as a work of art we may well consider it to be superior. It is, in the first place, very much shorter. Length is to the novelist what flesh is to the pedestrian; he cannot "stay the distance." But the comparative brevity of *Micah Clarke* enables Mr. Doyle to maintain the same rapid pace throughout with unflagging vigour and undiminished speed. In the second place, though Micah Clarke is a Hampshire Jan Ridd in bravery, straightforward honesty, and herculean strength, he is morally elevated above his Devonshire rival by the strong puritan element in his character. A sweet refined gentle-woman like Lorna Doone, with her delicacy, culture, and aristocratic feeling, might have married Micah; she could never have been happy with the horny-handed plodding yeoman who was her husband. But enough of ungrateful comparisons between two admirable novels. I end as I began. Forget your prejudices against historical fiction, and read *Micah Clarke*.

Our Note Book
[Review of *The White Company*]

JAMES PAYN

There is quite a "boom" in the very last article in which a boom could be expected—namely, the historical novel. This species was supposed to have been extinct, and only specimens of it, dried and stuffed, which were not at all in demand, have been on view for many years. Now the author of that admirable story "The House of the Wolf" promises us another book of the past, and the author of "Micah Clarke" has given us a great improvement even on that life-like narrative in "The White Company." It is a very "Early English" story indeed, and yet there is such "go" and vigour in it that the reader is carried back by it through the centuries, and seems to live again the life of his forefathers. Mr. Conan Doyle (for I am told he has forsaken medicine for literature, and dropped the Dr. before his name) must, of course, have "read up" his subject; but he has treated it so naturally that the aroma of "cram" that clings to many historical novels (not excepting even "The Last Days of Pompeii") is entirely absent from it. There is enough fighting in it to satisfy the most truculent reader, but not of the too sanguinary kind. I have read nothing of the kind so good since "Ivanhoe," with which it has many points of resemblance. In the tournament scene, comparison with that masterpiece of Scott, the lists of Ashby de la Zouche, is too directly, and as I venture to think injudiciously, challenged; but not even the taking of Front de Bœuf's stronghold can surpass the sack of the Castle of Villefranche by the brushwood men, and the defence by the five heroes of its keep. Moreover, what is very rare in an historical novel, there is humour in "The White Company," as none who make "Sir Nigel's" acquaintance will deny.

Reprinted from *Illustrated London News* (14 November 1891): 622.

Literary Notes [1]
[Review of *The Refugees*]

Laurence Hutton

Three or four years ago, when *Micah Clarke* appeared, quite unheralded, the work of an unknown man, it was discovered that we possessed a new novelist with that rarest of endowments, the historical imagination. Now Dr. Conan Doyle has performed another deed of derring-do, for, in *The Refugees*, he has invited comparison with his own admirable work in the same kind. It is high praise to say that the result justifies his courage. The new tale is a brilliant and fascinating story. The period is the same as that of *Micah Clarke*, but, as the readers of the MAGAZINE do not need to be reminded, the scene is laid in France and in America, and the controlling event is the Revocation of the Edict of Nantes. One does not easily recall a more vivid picture of the court of Louis the Great, with its splendor, its misery, its meanness, its dignity, its culture, its ignorance, its intrigues, and bigotry, and scepticism, and piety, and indecency. Louis himself appears with certain attributes of kingship, if not of manhood, which make him a more dignified personage than Thackeray admits him to be. Madame de Montespan, the beautiful, the diabolical, dazzles from the page, and bows her haughty head only after a conflict on which the reader does not look unsympathizing. It is the figure of Madame de Maintenon, however, about which controversy will stir. Dr. Doyle concedes her to be a bigot, a prude, self-absorbed, even self-seeking. But he knows her better than any wight has known her these two hundred years. He has studied her smiles and frowns and wiles. He has seen the slow blood mantle her cheek and her white hand tremble. He has felt the steady gaze of her luminous gray eyes. He has heard the thrill in her vibrant voice. And he knows that despite her bigotry, her piety was sincere; despite her ambition, her love was profound and tender; despite her subtlety, she was Majesty's best friend and counsellor. Shall any late-plodding historian gainsay the witness of this on-looker and contemporary? If he breathes the atmosphere of courts, he knows the Paris of the citizen not less familiarly, and rural France, and the slow ocean voyage of 1685, and French and English colonial America, in Canada and the wild border settlements of New York. There is such a breathless whirl and rush of events in this book that at first one does

Reprinted from *Harper's New Monthly Magazine* (July 1893): 361.

not see what pains are spent upon the figures. De Catinat and Amos Green and the Seigneur de Sainte -Marie and De Lhut and Father Ignatius Marat are as actual as Louis himself. It was a horrible time, and the book is full of horrors. But a sense of art dominates all, and the reader is never asked to face what he cannot bear. And, indeed, it is less dreadful than Baird's story of the Huguenot persecution in France, or Parkman's, of the French and Indian wars in America. For the historian must see the victims perish; but the novelist, while he is true to truth, may yet be the Earthly Providence who shall save his people from the very jaws of death. The reality and rotundity, so to speak, of these Huguenots and Catholics rouse in the critical reader a misgiving that they may be nineteenth-century comrades, after all, masquerading in the flowing wigs and high-heeled shoes of the seventeenth. But he is reassured on perceiving that they are really of their time, in thought, habit, and action, and that it is their intense vividness which gives them their illusive modernity. If Dr. Conan Doyle, who knows all about shields and crests and quarterings, has no family motto (which it is perhaps profanation to suppose of any well-to-do Englishman), a literary Herald's College, examining his pretensions through his books, would promptly accord to him the honorable legend, *Palman qui meruit, ferat.*

Literary Notes [2]
[Review of *Round the Red Lamp*]

LAURENCE HUTTON

In another new volume, lately published, Dr. Doyle succeeds in exhibiting realism in which there is no romance whatever. It is a collection of fifteen short tales of professional experience, told *Round the Red Lamp*, by a group of physicians and surgeons. "The Red Lamp," the author explains, is the usual sign of the general practitioner in England, and it casts, in nearly all these instances, a dazzling glare upon Dr. Doyle's pages which is sometimes trying to the eyes and the nerves. An expression of one of the story-tellers as applied to a story told by somebody else, that it is "creepy," seems to fit most of the stories in the book. In "His First Operation" the reader is treated to a popliteal aneurism, to a Colle's fracture, to a spina bifida, to a tropical abscess, and to an elephantiasis, all in a single paragraph. He is asked to inspect a long line of knives, tenacula, saws, canulas, forceps, and trocars; and he is introduced to Peterson, the skin-grafting-man; to Anthony Browne, who took a larynx out last winter; to Murphy, the pathologist, and to Stoddart, the eye-man. All of which is certainly "creepy" enough.

Dr. Doyle, in his Preface, expresses his belief that "a tale which may startle the reader out of his usual grooves of thought, and shocks him into seriousness, plays the part of the alterative and tonic in medicine, bitter to the taste, but bracing in the result." The bitterness to the taste is evident; and, with all due respect to the doctor, the patient will get more lasting benefit out of the prescriptions called "Sweethearts" and "The Straggler of '15," which act as sedatives, than out of all the bitter tonics contained in "The Third Generation" or "The Curse of Eve," which shock us into a state of seriousness far less bracing than bitter.

Some of Dr. Doyle's observations about the use of medicines in popular fiction, as coming from an expert in fiction as well as in medicine, are well worth careful reading. They are contained in the chapter called "A Medical Document," to which the reader is referred. "Nobody ever gets shingles, or quinsy, or mumps in a novel," he says in closing. "All the diseases, too, belong to the upper part of the body. The novelist never strikes below the belt." In one of these tales, "The Case of Lady Sannox," we recognize the

Reprinted from *Harper's New Monthly Magazine* (April 1895): 449–50.

Mr. Doyle of the Detective Series. Mr. Sherlock Holmes, however, would have begun at the other end of the case, and would have made the mystery before he solved it. This is the only story in the collection which is bitter and bracing at once.

Mr. Irving Takes Paregoric
[Review of *A Story of Waterloo*]

GEORGE BERNARD SHAW

Any one who consults recent visitors to the Lyceum, or who seeks for information in the Press as to the merits of Mr. Conan Doyle's "Story of Waterloo," will in nineteen cases out of twenty learn that the piece is a trifle raised into importance by the marvellous acting of Mr. Irving as Corporal Gregory Brewster. As a matter of fact, the entire effect is contrived by the author, and is due to him alone. There is absolutely no acting in it—none whatever. There is a make-up in it, and a little cheap and simple mimicry which Mr. Irving does indifferently because he is neither apt nor observant as a mimic of doddering old men, and because his finely cultivated voice and diction again and again rebel against the indignity of the Corporal's squeak-ings and mumblings and vulgarities of pronunciation. But all the rest is an illusion produced by the machinery of "a good acting play," by which is always meant a play that requires from the performers no qualifications beyond a plausible appearance and a little experience and address in stage business. I had better make this clear by explaining the process of doing without acting as exemplified by "A Story of Waterloo," in which Mr. Conan Doyle has carried the art of constructing an "acting" play to such an extreme that I almost suspect him of satirically revenging himself, as a literary man, on a profession which has such a dread of "literary plays." (A "literary play," I should explain, is a play that the actors have to act, in opposition to the "acting play," which acts them.)

Before the curtain rises, you read the playbill; and the process com-mences at once with the suggestive effect on your imagination of "Corporal Gregory Brewster, age eighty-six, a Waterloo veteran," of "Nora Brewster, the corporal's grandniece," and of "Scene—Brewster's lodgings." By the time you have read that, your own imagination, with the author pulling the strings, has done half the work you afterwards give Mr. Irving credit for. Up goes the curtain; and the lodgings are before you, with the humble breakfast table, the cheery fire, the old man's spectacles and bible, and a medal hung up in a frame over the chimneypiece. Lest you should be unobser-vant enough to miss the significance of all this, Miss Annie Hughes comes

Reprinted from *Saturday Review* [London] (11 May 1895): 619–621.

in with a basket of butter and bacon, ostensibly to impersonate the grandniece, really to carefully point out all these things to you, and to lead up to
the entry of the hero by preparing breakfast for him. When the background
is sufficiently laid in by this artifice, the drawing of the figure commences.
Mr. Fuller Mellish enters in the uniform of a modern artillery sergeant, with
a breech-loading carbine. You are touched: here is the young soldier come
to see the old—two figures from the Seven Ages of Man. Miss Hughes tells
Mr. Mellish all about Corporal Gregory. She takes down the medal, and
makes him read aloud to her the press-cutting pasted beside it which describes
the feat for which the medal was given. In short, the pair work at the picture
of the old warrior until the very dullest dog in the audience knows what he
is to see, or to imagine he sees, when the great moment comes. Thus is
Brewster already created, though Mr. Irving has not yet left his dressing-
room. At last, everything being ready, Mr. Fuller Mellish is packed off so
as not to divide the interest. A squeak is heard behind the scenes: it is the
childish treble that once rang like a trumpet on the powder-waggon at
Waterloo. Enter Mr. Irving, in a dirty white wig, toothless, blear-eyed,
palsied, shaky at the knees, stooping at the shoulders, incredibly aged and
very poor, but respectable. He makes his way to his chair, and can only sit
down, so stiff are his aged limbs, very slowly and creakily. This sitting down
business is not acting: the callboy could do it; but we are so thoroughly
primed by the playbill, the scene-painter, the stage-manager, Miss Hughes
and Mr. Mellish, that we go off in enthusiastic whispers, "What superb
acting! How wonderfully he does it!" The corporal cannot recognize his
grandniece at first. When he does, he asks her questions about children—
children who have long gone to their graves at ripe ages. She prepares his
tea: he sups it noisily and ineptly, like an infant. More whispers: "How
masterly a touch of second childhood!" He gets a bronchial attack and gasps
for paregoric, which Miss Hughes administers with a spoon, whilst our faces
glisten with tearful smiles. "Is there another living actor who could take
paregoric like that?" The sun shines through the window: the old man would
fain sit there and peacefully enjoy the fragrant air and life-giving warmth of
the world's summer, contrasting so pathetically with his own winter. He
rises, more creakily than before, but with his faithful grandniece's arm fondly
supporting him. He dodders across the stage, expressing a hope that the flies
will not be too "owdacious," and sits down on another chair with his joints
crying more loudly than ever for some of the oil of youth. We feel that we
could watch him sitting down for ever. Hark! a band in the street without.
Soldiers pass: the old warhorse snorts feebly, but complains that bands don't
play so loud as they used to. The band being duly exploited for all it is
worth, the bible comes into play. What he likes in it are the campaigns of
Joshua and the battle of Armageddon, which the poor dear old thing can
hardly pronounce, though he had it from "our clergyman." How sweet of
the clergyman to humour him! Blessings on his kindly face and on his silver

hair! Mr. Fuller Mellish comes back with the breechloading carbine. The old man handles it; calls it a firelock; and goes crazily through his manual with it. Finally, he unlocks the breech, and as the barrel drops, believes that he has broken the weapon in two. Matters being explained, he expresses his unalterable conviction that England will have to fall back on Brown Bess when the moment for action arrives again. He takes out his pipe. It falls and is broken. He whimpers, and is petted and consoled by a present of the sergeant's beautiful pipe with "a hamber mouthpiece." Mr. Fuller Mellish, becoming again superfluous, is again got rid of. Enter a haughty gentleman. It is the Colonel of the Royal Scots Guards, the corporal's old regiment. According to the well-known custom of colonels, he has called on the old pensioner to give him a five-pound note. The old man, as if electrically shocked, staggers up and desperately tries to stand for a moment at "attention" and salute his officer. He collapses, almost slain by the effort, into his chair, mumbling pathetically that he "were a'most gone that time, Colonel." "A masterstroke! who but a great actor could have executed this heart-searching movement?" The veteran returns to the fireside: once more he depicts with convincing art the state of an old man's joints. The Colonel goes; Mr. Fuller Mellish comes; the old man dozes. Suddenly he springs up. "The Guards want powder; and, by God, the Guards shall have it." With these words he falls back in his chair. Mr. Fuller Mellish, lest there should be any mistake about it (it is never safe to trust the intelligence of the British public), delicately informs Miss Hughes that her granduncle is dead. The curtain falls amid thunders of applause.

Every old actor into whose hands this article falls will understand perfectly from my description how the whole thing is done, and will wish that he could get such Press notices for a little hobbling and piping, and a few bits of mechanical business with a pipe, a carbine, and two chairs. The whole performance does not involve one gesture, one line, one thought outside the commonest routine of automatic stage illusion. What, I wonder, must Mr. Irving, who of course knows this better than any one else, feel when he finds this pitiful little handful of hackneyed stage tricks received exactly as if it were a crowning instance of his most difficult and finest art? No doubt he expected and intended that the public, on being touched and pleased by machinery, should imagine that they were being touched and pleased by acting. But the critics! What can he think of the analytic powers of those of us who, when an organized and successful attack is made on our emotions, are unable to discriminate between the execution done by the actor's art and that done by Mr. Conan Doyle's ingenious exploitation of the ready-made pathos of old age, the ignorant and maudlin sentiment attaching to the army and "the Dook," and the vulgar conception of the battle of Waterloo as a stand-up street fight between an Englishman and a Frenchman, a conception infinitely less respectable than that which led Byron to exclaim, when he heard of Napoleon's defeat, "I'm damned sorry"?

*   *   *

I hope I have not conveyed an impression that the triple bill [A.W. Pinero's *Bygones*, A.C. Doyle's *A Story of Waterloo*, and W.G. Wills's *A Chapter from Don Quixate*] makes a bad evening's entertainment. Though it is my steady purpose to do what I can to drive such sketches as "A Story of Waterloo," with their ready-made feeling and prearranged effects, away to the music-hall, which is their proper place now that we no longer have a "Gallery of Illustration," I enjoy them, and am entirely in favour of their multiplication so long as it is understood that they are not the business of fine actors and first-class theatres.

Dr. Conan Doyle's Latest Case [1]
[Review of *Rodney Stone*]

Max Beerbohm

I believe the Doctor sold his practice some years ago, after his first success in fiction. Yet, though I have read much of his writing, I never regard him as anything but a medical man. He is the first to have carried the bedside-manner into literature, and I rather like him for it. He is so strong, and shrewd, and brisk, and kindly. The very touch of his large cool hands is soothing. In the very glint of his gold-rimmed glasses there is something which inspires me with confidence. None would commend more heartily than I the skill and patience he has brought to the treatment of many notable cases. But, I confess, my heart misgave me when I heard that, forsaking his old patients, he was plying a free lance over the rigid corpse of Beau Brummell. Had the good Doctor brought back to us from that dark ravine, where they lie bleaching, Sherlock's bones, I had rejoiced in his reconstruction of them. That he should be tampering with those exquisite remains, embalmed so piously by the alien hand of D'Aurevilly and sprinkled with paper-flowers from my own hand, ah, outrage of temerarious outrage! But, strangely enough, now that I come to gaze with my own eyes upon the autopsy, my wrath for its victim is swallowed up in pity for its performer. I have seen many failures made by well-meaning men; not one more pitiable than this.

A series of detective stories written by Mr. Austin Dobson might make a parallel with the Doctor's account of the Dandiacal Age. Yet, it is probably that Sherlock, as created by our *rococoiste*, would cut a more presentable figure than does Sir Charles Tregellis, standing before us (such is the Doctor's idea of a foppish attitude) "with one thumb in the arm-pit." We are not surprised, after this, at Sir Charles's mode of speech. "Our stuffs," says he, "lack taste and variety," and he boasts of having once discovered "a new waistcoating which for a time became all the rage." But in the diction of modern haberdashery he is surpassed, I think, by a fellow-dandy, who says, in reference to a buff vest, that "a touch of red sprig would give it the finish which it needs." Elsewhere, the baronet comments on a friend's absence from "the Marchioness of Dover's ball," and to some request or other he accedes with the words "Very good!" He shows his collection of curios, remarking that

Reprinted from *Saturday Review* [London] (26 December, 1896): 665–66.

193

"They are *des petites cadeaux*, but it would be an indiscretion for me to say more." It was an indiscretion for Doctor Doyle, being shaky in his French genders, to say so much. Nor was there any need of process-blocks—apt illustrations though they are—to drive home for us the image of this Baker Street Beau.

Doctor Doyle's failure to portray the manners of a dandy is not more complete than his failure to see a dandy's soul. Sir Charles Tregellis is supposed to be the pink of dandyism, the beacon of affectation. The first thing we hear of him is that he wishes his lap-dog, tired after a journey, to be given a half-pint of warm milk with six drops of pure brandy. The last thing we hear of him is that, seceding finally from the town, he takes to his bed because he cannot prevent velvet collars from becoming fashionable. Well, we know there were men of that kind in the Georgian era. They will always fascinate the historian, the psychologist. In "Beau Austin" [a play by William Ernest Henley, 1892] we have a curious and careful study of one of them. But the play is hardly dramatic. Indeed, the authors, by trying, towards the end, to make the Beau a fine and sympathetic fellow, have made it clear to us how hopeless a theme for drama true dandyism is. And poor Doctor Doyle, unable to interest his readers in what is unintelligible to himself, has slyly endowed his hero with many extraneous qualities.

We are Berties, Hughies, Archies,
    In the Guards, don't you know?
Twirling silky long moustaches,
    Being Guards, don't you know?
Not a regiment that marches
    Like the Guards, don't you know?
Dandies? Yes! But Dandy-*Lions*
    In the Guards!

So are we assured that Sir Charles Tregellis was a man at heart. "His lips were set and his eyes shining, with just a little flush upon each pale cheek," as he tore, for a wager, along the Brighton Road. At a prize-fight, he showed "a quiet air of domination amongst these fierce fellows, like a huntsman walking carelessly through a springing and yapping pack." And all the rest of it. Doctor Doyle tries to explain the contradiction by showing us that this dandy did not take his affectations seriously. What dandy ever did? Affectations, seriously taken, become convictions, and he who so takes them is no dandy. But, at the same time, affectations do absorb the whole dandiacal being, and it were impossible that a man so permeated with vain foibles as was Sir Charles Tregellis should be distinguished for any prowess in sport or in athletics. Of course, the Doctor had to work in his good descriptions of a driving-race and of a prize-fight, but then why did he not present Sir

Charles as an ordinary gentleman of the period? Why this forlorn, laborious effort to draw a dandy? Why?

Had the fumbled figure, Sir Charles Tregellis, been central in some well-made plot, he had mattered less. But such slight plot as there is bobs up only at the beginning and end of the book. The Doctor evidently relies upon his dandy, surrounded with certain stock accessories—mouthing effigies of Fox and Sheridan, Lord Dudley and the Duke of Queensberry. He gives us, also, the Regent (with a snub nose!), and trots out the old, exploded fable that the Regent was warned off the Turf. He gives us a glimpse of Pitt: "Look at the barouche with the sharp-featured man peeping out of the window." Surely he underrates our memory. Who has forgotten Thackeray's superb impression: "If you and I had been alive then, and strolling down Milsom Street—hush! we should have taken our hats off, as an awful, long, lean, gaunt figure, swathed in flannels, passed by in its chair, and a livid face looked out from the window—great fierce eyes staring from under a bushy, powdered wig, a terrible frown, a terrible Roman nose—and we whisper to one another, 'There he is! There's the great commoner! There is Mr. Pitt!' " Doctor Doyle may think it rather cruel of me to compare him with Thackeray, but, indeed, he must pay the penalties of his presumption. I am quite ready to believe that he has done his best. The list of authorities, which he claims, in his preface, to have read, is long and creditable. But he might as well have been reading "Frere on Tonsilitis" or the back numbers of the "Lancet," for all he has contrived to catch of grace or sentiment or understanding. He has bungled the post-mortem horribly. And yet he is quite pleased with himself, this obstinate medico. He hints that he means to perform, shortly, a second operation.

No, no, Doctor Doyle! You're a very good general practitioner, I've no doubt. But you've bungled the post-mortem. Operations of this kind require great special knowledge and most delicate handling. Come! Roll down your shirt-sleeves! Put on your coat! It's a pity for your professional reputation that you ever undertook the case. You had far better have stuck to your ordinary practice. Pack up your instruments, my good sir! Jump into your brougham!

Dr. Conan Doyle's Latest Case [2]
[Exchange of Letters]

ARTHUR CONAN DOYLE AND MAX BEERBOHM

To the Editor of the *Saturday Review*.

Reform Club, Pall Mall, S.W.

SIR,—I observe that Mr. Max Beerbohm differs very widely from me in his conception of the dandy of the early part of this century. The lists are open to all, and if he wishes to depict a fop of his own it will, no doubt, meet with the success which it deserves. But in the meanwhile you will perhaps allow me space to point out some of the historical and social errors which appear in his short article.

Mr. Beerbohm is severe because I do not describe the younger Pitt. There was no reason why I should describe him, as he does not—save for a reference in conversation—appear in the book. But, in order to show me how it should have been done, Mr. Beerbohm quotes what he describes as the well-known description by Thackeray. It is a well-known description—but it is evidently not a well-known one to Mr. Beerbohm, for it does not refer to the person of whom he is talking at all. "An awful figure in a chair," says Thackeray. "A livid face . . . powdered wig . . . a Roman nose. There he is! There is the great Commoner." How could anyone imagine that this was the younger Pitt, who probably never rode in a chair or wore a wig in his life—and who certainly never had a Roman nose! The description is of Pitt's father, afterwards Earl of Chatham. It may be a venial offence to confound the one Pitt with the other, but what are we to say of the failure to recognize the internal evidence which is contained in the quotation itself? I trust that Mr. Beerbohm will "scatter no more paper flowers" about that epoch until he has read something more reliable than D'Aurevilly's lively but inaccurate essay.

Mr. Beerbohm is contemptuous because a fop has been described in the text as standing with his thumb in his armpit. He also alludes to Brummell in terms which suggest that he knows something of him. If so, he must know that this was one of the Beau's characteristic attitudes. Contemporary sketches depict him in it. The student can refer to one of them in the

Reprinted from *Saturday Review* [London] (2 January 1897): 15–16.

frontispiece of the second volume of Gronow's Memoirs. There the Beau stands, thumb in armpit, in this impossible attitude for a fop.

Mr. Beerbohm then alludes to "the old exploded fable" that the "Regent was warned off the Turf." After the foregoing specimens of Mr. Beerbohm's historical accuracy, it will take more than his mere assertion to establish that this is a fable. He cannot even state the case without blundering, for it was in 1791—twenty years before George became Regent—that the incident occurred. It is true that the Prince of Wales was not warned off by name—this would have been too daring even for the autocrats of the Jockey Club—but his jockey, Sam Chifney, was suspended, which answered the same purpose. Chifney's own account of the matter will be found in the little pamphlet by him called "Genius Genuine."

Mr. Beerbohm denies that the Prince had an upturned nose. He must settle that with Mr. Lawrence the painter, who has depicted him with one. Mr. Beerbohm in commenting upon my picture of the times implies that, though I may have the facts, I have not caught the spirit. I cannot say the converse of him, but, at least, I can assure him that he is very far from having caught the facts. He may be upon safe ground when he refers to my bedside manner and gold-rimmed glasses, but he is very ignorant of the period about which he writes.—Yours faithfully,

A. Conan Doyle.

SIR,—This letter bears traces of suppressed emotion and a feverish haste. Does the Doctor *really* suppose that I had confused the two Pitts? Apart from any special reading I may have done for my own pleasure, I am far too fresh from school to have forgotten which was called the Great Commoner and which moved in the politics of the Regency. The Doctor's description of the latter, looking out of a barouche, was obviously inspired by Thackeray's fine description of the former, looking out of a Sedan chair. In comparing the two passages, I merely suggested that the Doctor had made a very feeble plagiarism, nor did there seem any need to assure my readers that the father was not his own son. The terrible phrase, "one thumb in the armpit," were applicable perhaps to Mr. Bumble, but not to Mr. Brummell. Count D'Orsay wore a large hat, but we should hesitate to call it "a topper jammed on to his nose." If the Doctor cannot understand that, I am very sorry. Facts are easier than style, and I am glad the Doctor has admitted that the Regent—one may speak, generally, of the Regent—was not warned off the Turf. But I cannot accept his contention that a dishonest jockey must needs be the servant of a dishonest master. As a matter of fact, there never was a shadow of evidence that George behaved dishonourably in the Chifney affair, and I think that no one, not even a dead king, should be slandered for the sake of a trumpery effect in fiction. I have seen many pictures of George, by Lawrence and others. He had, of course, the regular Hanoverian nose, arched and drooping. Lastly, I may point out that D'Aurevilly's "Du Dandysme et de Georges Brummel," being a work split up into twelve chapters, is not an essay, and that it is not, and was not meant to be, in the least lively. "Physician, heal thyself!"—Yours, & c.

Max Beerbohm.

Dr. Conan Doyle's Latest Case [3]

ARTHUR CONAN DOYLE

To the Editor of the *Saturday Review*.
Greyswood Beeches, Haslemere, 4 *Jan.*, 1897.

SIR,—I note the various concessions which have to be made to Mr. Beerbohm in order to save the situation. If his conscience will pass them I will do the same. And I especially applaud his excellent contention that because George was at one time of his life a Regent, it is permissible to describe him at all times as the Regent. I would suggest that the same argument would justify us in describing any historical character as "The Baby"—which would simplify matters very much.

Here's "good hunting" for the New Year to Mr. Max Beerbohm.— Yours faithfully,

A. Conan Doyle.

Reprinted from *Saturday Review* [London] (9 January 1897): 40–41.

Chromoconanography
[Review of *Uncle Bernac*]

MAX BEERBOHM

Those who have watched Doctor Conan Doyle's career will remember that he engaged with me, some months ago, in a queer little combat over his novel of Georgian manners, "Rodney Stone." He came off, if I may say so, second-best, but he took his defeat with such good-humour, and his tone was so courteous and contrasted so favourably with mine, which was most provocative, that I could not help crediting him, in my heart, with a moral victory. I liked his deportment very much, and have thought kindly of him ever since, and when, some days ago, there came to me, in a consignment from a circulating library, another book of his, "Uncle Bernac," I sat down to read it with all prejudice in its favour. I was pleased to find that the first chapter was really not half bad. How a young *emigré*, eager to serve the usurper whom his father had hated, crossed the channel in a lugger and was rowed, under a gathering storm, by two rascally seamen, to the beach of his beloved France, and how, in his great joy, he knelt down and pressed his lips "upon the wet and pringling gravel"—all this was told with force and sentiment, and with a literary style which no imitator of Stevenson need blush to acknowledge as his own. The succeeding chapters were not less good. I liked the storm and the salt-marsh and the mysterious stranger and the hair-breadth 'scape in the ruined cottage. As the hero and his host crept into the secret passage from the chalk-pit, I felt sure they would soon emerge upon a very respectable Romance. Emerge they did, in the Castle of Grosbois, where the hero was presented to a beautiful girl, whose mode of speech seemed to me rather too melodramatic to be really romantic. Still, I was full of hope. There were all the materials for a good story of its kind, when lo! the hero was summoned to the Camp of Boulogne, leaving the story behind him, and was whirled into the midst of Mrs. Jarley's wax-works. Here he was kept, doing nothing in particular, and was released, just before the end of the volume, to pick the story up again if he could—"adventures which," as Doctor Conan Doyle says with irresistible *naïveté*, "might have been of some interest in themselves had I not introduced the figure of Napoleon." Why, then, drag in Napoleon? Or, at any rate, why drag in the story? To

Reprinted from *Saturday Review* [London] (10 July 1897): 31–32.

this question the Doctor has a ready answer: "if it had not been for that story I should not have had an excuse for describing to you my first and most vivid impressions of Napoleon, and so it has served a purpose after all." But has it? It seems to me, rather, one of two stools between which Doctor Conan Doyle has fallen badly. There are two ways of introducing a great historical figure into fiction. One is to make him the protagonist, around whom all the action revolves; the other is to sketch him in slightly, incidentally. The former mode has been adopted by my neighbour, "G.B.S.," who has presented Napoleon as the predominant figure in a dramatic episode, and has analysed him from the standpoint of a very clever civilian. Had Doctor Conan Doyle, likewise, made Napoleon the true pivot for a romance, he might have given us a worthy companion-picture for that which has been given by "G.B.S." In "Uncle Bernac," as it stands, Napoleon has no business save as an incidental figure, and yet he is allowed to overshadow all the other figures, until, without interesting us in himself, he succeeds in robbing us of any interest we may have taken in them. Doctor Conan Doyle, as we all know, has written for the stage; what would he say of a dramatist who allowed one of the supers in his play to have the stage all to himself throughout the second and third acts? He would say that such a dramatist was an unmitigated bungler. And that is what I feel bound to say of Doctor Conan Doyle.

"G.B.S." would not pretend that he had given us a perfect picture of Napoleon. But at least he has given his Napoleon something to do, has shown us the man's moods changing, in a natural sequence, under stress of certain incidents. His Napoleon convinces one more than the Doctor's in exactly the same ratio as an animatograph convinces one more than an album of kodaks. (Lest my neighbour blush as he reads this, let me explain that I seek not to crown him, but only to bonnet the Doctor.) In the "Man of Destiny," even though one read the play merely, and see not Mr. Murray Carson's acting, Napoleon is shown to us as a human being. In "Uncle Bernac," he is the sorriest of lay-figures, faked and padded, with his stiff joints adjusted, now to this, now to that, of the requisite altitudes, while the Doctor reels off a running commentary with "improving" digressions, in the manner of Little Nell. "The camp of Boulogne contained at that time one hundred and fifty thousand infantry, with fifty thousand cavalry, so that its population was second only to Paris among the cities of France. It was divided into four sections, the right camp, the left camp, the camp of Wimereux, and the camp of Ambleteuse, the whole being about a mile in depth, and extending along the seashore for a length of about seven miles." Heavens! The Doctor does not fail through lack of industry, at all events. If mere industry could do the trick, he would have triumphed indeed. In his reconstruction of Napoleon, he has omitted nothing, except Napoleon. With laborious accuracy are enumerated all the Emperor's peculiarities, compiled from all the best authorities—his "plump white legs," his quick temper, his indelicacy, his thin hair, his boyish smile, his boots, his charger, his

brutal *amours*, his abstemiousness, his vanity, his bad penmanship, his "marvellous grasp of fact," his stoop, his parsimony, his snuffbox, "the brusque
manner which he adopted to women," "the caressing gesture that was peculiar
to him" and "the singular epileptic gesture which was peculiar to him."
Insatiate Doctor! Floundering on from detail to detail, lumping in everything
without selection, dragging in everyone by the hair of their heads—Talma,
Grétry, Josephine, Robert Fulton, and all the Marshals—plunging among
the dry-bones of history as a water-horse plunges among the water-reeds, is
this, I ask you, *is* this the way to write a book? You have a great admiration
for Napoleon, and you wished to make him vital in a romance. You are
industrious and enthusiastic, and you are no amateur in writing. Surely you
might have foreseen that your method was crazy and foredoomed. Suppose
that you will be re-incarnated towards the end of the next century and that
your historical reading will inform you with an overpowering interest in the
career and character of (say) Lord Randolph Churchill; and suppose that you
will sit down with the purpose of portraying Lord Randolph in fiction. Shall
you not, under these circumstances, take some phase or phases of his public
life and so pave the way for a well-formed romance, in which his character,
as it seems to you, may be effectively illustrated in action? Shall you not be
careful to eliminate from the scheme of your book all extraneous matter that
would but confuse your readers and hamper you in your chief aim? Or shall
you (supposing that you can remember your experiences in this century)
deliberately repeat the method of your "Uncle Bernac"? Shall you begin with
an exciting tale about a young man, who, in the year 1885, fell in with a
gang of Anarchist conspirators in Soho, and was, after many marvellous
adventures, rescued by his uncle, and taken to see Lord Randolph Churchill
at his room in the India Office? Would you then occupy pages with a
catalogue of Lord Randolph's peculiarities, his large moustache, his prominent eyes, his slight lisp, the amber mouthpiece through which he smoked
cigarettes? Shall you make him say at once "the duty of an Opposition is to
oppose," "Mr. Gladstone is an old man in a hurry" and any other of his most
famous utterances that you could remember? Shall you then make him engage
the young man as private secretary, and, having cast his eye over a bundle
of most complicated despatches, (astonishing one of the permanent officials
by the rapidity with which he mastered them), jot down some notes for a
speech to be delivered that evening at Birmingham, see that his fishing-
tackle was ready for an imminent trip to Norway and make up his book for
the Oaks, just in time to receive the Premier and have a stormy scene with
Mr. W. H. Smith, and then, after a mood of deep despondency, hear that
the Liberals had been defeated at a bye-election and jump up on to a chair,
waving his hat round his head and cheering with all his might? After some
chapters of this kind of thing, shall you then make Lord Randolph the means
of this secretary marrying a young lady to whom he was deeply attached and
living happily ever after? If, Doctor, you pursue this plan, shall you imagine

that you have given a true or worthy or convincing picture of a tragic and fascinating figure in history?

I know that a great man cannot be perfectly described save by a great writer, but I know, also, that Doctor Conan Doyle might, if he had sought my advice at the outset, have made a respectable little book out of the Napoleonic Legend. I see that he hints at a sequel, (oh these sequels!), but would it not have been better had he written the sequel at once, and satisfied his publishers by substituting it for the portrait of Napoleon? The portrait of Napoleon is simply a trumpery and twopence-coloured supplement slipped in without rhyme or reason. It is a more terrible example of chromoconanography than even the portrait of George IV. which was given away with "Rodney Stone." Doctor Conan Doyle can write coherent stories—otherwise he would never have been the popular author that he is—and I warn him that, unless he pull himself together, he will find the public buying fewer of his books. The reviewers still ransack their vocabularies for words of ecstatic praise, but let Doctor Conan Doyle listen to me, nevertheless, rather than to them. I myself have enjoyed several of his earlier books, and I am quite honest in wishing him every success. Indeed, I have felt great compunction in writing this article at all, especially as Mr. Le Gallienne has been chiding me, not unkindly, in the "Star," for "baiting popular favourites." I feel rather nervous, now that I know Mr. Le Gallienne has his eye on me. Surely "baiting" is an inappropriate word. "Gibbeting" were better. *Faut vivre, mon chére.* Someone's got to be public hangman. The post is not attractive nor romantic, I know. But he who holds it is, in his modest way, on the side of the Angels. I am quite a decent sort of person really. I, too, have gentle tastes, (when I am off duty), and love

> to hear the little brook a-gurgling,
> (Brook a-gurgling,)
> and listen to the merry village chime
> (Village chime.)

My Contemporaries in Fiction.
XIII.—The Young Romancers

David Christie Murray

In the combined spelling and reading book which was in use in schools more than forty years ago there was printed a story to the following effect: Certain Arabs had lost a camel, and in the course of their wanderings in search of him they met a dervish, whom they questioned. The dervish answered by offering questions on his own side. "Was your camel lame in one foot?" he began. "Yes," said the owners. "Was he blind in one eye?" he continued. "Yes," said the owners again. "Had he lost a front tooth?" "Yes." "Was he laden with corn on one side and with honey on the other?" "Yes, yes, yes. This is our camel. Where have you seen him?" The dervish answered: "I have never seen him." The Arabs, not without apparent reason, suspected the dervish of playing with them, and were about to chastise him, when the holy man asked for a hearing. Having secured it, he explained. He had seen the track of the camel. He had known the animal to be lame of one foot because that foot left a slighter impression than the others upon the dust of the road. He had argued it blind of one eye because it had cropped the herbage on one side of the road alone. He knew it to have lost a tooth because of the gap left in the centre of its bite. Bees and flies argued honey on one side of the beast, and ants carrying wheat grains argued wheat on the other. The name of this observant and synthetic-minded dervish was not Sherlock Holmes, but he had the method of that famous detective, and in a sense anticipated the plots of all the stories which Dr. Conan Doyle has so effectively related to him. Possibly the best stories in the world which depend for their interest on this kind of induction are Edgar Allan Poe's. "The Gold Bug," "The Murder in the Rue Morgue," and "The Stolen Letter," have not been surpassed or even equalled by any later writer; but Dr. Doyle comes in an excellent second, and if he has not actually rivalled Poe in the construction and development of any single story, he has run him close even there, and has beaten him in the sustained ingenuity of continuous invention. The story of "The Yellow Band" has a flavour almost as gruesome and terrible as Poe's "Black Cat," and an unusual faculty for dramatic narrative is displayed throughout the whole clever series. The Sherlock Holmes stories are far,

Excerpted and reprinted from *Canadian Magazine* [Toronto] (October 1897): 498–500.

indeed, from being Dr. Doyle's best work; but it is to them that he mainly owes his popularity. They took the imaginative side of the general reader, and their popular properties are likely to keep them before the public mind for a long while to come. To estimate Dr. Doyle's position as a writer one has to meet him in "The Refugees," in "The White Company," and in "Rodney Stone." In each of these there is evident a sound and painstaking method of research, as well as a power of dramatic invention; and in combination with these is a style of unaffected manliness, simplicity, and strength, which is at once satisfactory to the student and attractive to the mass of people who are content to be pleased by such qualities without knowing or asking why. The labour bestowed on "The White Company" may very well be compared to that expended by Charles Reade on "The Cloister and the Hearth." It covers a far less extent of ground than that monumental romance, and it has not (and does not aim at) its universality of mood, but the same desire of accuracy, the same order of scholarship, the same industry, the same sense of scrupulous honour in matters of ascertainable fact, are to be noted, and being noted, are worthy of unstinted admiration. It is, perhaps, an open question as to whether Dr. Doyle, in his latest book, has not run a little ahead of the time at which a story on such a theme could be written with entire safety. "Rodney Stone" is a story of the prize-ring, and of the gambling, hard-drinking and somewhat brutalized days in which that institution flourished. There are many of us (I have made public confession half-a-score of times) who regret the abolition of the ring, on grounds of public policy. We argue that man is a fighting animal, and that in the days of the ring there was a recognized code of rules which regulated his conduct at times when the combative instinct was not to be restrained. We observe that our commonalty now use the knife in quarrel, and we regret the death of that rough principle of honour which once imposed itself upon the worst of rowdies. But there is little doubt that the feeling of the community at large is overwhelmingly against us, and it is for this reason that I am dubious as to the success of Dr. Doyle's last literary venture. The makings of romance are in the story, and are well used. There are episodes of excellent excitement in it; notable amongst these being the race on the Godstone roads, which is done with a swing and passion not easy to overpraise. In the narrative of the fight and of the incidents which preceded it the feeling of the time is admirably preserved and the interest of the reader is held at an unyielding tension. But the prize-ring is a little too near as yet to offer unimpeachable matter for romance; and people who can read of the bloodthirsty Umslopogaas and his semi-comic holocausts with an unshaken stomach, or feel a placid historic pleasure in the chronicles of Nero's eccentricities, will find "Rodney Stone" objectionable because it chronicles a "knuckle fight," and because a "knuckle fight" is still occasionally brought off in London, and more occasionally suppressed by the police.

But a more serious criticism awaits Dr. Conan Doyle's last work. It is offered respectfully, and with every admiration for the high qualities already noticed. In the re-embodiment of a bygone age in fiction three separate and special faculties are to be exercised. The first is the faculty for research, which must expend its energy not merely on the theme in hand, but on the age at large. The second is the imaginative and sympathetic faculty, which alone can make the dry bones of social history live again. The third is the faculty of self-repression, the power to cast away all which, however laboriously acquired, is dramatically unessential. Two of these powers belong in generous measure to Dr. Conan Doyle. The third, which is as necessary to complete success, he has not yet displayed. In "Rodney Stone" an attempt has been made to cover up this shortcoming, in the form in which the story has been cast, and in the very choice of its title. But when the book comes to be read it is not the tale of Rodney Stone (who is a mere outsider privileged to narrate), but of his fashionable uncle's combat with Sir Lothian Hume, with the ring in which their separate champions appear as a battle ground. Many pages are crowded with people who are named in passing and forgotten. They have no influence on the narrative, and no place in it. Their presence assuredly displays a knowledge of the time and its chronicles, but they are just so many obstacles to the clear run of the story, and no more. This is really the only fault to be found with the book, but it is a grave fault, and the writer, if he is to take the place which his powers and his industry alike join in claiming for him, must learn to cast "as rubbish to the void" many a painfully acquired bit of knowledge. To be an antiquary is one thing, and to be an antiquarian romancer is another. Mr. Doyle has aimed at being both one and the other in the same pages. A true analogy may be taken from the stage, where the supernumeraries are not allowed to obscure the leading lady and gentleman at any moment of action.

Mr. Stanley Weyman, who is not Dr. Doyle's equal in other matters, is in this sole respect his master. He keeps his hero on the scene, and his action in full swing. He gives no indication of a profound or studious knowledge of his time, but he knows it fairly well. Dr. Doyle's method is at bottom the truer, when once the detailed labour is hidden, but when it bares its own machinery it loses most of its gain.

A Novelist's Verse
[Review of *Songs of Action*]

LITERATURE

That Dr. Conan Doyle could write good, stirring verse he showed long ago. There is nothing better in this book than "The Song of the Bow," which has the elemental qualities of a song that is meant to be sung, and which made its appearance many years back in "The White Company." If all the other pieces were up to this level, we should have to rate Dr. Conan Doyle's poetical talent high. As it is, the volume shows his versatility, and will give real pleasure to all who still possess healthy emotions to be moved by swinging metres and themes to suit. The author's aim in nearly all these "songs of action" is that which guided Mr. Henley when he made the choice of pieces for his *Lyra Heroica*—"to set forth the beauty and the joy of living, the beauty and the blessedness of death, the glory of battle and adventure, the nobility of devotion, the dignity of resistance, the sacred quality of patriotism." In such a ballad as "Corporal Dick's Promotion" we have all these ideals finely illustrated. Told in the simplest words and without melodramatic artifice, this tale of the rough soldier—"a hard-faced old rapscallion"—who gives his life in the Egyptian desert to save a boy comrade from the Arabs, goes straight to the heart. Dr. Conan Doyle does not often get Mr. Rudyard Kipling's irresistible lilt into his stanzas, nor have they quite the same finish and masterly choice of words as Mr. Newbolt's ballads; but in "heart" they are never wanting, and this should win them wide hearing and favour. The verse is sometimes a little hard in quality—not flexible enough to set itself instantly to music in the reader's head, as nearly all Mr. Kipling's does. Still, there is a good deal in the volume to which this does not apply. The chorus to the "Ballad of the Ranks," for instance, is eminently musical, though the verse-part goes just a shade too stiffly.

> Who carries the gun?
> A lad from over the Tweed.
> Then let him go, for well we know
> He comes of a soldier breed.
> So drink together to rock and heather,

Reprinted from *Literature* (18 June 1898): 693.

> Out where the red deer run,
> And stand aside for Scotland's pride—
> The man that carries the gun!
> For the Colonel rides before,
> The Major's on the flank,
> The Captains and the Adjutant
> Are in the foremost rank.
> But when it's "Action front!"
> And fighting's to be done,
> Come one, come all, you stand or fall
> By the man who holds the gun.

The songs are not nearly all about fighting—not even about heroism in other fields than those of battle. There are several fine hunting ballads. "'Ware Holes" is a moving story told with effect and without the touch of sentimentalism which would have spoiled it. In "With the Chiddingfolds" Dr. Conan Doyle seems to have introduced a reminiscence of "John Peel" just as a composer will, by clever scoring, throw in a hint of some familiar air that is akin to his theme. Racing and golf are sung also, though with scarcely so much success. The poet of the putting-green has yet to appear, and Dr. Conan Doyle's "Farnshire Cup" can hardly bear comparison with Adam Lindsay Gordon's thrilling tales of close races. On the other hand, "The Groom's Story" (which was lately amusing readers of the *Cornhill*) is vastly humorous, and shows the author in a vein in which he need fear no comparisons. The idea of the "big, bay 'orse" which had never shown any pace until he was harnessed to a motor-car that suddenly ran away and pushed him ahead at a terrific speed is comic in itself, and it loses nothing by its treatment—

> Master 'eld the steerin' gear, an' kept the road all right,
> And away they whizzed and clattered—my aunt! it was a sight.
> 'E seemed the finest draught 'orse as ever lived by far,
> For all the country Juggins thought 'twas 'im wot pulled the car.
>
> 'E was stretchin' like a grey'ound, 'e was goin' all 'e knew;
> But it bumped an' shoved be'ind 'im, for all that 'e could do;
> It butted 'im an' boosted 'im an' spanked 'im on a'ead,
> Till 'e broke the ten-mile record, same as I already said.
>
> Ten mile in twenty minutes! 'E done it, sir. That's true.
> The only time we ever found what that 'ere 'orse could do.
> Some say it wasn't 'ardly fair, and the papers made a fuss,
> But 'e broke the ten-mile record, and that's good enough for us.

How Mr. Kipling (whose name in this connexion is like King Charles' Head and cannot be kept out when one writes of this kind of poetry) has "made school," to borrow a phrase from the studios, may be seen here, as in so many other writers of less note than Dr. Conan Doyle. The matter of "The Frontier Line" shows his influence as much as the manner of "The Rover's Chanty." The former, with its queries to the inhabitants of the distant parts of the earth, "What marks the frontier line?" draws the answer that it is marked by none of the natural features of division:—

> But be it east or west,
>   One common sign we bear,
> The tongue may change, the soil, the sky,
> But where your British brothers lie,
> The lonely cairn, the nameless grave,
> Still fringe the flowing Saxon wave.
>   'Tis that! 'Tis where
>   *They* lie—the men who placed it there,
> That marks the frontier line.

The chant has all the swing and inconsequence that usually mark this kind of composition, and one would wish to turn the capstan to no better rhyme.

Two very neat epigrams give a flavour to the make-weight of various verse that comes towards the end of the volume. "A Parable" (Dr. Conan Doyle might have added "for philosophers") is particularly happy in packing a commentary upon so vast a question into so small a space:—

> The cheese-mites asked how the cheese got there,
>   And warmly debated the matter;
> The Orthodox said that it came from the air,
>   And the Heretics said from the platter.
> They argued it long and they argued it strong,
>   And I hear they are arguing now;
> But of all the choice spirits who lived in the cheese,
>   Not one of them thought of a cow.

For many reasons we are glad to be able to welcome this volume of Dr. Conan Doyle's—not least because there is a decided tendency in England for men of letters to be tied down too much to a particular line. In France, on the contrary, there is scarce a writer of distinction who has not published, at any rate, some verse, and in poetry (which every one writes, though they may not publish) we often find unexpected qualities of mind and felicities of phrasing that have been to seek in other forms of literary expression.

[Review of *A Duet with an Occasional Chorus*]

LITERATURE

In this latest of his novels Mr. Conan Doyle has apparently determined to show the admirers of his stirring romances and ingenious detective stories that he can be mildly "domestic" enough to satisfy the fiercest thirst for literary milk-and-water. "A Duet with an Occasional Chorus" is simply a story of the married life of a very commonplace young man and a quite colourless young woman—a story beginning with the interchange of love letters between the young couple and ending with the birth of the first baby. Frank Crosse is an assistant accountant in an insurance office at £400 a year. Maude Selby has a *dot* of £50 per annum, and on this they set up housekeeping in the usual small suburban villa, where the usual troubles with their servants and the tearful wrestlings of the inexperienced young housewife with "Mrs. Beeton" are duly chronicled in a manner not much more remarkable, to tell the truth, than that of the familiar jesters on the subject in the pages of the cheap weekly papers. The method employed by Mr. Doyle to lift his novel above this level and give a "cultured" tone to it has a certain innocence of its own. Before their marriage the young couple meet for an afternoon "outing," and having discussed the rival claims of a *matinée* and of the "Australians at the Oval," they finally decide on doing Westminster Abbey. Whereupon there follows a couple of chapters of "adapted guide-book" after this style:—

> Tennyson, the last, almost the greatest of that illustrious line, lay under the white slab upon the floor. Maude and Frank stood reverently beside it.
>
> > Sunset and Evening Star.
> > And one clear call for me.
>
> Frank quoted. "What lines for a very old man to write. I should put him second only to Shakespeare had I the marshalling of them."
> "I have read so little," said Maude.
> "We will read it together after next week. But it makes your reading so much more real and intimate when you have stood at the grave of the man who wrote it. That's Chaucer, the big tomb there. He is the father of British poetry. Here is Browning beside Tennyson—united in life and in death. He was the more profound thinker, but music and form are essential also."

Reprinted from *Literature* (1 April 1899): 345.

"Who is that standing figure?"

"It is Dryden. What a clever face, and what a modern type. Here is Walter Scott beside the door. How kindly and humorous his expression was."

And so forth, and so forth. Again, after a few pages of postnuptial billing and cooing, we have a couple of chapters about Mr. Samuel Pepys, including an account of a visit to his tomb in St. Olave's, and familiar reflections on the relation between Pepys and his wife. Then there comes a little money trouble of the young couple, followed by an abortive attempt on the part of the ladies of Woking—the only real touch of comedy in the book—to form a Browning Society. Then the mild excitement of a visit paid to the wife by an old flame of the husband's—a lady of the "siren" order—who is touched (see penny novelette *passim*) by the sweetness, and goodness, and simplicity, of the young wife, and repents her of her mischief-making intentions, and "suddenly puts her arms round Maude and kisses her on the cheek," exclaiming "You are a good sort and I hope you will be happy." After which we get a chapter entitled "No. 5; Cheyne Row," describing a visit to the Carlyle Museum, and containing informing passages of this description:—

> They spent their early years in Scotland, you know, and he was a man going on to the forties when he came to London. The success of *Sartor Resartus* encouraged him to the step. His letter describes all the incoming. Here is his comment written after her death.

By this time we have reached the "last note of the duet." It is turned into a trio by the birth of the baby, and after a final letter to the author from the young mother containing a most vivid and graphic description, a whole page long, of the behaviour of the infant in his bath and his attitude towards his feeding bottle, the "story" comes to an end.

Of course it is not impossible to construct an amusing, an interesting, even a powerful novel on materials as slender as these; but unfortunately it requires qualities which are far from being conspicuous in Mr. Doyle. Subtlety of observation and delicacy of character-drawing are not his forte; and though he is not lacking in the humorous faculty, it requires a broader canvas and more strongly contrasted individualities to allow it adequate scope. It is apparently his consciousness of his inability to interest his reader in the singularly commonplace life-story of his personages which has led him to resort to the artless device of making them exchange views with each other on the denizens of Poets' Corner, and the matrimonial relations of Mr. and Mrs. Carlyle. The result is a book, which is certainly quite unworthy of Mr. Conan Doyle's reputation, and which, indeed, considering the sort of work that he has accustomed his numerous admirers to expect from him, is, we cannot refrain from saying, a rather daring experiment on the docility of his public.

Boer Critics on *The Great Boer War*

EDITORS OF *CORNHILL MAGAZINE*

Last winter some copies of Dr. Conan Doyle's book, "The Great Boer War," were sent through the Colonial Office to the Boer prisoners of war in Ceylon. A warm letter of thanks was received, and the suggestion followed that the author would be much interested in any criticisms on his work which the prisoners of war might offer. Thanks to the courtesy of the Colonial Office and of the civil and military authorities in Ceylon, the Editor prints the following expressions of opinion from some of those who fought against the British arms.

The most important criticism is signed by W. G. H. Koenneker, who describes himself as "one of Kruger's Mercenaries."

CONAN DOYLE'S "THE GREAT BOER WAR."

I have been asked to give my impressions of the above work, and have done so with pleasure even at the disadvantage of using a language not my own, because it has appealed to me very strongly and pleasantly. But I must insist that they represent exclusively my personal opinion, given, moreover, at a time when I am a prisoner of war still, and therefore not able yet to look at the events treated therein, either from the broad point of view given through general knowledge or information from both sides, or with the well-weighed criticism exercised over past experiences.

The introduction is a masterwork in its way for the unbiassed valuation of the good and bad qualities of the Dutch race, deducing them from and explaining them by the racial composition and the gradual development and conditions of life of the South African Dutch, and for the brief but clear summary of the causes of the great struggle and the final complications which led up to its outbreak. Yet there might have been still more allowance made for the pernicious influence of red-tapeism and the often displayed incapability of British authorities to adapt themselves to the way of thinking of a people who have gained everything they possess by incessant fighting, are highly self-reliant and conservative, and therefore naturally distrustful against all innovations.

Reprinted from *Cornhill Magazine* #11 (September 1901): 292—97.

Especially their misunderstanding of the principles according to which the British claimed full human rights for the black population cannot be counted high enough as one of the reasons for such mistrust, considering that there is scarcely a Boer family to be found who has not lost, *i.e.* had slaughtered and mutilated, some of its members in one or other of the innumerable Kaffir wars, while, on the other hand, the average Boer is not given much to general literature, and therefore little amenable to reason and progressive ideas.

The healthy influence which the author ascribes to the many points in common between the two races, as religiousness, personal bravery, love for sports, respect for women, &c., was certainly existent but more than counterbalanced by the influence of education which all over the Transvaal and a great part of the Free State was in the hands of Hollanders, who, for the outlying districts at least, were often recruited among a very low class of men of all trades and all shades of morality. Having gained a comparatively great influence by their readiness to adapt themselves to Boer fashion, and by the fact that in their districts they were generally the only men who were in constant touch with the outer world, they did everything to prohibit British influence and a better understanding from growing, because they knew full well that, as soon as those gained a secure foothold, their *rôle* would be played out.

Besides there was the cherished tradition of victories gained over the British before, which in so tenacious, old-fashioned people was a greater hindrance to their acceding to any British demands than any modern European can realise.

A minor point to be mentioned is the weight which the author attached to the great Uitlander petition of '94. Though the justice of the demands raised is undeniable, yet there might be less boasting of the number of 35,000 inscriptions, since the memory of the more than dubious way in which a great part of these inscriptions have been brought together is too fresh still.

For the rest I think that he weighs each party's share in the bringing about of the war with admirable impartiality and fairness, especially in such matters as the influence of Cecil Rhodes' personality on South African politics and other similar ones. In one instance only I consider his judgment somewhat harsh, viz. in qualifying as "wanton" the way in which the Free State threw in its lot with the Transvaal.

It is and will probably always remain impossible to decide exactly by which motives the leaders of the former were caused to prepare an offensive and defensive alliance long before the crisis. There is even a strong inclination on the part of many, who have been able to follow political life before the war narrowly, to believe that in President Steyn's decision personal ambition and the hope of replacing the older and less diplomatic President Kruger in the position of leading spirit of the South African Dutch have played a great part. However that may be, there cannot be any doubt that the overwhelming majority of the Free Staters themselves were moved solely by a strong feeling of sympathy with their brethren in the Transvaal, and of fear that if those were allowed to be conquered by Great Britain, their own turn to give up their independence would soon come too.

About the actual history of the different movements and actions of the war as described by C. D. I can judge very superficially only, since during the first ten months, until I was made prisoner, I was continually with our commander at the front, and therefore unable to gather much information about things which did not concern us directly. Besides that, the author views the course of events from the British centre, while the scanty information we got concerns more the movements on our own side, but the general observations which I have found I can for the greater part fully and entirely endorse.

There is first of all the underrating of the enemy, which was carried on to the same extent in both sides. The fault of not following up advantages gained on the Boer side, the pedantic sticking to obsolete military traditions and consequent waste of blood on the British side, the respective advantages and drawbacks of the two so fundamentally different methods of warring, the difficulty and ever changing conditions of the fighting ground, the mutual relations and influences of far distant actions, are all so splendidly and clearly discussed that for the casual observer nothing remains to add.

But the thing which in my opinion gives the book its intrinsic and lasting value is here again the absolute impartiality with which the author treats friend and foe alike. With loyal admiration he values everywhere the much enduring bravery, the dour tenacity of a people of herders and peasants fighting against the trained troops of a mighty empire, their military qualities developed in the hour of need, and their touching devotion to their country which makes them sacrifice everything for the one all absorbent aim for freedom and independence. And, on the other hand, the gallant pluck, the death-contemning bravery of those British troops, who ever on the attacking side pave with their dead and wounded the slopes of the hills from whose crest the enemy must be driven, yet never look back at the cost as long as the price is won; their stolid endurance when being marched to utter exhaustion after a slippery enemy on half or quarter rations, with a heavy weight to carry under a blazing sun and with scanty cover during the chilly nights—they are related in a language worthy of the subject and illustrated by dates and facts.

Again, when the parts are reversed, the Boers storming right up to the British rifles with supreme dash, or a small British garrison keeping an exposed position, an open townlet, against overwhelming odds with downright bulldog tenacity, one seems to read a tale of knightly time of old and not an episode of our modern century of crass materialism. Surely such books are not written in vain, and will be read by generations to come on both sides.

There are, of course, many things which the man on the other side must find difficult to understand or explain, chief amongst them the insignificance of the losses on the Boer side in many engagements as compared with those on the British side. Yet the fact is there, and even on occasions where the Boers were the attacking party, their casualties were far beneath the author's estimate. So were, for instance, on January 6th in the storm on Ladysmith (Platrand) our losses all round in killed and wounded well under three hundred, *i.e.* less than half as much as presumed by the author.

But on the whole his exposition of the great drama is clear and consequent, and apparently based on much studious and careful collecting and sifting of detailed intelligence.

And now the chapter entitled "On End of the War." Well may the author be excused for his sanguine anticipation of the end, since, from a European point of view, the taking of both capitals, of the principal towns and lines of communications, and the keeping in captivity of about one-fourth of the entire fighting strength of the enemy would indeed indicate that all was over. But subsequent events have shown clearly enough that such was not the case and that the expectation of a final settlement, honourable for both parties, was not to be realised yet.

How all will end we do not know even yet, but it is sincerely to be hoped that the long-drawn fighting will not embitter both parties past redemption, and that those lately employed measures which may or may not be necessitated by the exigencies of warfare will not separate two fine races so far that no friendly understanding or blending may be looked forward to in later years.

In that respect there should be praised, too, the good taste of the author in refraining from chronicling all the regrettable incidents, where the strict rules of civilised warfare have been disregarded on either side. Insignificant facts in themselves and generally caused by irresponsible individuals or by misunderstanding, they are yet able to create more ill feeling than anything else if dwelt upon too much.

To discuss the merits of "Some Military Lessons of the War" I must leave to more competent judges, but I should think that they are at least founded on sound common sense and derived from practical experience. Especially where the author insists on the necessity of giving young officers a more scientific and thoroughly professional military training to temper their fine natural courage and sporting instincts, one would take the author's advice as doubly valuable, since from such a training of the officers all other improvements would automatically result in the course of time.

However that be, honour to the man who wrote "The Great Boer War" in the way he did, while the din of battle was still filling the air.

Ragama Camp, Ceylon,
28.3.1901.

* * *

In addition to this, Lieut.-Colonel A. C. Vincent (the English officer through whom the books were presented to the Boers) summarises some further expressions of opinion as follows:

General Roux admits that the book is written in a most fair spirit, though not strictly accurate from an historical point of view, it being very evident to him that the descriptions of battle scenes are not those of an eye-witness, but gathered from hearsay.

Commandant Runck, leader of the German commando, says that from his own personal knowledge no reliance can be placed on Conan Doyle's figures, or minor details. The numbers of Boers engaged in various actions, the numbers they lost in killed and wounded, and the estimate of the guns they had in action, are all greatly exaggerated.

This is the opinion of the other Boer officers who have read the book.

Several English-speaking Burghers who have read the book praise it as by far the fairest one written from an English point of view, but they question its details. They all condemn Conan Doyle's strictures on the British artillery, and say that the guns were certainly outranged, but the practice of the British gunners was superb, and our shell-fire did much more execution than our infantry fire.

9th May, 1901.

To the last two criticisms Dr. Conan Doyle makes reply:

NOTE TO COMMANDANT RUNCK'S STATEMENT.

We have captured up to date about 20,000 Boer fighting men, and roughly a hundred guns large and small. By no calculation can the total number of their armed men at the outset be placed under 50,000. This large number of men and guns must have been employed, and if I have over-estimated them at one point I have probably under-estimated them at another. Occasionally I have been able to check my figures from Boer sources.

NOTE TO THE CRITICISM ABOUT ARTILLERY.

This is a misapprehension. My actual words are: "In dealing with our artillery it must be acknowledged that for personal gallantry and general efficiency they take the honours of the campaign." My criticism was directed towards their armament and some details of their drill.

Review of *Collected Edition of A. Conan Doyle's Novels*

ATHENAEUM

It is not given to many authors to secure themselves in the warm favour of the public so early and so firmly as Sir A. Conan Doyle; and it is the privilege of fewer still to celebrate that popularity by a formal *édition de luxe* of their works. Stevenson, the collected edition of whose works was one of the successful ventures of publishing some ten years back, was of another quality than Sir A. Conan Doyle, and reached a different level. Mr. Kipling is probably the first figure in the public eye, almost as famous to-day as was Dickens in his generation, and the issue of a limited edition in his case justified itself. We cannot but think that Sir A. Conan Doyle has greatly dared in joining the ranks of these greater names, though in one instance, to be noted later, he has equalled, if not surpassed, their fame. After all, the limited edition is in some sort the evidence of permanence, and Sir A. Conan Doyle modestly wonders "if there are any elements of permanence" in his work. At the same time there can be no doubt in the minds of his admirers as to the value of this handsome library edition. The paper is excellent, the type is large and clear, the size is not too ponderous, and the illustrations, of which there are only two to each volume, are interesting. For collectors there is the additional satisfaction that the edition contains only one thousand sets, and that the first volume of each set is signed by the author.

Sir A. Conan Doyle would appear to be deserting letters for affairs, so that it is difficult at present to judge of his true quality as a writer of fiction. Evidently he began with a more romantic feeling and a finer sense of the adventurous than he went on with. His fire seems to have decreased; he gives the impression of becoming more deliberate and less imaginative, and of attaining philosophy inconsistent with true artistry. It looks as if in his maturer years this ready writer were precipitating in the average British way. He always had an element of deliberation, such as one dissociates at once from inspiration and the "dæmonic" force of art. Yet what an admirable piece of work was "The White Company," which suffered no whit because it was descended from "The Cloister and the Hearth" and "Quentin Durward." "Micah Clarke," too, stands high among historical novels. In the prefatory

Reprinted from *Athenaeum* (9 January 1904): 40.

note to this romance the author writes his own criticism for good or ill: "To me," he says, "it always seems that the actual condition of a country at any time, a true sight of it with its beauties and its brutalities, its life as it really was, . . . are of greater interest than the small aims and petty love-story of any single human being." There speak the virtues and defects of the author. It may be history which he hankers after in those sentences—it is not fiction. And, though this defect pursues him from the outset of his career, it is not until such a book as "Rodney Stone" that it becomes an obsession. "Rodney Stone" is not a tale, but a cinematograph of the Regency period. It is vivid, wonderfully well studied, and understanding to a fault; but it falls short of fiction. The same hole may be picked in "The Stark Munro Letters," which, for all that, contain some of the best material that the author has put together. It strikes one as odd and unfortunate that, with the author's power of visualizing a scene, he should have been, on the whole, so little successful in visualizing a character. He has invented some, no doubt and several of these are in "Micah Clarke." He has also hit upon an excellent type in Brigadier Gerard. But he shows no gallery of portraits; they lack life, but are set generally in a moving landscape. It is some kink in the imagination. The work that has made this author popular is the series of tales, admirable in their way, associated with Sherlock Holmes, a character, as is now generally known, imitated from Poe. Sherlock Holmes has so seized the popular ear that he almost alone of the abundance of men and women provided by living authors supplies a familiar reference used everywhere, an ineffaceable part of the English language. Such impression of a figure on the public is an achievement of the rarest (it is only equalled, as far as we recall at the moment, by the case of Jekyll and Hyde), but in this case it is an achievement which has little to do with letters.

The Novels of Sir Arthur Conan Doyle

ANDREW LANG

If this country's education were conducted on truly scientific principles, we ought to have statistics of the great Novel industry. It is not enough to know how many copies of popular novels are sold; on that point the publishers often give us ample information. From 80,000 to 150,000 copies of a novel that really reaches the heart of the English people are promptly disposed of; and, allowing only ten readers for each copy, the millions are plainly being influenced by our authors of genius. This is a grave thought for conscientious novelists; the making of the spiritual life of England is in their hands. They feel it, and are all but overborne by the too vast orb of their responsibilities. In their photographs, which accompany the reports of interviews with them, we mark with sympathy the ponderous brow, supported by the finger so deft on the type-writing machine; and, as we read the interview, we listen to the voice that has whispered so many thousands of words into the phonograph.

The popular novelists of England and of America are serious men; they occupy at least in their own opinion a position which, since the days of the great Hebrew prophets, has been held by few sons of earth. Now and again they descend, as it were, from the mountain and wearily tell the world the story of their aims, their methods, and their early struggles, before they were discovered by enterprising publishers, before their books provided the text of many a sermon, just as did Mr. Richardson's "Pamela."

These men and women are our social, spiritual, religious, and political teachers. This is an important fact, for their readers take fiction seriously; their lives are being directed, their characters are being framed, by authors such as Mr. Hall Caine, Miss Marie Corelli, Mr. Anthony Hope, Mr. Rudyard Kipling, and Sir Arthur Conan Doyle. Unluckily we have, for lack of statistics, no means of knowing the nature and limits of the moulding of character and direction of life exercised by these energetic authors. Can it be possible that they sometimes neutralize each other's effects, and that the earnest reader of Mr. Wells finds the seeds of his doctrine blown away on the winds of the mighty message of Mr. Hall Caine? Does the inquirer who sets out to follow the star of Miss Marie Corelli become bewildered and "pixy-led," as they say in Devonshire, by the will-o'-the-wisps of Mr. Kipling?

Reprinted from *Quarterly Review* (July 1904): 158–79; reprinted in *Living Age* [Boston], (10 September 1904): 641–54.

The serious writers on "the Novel," in the Press, like the late Mr. Norris, author of "The Octopus," assure us that all is well, that the Novel is, or ought to be, everything; that the novelist is our inspired teacher in matters theological, social, political, and perhaps (when we think of Mr. H. G. Wells) scientific; not to mention that the historical novelist writes the only sort of history which should be, and which is, read by the world. But the pity of it is that novelists, like other teachers, differ vastly in doctrine among themselves; so that, if we read all the popular authors, we "come out," like Omar Khayyám, "no wiser than we went," but rather perplexed in our intellects.

The owners of the stores in America which gave away a celebrated British novel as a bounty on soap, are said to have expressed themselves thus:—

> Our hands were never half so clean,
>   Our customers agree;
> And our beliefs have never been
>   So utterly at sea.

The beliefs of the public may, of course, be brought back to dry land by some more orthodox novelist, but the whole process is unsettling. Yet it may be that the populace, in various sections, cleaves to one teacher, neglecting others. Do the devotees of Miss Marie Corelli read the discourses of Mr. Hall Caine; and do the faithful of Mrs. Ward peruse either, or both, of the other two spiritual guides? Lacking the light of statistics we can only guess that they do not; that the circles of these authors never intersect each other, but keep apart; just as a pious Mussulman does not study "Hymns Ancient and Modern," while a devotee of Mr. Swinburne seldom declines upon "The Christian Year." Meanwhile the mere critic fails to extract a concrete body of doctrine from the discourses of any of our teachers.

Concerning Sir Arthur Conan Doyle, who is, we trust, nearly as popular as any teacher, it may be said with gratitude that he aims at entertaining rather than at instructing his generation. We venture to think that the contemplative and speculative elements in his nature are subordinate to the old-fashioned notion that a novelist should tell a plain tale. A handsome and uniform edition of his works lies before us, with manly, brief, and modest prefaces by the author. The volumes are fair to see; the type and paper are good, though the printing is not incapable of correction, and the spelling is sporadically American.

There are authors whom we like best in stately "library editions," others whom we prefer in first editions—of such are Keats and Charles Lamb; and, handsome as is the *format* of Sir Arthur's collected works, there are a few of them which please us most "in the native pewter." Now the native pewter of Sherlock Holmes is a sixpenny magazine, with plenty of clever illustrations; he takes better in these conditions than in a sumptuous text with only one or two pictures. Sir Arthur is an unaffected writer. His style is not "a separate ecstasy," as in the case of Mr. R. L. Stevenson's writings; his is a simple narrative manner. He does not pass hours in hunting for *le mot propre*; and a phrase is apparently none the worse in his eyes because it is an old favorite of the public, and familiar to the press and the platform. However, like Aucassin in the *cantefable*, "we love a plain tale even better than none," and love anything better than the dull and tormented matter of the prigs who, having nothing that deserves to be said, say it in a style which standeth in an utterly false following of Mr. George Meredith. "The Author's Edition" is a delightful set for a smoking room in a club or in a country house.

By a laudable arrangement, Sir Arthur has confined his speculative and contemplative exercises to a pair of books, "The Stark Munro Letters" and "A Duet." In the former, a young man has his "first fight" (not at all in the style of the author's "Rodney Stone") "with the spiritual and material difficulties which confront him at the outset of life. There is no claim that his outlook is either profound or original." Indeed his outlook is not remarkable for subtlety or distinction. Sir Arthur is not a Pascal; and, if he were, his "Pensées," presented in a work of fiction, would fail to exhilarate. As he says, Tom Jones and Arthur Pendennis and Richard Feverel "do not indicate their relation to those eternal problems which are really the touchstone and centre of all character." Thank heaven they do not!

An eternal problem can hardly be "the centre of a character"; and, if it were, we do not always pine to read a novel about an eternal problem. A little of "Obermann" goes a long way. If a problem is eternal it has obviously never been solved; and what chance had Thomas Jones, a foundling, of solving eternal problems. As for Pen, he frankly abandoned the attempt. The narrator in the "Stark Munro Letters" ends his speculation by deciding that "something might be done by throwing all one's weight on the scale of breadth, tolerance, charity, temperance, peace, and kindliness to man and beast." Having arrived at this acceptable solution, we do not care to follow the mental processes by which the young thinker reaches the result. We have ever been of his mature opinion, which, moreover, has the sanction of the Church, and of the best heathen and Christian philosophers.

There is no speculation and no preaching of doctrines, no nonsense about a "message" or a "mission," in the rest of Sir Arthur's books, where the good people are plucky, kind, and honorable, while the bad people are usually foiled in their villainous machinations. The quality which recommends Sir Arthur's stories to his readers, and to ourselves, is a quality which cannot be taught or learned; which no research, or study, or industry can compass; which is born with a man; which can hold its own without the aid of an exquisite style; and which is essential. Sir Arthur can tell a story so that you read it with ease and pleasure. He does not shine as a creator of character. Perhaps Micah Clarke, an honest English Porthos, is the best of his quite serious creations; while Sherlock Holmes, not so seriously intended, has become a proverb, like Monsieur Lecoq. But Brigadier Gerard is Sir Arthur's masterpiece; we never weary of that brave, stupid, vain, chivalrous being, who hovers between General Marbot and Thackeray's Major Geoghegan, with all the merits of both, and with others of his own.

The ladies who pass through the novels play their parts, and are excellent young women in their rôles, but they are not to be very distinctly remembered, or very fondly adored. There is not a Sophia Western, an Amelia, a Diana Vernon, a Becky Sharpe, an Anne Elliot, a Beatrix Esmond, or a Barbara Grant, in their ranks; and indeed such characters are scarce in all fiction. The greatest masters but seldom succeed in creating immortal women; only Shakespeare has his quiver full of such children as these. In short, we read Sir Arthur Conan Doyle for the story, and are very glad that we have such stories to read; rapid, varied, kindly, and honest narratives. As Mr. Arthur Pendennis remarked about his ancestral claret, "there is not a headache in a hogshead" of them.

We shall first glance at Sir Arthur's historical novels, "Micah Clarke," "The White Company," "The Refugees," and "Rodney Stone." The public is very far from sharing the opinion professed by James II in exile, that "history is much more instructive than novels, and quite as amusing." For ourselves we deem his Majesty's own historical work vastly more entertaining than any novel written during his lifetime; but, in the opinion of the public, history only exists as material for historical romances, just as the engineer said that rivers exist for the purpose of feeding navigable canals.

Sir Arthur's earlier historical novels are influenced, more than he probably suspects, by those of Sir Walter Scott. "Micah Clarke," like Mr. Blackmore's "Lorna Doone," is a tale of the last romantic rebellion with a base in England—the futile attempt of Monmouth. The big Porthos-like hero is, in some ways, akin to John Ridd; but he occupies, as regards politics and religion, the *juste milieu* that Sir Walter favored when he wrote history, and assigned to such romantic heroes of his own as Henry Morton, and even Roland Graeme. Though "a simple-hearted unlettered yeoman," Micah Clarke is really wise with the wisdom of the later Victorian time, and, in one remark, speaks as if he had read Mr. Herbert Spencer with approval, so far as the problems of religion are concerned. He takes a calm view of history, and is no fanatic of the Protestantism of his period—that of Titus Oates. "The mob's ideas of Papistry were mixed up with thumbscrews" (not a Catholic implement, by the way) "and Fox's Martyrology." Micah is the son of a church-woman, and a Puritan, and himself has no particular bent, except in favor of freedom and fighting. "I believe that there was good in Papistry, Church, Dissent, but that not one was worth the spilling of human blood." King James was the rightful King, and Monmouth, black box and all, was a bastard, to Micah's mind; but, as fighting was toward, he fought for the son of Lucy Walters.

Decimus Saxon, the pedantic soldier of fortune, a most entertaining character, with his Latin and his professional skill, his indifference as to the cause for which he draws his sword, and his eye for "caduacs and casualties," is an English Dalgetty, and almost as amusing as the immortal laird of Drumthwacket, "that should be." He is a grandson, as it were, of Dugald's father, Sir James Turner, who was learned, but not pedantic, and a far better-hearted man than either Decimus or Dugald. Indeed Decimus "doth somewhat lean to cutpurse of quick hand." A more original character is the "Malignant" Monmouthite, the ruined, kind, dandified, and reckless Sir Gervas Gerome, so full of fight and foppery.

Rather to the surprise of the reader, at a given moment, while escorting a preacher and his rustic flock of "slashing communicants" to join Monmouth, Decimus suddenly ceases to be Dalgetty, and becomes John Balfour, called Burley. A cornet of the King's Horse approaches the psalm-singing conventicle with a flag of truce, and we quote what follows.

"Who is the leader of this conventicle?" he asked.

"Address your message to me, sir," said our leader from the top of the wagon, "but understand that your white flag will only protect you whilst you use such words as may come from one courteous adversary to another. Say your say or retire."

"Courtesy and honor," said the officer with a sneer, "are not for rebels who are in arms against their lawful king. If you are the leader of this rabble, I warn you if they are not dispersed within five minutes by this watch"—he pulled out an elegant gold time-piece—"we shall ride down upon them and cut them to pieces."

"The Lord can protect His own." Saxon answered, amid a fierce hum of approval from the crowd. "Is this all thy message?"

"It is all, and you will find it enough, you Presbyterian traitor," cried the dragoon cornet. "Listen to me, you fools," he continued, standing up upon his stirrups and speaking to the peasants at the other side of the wagon. "What chance have ye with your whittles and cheese-scrapers? Ye may yet save your skins if ye will but give up your leaders, throw down what ye are pleased to call your arms, and trust to the King's mercy."

"This exceeds the limits of your privileges," said Saxon, drawing a pistol from his belt and cocking it. "If you say another word to draw these people from their allegiance, I fire."

"Hope not to help Monmouth," cried the young officer, disregarding the threat, and still addressing his words to the peasants. "The whole royal army is drawing round him and—"

"Have a care!" shouted our leader, in a deep, harsh voice.

"His head within a month shall roll upon the scaffold."

"But you shall never live to see it," said Saxon, and stooping over he fired straight at the cornet's head. At the flash of the pistol the trumpeter wheeled

round and rode for his life, while the roan horse turned and followed with its
master still seated firmly in the saddle.

Here we have Drumclog, and Cornet Graham, and Burley's slaying of
him under a flag of truce, with his excuse for so doing, all over again; whereof
the author must have been as unconscious as Sir Walter himself when he
annexed a verse by the poetical valet of his friend Rose. The Shirra justly
said that, like Captain Bobadil, he "had taught many gentlemen to write
almost or altogether as well as himself." This English Drumclog ends like
the other, after a pretty fight; and the adventures reach Taunton, where the
condition of that unhappy and pious town, and of Monmouth's scythemen
and other rude levies, is depicted with much fire and energy. The hero, with
great self-sacrifice, hands over the love-making business to a humorous friend
named Reuben, and is free to devote himself to manly adventure. At this
point comes the news of the failure of Argyll; and Sir Patrick Hume of
Polwarth and Sir John Cochrane (whom Claverhouse had prophetically
damned) receive from Decimus the same critical hard measure as Macaulay
gives them. "The expedition was doomed from the first with such men at
its head," says Decimus—with truth; for Argyll, if alone, would have been
safe, though the Lowland leaders, in any case, being odious to the Remnant,
could have raised no stir in Scotland.

Monmouth himself appears to us to be very well designed, though he
was more fair to outward view than he seemed in the eyes of Micah Clarke.
Though his Stuart blood was doubted by all but Charles II, his weakness,
waywardness, and loss of nerve when [the] Sedgemoor fight went against
him, were quite in the vein of the Chevalier de St. George at Montrose, of
Queen Mary at Langside, and of Charles Edward in the first hours after
Culloden. Each one of that forlorn four had shown courage enough on other
fields, but as leaders of a lost hope the terror of betrayal overmastered him.
Unlike the rest, Monmouth was a sentimentalist of the most modern fashion.
A worse commander could not have been found for a very bad cause.

Robert Ferguson is described as almost a maniac from sheer vanity; but
the unique character of the Plotter cannot be unriddled in a novel, if it can
be unriddled at all. Still, we do not recognize him when he speaks to
Monmouth in the wildest manner of the Remnant. "Why was Argyll cutten
off? Because he hadna due faith in the workings o' the Almighty, and must
needs reject the help o' the children o' light in favor o' the bare-legged
children o' Prelacy, wha are half Pagan, half Popish." The terms do not
apply to the Campbells; and Ferguson had humor enough if Dalrymple says
truly that he tided over a day's lack of supplies by inducing Monmouth to
proclaim a solemn fast for the success of his arms. Probably Sir Arthur bases
his account of Ferguson's demeanor on a passage of Burnet: "Ferguson ran
among the people with all the fury of an enraged man that affected to pass

for an enthusiast, though all his performances that way were forced and dry." He would not perform in this forced way before Monmouth.

Micah's personal adventures are excellent romantic reading, especially his captivity in a mysterious dungeon whence the most experienced reader, though he knows that the hero must escape, cannot imagine how he is to do it. Through "The Onfall at Sedgemoor" the author, like Scott at Flodden, "never stoops his wing," for Sir Arthur is a master in the rare skill of describing a battle with lucidity and picturesque vigor. There is no better account of Waterloo, from the private soldier's point of view, than that given in his brief novel, "The Great Shadow"; and Sedgemoor also is excellent.

The picture of Judge Jeffreys may be cited: probably it is quite accurate; yet Dryden admired this man!

Last of all, drawn by six long-tailed Flemish mares, came a great open coach, thickly crusted with gold, in which, reclining amidst velvet cushions, sat the infamous Judge, wrapped in a cloak of crimson plush with a heavy white periwig upon his head, which was so long that it dropped down over his shoulders. They say that he wore scarlet in order to strike terror into the hearts of the people, and that his courts were for the same reason draped in the color of blood. As for himself, it hath ever been the custom, since his wickedness hath come to be known to all men, to picture him as a man whose expression and features were as monstrous and as hideous as was the mind behind them. This is by no means the case. On the contrary, he was a man who, in his younger days, must have been remarkable for his extreme beauty.* He was not, it is true, very old, as years go, when I saw him, but debauchery and low living had left their traces upon his countenance, without, however, entirely destroying the regularity and the beauty of his features. He was dark, more like a Spaniard than an Englishman, with black eyes and olive complexion. His expression was lofty and noble, but his temper was so easily aflame that the slightest cross or annoyance would set him raving like a madman, with blazing eyes and foaming mouth. I have seen him myself with the froth upon his lips and his whole face twitching with passion, like one who hath the falling sickness. Yet his other emotions were under as little control, for I have heard say that a very little would cause him to sob and to weep, more especially when he had himself been slighted by those who were above him.

"Micah Clarke" is a long novel of five hundred and seventy pages; but nobody, when he has finished it, remembers that it is long—which is praise enough for any romance.

In the preface to "Micah Clarke" the author says:—

---

* "The painting of Jeffreys in the National Portrait Gallery more than bears out Micah Clarke's remarks. He is the handsomest man in the collection." (Author's note.)

To me it always seems that the actual condition of a country at any time, a true sight of it with its beauties and brutalities, its life as it really was, its wayside hazards and its odd possibilities, are [*sic*] of greater interest than the small aims and petty love story of any human being. The lists, the woodlands, and the outlaws are more to me than Rebecca and Rowena.

Passe pour Rowena, but surely Diana Vernon or Beatrix Esmond is not of inferior interest to Locksley, Friar Tuck, and the lists of Ashby de la Zouche? "To others the story of one human heart may be more than all the glamor of an age, and to these I feel that I have little to offer."

This is very true, and marks one of Sir Arthur's limitations. He does not interest us in love affairs, or in his women. Fielding could not only give us life "with its wayside hazards," but also bring us acquainted with Amelia and Sophia, whom to have known is [a] great part of a liberal education, in the famous old phrase. In "The White Company" we have lists, indeed, and a scene reminiscent of that immortal passage in "Ivanhoe," where the Disinherited Knight smites, with the point, the shield of the Templar. Sir Arthur's romance of Froissart's age in some ways resembles "The Cloister and the Hearth"; its main interest lies in its "wayside hazards," whether in England, or with the wandering White Company in southern France. The hero, leaving the monastery where he has been educated with that useful old favorite, a gigantic, hard-hitting lay-brother, John of Hordle, marches to join a very good knight of fantastic chivalry, Sir Nigel Loring, and fights under his standard, south of the Pyrenees. It is a tale of swords and bows, and we cannot refrain from quoting "The Song of the Bow," which provokes the very unusual wish that the author had written more verse.

> What of the bow?
>   The bow was made in England:
> Of true wood, of yew wood
>   The wood of English bows;
>   So men who are free
>   Love the old yew-tree
> And the land where the yew-tree grows.
>
> What of the cord?
>   The cord was made in England:
> A rough cord, a tough cord.
>   A cord that bowmen love;
>   And so we will sing
>   Of the hempen string
> And the land where the cord was wove.
>
> What of the shaft?
>   The shaft was cut in England:
> A long shaft, a strong shaft.

Barbed and trim and true;
So we'll drink all together
To the gray goose feather
And the land where the gray goose flew.

What of the mark?
Ah, seek it not in England:
A bold mark, our old mark
Is waiting oversea
When the strings harp in chorus
And the lion flag is o'er us
It is there that our mark shall be.

What of the men?
The men were bred in England:
The bowmen—the yeomen—
The lads of dale and fell.
Here's to you—and to you!
To the hearts that are true
And the land where the true hearts dwell.

The roadside adventures, especially that of the man who has taken
sanctuary, and of the pursuing avenger of blood, are brilliant studies of life
in Chaucer's time; and, though they are many, they are not too many. The
little fighting Sir Nigel, the soul of chivalry, is a very tall man of his hands—
almost too excellent a swordsman for his weight and his inches—while the
very plain middle-aged wife whose favor he wears, proclaiming her *la plus
belle du monde*, is a figure as original as her lord. He is an expert in heraldry,
and, his sole object being "advancement" in the way of honor, he holds his
own in single combat with du Guesclin, though the natural odds are those
of Tom Sayers against Heenan. Like the hero of the old song who

Met the devil and Dundee
On the braes of Killiecrankie,

Sir Nigel "fought by land and fought by sea"; and the adventure of the
"Yellow Cog" with the rover galleys is one of the best fights in a book
full of fighting. Even after "Ivanhoe" the tournament at Bordeaux and the
adventure of the unknown knight seem fresh and stirring; and the unknown
knight, du Guesclin, is quite equal to his reputation, when we reach the
Jacquerie, which was a predestined incident. The siege of a house is always
a lively affair, though the artist does not represent the bald and unhelmeted
Sir Nigel as a very dangerous opponent; his attitude of self-defence rather
resembles that of Mr. Pickwick, which was "paralytic"; indeed he is offering
a tame and unheard-of kind of lunge, or rather poke, from the shoulder at
an almost naked adversary, who "takes it very unconcernedly." When an

archer shoots six hundred and thirty paces, we must presume that the author
has warrant for such a prodigious deed with the long bow; to be sure the
bowman makes use of his feet, "turning himself into a crossbow." Sir Arthur
relies on "one chronicler," criticized by Mr. C. J. Longman in the Badminton
"Book of Archery"; and that chronicler, Giraldus Cambrensis, does not stand
the test of modern experiment.

As Sir Arthur adds historical notes, he might as well name his "old
chroniclers," with their dates; otherwise their evidence is of no great value.
The novel reader, who is terribly afraid of coming to know anything accurately, is not likely to look at the notes, and be frightened away by a name
and a date. "The White Company" is a lively romance, and very good reading
for boys and friends of old times and tall knights. There is a love story; but,
by separating hero and heroine early in the tale, the author ingeniously avoids
a subject in which he does not pretend to shine. The mystic Lady Tiphaine,
wife of du Guesclin, with her limited clairvoyance, is not a success; and the
author has never distinguished himself in dealing with the supernormal. In
consulting with seeresses, "physical contact" is very properly "barred," so as
to avoid "muscle-reading"; but Lady Tiphaine (who has a view of the future
glories of the British Empire) "would fain lay hands upon someone" when
she practices her clairvoyant art. After her success with the vision of the
Union Jack, or the English banner, at all events,

> "It is over," said du Guesclin, moodily. . . . "Wine for the lady, squire.
> The blessed hour of sight hath passed!"

Here the author is more patriotic than imaginative, though du Guesclin was
naturally vexed, being a good Frenchman, at hearing of our superior colonial
expansion.

"The Refugees," a tale of the court of Louis XIV, about the time of the
revocation of the Edict of Nantes, ends in the Iroquois country, whither the
Huguenot characters have fled. The story, though full of life and action,
deals with a theme which does not "set the genius" of the author. He has
not the finesse for a romance of the court of France; and his foil to all its
artificialities, Amos Green, a young English colonial trapper, is of incredible
simplicity. He certainly would not have been allowed to shoot at casual birds
in the streets of such rising American townships as Boston and New York,
and he could not have expected such sporting privileges in Paris. Yet he is
amazed and annoyed when he is not permitted to go about gunning in the
midst of the French capital. He is, of course, very shrewd, much too shrewd
to be so innocently simple, and he is our old friend the useful Porthos of the
novel, like John of Hordle in "The White Company." It is well to have a
character who can open any door without a key, and fight more than the
three enemies at once, whom Major Bellenden, in "Old Mortality," found
too many for any champion except Corporal Raddlebanes. As to the Iroquois,

we know their fiendish cruelties even too well from the "Lettres Edifiantes" of the Jesuit missionaries, and we do not care to make closer acquaintance with them in a novel. The following passage shows the courtiers waiting for the king to get out of bed.

Here, close by the king, was the harsh but energetic Louvois, all-powerful now since the death of his rival Colbert, discussing a question of military organization with two officers, the one a tall and stately soldier, the other a strange little figure, undersized and misshapen, but bearing the insignia of a marshal of France, and owning a name which was of evil omen over the Dutch frontier, for Luxembourg was looked upon already as the successor of Condé, even as his companion Vauban was of Turenne. . . . Beside them, a small, white-haired clerical with a kindly face, Père la Chaise, confessor to the king, was whispering his views upon Jansenism to the portly Bossuet, the eloquent Bishop of Meaux, and to the tall, thin, young Abbé de Fénelon, who listened with a clouded brow, for it was suspected that his own opinions were tainted with the heresy in question. There, too, was Le Brun, the painter, discussing art in a small circle which contained his fellow-workers Verrio and Laguerre, the architects Blondel and Le Nôtre, and sculptors Girardon, Puget, Desjardins, and Coysevoix, whose works have done so much to beautify the new palace of the king. Close to the door, Racine, with his handsome face wreathed in smiles, was chatting with the poet Boileau and the architect Mansard, the three laughing and jesting with the freedom which was natural to the favorite servants of the king, the only subjects who might walk unannounced and without ceremony into and out of his chamber.

"What is amiss with him this morning?" asked Boileau in a whisper, nodding his head in the direction of the royal group. "I fear that his sleep has not improved his temper."

"He becomes harder and harder to amuse," said Racine, shaking his head. "I am to be at Madame de Maintenon's room at three to see whether a page or two of the 'Phédre' may not work a change."

This passage cannot but remind us of the scene with the wits at Button's in "George de Barnwell," and also of an imaginative reporter's account of people at a private view, or some such function. At the period indicated, we need not be told, as we are, that people were not talking about "the last comedy of Molière" or of "the insolence of Pascal." Molière was dead; Pascal was dead; and Paris did not talk for ever about the "Lettres Provinciales." The rivalries of Madame de Montespan and Madame de Maintenon, the night ride of Amos—as adventurous, for a short distance, as that of the musketeers to Calais—remind us of Dumas, and do not bear the comparison. Montespan's attempt to have his wife beheaded is much less convincing than the decapitation of Milady. Here it is.

And thus it was that Amory de Catinat and Amos Green saw from their dungeon window the midnight carriage which discharged its prisoner before their eyes. Hence, too, came that ominous planking and that strange procession in the early morning. And thus it also happened that they found themselves looking down upon Françoise de Montespan as she was led to her death, and that they heard that last piteous cry for aid at the instant when the heavy hand of the ruffian with the axe fell upon her shoulder, and she was forced down upon her knees beside the block. She shrank screaming from the dreadful red-stained, greasy billet of wood; but the butcher heaved up his weapon, and the seigneur had taken a step forward with hand outstretched to seize the long auburn hair and to drag the dainty head down with it when suddenly he was struck motionless with astonishment, and stood with his foot advanced and his hand still out, his mouth half open, and his eyes fixed in front of him.

We think of the terrific scene when Barbazure's head was struck from his cruel shoulders as he was directing the execution of his innocent and injured spouse, for,

> Quick as a flash de Catinat had caught up the axe, and faced de Montespan with the heavy weapon slung over his shoulder, and a challenge in his eyes.
> "Now!" said he.
> The seigneur had for the instant been too astounded to speak. Now he understood at least that these strangers had come between him and his prey.

However, Montespan stabs "his bearded seneschal through the brown beard and deep into the throat"—strange doings in the golden prime of Louis XIV. The Iroquois adventures are more plausible, and very exciting; while for villain, we have a Franciscan, more fierce and tenacious than any Dominican, who pursues a French heretic into the heart of the Iroquois country, where he gets his end more easily than the brave Père Brébeuf.

A more interesting novel, despite the wild improbabilities of the plot, is "Rodney Stone," where the author is on English soil, among the bloods of the Regency and the heroic bruisers of an heroic age. The prize-fighters and country folk may be more truly drawn than the dandies; but every one who, like the Quaker lady known to George Borrow, adores "the bruisers of England" will find this a book to his heart's desire. From the old champion, Harrison, to that Sir Nigel Loring of the fancy, young Belcher, and the strange old Buckhorse with his bell-like cry, all Sir Arthur's fighting men are painted in a rich and juicy manner, with a full brush; and his hard-driving Corinthian blackguards are worthy of them, while the Prince Regent is more successful, as an historical portrait, than Louis XIV. There are plenty of "spirited rallies" and "rattling sets-to" in Sir Arthur's short stories; but "The Smith's Last Battle" is his masterpiece, and the chivalrous honesty of that excellent man would have made him justly dear to Borrow's Quakeress.

The best of the author's tales of times past, we have little doubt, are collected in the volume of "The Exploits of Brigadier Gerard." This gallant, honest, chivalrous, and gay soldier represents a winning class of Frenchmen of the sword, with a considerable element of sympathetic caricature. The vanity of the Brigadier and his extreme simplicity are a little exaggerated; perhaps the author did not know at first how dear Gerard was to grow to himself and to his readers. In Napier's famous "History of the Peninsular War" we meet many young French officers doing things as desperate as Gerard does, and doing them, like the great Montrose, with an air, with a flourish, with a joyous acceptance of a dramatic opportunity. The English officer who captures Gerard, and plays a game of *écarté* with him for his liberty, was just such another as himself; but "Milor the Hon. Sir Russell. Bart" could never have told his own story. Like Thackeray's General Webb, and like General Marbot, the Brigadier "is not only brave, but he knows it," and is not at all diffident in making his hearers aware of his prowess. His fight with the Bristol Bustler is not the least audacious of his combats, though, being ignorant of the rules of the fancy, the Brigadier kicked his man. "You strike me on the head, I kick you on the knee"; he thinks that this is perfectly legitimate. "What a glutton he'd have made for the middle-weights," exclaims the Bustler's admiring trainer, after observing, "it's some-thing to say all your life, that you've been handled by the finest light-weight in England." The Bible, as Izaak Walton observes, "always takes angling in the best sense"; and Sir Arthur takes boxing in the same liberal way. Keats would have sympathized with him deeply, for the poet was a man of his hands, and is said to have polished off a truculent butcher. But the Brigadier, of course, shines most with the sword, and mounted; and there is not a tale in the collection which we cannot read with pleasure more than once; indeed they are so equally good that it is hard to select a favorite. Perhaps "How Gerard Won his Medal" and "The Brothers of Ajaccio" come back most pleasantly to the memory, with the Brigadier's remarkable feat in saving the Emperor at Waterloo.

To prefer this book among Sir Arthur's is as much as to say that we deem him better at a *conte* than in the composition of a novel of the conventional length. This is natural, as adventure and description, rather than character and analysis and love stories, are his forte. He has omitted "The Firm of Girdlestone" from this collection, though we prefer it to "A Duet," where the story is one of young married affection, and there are neither swords in the sun nor wigs on the green. Ladies may write love letters about merinos and alpacas, and "a little white trimming at neck and wrists, and the prettiest pearl trimming. Then the hat *en suite*, pale gray *lisse*, white feather, and brilliant buckle." These things may be written, but the wooer would be as much bored as Bothwell probably was by Queen Mary's sonnets, if she really defied "the laws of God, and man, and metre" (especially metre) in the poems attributed to her by her enemies.

> Not here, oh Apollo,
> Are haunts meet for thee.

We cannot pretend to be interested in Frank and Maude, and "the exact position of the wife of the assistant accountant of the Co-operative Insurance Company"—certainly no lofty position for a bride whose father, we learn, had a billiard-room of his own, and everything handsome about him, at "The Laurels, St. Albans." Francis writes "critical papers in the monthlies," and here is an example of his discourse when, with his bride, he visits Westminster Abbey:—

> What an assembly it would be if at some supreme day each man might stand forth from the portals of his tomb. Tennyson, the last and almost the greatest of that illustrious line, lay under the white slab upon the floor. Maude and Frank stood reverently beside it.
>
> > Sunset and evening star
> > And one clear call for me,
>
> Frank quoted. "What lines for a very old man to write! I should put him second only to Shakespeare had I the marshalling of them."
>
> "I have read so little," said Maude.
>
> "We will read it all together after next week. But it makes your reading so much more real and intimate when you have stood at the grave of the man who wrote. That's Chaucer, the big tomb there. He is the father of British poetry. Here is Browning beside Tennyson—united in life and in death. He was the more profound thinker, but music and form are essential also." . . .
>
> "Who is that standing figure?"
>
> "It is Dryden. What a clever face, and what a modern type. Here is Walter Scott beside the door. How kindly and humorous his expression was! And see how high his head was from the ear to the crown. It was a great brain. There is Burns, the other famous Scot. Don't you think there is a resemblance between the faces? And here are Dickens, and Thackeray, and Macaulay. I wonder whether, when Macaulay was writing his essays, he had a premonition that he would be buried in Westminster Abbey. He is continually alluding to the Abbey and its graves. I always think that we have a vague intuition as to what will occur to us in life."
>
> "We can guess what is probable."

To find a likeness in the faces of Burns and Scott is certainly original criticism. These young married people certainly "do not overstimulate," whether they moralize in Mr. Carlyle's house or in the Abbey.

It may be a vulgar taste, but we decidedly prefer the adventures of Dr. Watson with Mr. Sherlock Holmes. Watson is indeed a creation; his loyalty to his great friend, his extreme simplicity of character, his tranquil endurance of taunt and insult, make him a rival of James Boswell, Esq., of Auchinleck. Dazzled by the brilliance of Sherlock, who doses himself with cocaine and is amateur champion of the middle-weights, or very nearly (what would the Bustler's trainer say to this?), the public overlooks the monumental qualities of Dr. Watson. He, too, had his love affair in "The Sign of Four"; but

Mrs. Watson, probably, was felt to be rather in the way when heroic adventures were afoot. After Sherlock returned to life—for he certainly died, if the artist has correctly represented his struggle with Professor Moriarty—Mrs. Watson faded from this mortal scene.

The idea of Sherlock is the idea of Zadig in Voltaire's *conte*, and of d'Artagnan exploring the duel in "Le Vicomte de Bragelonne," and of Poe's Dupin, and of Monsieur Lecoq; but Sir Arthur handles the theme with ingenuity always fresh and fertile; we may constantly count on him to mystify and amuse us. In we forget what state trial of the eighteenth century, probably the affair of Elizabeth Canning, a witness gave evidence that some one had come from the country. He was asked how he knew, and said that there was country mud on the man's clothes, not London mud, which is black. That witness possessed the secret of Sherlock; he observed, and remembered, and drew inferences, yet he was not a professional thief-taker.

The feats of Sherlock Holmes do not lend themselves as inspiring topics to criticism. If we are puzzled and amused we get as much as we want, and, unless our culture is very precious, we *are* puzzled and amused. The *roman policier* is not the roof and crown of the art of fiction, and we do not rate Sherlock Holmes among the masterpieces of the human intelligence; but many persons of note, like Bismarck and Moltke, are known to have been fond of Gaboriau's tales. In these, to be sure, there really is a good deal of character of a sort; and there are some entertaining scoundrels and pleasant irony in the detective novels of Xavier de Montépin and Fortuné du Boisgobey, sonorous names that might have been borne by crusaders! But the adventures of Sherlock are too brief to permit much study of character. The thing becomes a formula, and we can imagine little variation, unless Sherlock falls in love, or Watson detects him in blackmailing a bishop. This moral error might plausibly be set down to that overindulgence in cocaine which never interferes with Sherlock's physical training or intellectual acuteness. Sir Arthur writes in one of his prefaces:—

> I can well imagine that some of my critics may express surprise that in an edition of my works from which I have rigorously excluded all that my literary conscience rejects, I should retain stories which are cast in this primitive and conventional form. My own feeling upon the subject is that all forms of literature, however humble, are legitimate if the writer is satisfied that he has done them to the highest of his power. To take an analogy from a kindred art, the composer may range from the oratorio to the comic song and be ashamed of neither so long as his work in each is as honest as he can make it. It is insincere work, scamped work, work which is consciously imitative, which a man should voluntarily suppress before time saves him the trouble. As to work which is unconsciously imitative, it is not to be expected that a man's style and mode of treatment should spring fully formed from his own brain. The most that he can hope is that as he advances the outside influences should decrease and his own point of view become clearer and more distinctive.

Edgar Allan Poe, who, in his carelessly prodigal fashion, threw out the
seeds from which so many of our present forms of literature have sprung, was
the father of the detective tale, and covered its limits so completely that I fail
to see how his followers can find any fresh ground which they can confidently
call their own. For the secret of the thinness and also of the intensity of the
detective story is that the writer is left with only one quality, that of intellectual acuteness, with which to endow his hero. Everything else is outside the
picture and weakens the effect. The problem and its solution must form the
theme, and the character-drawing be limited and subordinate. On this narrow
path the writer must walk, and he sees the footmarks of Poe always in front
of him. He is happy if he ever finds the means of breaking away and striking
out on some little side-track of his own.

Not much more is left to be said by the most captious reviewer. A
novelist writes to please; and if his work pleases, as it undeniably does, a
great number and variety of his fellow-citizens, why should his literary
conscience reject it? If Poe had written more stories about Dupin—his
Sherlock Holmes—and not so many about corpses and people buried alive,
he would be a more agreeable author. It is a fact that the great majority of
Sherlock's admirers probably never heard of Poe; do not know that detective
stories date from Dupin, and stories of ciphers and treasure from "The Golden
Bug," or beetle, as the insect is usually styled in English. Of Sir Arthur's
debt to Poe there is no more to say than he has said. Perhaps he has not
himself observed that his tale of "The Man with the Twisted Lip" is a variant
of the adventure of Mr. Altamont in the "Memoirs of James Fitzjames de la
Pluche." The "mistry" of that hero's "buth," by the way, seems to have
revealed in his Christian names, which, like the motto of Clan Alpine,
murmur, "My race is royal." Readers who remember the case of Mr. Altamont are not puzzled by the disappearance of Mr. Neville St. Clair.

Possibly the homicidal ape in "The Murders in the Rue Morgue" suggested the homicidal Andaman islander in "The Sign of Four." This purely
fictitious little monster enables us to detect the great detective and expose
the superficial character of his knowledge and methods. The Andamanese are
cruelly libelled, and have neither the malignant qualities, nor the heads like
mops, nor the weapons, nor the customs, with which they are credited by
Sherlock. He has detected the wrong savage, and injured the character of an
amiable people. The *bo:jig-ngijji* is really a religious, kindly creature, has a
Deluge and a Creation myth, and shaves his head, not possessing scissors.
Sherlock confessedly took his knowledge of the *bo:jig-ngijji* from "a gazetteer," which is full of nonsense. "The average height is below four feet!" The
average height is four feet ten inches and a half. The gazetteer says that
"massacres are invariably concluded by a cannibal feast." Mr. E. H. Man,
who knows the people thoroughly, says "no lengthened investigation was
needed to disprove this long-credited fiction, for not a trace could be discovered of the existence of such a practice in their midst, even in far-off times."

In short, if Mr. Sherlock Holmes, instead of turning up a common work of reference, had merely glanced at the photographs of Andamanese, trim, elegant, closely-shaven men, and at a few pages in Mr. Man's account of them in "The Journal of the Anthropological Institute" for 1881, he would have sought elsewhere for his little savage villain with the blow-pipe. A Fuegian who had lived a good deal on the Amazon might have served his turn.

A man like Sherlock, who wrote a monograph on over a hundred varieties of tobacco-ash, ought not to have been gulled by a gazetteer. Sherlock's Andamanese fights with a blow-pipe and poisoned arrows. Neither poisoned arrows nor blow-pipes are used by the islanders, according to Mr. Man. These melancholy facts demonstrate that Mr. Holmes was not the paragon of Dr. Watson's fond imagination, but a very superficial fellow, who knew no more of the Mincopies (a mere nickname derived from their words for "come here") than did Mr. Herbert Spencer.

Sherlock is also as ignorant as Dickens was of a very simple matter, the ordinary British system of titles. He has a client, and he looks for that client in another "book of reference," not the light-hearted gazetteer which he consults with the pious confidence that Mrs. Gallup bestows on the "Encyclopædia Britannica." He discovers that the client's name is "Lord Robert Walsingham de Vere St. Simon, second son of the Duke of Balmoral"—not a plausible title at best. Yet, knowing this, and finding, in the "Morning Post," the client's real name, both Sherlock and the egregious Watson speak of Lord Robert St. Simon throughout as "Lord St. Simon"! The unhappy "nobleman," with equal ignorance of his place in life, signs himself, "Yours faithfully, St. Simon."

Of course we expect that so clumsy a pretender to be the second son of a duke will be instantly exposed by the astute Sherlock. Not so; Sherlock "thinks it all wery capital." Now would Sherlock have called the late Lord Randolph Churchill "Lord Churchill," or would he have been surprised to hear that Lord Randolph did not sign himself "Churchill"? Anthropology we do not expect from Sherlock, but he really ought to have known matters of everyday usage. The very "page boy" announces "Lord Robert St. Simon"; but Sherlock salutes the visitor as "Lord St. Simon," and the pretended nobleman calls his wife "Lady St. Simon." But do not let us be severe on the great detective for knowing no more of anthropology than of other things! Rather let us wish him "good hunting," and prepare to accompany Dr. Watson and him, when next they load their revolvers, and go forth to the achieving of great adventures.

[Review of *Sir Nigel*]

BOOKMAN

If the inimitable Sherlock Holmes is really dead, we could wish for nothing better than to renew our friendship with the stalwarts of the White Company, to which "Sir Nigel" forms a prelude. It is, in brief, the story of how young Nigel Loring won his spurs and his bride, and of how he first met the incomparable Aylward. There is nothing novel or ambitious about the book; this kind of work has been done often enough before, though rarely with such spirit and gusto as Sir Conan Doyle brings to the task. But after the psychological miasma of much modern fiction of the Ibsenical sort it is like a breath of fresh sea air to find ourselves once more in the open, riding side by side with these simple-hearted knights, who batter each other so cheerfully, each seeking some one upon whom he may "do some small deed." The phrase is quaintly reminiscent of the habit (*horresco referens*) of drunken soldiers, who are said in the expressive vernacular to "look for trouble." Nigel Loring was always "looking for trouble," and rarely had much difficulty in finding it, but his naive joy in his exploits has its own boyish charm, and we are fain to confess that, like Alan Breck, he was a "bonny fighter." Sir Conan Doyle describes a battle with keen relish, and no living writer can paint a more vivid picture of the emblazoned pageantry of mediæval warfare. There is a breezy, open-air freshness about the book, and Sir Conan Doyle has used his intimate knowledge of the Surrey hills to splendid effect. Steeped as he is in the history of the period, the author of "The White Company" is studiously accurate in detail, but he is too good a story-teller to be tiresomely instructive. The story breathes the spirit of healthy patriotism, and there is a sufficient love interest, as much as the normal boy expects and no more. In short, "Sir Nigel" is the boy's book of the year.

Reprinted from *Bookman* [London] (January 1907): 191.

Morals and Morality:
Sir A. Conan Doyle's *Fires of Fate*

"Dramaticus"

Is Suicide Justifiable?

The *Fires of Fate*, just produced at the Adelphi by Mr. Waller, is a play which must have made Mr. Redford's heart rejoice. Here there was nothing to censor! It is concerned with straightforward, manly morality. There is no pandering to cowardly decadent views. It is a play which boldly sets forth that a man's life is not his own to live or leave as it pleases him, but a thing to be lived through, to the bitter end if necessary, because, though no good may come of it to you, good may come to others. The hero, Colonel Egerton, is in the mood to end his life when the play begins, but the Church, in the person of a sturdy Nonconformist minister, tells him nay, and he bows to the Church and has no cause to be sorry.

In the Consulting Room

Colonel Egerton, not feeling well, goes to consult an eminent M.D. That is the first act. The eminent M.D. puts him through his paces—makes him count ninety-nine, hits him under the knee, tests his brain, and so forth, and finds that he has sclerosis of the spine in a form which will kill him in about a year, and during most of that time he will be a miserable invalid. Now, Colonel Egerton is a brave man, but he shrinks from this prospect. He has no ties, no one belonging to him, and he decides to chuck up the sponge. Better die like a man now than drag out a miserable year of existence a burden to other people. Then in comes the minister to say "No. Your life is not your own. Even in that year there may be work for a soldier to do." And Colonel Egerton, like the sturdy soldier that he is, says, "Right."

Reprinted from Supplement to the *Graphic* Midsummer Number (26 June 1909): 868.

In Egypt

So, instead of putting a bullet through his brains, he joins the doctor and his minister brother on a holiday trip to Egypt, and on the Nile he meets pretty Sadie Adams, of Mass., U.S.A., and falls in love with her very deeply. How is a man, though, who will die in a year of a distressing disease to propose to a girl on the threshold of life? He cannot do it, so he adds heart trouble to spine trouble, and suffers in silence. Then the party, which includes several other people, go on a journey up country, and are captured by Dervishes, and this is where the *Fires of Fate* business comes in. Their troubles and disasters bring out all their best qualities. They stand true to their religion, though threatened with the knife or Islam. A young Englishman refuses to make his own escape if the others cannot escape also, and the one man of the party who has a revolver hands it over to Sadie Adams's chaperon to make use of if the worst comes to the worst, and there is a terrible fate in store for the pretty American. But it is Colonel Egerton, sorely wounded, with a crack on the head, who manages to crawl to a rock and signal to a young British officer miles away that they are in sore straits.

The Rescue

Of course, we know that a British force will arrive in time to prevent anything more disastrous than a little privation happening to Mr. Lewis Waller, Miss Evelyn D'Alroy, Mr. Evelyn Beerbohm, Mr. A. E. George, Mr. Michael Sherbrooke, and the rest of the clever company, and, sure enough, it does, led by that excellent young actor, Mr. Charles Maude. He is delightfully breezy, and gives you a capital picture of the best type of young English officer, keen as mustard on active service, but regarding it rather as a form of sport. The only trouble is that a young married couple have been killed. They have been given no chance of being purified and ennobled by the fires of fate, and I should have felt more distressed about them if they had not been so very uninteresting.

The Uses of a Blow on the Head

Now, Sir Arthur Conan Doyle is a doctor, and I have no doubt that his medical lore is all right, so I will not explain how he cures Mr. Waller, because, though a little British army has turned up and saved the tourists, even a large British army could not cure sclerosis of the spine, and while this remains an active evil there can, of course, be no marriage between Colonel Egerton and Miss Sadie Adams. Well, it was the blow on the head that did the trick. When the gallant Colonel saw the eminent M.D. in the first act he asked if there was any cure for his complaint, and was told that the only man known to science who was cured of it found the remedy in the shock of a railway accident. Well, that did not sound very hopeful. You cannot go travelling round hoping for a railway accident, and even if you struck one I should fancy that it would be rather a kill or cure kind of a remedy. What the M.D. did not say was that a blow on the head from a Dervish would do just as well. I suppose he did not know it. In any case, it cured the Colonel, and so the old minister was right. Through not committing suicide he was instrumental in saving the lives of his friends and earned happiness for himself. This is an excellent moral, and as the play is a capital, stirring drama, well mounted and well acted, I am sure it will prove a good all-round success.

[Review of *The House of Temperley*]

ATHENAEUM

"A Melodrama of the Ring" its author styles this play with pleasing frank-
ness, and he is right. It is good melodrama, and it is full, as pieces of its
class should be, of bustle, excitement, and incident. It calls up in an extremely vivid fashion the days when pugilism was a sport patronized by high
and low, and practised by professionals and amateurs prepared to take and
give hard blows without wincing under punishment or seizing an unfair
advantage. The democratic nature of the sport is well brought out in the
scenes which show men of all ranks mixing on almost equal terms, and as
ready, many of them, to put on the gloves as to watch others fighting for
their amusement.

The ring scenes are, needless to say, the great features of the play—
indeed, they are the play; and it is on the realism of such pictures of the
Regency era as the supper party and boxing match in Tom Cribb's saloon,
and the grand encounter fought in the meadow on a Sussex farm that the
appeal of "The House of Temperley" depends. The playwright does not
shrink from exhibiting the brutal side of the sport, just as he does not deny
that there were rogues as well as honest enthusiasts among its followers; but
he also suggests that in the noisy, hard-drinking, wild sportsmen of the third
George's reign, the cult at its best encouraged manliness and a friendly and
companionable spirit.

Only those who attend a performance of the piece can have any idea
how life-like these passages are made on the stage, how naturally members
of the crowd shout and quarrel and cheer, how excited they get during the
fights, what animation there is throughout every moment of the action. Sir
Arthur owes a great debt to his stage-manager, and scarcely less to his actors.
Not since "Strife" was produced have we had masses of "supers" so well
handled, and every one of the four players called upon to box—Mr. Gwenn,
Mr. Homewood, Mr. Reginald Davis, and Mr. Charles Maude—takes to
the business as if he really enjoyed it. Such zest cannot but affect an audience,
and the play obtained the heartiest first-night reception of any of the year.

That there are many faults in the work it would be impossible to deny.
The love-scenes have a strange air of unreality. We are never interested in

Reprinted from *Athenaeum* (1 January 1910): 23.

the heiress who throws over the generous-hearted soldier she loves, Capt. Jack Temperley, and accepts his spendthrift brother Sir Charles, merely to save the honour of the family. The plot in general, too, is thin besides being conventional. It all turns on a challenge which Sir Charles accepts from his greatest creditor, and backs with all he has, to produce a man who can beat this creditor's pugilist protégé; and such story as there is treats of the kidnapping of the baronet's nominee, and his brother's undertaking at the last moment to support his colours in the ring. Would any referee have accepted on the stroke of time such a substitute when bets had been laid on or against the original choice? Then, again, the episode in which Sir Charles's enemy is expelled from his club on the evidence of a barmaid and a self-confessed blackguard is far from convincing. Finally, the epilogue, as it might be called, in which we see the baronet sacrificing his life to save his brother's during the Peninsular War, comes with a shock of surprise, because it is introduced without any preparation. But these are the defects of a good melodrama, and therefore immaterial.

Where all the men do well, it seems unfair to particularize. But an exception must be made in favour of Mr. Ben Webster, who as Sir Charles does wonders with a part that is little more than costume and manner; nor should Mr. Rock's vehemence in the character of the blustering villain go unnoticed. The honours, however, go to the players already mentioned who have fighting opportunities.

Notes on Conan Doyle

ARTHUR BARTLETT MAURICE

I

Entirely too much has been written about Conan Doyle as the creator of Sherlock Holmes, the most widely known character in all fiction, and entirely too little about him as the author of *Rodney Stone, The White Company, The Adventures of Gerard, The Refugees, Uncle Bernac* and *The Great Shadow*, not to mention the very delightful book of essays, *Through the Magic Door*. As a matter of fact we wonder how many persons there are, considering themselves familiar with his works, who will be just a little bit puzzled by some of these titles. How many of them will recall readily *Beyond the City*, or *The Doings of Raffles Haw*? Yet it is in these comparatively neglected books, and not in the Sherlock Holmes stories, that Conan Doyle's best work has been done. Not only that, but his heart was never in the making of Sherlock Holmes as it was in the making of Colonel Etienne Gerard. He loved Gerard for his dash, his daring, and his devotion, and still more for the very human shortcomings with which he endowed him. This partiality has always been marked, ever since the day, in *Uncle Bernac*, he first introduced a Gerard quite as different from the Brigadier of the later stories as the embryonic Sherlock Holmes of *A Study in Scarlet* was different from the Sherlock Holmes of "The Final Problem."

II

Keen as has been Conan Doyle's interest in the Hundred Years War between France and England (*The White Company* and *Sir Nigel*) the Rebellion of Monmouth (*Micah Clarke*), and the court of Louis the Magnificent (*The Refugees*), to him the supreme dramatic chapter of all history is that which tells the story of the great Napoleon and the men with hairy knapsacks and hearts of steel whose tramp shook the continent for so many years. In the twenty odd stories which tell of the exploits of Gerard he has shown us every

Reprinted from *Bookman* [New York] (July 1914):498–505.

phase of that epic struggle. Throughout, if we except the brief appearance on the scene in *Uncle Bernac*, the Brigadier is always consistent. He is lacking in subtle perception, as became a dashing lieutenant-colonel of Hussars of the Napoleonic campaigns, but is by no means devoid of native wit. That he is brave and generous goes without saying. In the babble of his old age he is reminiscently vain of his early physical prowess and personal fascinations, although he is always discreet, and always stops short of mentioning the lady of the particular story by name. There was hardly a corner of Europe in which he had not served. He had been a prisoner in England and there engaged in fisticuffs, to his wondering discomfiture, with the Bristol Bustler. In the terrible retreat from Russia he had found shelter in the carcases of dead horses. At Waterloo, had not the face of history been against him, as the face of history was against Athos, Porthos, Aramis and d'Artagnan in their efforts to save the head of Charles I, his individual stratagem would have turned the fortunes of the day and made Napoleon once more master of Europe.

III

But it was in Spain that Gerard was at his best. Countless there were his performances of dash and intrepidity. To the end of his days he delighted in narrating the story of his uninvited participation in the fox hunt of the English officers, outriding them all, cutting the fox in two with a sweep of his sword, and riding away with the profound belief that the yells of execration at the unhallowed deed were simply shouts of generous admiration. Perhaps as typical an exploit as any was that which brought him into the merciless hands of the Portuguese "Smiler." Massena was about to retreat and wished to apprise another French army, that was seriously threatened, of his move. The beacon that had been prearranged for this signal was on top of a mountain held by the bandit. Two French officers had been sent to light it, and had apparently met dreadful fates. It was Gerard's turn. After various adventures the Brigadier fell into the hands of the "Smiler." The latter offered him his choice of deaths in return for certain information. Gerard had an inspiration. He gave the information and then made his conditions. "I choose to be burned on yonder beacon at the stroke of midnight." Even with the final fall of the Empire Gerard's activities do not cease. In a fast adventure we find him, some six years after Waterloo, on an expedition to St. Helena to set the Emperor free. It is too late. Gerard arrives only to witness strange ceremonies and to catch one brief glimpse of the dead face of the master he has served so long and so well. To Conan Doyle the story of the Napoleonic years is the story of all stories and Gerard is its personification.

IV

To say that in the veins of Arthur Conan Doyle are commingled the three bloods that flowed at Fontenoy and the battle of the Boyne is far from being a mere rhetorical flourish. It is in expressing it in just that way that the significance lies. When associated with his work it suggests the British sturdiness, tempered by the Irish wit and mellowness, and the French *finesse* and dash. It explains the catholicism of his personal enthusiasms, and his unvarying historical partiality whether the background of the story be Gascony during the Hundred Years War, or the Iberian Peninsula, when Wellington was grappling with Napoleon's marshals. Always the dominant note is one of generous appreciation of a valiant enemy. His British heroes who fought at Waterloo never fail in giving credit to that last intrepid stand of the Old Guard. His weather-beaten naval officers who served under Nelson cannot find epithets strong enough to express their hatred of the French and of the French leader. Yet that does not prevent them from being outspoken in the recognition of the prowess of a worthy foe. Gerard himself is contemptuous in speaking of those who are so blind as to imagine that the virtues of valour and fortitude belong exclusively to any one nation. "I who have fought in all countries," he tells us in one story, "against the Russians, the Prussians, the English, the Austrians, the Italians, the Spaniards—against all the world in short, tell you, my children, that the soldiers of all these countries are equally brave. Except," he adds with a touch of gorgeous Gascon naïveté, "that the French have rather more courage than the rest." Mr. Sherlock Holmes upon one occasion imparted to Watson the information that his grandmother had been a French woman. Inevitably, some day, in a similar sudden burst of confidence, he will allude to another line of his ancestry which will carry superbly back to the Irish kings.

V

If a certain famous romance is called a novel without a hero, Conan Doyle may be regarded as a novelist without a heroine. For certainly, there has never been another writer of equal achievement in whose books woman has played so Oriental a part. The name of Conan Doyle conjures up a great number and variety of men, all distinct, definite, sharply outlined. Etienne Gerard swings lightly into the saddle. Buck Tregellis superbly crushes a bore's presumptuous familiarity. Sir Nigel Loring makes a knightly vow. Corporal Gregory Brewster shakes his head and mutters, "It wouldn't have done for the Duke." To ascribe to any one of these male characters the action or the words belonging to another would be a glaring inconsistency. But the women of his books! Is there a Doyle heroine who can be regarded as much more than a marionette? How many of them are remembered at all? In what story does Winnie LaForce appear? Who is the heroine of *The Firm of Girdlestone?* Of *Micah Clarke?* Of *The Refugees?* True, there is individuality in the historical characters, the Empress Josephine, Lady Hamilton, Madame de Maintenon. Doyle is too good a transmuter to have failed there. But out of the Doyle heroines in the strict sense of the term we know only that she is a well-behaved young person, fond of lawn tennis, and addicted to afternoon tea. Perhaps it is enough.

VI

Some Frenchman has said that the most dramatic situation in all literature is where Robinson Crusoe finds the human footprint in the sand. That is an opinion with which a good many of us will be inclined to take issue. To the modern way of thinking it is not enough for a writer to present a great situation. He must prepare the reader's mind to receive it in the proper spirit. The stage must be set. There must be the preliminary period of suspense. The finding of the footprint in *Robinson Crusoe* comes at the beginning of a chapter, out of a clear sky. It surprises but it does not thrill. It was precisely the same fundamental idea that Doyle used at the beginning of *The Hound of the Baskervilles*. To point out that the modern writer made the most of it does not in the least imply any comparison of the two books. But in the Doyle story the reader listened to the strange old-world legend of the demon hound that tore out the throat of the evil Sir Hugo Baskerville. He caught the spirit of the lonely moor, and something of the fear that inspired Sir Charles. He heard the story of the Baronet's sinister death—the tales of the peasantry about the hound and the uncanny sounds coming from the Grimpen Mire—in a word, he was keyed up to just the proper pitch to receive the climax. Dr. Mortimer contradicted the statement that had been made at the coroner's inquest that there were no traces upon the ground near Sir Charles's body. He had seen some, fresh and clear. "Footprints? Footprints. A man's or a woman's?" "Mr. Holmes, they were the footprints of a gigantic hound."

VII

In contemporary fiction one must look far for a more dramatic incident than the rescue of Sir Nigel and Bertrand du Guesclin by the English archers in *The White Company*. Here again the basic idea is one of the conventional stock properties of fiction. It is the idea that found expression, for example, in verse when associated with the siege of Lucknow during the Sepoy Rebellion. Within the citadel, the hard-pressed little English garrison. Outside the merciless enemy. Hope practically gone, when a Scotch lassie, Jessie Brown, wakes from sleep, crying that she has heard the pipes of the Highlanders. The elation of a moment is followed by deeper depression.

> The Colonel shook his head
> And they turned to the guns once more.

Soon, however, others besides Jessie Brown start and listen, and a great cheer goes up.

> It was the pipes of the Highlanders,
> And now they played "Auld Lang Syne."
> And it came to our men like the voice of God,
> And they shouted along the line.

The last two lines may be very mediocre verse, but the situation is one of sound dramatic force. In *The White Company*, the castle in which Sir Nigel and Du Guesclin are guests is attacked by a savage peasantry. Side by side the Englishman and the Gascon hold the stair. There, too, hope is practically gone, and the flames are leaping high, when there comes to the ears of the besieged, borne on the night wind, the marching song of the rescuing archers:

> What of the bow?
> The bow was made in England,
> Of yew wood, of true wood,
> The wood of English bows.

VIII

In a decidedly lower key but no less essentially dramatic is an episode in *Beyond the City*. Again it is an old idea presented with surprising freshness. Admiral Hay Denver, after years of splendid service, is living in comfortable retirement. He learns that his son's honourable name is threatened by the defalcation of a rascally partner. At any cost disaster must be averted. The Admiral decides to sell his pension outright and go back to the sea for a living. He applies at a shipping office for a position as first or second mate.

The manager looked with a dubious eye at his singular applicant.
"Do you hold certificates?" he asked.
"I hold every nautical certificate there is."
"Then you won't do for us."
"Why not?"
"Your age, sir."

"I give you my word that I can see as well as ever, and am as good a man in every way."

"I don't doubt it."

"Why should my age be a bar then?"

"Well, I must put it plainly. If a man of your age, holding certificates, has not got past a second officer's berth, there must be a black mark against him somewhere. I don't know what it is, drink or temper, or want of judgment, but something there must be."

"I assure you there is nothing; but I find myself stranded, and so have to turn to the old business again."

"Oh, that's it," said the manager, with suspicion in his eye. "How long were you in your last billet?"

"Fifty-one years."

"What!"

"Yes, sir, one-and-fifty years."

"In the same employ?"

"Yes."

"Why, you must have begun as a child."

"I was twelve when I joined."

"It must be a strangely managed business," said the manager, "which allows men to leave it who have served for fifty years, and who are still as good as ever. Whom did you serve?"

"The Queen. Heaven bless her!"

"Oh, you were in the Royal Navy. What rating did you hold?"

"I am admiral of the fleet."

IX

If among the many literary influences which have moulded Conan Doyle's work any one influence is paramount, it is that of Macaulay. Doyle has always held that Macaulay could have written a great historical novel. "He could have made the multiplication table interesting reading." True, Macaulay was a great transmuter, and, in a lesser way, a great transmuter is Arthur Conan Doyle. The very heart of Froissart's *Chronicles* went to the making of *The White Company*. In addition over one hundred and fifteen volumes, French and English, dealing with the period, were mastered before he wrote one line of the manuscript. *Micah Clarke*, which dealt with the Monmouth Rebellion, was the result of a year's reading and five months' writing. For the American chapters of *The Refugees* he drew freely from Parkman. To all kinds of obscure memoirs he turned for the building of his perspective of the Napoleonic legend. The inspiration of *Rodney Stone* is to be found in the several crude volumes dealing with the British prize ring when that institution was at its apogée—from 1795 till 1810—and if one would see how the master workman can take inferior material and illumine it with the fire of his own talent, let him read through the stilted and grotesque pages of *Pugilistica*, and *Boxiana*, with the battered slang, the pompous jokes, the abominable verse, and then turn to *Rodney Stone*.

X

Rodney Stone has been called "the best story of the ring ever written." It is that and it is a great deal more. Designed, first of all, as a rousing tale, it possesses a plot that is almost flawless; and the manner in which event after event, with cumulative intensity, leads up to the battle on Crawley Downs, and the interests of all concerned hang upon the issue of that struggle, raising it from a mere contest between two professional bruisers to an almost epic dignity, is real dramatic art. But above all is the atmosphere of the tale. The book begins as countless other books begin—the man of mellow age jotting down his story for the grandchildren that gather about his knee. But the triteness goes no farther. Contrast the simplicity and genuineness of the opening of this story with the stilted tone and the purely artificial style of even so fine a novel as *Lorna Doone*. The England that Rodney Stone recalls is still very near and vivid to him. Again in memory he feels the national dread of the Corsican—"that great and evil man." Again he sees the beacons on the white cliffs, and strains his eyes, peering out over the Channel for the war ships of the tricolour. He kindles with the reminiscent thrill of war, and his heart beats fast as he remembers the tales of splendid sea fights told in the village taverns. Once again he is a boy about to leave his mother's side and his simple home at Friars Oak, to go up to the great world of London, to meet the Prince, and the Corinthians, and the men of the ring, and the officers of Nelson's fleet in the company of his famous uncle, Sir Charles Tregellis. Had *Rodney Stone* no other merit, it would deserve a niche for this character alone. All that history has to tell of Brummel serves only to make him seem pale and colourless when placed side by side with the strange, preposterous, impertinent, yet wholly likeable fribble of Conan Doyle's book.

XI

One day some ten years ago the writer of these notes was discussing various bookish matters in the library of the Liverpool home of the late Dr. John Watson. The conversation ranged from the novels of Balzac to the shockers of Ponson de Terrail, a writer who has been called "the Shakespeare of secret murder." Finally it found its way to the fiction of Conan Doyle. The author of *The Bonnie Briar Bush* was emphatic in his appreciation. "Doyle is a splendid workman. He possesses a wonderful gift of narrative and he knows how to make everything that he reads count. But his books are entertaining to a degree that is at times unfortunate. People find his yarns so amusing as

yarns that they are inclined to overlook entirely how well they are written."
Commenting upon this verdict, it may be said that most persons considered
Ian Maclaren during his lifetime so exclusively as a spinner of tales of the
Scottish kailyard that they failed utterly to appreciate him as a sound judge
of literary matters. Remote as Drumtochty was from the scenes of *Madame
Bovary* and *Bel-Ami*, its historian was a close student of his Flaubert and his
Maupassant. But if Conan Doyle has never been appreciated for what he
really is, the case is far from being an isolated one. It is very seldom that a
man who is regarded essentially as a story-teller is generally appraised at his
real value as a literary workman. For his full mead of serious appreciation he
has to look to a small circle of men of his own profession. To them Conan
Doyle is not merely a writer who happened to stumble upon a character
which has become the most widely known in all fiction. He is an author of
unusual imagination, of fine constructive powers, the possessor of an effective
style, in short, a craftsman to be placed, by virtue of many sturdy attributes,
not very far below the apex among contemporary English story spinners.

The Science Fiction of Arthur Conan Doyle

George E. Slusser

At first glance Conan Doyle's tales might seem to have little to do with science fiction. Indeed, in those stories that deal with the otherworldly, the author appears more interested in occult phenomena than in scientific occurrence, turned more toward the prehistoric past than the future, toward lost worlds rather than new ones. And yet, despite surface appearances, these stories clearly address what many theorists still consider the central problem of the genre: what Isaac Asimov calls "the impact of scientific advance upon human beings." What is ultimately important is to determine the manner in which his works address this problem and to define the thematic and formal configurations that result. The tales in question span, essentially, a period from the *fin de siècle* to the 1920s, a historical moment dominated by World War I and marked by the final extension and beginning dissolution of empire. In them, science is not considered as an epistemological problem so much as an agent of change and movement, as technology. And if then this science, in turn, has become a menace, it is again not to man's perceptual or conceptual security but to his physical existence itself. During this period changing and increasingly violent social and cultural conditions not only give new urgency to the theory of evolution, but in doing so seem to bring about a greatly altered relationship between positivistic science and a natural world suddenly become more than simply recalcitrant, but now terrifyingly atavistic, cataclysmic even. Throughout more than four decades of work in diverse story forms—many like the "lost-race" and "future-war" narrative and the tale of occult "science" considered forerunners of the genre or tangential to it—Conan Doyle develops consistent strategies to deal with the contradictory impact of contemporary science, with simultaneous belief in technological progress and fear of evolutionary regression. This preoccupation places Doyle firmly in the British tradition of science fiction that reaches from Wells to recent writers like Aldiss and Clarke.

Less a purist than Asimov, Kingsley Amis sees as the fundamental condition for the creation of science fictional situations "some innovation in science or technology, or pseudoscience and pseudotechnology." And to be

Reprinted from *The Best Science Fiction of Arthur Conan Doyle*, edited by C. G. Waugh and M. H. Greenberg (Carbondale and Edwardsville: Southern Illinois University Press, 1981), vii–xix). Reprinted by permission.

sure, in the tales considered here, pseudoscience always seeks to cover the supernatural, and instead of mediums and seances we have "psychometry." The technological innovations they describe, on the other hand, are very real: new motors, dynamos, airplanes, submarines. Be it pseudoscience or real technology, however, practical concerns invariably take precedence over speculative or purely theoretical ones. The reason for this is that both science and technology seem to have, for Doyle, the same function: to uncover and ultimately harness the primal powers of nature. To this end, both provide means of actual physical exploration. Psychometry, for instance, posits that spirit inheres in objects in such a way that they may act as vehicles to carry one elsewhere, or even back in time, to the place where they were first charged with the emotional energy they convey. Yet this search to control primal forces can and does lead to an unleashing of the uncontrollable, the pursuit of innovation paradoxically to resurgence of some horrible primitive past. Thus in "The Leather Funnel," a story bearing many similarities with the ones in this Collection, the psychometric exercise summons nameless terrors that cause the experimenter to retreat to his well-ordered present: "I writhed, I struggled, I broke through the bonds of sleep, and I burst with a shriek into my own life. . . . Oh, what a blessed relief to feel that I was back in the nineteenth century—back out of that medieval vault into a world where men had human hearts within their bosoms." Emblematic perhaps of the paradox of scientific "research" in Conan Doyle is the climactic scene of the novel *The Lost World*, too long to be included here, although the collection contains two stories featuring its protagonist. Here Professor Challenger, the archetypal scientist whose very name is innovation, comes to unleash—in the guise of scientific demonstration, as "proof" of the existence of the world he has discovered—a hideous pterodactyl in the midst of the assembled Zoological Society.

The obverse of science then seems to be horror. And again and again in Conan Doyle we see the importance of horror to a genre which Darko Suvin, in a recent definition, claims has always been dominated by a rationalist vision. "Estrangement" in science fiction, for Suvin, exists to serve cognition. As a formal device it is used to generate a fictional *novum*, a new world which must be validated by cognitive means, for only cognition can guarantee such concepts as purposive change, progress, futurity. Conan Doyle's tales turn these terms around. Cognition quite literally serves estrangement, for to pursue rational inquiry or orderly advance, such as the aviator rising step by calculated step in "The Horror of the Heights," invariably leads to an encounter with regressive, atavistic forces that shatter all pretense at cognitive advance. Suvin may be wrong then to place his generic boundary at a point separating science fiction and horror as cognitive and anticognitive modes. What we seem to have, rather, are elements in the same generic system. The presence of the anticognitive need not signal a qualitative shift from the empirical to the supernatural realm, but rather a reversal occurring entirely within natural space, the assertion of an irrational and monstrous "nightside" to the idea of scientific progress. In fact, this dayside and nightside is portrayed with such acuity in Conan Doyle's fiction that it forms, as a set of contrasting images, its distinctive organizing polarity. Loving and detailed descriptions of man-made objects, such as the Paul Veroner monoplane in "The Horror of the Heights" with its "ten cylinder rotary Robur engine" and "all the modern improvements—enclosed fusilage, high-curved landing skids . . . gyroscopic steadiers, and three speeds, worked by an alteration of the angle of the planes upon the Venetian blind principle," constantly call forth nightmare images from the biological realm. The "horror" encountered in the upper air is both "loathsome" and predatory: "The vague, goggling eyes which were turned always upon me were cold and merciless in their viscid hatred." Likewise, the creature Professor Challenger retrieves and unleashes on civilization in *The Lost World* summons from the narrator a series of atavistic images. It has a face "like the wildest gargoyle," a savage mouth full of a "double row of shark-like teeth"; it is "the devil of our childhood," emitting a "putrid and insidious odor" as it soars from the room. In a sense, this monstrous reversion of airplane to flying monster symbolizes what is, generally in Conan Doyle, retreat from the future to the past, from science to myth. What is more, the cause of such reversals appears to be cognition itself, the process of knowing or seeking to know. With the rigor of an equation, the aviator's obsessive search for knowledge through his machine in "The Horror of the Heights" releases the implacable hate of the airborne monster that displaces him. In like manner, Challenger's rational demonstration culminates by invoking the ultimate irrationality, a devil in flesh and blood.

At work here then is a particular compensating dynamic—where technology, mind-imposed order, calls forth organic monstrosity, mind-shattering chaos—probably born in the renaissance of conflict between an emerging modern science and a resisting medieval world order, and representing a psychic need on the part of man to maintain himself, as creature formed of mind and body, at the normative center of a natural world now conceived in terms of process and change. Indeed, a system of compensation is already fully at work in Swift's *Gulliver's Travels*, where the projective schemes of science invariably lead to those monstrous physical regressions symbolized by the endlessly decaying *struldburgs*. This dynamic was given greater amplitude, however, by the accelerated rhythm of scientific speculation in the 19th century, especially by the hopes and fears raised with evolutionary theory, where all excitement at man's intellectual domination of nature is perpetually dampened by vistas of purposeless, monstrous forces called forth by this bold theorizing itself. In this context Conan Doyle's tales, which as "popular" works seem so open to the collective fears and aspirations of this scientific century, force comparison with the narrative mode most probably their true successor—the science fiction film. Not only are both dominated by the same system of images—and Doyle's stories are eminently "filmic" in their structure, based on sharp visualized contrasts—but they are essentially cathartic in nature, affecting reader and viewer alike as rites of humbling which paradoxically do not displace man from the center so much as reinstate him (if in diminished form) in that position. Both modes then are, in essence, antievolutionary in nature, governed not by a complex rhythm of struggle and change so much as by a simpler binary logic reminiscent of the Pascalian "contrariety"—as man rises he is lowered, as man falls he is raised up.

In a sense, the dynamic of the science fiction film could serve as gloss for Conan Doyle's tales. It centers on the constant relationship of man to machine and organism, to his extensions and his origins, to the future he would build in hopes of escaping his biological destiny by using and perhaps ultimately becoming a machine, and the past he would renounce only to have it recur in the most primitive forms to remind him of his median position between these two impulsions. Increasingly, from the 19th century on, organic process has been seen in an evolutionary light as random tooth-and-claw violence in need of control through technology, the construction of a mechanized landscape to replace the natural one. To do so, however, is to invite resurgence of this repressed organic force—in forms all the more monstrous for their repression—through some unexpected or forgotten chink in the mechanistic structure. In the film, in fact, we learn that the most frequent channel of reentry is "dehumanized" man himself, to whom the organic recurs as "thing" from his cultural, racial, or biological past. Thus, within the ordered world of *Metropolis*, the mechanized future city with its upper and lower layers, emerges a parallel structure from the dark Gothic past, also with its upper and lower areas, Rotwang's primeval hut and Maria's catacombs, an inverted funnel through which black magic invades white, then explodes as destructive, organic chaos into the city itself. A recent film like *Alien* places this dynamic on a basic morphological level, where expulsion of the organic becomes the direct cause of its monstrous resurgence. Into the overly mechanized world of their spaceship—a metal womb and tomb presided over by a travesty of the procreative forces, a family unit where "father" is the Company, "mother" the central computer that does its bidding, their offspring the robot science officer Ash—the crew in pursuit of its mission reintroduces a primal organic form whose subsequent (and destructive) evolutionary course literally transforms machine landscapes into writhing living shapes, turns cords and cables into intestines, digestive rather than thinking entities.

If anything, Conan Doyle's science fictional vision is even more restrictive in its depiction of the dilemma of modern technological man. As vision, it not only radically qualifies the turn-of-the-century myth of empire built on technological mastery of the natural environment, on the taming of elemental and racial savagery into institutionalized civility, but also contradicts the world view that sustains Doyle's own creation, Sherlock Holmes, the age's most popular incarnation of rationalistic positivism. Instead we have man cleaving in almost agoraphobic fashion to the streamlined shells he has constructed—the well-ordered world of social conveniences and railroad schedules—in terror of primal forces lurking beyond. Yet in his isolation he must be reminded that he too—both in his body and in the very energy that drives him to achieve "progress"—not only partakes of these forces but even provides, in the act of moving to exclude them, a conduit for their violent reentry into the closed spaces his technology has built. With Doyle then we have, more than simply a dionysian "underside," a total encirclement of fragile human order akin to the landscape of *Beowulf*, where man's efforts are a feeble point of light surrounded on all sides by Grendel's darkness. In most of Conan Doyle's science fiction tales, technology has provided merely the thinnest film of order, a delicately suspended *status quo*. From this plane the least foray into surrounding spaces, each act of scientific curiosity or exploration, leads to the monsters Doyle sees lurking everywhere—in the earth or in the air, in the past and in the future. Only this flattest of presents is safe ground. And it is safe, apparently, only because it is continually reaffirmed by these incursions into monstrous space, through almost ritualistic encounters with chaos that lead to those miraculous reprieves epitomized by the last line of "The Lift": "By Jove, that was a close call!"

And yet, however restrictive the landscape of Doyle's tales may seem, the pattern that emerges from this interplay of basic images—man, machine and monster—is ultimately both complex and suggestive. This interplay suggests first of all, on its simplest level, the ambiguity of technology as a mode of action. For the force that constructs present order by banishing the chaotically organic into the past or the future at the same time provides both the lure and the means of adventuring out of that present to lands that time forgot or, through controlled transmission of spirit, toward worlds to come. The machine then that would expel monsters actually begets them, in both directions indiscriminately, and in spatial and temporal realms alike. In this sense, then, Doyle provides a link between Wells's entropic future in *The Time Machine* and a work like Brian Aldiss's *Cryptozoic!*, which posits absolute reversibility of future and past and offers the possibility that our evolutionary end is actually one with our beginning in primal chaos. It is, in fact, just such a possibility that raises for Doyle a second, deeper question. For technology here appears in danger of becoming a self-regulating process, an automatic exchange on the machine-monster axis from which man, at the point where he ceases to use machines and begins to be used by them, vanishes altogether as active term, becomes at best a passive onlooker or victim. In his insistence, however, on locating man in this otherwise binary landscape as a third connecting term, Doyle not only asserts man's involvement in the process of making machines but raises the question of human responsibility as well. Paradoxically, many so-called parables of technology actually seek to efface the question of technology—the relation of man to machine—by excluding man from the equation through this very act of revealing the machine itself to be the monster. The pivot here is often a concept like "sentience," which delineates the moment when, magically, the machine is given independent will and turns to dominate its maker. We see this sudden, unmediated conflation of poles in a tale like Harlan Ellison's "I Have No Mouth and I Must Scream," where a giant computer "born" of man's hate finally effaces man altogether by making him a monstrous blob of flesh, and thus suspending the struggles of technological man in a juxtaposition of machine and monster as mirror doubles. The same fusion constantly operates in the imagistic configurations of films: Rotwang's robot is instantly transmuted into the monstrous "false" Maria; the Frankenstein monster, spawned of the apparatus in the film's famous laboratory, emerges an amalgam, with plugs on its head and creaking gait, of the organic and the mechanical; finally the gradual animation of the machine landscape in *Alien* reduces man to the role of horrified spectator, unable to reflect that he, initially, built the machine that begat the monster. With Doyle, however, a different pattern of imagery occurs. Here the process of conflation turns upon the inclusion of man rather than his exclusion, and the result is a series of hybrid forms whose position is determined by this common term, a system of shifts built on such couplings as beast-man and man-machine, and distributed along an axis that remains centered in man. Literally, visually, in Doyle man cannot make a machine and loose it on the world without remaining part of it himself, thus through this hybridization marking it as an extension of his will rather than a separate entity. The difference here is subtle but crucial, for man in making his machine does not simply make a monster so much as he, in the process of creating it, becomes a monster himself. Monstrosity here then is ultimately of a very different form, one which visually, in these hybrids, both subsumes and mirrors man's moral responsibility by grotesquely distorting it, by insistently linking the sought-for extremes of machine and primal organism to a perniciously abiding human center. In a sense then this rhythm, at the price of restoring homocentricity, delineates these extremes, and by doing so resists the dehumanization of technology that increasingly marks later science fiction.

This particular mode of resistance is not unique to Conan Doyle, however, but rather places him solidly in a tradition of British science fiction that runs from Wells to Clarke. Let us work backwards from a striking, and very Doyle-like example in Clarke, "A Meeting with Medusa." At the core of this story's action we have the clear formation, become now almost a formulaic exercise, of a balancing set of hybrid forms. The prophesy of a machine future ("Someday the real masters of space would be machines, not men.") instead leads cyborg Howard Falcon to encounter his biological past on Jupiter in the monstrous form of the great floating "Medusa," an alien that ironically resembles this most primitive of earth creatures. What is more, his atavistic terror and fall in the face of this "Medusa"—a literal reversion to the beast-man—renders all the more grotesque his subsequent assertion of mechanically aided superbeing, rising "on his hydraulics to his full seven feet of height." The pattern that emerges is neither regressive nor progressive, for Falcon is as unable to abandon the machine as he is to become one. In fact, beneath a pretense of evolutionary drama, Clarke's shifts in perspective actually reinstate a static view of man as unchanging norm. In its vertical rhythm of rising and falling forms, Clarke's tale reminds us of Doyle's "The Horror of the Heights." Here an aviator exceeds what he sees as the limits set by the "Creator," and reaches the "jungles" of the upper air only to be hurled back to earth by the very real monsters that exist there. Once again, however, the outer rhythm contains an inner one, where the accent has shifted from man meeting monster to man actually becoming one, both in his technological ascension and in his subsequent atavistic fall. The aviators in this story in fact, in their obvious physical love of their airplanes, literally meld with them as if they were mechanical extensions of their inquiring spirit. But as these explorers are hurled back to earth, the body of one, Lt. Myrtle, is found missing its head. In a very real sense then, the being who through mind would become a machine has instead become a monster without a mind at all. Another Doyle story of flight, "The Great Brown-Pericord Motor," transposes this same dynamic onto the horizontal plane. Published a month after the Wright brothers' success at Kittyhawk, this story tells how the ethereal genius Pericord conceives his great flying motor only to be forced, in order to build it, to associate with the crude and brutish engineer Brown. This titular association, on one hand, proves a most unstable hybrid, for Brown's attempt to steal the patent unleashes in Pericord a repressed animal violence that finally destroys him. On the other hand, however, and in contrary fashion, this title suggests that a union of body and spirit may be the proper fabric of human endeavor after all. Indeed, as each of these terms claims absolute status in the story, this union reasserts itself in the most grotesque manner. For just as Pericord's dream of disembodied machine flight is forced to bear, on its first and only voyage, the organic charge of Brown's dead body, so the inventor himself, as one who would sacrifice flesh to machine, discovers in turn that even mechanisms are not immune from organic inbalance, in this case his own ensuing madness: "It is the most delicate machine which is most readily put out of gear." The "flying machine" becomes, as its name suggests, a literal hybrid of organic and mechanical elements, and the final image of a "black bird with golden wings" heading out to sea simply points to the Byzantean nature of the construct, a machine that claims monstrous existence, a travesty of life.

At the heart of this dynamic of cancellation lies a paradoxical view of the machine itself, seen simultaneously as a progressive and a static entity. This paradox is immediately visible in a work like Clarke's *2001: A Space Odyssey*, where the machine not only leads man forward and backward at the same time—the use of tools is also the cultivation of destructive violence—

but also becomes, through the ever-present slabs, man's total environment, the envelope that encompasses and ultimately preserves him. Much the same pattern dominates Conan Doyle's narratives: the machine is constantly a force that moves only to assert itself as a fixed point, the dislocating menace that becomes at the same time man's huddling place, his sanctuary. In almost ritualistic fashion in these stories, machine becomes monster and monster machine, future summons past and pure mind organic chaos only so that these cancelling forces may drive man back to the center, reaffirm that comfortable present which technology has achieved yet fears forsaking to adventure in either direction. In "The Great Brown-Pericord Motor" it is precisely because of these counterthrusts of organism and mechanism, of mind and body, that ultimately nothing moves, that the progress of Kittyhawk is suspended and the world spared the effects of manned flight and potential destruction from the air. And in a much later tale, "The Disintegration Machine," we find the same paradox: fascination with the possibility of change through technology, here raised to cataclysmic power, countered by the desire to reverse directions entirely, to affirm a present unchanging in its power to balance and cancel opposing forces. As a figure, the inventor in this story combines the extremes of Brown and Pericord in one form: below the eyebrows he is pimply, slobbering, hunchbacked, above he displays a "splendid cranial arch." Morally, he is a hybrid of great "philosopher" and "vile crawling conspirator." His search to "disintegrate"—on the high level to reduce solid bodies to pure essence, on the low to destroy London and a political enemy—leads him to encounter the solid figure of Professor Challenger, who functions here less as Europe's leading scientific speculator or as incarnation of man's instinctual past, than as their stable union, the guardian of the status quo. Significantly, he does not disintegrate the would-be disintegrator so much as execute him by tricking him into his machine, which in the act comes to resemble one of those electric chairs that so fascinated Conan Doyle as terrible instruments of social order.

The result is a fictional dynamic that celebrates stasis. Indeed, behind the paradoxical destinies of these technological explorers—be they aviators or inventors—lies a precise literary model, one often invoked in the context of modern science from Tennyson to Clarke, Ulysses, the hero whose fabulous voyage is simultaneously a homecoming, whose travels join the poles we ultimately encounter in Conan Doyle—the alien and the mundane. Interestingly, however, the archetypal incarnation of this Odyssean rhythm in British science fiction is not a man but a machine: Wells's time machine chair. Here the mechanical vehicle, conspicuously opposed to the monstrous shapes it encounters, remains all the while an obvious extension of the contemporary Englishman's domestic immobility, a seat onto which the traveller can "clamber" in safety. In Wells's novel, it is this time machine then which resumes all opposite impulses, taking man to meet the monsters of the future and in the same movement thrusting him back, a dishevelled monster himself, into the polite dinner-table world from which he started. In its very form the time machine equates the going out with the coming home, and frames the fabulous sweep of technology and man's fears of terrible encounters in time in a thoroughly domestic space. This time-space nexus is defined, emblematically, as the returning traveller recrosses the path of his forward-moving housekeeper Mrs. Watchett and reverses it: "I think I have told you that when I set out . . . Mrs. Watchett had walked across the room, travelling . . . like a rocket. As I returned, I passed again across that minute when she traversed the laboratory. But now her every motion appeared to be the exact inversion of her previous ones. The door at the lower end opened, and she glided quietly up the laboratory, back foremost, and disappeared behind the door by which she had previously entered." It is not, then, that we have never moved, or that our movement through technology is a dream. Rather technological man, in works from Wells through Doyle to Clarke, seems to move only to bestow on his own present a sacred, almost numinous quality: Mrs. Watchett's banal trajectory transfigured by its marvelous acceleration and reversal.

The world of Doyle's tales may itself then seem a self-regulating machine, a structure resumable in the very objects, the motors and lifts, that mark their titles and excluding man altogether as purposive agent. Ultimately, however, Doyle does grapple with the possibility at least of some Odyssean being, unifying the contrary impulses of past and future, technology and organic vigor, emerging at the focal point of this triple rhythm of man, machine and monster. Even so, most of his stories focus on the negative aspect of this problem, on that tenacious split between body and mind faced by modern man, that extension of the primal fall of man caused by the scientific enterprise itself. This is an abiding preoccupation that ties together the most diverse categories of tales in Conan Doyle. The problem of the separation of mind and body is perhaps most apparent in his pseudoscientific tales of spiritual transmigration. Interestingly, these function in quite the opposite manner from stories in the occult tradition of Hoffman. For where the latter present (and applaud) the constant attempts of spirit to throw off its material trammels, Doyle's celebrate instead the process whereby the wandering spirit is inexorably drawn back to the precise material object that gave rise to it originally. Some of Doyle's tales are cautionary in this respect, and would show us this: if the spirit in its scientific investigations would wander away from its proper place, it will discover that some other, more horrible, force may occupy that place instead. In the farcical German student story, "The Great Keinplatz Experiment," that place is literally shown to be here or no place. The experiment that would prove the spirit can exist apart from its body results only in a grotesque transposition of minds, which leads in turn to a slapstick of drunken brawls and pratfalls. The implications of a tale like "Through the Veil," however, are much more ominous, for it is suggested here that the ordered surface of contemporary society itself holds only by suspending some deeper relation between spirit and body, in this case between modern man and his racial memory rooted in the native soil. Again it is science—here the archeological excavation of an old Roman ruin in Scotland—that leads to the protagonist's terrible dream and the realization that her present marriage may conceal the barbarous murder of her former self's Roman lover by the past incarnation of her present husband. The savage, twisted violence of these beginnings has not resolved itself in time, but on the contrary remains incarnate in the marked racial opposition of husband and wife, ever ready to erupt into the seemingly placid present. We find similar warnings in Doyle's "future war" tales. In "Danger!," written eighteen months before the outbreak of World War I, technology in the form of the submarine raises dark subterranean forces—a reversion from the chivalric codes of warfare to a Darwinian struggle for survival—to attack an empire built on overextension, the dissipation of spirit, through conquest and economic exploitation, away from its proper roots in the soil of the homeland, now neglected and unable to sustain its own. "The Last Galley," a future war tale in reverse, again places the prophesied decline of the British empire in a general context of the necessary split between the quest to conquer and the pull of the native soil. The lesson here is less the fall of Carthage than the spectacle of the "lean, fierce galleys" of the Roman conquerer, himself now forced to roam far from home, pulled down by the dying gesture of the dark rover captain in sight of Carthage. Here again the bright future is engulfed in the dark vortex that opens at the feet of those who would turn their back on the past.

Doyle's "lost world" tales are similarly cautionary. The difference, however, is that they locate this relation of mind to body in time rather than in space. If in "The Horror of the Heights" man pursues his space flight future only to be hurled back to earth, in "The Terror of Blue John Gap" he seeks his prehistoric past in this dark subterranean realm beneath the old Roman mine. But in his utter revulsion at the incomprehensible, shapeless form he encounters, the modern explorer remains irrevocably cut off from a being less his evolutionary ancestor than his exact opposite, an absolute, detached physical force, the sightless dweller in dark regions the sighted can never penetrate. The story "The Lift" is even more interesting, for it sets this same divergence of mind and body, of dark and light impulses, squarely within the temporal frame of the present. Here, in a post-war world returned to blue-sky happiness, on an observation tower in a mechanized pleasure garden which actualizes the desire of modern man to elevate himself above the primal soil, Commander Stangate's dark premonitions announce the eruption of organic chaos into this well-ordered world. In the figure of Jim Barnes, the mechanic who would hurl this holiday crowd to their deaths, we see an atavistic physique—great straggling limbs, a hooked nose and flowing beard—twisted into madness. Ironically, it is the new perspective afforded by modern technology that reawakens irreconcilable, primitive visions in the heart of "peaceful England." Original sin reenters the garden of technology as Jim looks down at the crowd from the girders and sees "the wicked dotting the streets" beneath him.

These are all tales of separation. But are there any, finally, that explore the possibility of union between mind and body, between man's past and his future? Where such union is hinted at, it occurs invariably in an individual rather than a social context. "The American's Tale" is an interesting case in point. We find more here than just another lost world in the strange "Arizona" covered with "orchidlike umbrellas" and man-eating flytraps. We have instead an odd interpenetration of forces: the uneducated American enters the world of polite London scientific societies to tell of the quiet Englishman Tom Scott, who on the American frontier seems able to mingle civilized codes of honor with an uncanny affinity for monstrous flytraps. Though this story ends with a plea to unite the American eagle and the British lion, this hybrid merely covers the fact that any true fusion here takes place on the level of the lone figure of Scott, who seems to have harnessed organic monstrosity in the service of human order. In another American tale, "The Los Amigos Fiasco," organized technology's attempt to eradicate dark chaos is opposed by the figure of the amateur scientist Peter Stulpnagel, who alone sees that larger and larger doses of electricity will not kill criminal Duncan Warner, but on the contrary fortify and rejuvenate him. And yet this triumph merely serves to transpose the initial rift onto another level. For though he can proclaim that "electricity is life," Stulpnagel remains a harmless, foolish figure isolated from this force incarnated by Warner with his tangled locks and black flowing beard. The one figure in Doyle who unites, at least iconically, these two extremes is Challenger himself, the figure who remains not only his ultimate science fictional character but his ultimate character in every sense. Challenger is "a primitive cave man in a lounge suit"; he is "the greatest brain in Europe, with a driving force behind it that can turn all his dreams into facts." The unity of body and mind found in Challenger, however, is in many ways more bravado than conviction. For his absolute experiment, and culminating act of union, remains, in the story "When the World Screamed," little more than a rape. In thrusting the dart of technology into what he has discovered to be the living epiderm of our Earth, this physical center of Doyle's fictional universe reveals himself to be an emotional child: "I propose to let the earth know that there is at least one person . . . who calls for attention."

SPIRITUALISM
♦

Sir Arthur Conan Doyle and His Spooks

E. T. RAYMOND

It is related of Congreve that in his later years he affected a disdain for his own works, and expressed annoyance when they were praised. Voltaire, visiting England, began in his innocence to congratulate the old dandy on being the only English comedy writer who could touch the skirts of Molière. Congreve replied that *The Way of the World* and *Love for Love* were only the diversions of an idle youth, and begged his visitor to think of him only as a private gentleman. The retort was prompt. "I could have met a gentleman," said Voltaire, "without leaving France."

This precise form of foppery is no longer met with, but many clever men are still afflicted with the weakness of which it was one manifestation. They are contemptuous of their strong sides, and ludicrously proud of qualities which, at the best, they share with a crowd. Born songsters pride themselves on their economics; good romancers talk bad politics; popular preachers slop about in the morasses of Higher Criticism; men with illimitable fairy tales in them argue on Socialism or the price of coal; budding Romneys deviate into all the various lunacies which end in "ism"—and (one hopes) in bankruptcy.

But perhaps the most remarkable case is that of Sir Arthur Conan Doyle. A genuine craftsman, having found his precise medium, having achieved a success as complete as it was deserved, finds no happiness therein, thinks contemptuously of the happiness his art has brought to others, and turns with a sense of vocation to—it is difficult politely to specify what. He is not, of course, to be blamed for refusing to repeat himself to his life's end, like Nat Gould and others. He is said to have become so weary of Sherlock Holmes that he murdered the great detective with glee and resurrected him with extreme repugnance. All that is understandable; some tinge of the same feeling may have affected the most admiring reader. *Toujours perdrix* must be as monotonous for the cook as for the diner. But it is curious that an artist so considerable in the one special line never managed to strike out another fitting his peculiar gift.

Sir Arthur's incursions into historical romance cannot be called very successful. His *Micah Clark* is really a very bad kind of prig, D'Artagnan

Reprinted from *Living Age* [Boston] (3 January 1920): 31–33.

with a snuffle; *The White Company* is far from good company; *Brigadier Gerard* is too patently an Englishman who shrugs his shoulders and says "Parly-voo!" Nor can it be honestly said that Sir Arthur shines as historian or controversialist; for neither part has he the temper nor the judgment. He is, indeed, a rather singular example of the very limited man impatient of his limits, and always wanting, like his own Dr. Watson, to be trying another person's job. Dr. Watson was not a shining success, but his patients did not seem to complain, as Sir Arthur's readers must sometimes do.

What can now be the feelings of those readers over the latest vagaries of their old favorite? One can imagine the devout Doylist wringing his hands over every fresh appearance of Sir Arthur in the character of an exponent of spiritualism. For Sir Arthur the spiritualist makes cruel war on the great legend of the perfect detective. The peculiar charm of *Sherlock Holmes* is common sense penetrated with glamour; it is the romance of the ultra-prosaic. If Watson were a shade less commonplace, if the criminals were only a trifle more out-of-the-way, if the Anglo-Indian in *The Sign of Four* lived in a house less hideously real than the yellow-bricked villa at Brixton, the spell would cease to act. As things are, we are constantly hovering on the verge of skepticism and anti-climax when the requisite touch of natural stupidity or commonness assures us that it is all real, that we are veritably there in the frowsy suburban garden or the dusty attic, watching with Watson's own bewilderment the seeming irrelevances of the great consulting detective, or sharing his prejudice against the perky cocksureness of the regular man from Scotland Yard. Sherlock Holmes would be incredible if he ever deviated by a hair's-breadth from his line of inference from observation, if coincidence ever came to his help, if (in short) he were not always merely the personification of common sense, while Watson, his foil, is the personification of common stupidity.

Sir Arthur Conan Doyle, in his new character, is the exact opposite of his creation. Instead of common sense penetrated with glamour, we have here the wildest mysticism tamed down and vulgarized by a dreadful ordinariness. In the detective stories we do feel with a shudder that No. 10 Endymion Terrace, with its smug suburban front and its bow-window with an india rubber plant in a ten-and-sixpenny vase, is authentically one with Tophet; in the spiritualistic expositions we are made to feel that Paradise is very like, say, the Hampstead Garden Suburb, full of gramophones and Cockney jokers, with a sprinkling of superior persons.

Sir Arthur Conan Doyle describes it all much as if he had just returned from a week-end. "Happy circles," he says, "live in pleasant homesteads, with every nicety of beauty and of music. Beautiful gardens, lovely flowers, green woods, domestic pets—all these things are fully described in the messages of pioneer travelers who have at last got news back to those who linger in the old dingy home." There are no tiresome laws against divorce at will such as rouse Sir Arthur's indignation here below. The sullen husband

and the flighty wife are no longer the plague of their innocent partners, but find suitable "arrangements" for their happiness. The craftsman still labors at his job, but "for the joy of the work"—and one hopes his work gives joy to others. One hopes so, but there are obvious difficulties. For example, the joy of Mr. George Robey in his craft might mar the joy of Dr. Clifford. The joy of a critic of Sir Arthur Conan Doyle might not give joy to Sir Arthur Conan Doyle himself; if it did, the critic would have no joy, for what is the use of criticizing if the criticized, like the people in *Princess Ida*, "votes you quite delightful"? Sir Arthur apparently appreciates smoke and drink, for, according to him, there will be the "equivalents" of alcohol and tobacco in the Elysian fields. But will the shades of Sir Wilfrid Lawson and Mr. "Pussyfoot" Johnson be quite happy in such circumstances?

The description need not be continued, though it goes into much monstrous detail. Sir Arthur claims to have abolished, on the evidence of the mediums, the idea of "a grotesque hell and a fantastic Heaven." But his notion of evidence is a little different from that accepted in the King's Bench. For example, he states most confidently that early Christianity was simply spiritualism, and that the Founder of the Christian religion was the "most powerful medium the world has ever seen," who chose his disciples not because they were good or cultured but for their "psychic powers." "I am convinced," he says, as if that were an end of it. Yet he denounces as bigotry, narrow-minded obstinacy, and much else the convictions of the "orthodox"; the dogmas of Christianity, he says, "matter little," and have "added needlessly to the contentions of the world"; and he sweeps aside as of no account "all the haggling claims and the mythical doctrines which have grown up around the name of Christ."

When good Dr. Watson waxed too impossibly obtuse, Sherlock Holmes used to rally him with a "Really, my dear Watson." Is there nobody to bring up Dr. Watson's creator with a friendly remonstrance of the same kind? It appears to be called for.

Conan Doyle, Spiritualist, on Tour
[Review of *The Wanderings of a Spiritualist*]

JOSEPH JASTROW

The charitable treatment of this mission would be that of silence; and this the author would resent as an unwarranted condescension. A disrespectful critic, sampling the pages, put the book down with the comment, "Maunderings of a spiritualist." However ready to take the challenge of the volumes seriously, the responsible critic returns to it again and again as a pathetic human document. It is not the author's conviction of the return of the departed, revealed through the questionable performances of mediums, that forms the stumbling block to the respectful attention that one would extend to Sir Arthur Conan Doyle, M.D., but the puerile (or is it senile?) credulity that pervades the pages, and a curious combination of personal vanity and provincial prepossession. This it is that betrays the ineptness of his mind in the affairs of logic and psychology. The volume tells the story of the strange case of Conan Doyle.

The temper in which the propagandist pilgrimage to Australia was undertaken appears in the ceremony of a visit to a medium just before sailing. "I had the joy of a few last words with my arisen son, who blessed me on my mission and assured me that I would indeed bring solace to bruised hearts. The words he uttered were a quotation from my London speech at which Powell [the medium] had not been present, nor had the verbatim account of it appeared anywhere at that time. It was one more sign of how closely our words and actions are noted from the other side."

The tour through Australia is described as a triumphant enterprise, with crowded audiences, enthusiastic receptions, and acceptable box-office receipts, all devoted to the "cause." One doubts neither the sincerity nor the ability of the gifted advocate; but the ardor of a zealot, being so largely an emotional attitude, weakens the keenness of perception, alike of logic and fact. Sir Arthur was aware of the prevalent attitude which his statements aroused, but listened mainly to the approving words of his fellow believers.

"I was welcome enough as an individual, but by no means so as an emissary, and both the Churches and the Materialists, in most unnatural combination, had done their best to make the soil stony for me." The *Argus*

Reprinted from *Independent* [New York] (29 April 1922): 416, 418.

of Melbourne regarded the distinguished visitor as representing "a force which we believe to be purely evil"; another reported "the one thing clear is that Sir Conan Doyle's mission to Australia was a mournful and complete failure, and it has left him in a very exasperated state of mind." "My psychic photographs, which are the most wonderful collection ever shown in the world, were received in absolute silence by the whole press, though it is notorious that if I had come there with a comic opera or bedroom comedy instead of with the evidence of a series of miracles, I should have had a column." The papers, "timid as rabbits," were put down as examples of "reactionary intolerance."

What anyone in Sir Arthur's frame of mind—it matters little whether the mind is trained or untrained, with distinguished achievements or without them—persistently fails to understand is that his "miracles" are tainted with the suspicion of gross fraud in some instances, subtle delusion in others, logical misinterpretation in still others, and intensive prepossession through-out. What the critical reader or auditor looks for and listens for is the logical temper of the propagandist. He learns it by noting that Sir Arthur is as ready to credit discredited mediums as those sincerely contributing their personal revelations. A versatile medium by [the] name of Bailey produces "spirit hands," and from the same spiritual source birds and birds' eggs and birds' nests, Assyrian tablets, and what not. Sir Arthur admits that "there was a disturbing suggestion of cuffs about those luminous hands"; that the Assyrian tablets were forgeries, and that Bailey lied. But we are asked to remember that "to the transporting agency it is at least possible that the forgery, steeped in recent human magnetisms, is more capable of being handled than the original taken from a mound"; that "physical mediumship has no connection one way or the other with personal character, any more than the gift of poetry"; and that despite the exposures Sir Arthur "cannot doubt that he (Bailey) has been a great apport medium," who has a record of bringing from the "beyond" "eighty-seven ancient coins (mostly of Ptolemy), eight live birds, eighteen precious stones . . . seven inscribed Babylonian tablets, one Egyptian scarabaeus, an Arabic newspaper, a leopard skin, four nests," and many other things, including a "young live shark." It seems to Sir Arthur "perfect nonsense to talk about these things being the result of trickery," just as it seems quite as perfect nonsense to the rest of us to talk about them as being anything else.

Sir Arthur's credulity is staggering. He still believes that the fairies whose photographs (showing the marks of the shears) he published are as "genuine" as his other psychic photographs forming the protocol of the "Society for the Study of Supernormal Pictures"; he believes that by their "clairvoyant gifts" mediums can see as much as is revealed to merely medical eyes by X-rays and laryngoscopes; he believes that when restless and sleepless a special providence sent "a very distinct pungent smell of ether, coming in waves from outside" to calm his excited nerves; he believes that a similar miracle was performed in his behalf upon mosquitoes. "I prayed that my face would be spared" and "though my hands were like boxing-gloves and my neck all swollen, there was not a mark upon my face." He believes that a "psychic" dog had all the prodigious mathematical gifts attributed to him, "though age and excitement had now impaired them," and showed a knowing excitement in meeting so distinguished a fellow "psychic"; he believes in "ectoplasm," materialization, voices and usages from the beyond, and regards critical investigations as "fantastic precautions." To such a frame of mind ordinary argument loses its meaning; but the question of the defensive logic of prepossession remains.

Reliance is placed on photographs described as "almost too overwhelming for immediate propaganda purposes," which only when maturely considered bring the sense of "final proof . . . which no one with the least sense for evidence could reject. But the sense for evidence is not, also, a universal human quality." Unfortunately, true. But until the conditions under which these photographs were taken are minutely examined their "evidential" value of the thesis which they are made to support is precisely that of the proof that John Smith committed a murder, for here is a photograph of the place in which he did it; and photographs do not lie. They do not; but what truth they tell is not easily determined. On the other hand it is not the interpretation of evidence alone but the reliance upon fallacies that riddles the argument. "One positive result must always outweigh a hundred negative ones." It only needs one single case of spirit return to be established, and there is no more to be said. "How absurd is the position of those wiseacres who say 'nine-tenths of the phenomena are fraud.' Can they not see that if they grant us one-tenth, they grant us our whole contention?" Arguments of this kind are submitted to sophomores in courses on logic to cut their logical teeth on. In ordinary affairs of witness and evidence when 90 per cent is perjury, few juries trouble about the rest. But whether such supports function as real props to faith or as Freudian compensations, one cannot say.

For here we return to the pith of the problem. The spirit belief as advocated by Conan Doyle is a religious consolation; as such one would show it the respect of silence. But when the author of "The New Revelation" points to ectoplasm on the screen in one address and offers messages to the bereaved in another, the critic is at a loss to know what his duty in the matter may be. He must interpret it by his individual sense of responsibility. At the moment when Sir Arthur is bringing the same message to the United States and Canada, and is again speaking to crowded houses, it seems necessary to set forth in plain language the nature of the man and his message under the critical scrutiny of a scientific logic and a modern psychology.

It Seems to Heywood Broun

HEYWOOD BROUN

Of the author's early upbringing I know nothing, which is on the whole a help rather than a handicap, since it permits the amateur psychiatrist to speak freely. Accordingly, it is my guess that Sir Arthur did not like his father much and set about in later years to create one closer to the heart's desire. Sherlock Holmes is superbly the father image. His equipment consists of all wisdom, all courage, and all strength. No problem ever defied the wit of the big man in Baker Street. Men and women, heavy laden with perplexities, called at his door and found comfort. Even when death hissed all about them, Holmes needed no more than a few cigar ashes and, perhaps, some dry, caked mud, to find a pathway out of peril. Conan Doyle is himself a ruddy giant, and even so I hazard the opinion that he has found much in life to give him pause and panic. For his own purposes of relief he conjured up the helpful Holmes and it was a public benefaction to give this character to the world. Toward all of us who quaked and shivered when stairways creaked and strong winds blew, Holmes served as anti-bogey.

There is a tragic incompleteness in graven images. The ancient prohibition against these likenesses to be found in heaven, earth, and water still holds true. Anybody with a fair degree of imagination can make a god for himself and one eminently satisfactory for short hauls. But it is hard to cherish home-brew idols. So in those early days when Conan Doyle was fashioning the hero Holmes, the writer of detective fiction was already moving upon the first stage of a longer pilgrimage. If we had been wise enough we might have known that Sir Arthur was on his way to God. Most logically a belief in spiritism grows out of a faith and fondness for Sherlock Holmes. There is a wisdom in the psychology of that church which gives its members saints and martyrs as Indian clubs by means of which one may acquire a muscular Christianity capable of sustaining more weighty dogma.

I have no patience with those who sneer at Conan Doyle's preoccupation with mediums and ectoplasm. Once I heard him talk about his experiences with psychic phenomena and I was singularly unconvinced by his testimony. All I accepted was his sincerity. Still, it is no part of Sir Arthur's job to find a philosophy in which I may find peace and comfort. Since he has gained

Excerpted and reprinted from *The Nation* (21 September 1927): 277.

ease of mind for himself, and very likely for others, he would be a fool to drop the matter because of jibes from the side lines. Only one thing I hold against Conan Doyle. It is no kindly service which he performs in publicly exhibiting the bones of Sherlock Holmes. A gulf has been set up between the detective and his creator. Doyle has averted his face from the rooms in Baker Street. His mind is now engrossed with other themes which may be more important.

"Over There": Arthur Conan Doyle and Spiritualism

JEFFREY L. MEIKLE

Arthur Conan Doyle amazed his readers and casual acquaintances with an announcement in October 1916 of his conversion to spiritualism, a religion based on communication with spirits of the dead. The creator of Sherlock Holmes had previously seemed so "solid,"[1] his prose so blunt and workmanlike. Perhaps he had grown senile or had succumbed to grief over the war deaths of those close to him. Only two years earlier he had expressed a desire to devote his remaining years "to some serious literary or historical work,"[2] and no one, including Doyle himself, had expected him to engage in a vigorous campaign in the cause of spiritualism. Yet his interest in psychic phenomena was hardly sudden. As he insisted in his own defense, he had for thirty years investigated table rappings, hauntings, materialization, and thought transference.

Born in the year of *The Origin of Species*, Doyle rebelled against his family's Roman Catholicism, his apostasy made easier by his mother's merely nominal faith. He hated his Jesuit secondary school and renounced the career in art traditional in his family. Instead he entered upon a medical education at Edinburgh, where he found time also for immersion in the works of Huxley, Spencer, and Mill. For a period a professed agnostic, Doyle wrote his mother from school that he had attended a "capital" lecture by a Boston spiritualist on the topic, "Does Death end all?", and had found it "a very clever thing, indeed," but in the end "not convincing."[3]

Even so, Doyle was never a militant skeptic. The protagonist of his *Stark Munro Letters*—which fictionalize his early experiences as a struggling physician—finds Catholic theology to be "somewhere about the Early Pliocene," but concludes quite amicably that "religion is a vital living thing, still growing and working, capable of endless extension and development. . . ."[4] Like many another scientifically-inclined late Victorian, Doyle hoped to bring religion into accord with empirical evidence, or better yet to provide new evidence as substantiation of religious belief. Although Thomas Huxley refused on principle to attend a spiritualist seance, men nearly as

Reprinted from *The Library Chronicle of the University of Texas at Austin* n.s. #8 (1974): 23–37. Reprinted by permission.

eminent, among them William Crookes, Oliver Lodge, and Alfred Wallace, sought out the strongest sort of new evidence—proof of the soul's survival of physical death. Such scientifically-trained investigators measured forces exerted by spirits in seance rooms, ascertained unmistakable physiological changes in the bodies of mediums, and photographed materialized spirits under conditions which seemed to exclude fraud.

Inspired by reports of experiments by the newly-organized Society for Psychical Research, Doyle in 1882 joined Stanley Ball, an architect and fellow resident of Southsea, in attempts at thought transference, with Ball reproducing diagrams drawn by Doyle in an adjoining room. Four years later Doyle participated in table-tipping seances with an eccentric astronomer, Alfred Wilks Drayson, who supported a catastrophist theory of geology. But the young physician, still cautious, concluded that "our wills were concerned in bringing down the leg at the right moment."[5] A more convincing session, in which a trance medium advised Doyle not to bother reading a book he had been considering privately, prompted him to write a letter on telepathy to the spiritualist journal *Light*, published in July of 1887.

This was the beginning of his serious involvement with that publication, which, as Doyle's account books show, received from him contributions totaling £4,250 over a seventeen-month period from 1896 to 1898, when his annual income was about £12,000. Earlier, in December 1893, Doyle had joined the Society for Psychical Research, but his contributions to it, consisting only of annual subscription fees, reflect his disillusionment with its increasing conservatism and scientific caution as it sought to maintain respectability.[6] In 1894 Doyle satirized the SPR approach with a fictional professor who had "lectured, read papers, convened meetings, exposed a medium, conducted a series of experiments on thought transference," and who in so doing had "lost sight of human beings." Rejecting the idea that everything was "a case and a phenomenon," Doyle apparently desired his funding of *Light* to help produce the empirical evidence he required for belief.[7]

A coincidence brought Doyle and the physicist Oliver Lodge together in 1902. While waiting in an anteroom to be knighted, they "plunged at once into psychic talk"—Lodge the more positive of the two, but Doyle by his own account "quite sure about the truth of the phenomena, and only doubtful whether some alternative explanation might be found for a discarnate intelligence as the force at the back of them."[8]

When time permitted Doyle continued to read spiritualist literature and to investigate mediums. Sometime after the turn of the century he shelled out 10/6 to attend a seance at which "a big Afghan [was] one of the appearing materialisations," but he confessed to "grave doubts of their honesty."[9] His wife's death in 1906 might have triggered a conversion, but his second wife Jean Leckie, whom he married the following year, discouraged his interest—until she too had reason for concern, after her brother Malcolm's death at Mons, where soldiers reported seeing angelic hosts battling in the clouds.

Doyle conceived of the Great War as a spiritual conflict between forces beyond human comprehension in which the armies of Europe were mere pawns.[10] Early in the war Lily Loder-Symonds, the family's governess, lost three brothers, and Doyle eventually lost a son and a brother. When Lily developed the power of automatic writing and produced messages purporting to come from the spirit of Malcolm Leckie, the Doyles were converted to spiritualism. Not only did she provide proof of survival, since the messages contained information verified only later, but as a trusted member of the family her honesty was beyond question, unlike that of professional mediums. The former agnostic finally embraced a religion founded, as he supposed, on empirical evidence. To retreat now, he informed a friend, would be "like getting into a box & shutting the lid."[11]

After his public statement of belief Doyle began to lecture on spiritualism and was never free of speaking engagements. In his study hung a map of Great Britain on which he marked the towns that had received his message, and his correspondence reveals nearly a hundred spiritualist groups whose invitations he refused for lack of time. Those who heard him, whether in spiritualist churches or public auditoriums, learned of the religious significance of spirit communications.[12] Traditional seances, consisting of physical manifestations or evidential messages from deceased relatives, were valuable only for verifying scientifically the reality of survival. At that point, Doyle thought, an earnest inquirer should turn from the sensationalism of the seance room to study the increasing number of revelations from automatic writers and trance speakers concerning the afterlife. These mental mediums portrayed a universe of concentric spheres, each on a spiritually more refined plane, through which the soul of every human being was progressing toward a meeting with the divinity. Since most accounts agreed in major details, Doyle concluded that the general outline must be accurate and that the spiritual manifestations of the war years were a "new revelation" inaugurating a dispensation to replace that of the Christian era.

Following an article of Doyle's on psychic subjects in May 1917, Lodge wrote to thank him for his support. "It is a good thing that somebody of importance lets himself go every now and then. In these days of heavy artillery that is the only way to progress, the long-standing entrenchments of prejudice cannot otherwise be broken down." The new crusader himself thought public apathy toward spiritualism "a challenge to our manhood to attack and ever attack in the same bulldog spirit with which Foch faced the German lines."[13]

Doyle saw his work as a sacred mission and discussed the new faith with anyone who would listen. On 5 October 1918, shortly before the armistice, an unidentified officer wrote, regretting having missed dinner with the Doyles. He "had looked forward so much to a further chat about spiritualism, especially after the somewhat astounding results of our first effort in automatic writing." Jean Doyle by this time had "developed" as a medium, and her "description of life Over There" took "all the horror away from getting killed." Parents of soldiers slain in battle besieged Doyle with requests for aid in contacting their sons. Usually he advised them to pray, to attempt automatic writing on their own, and to consult Annie Brittain, his favorite trance speaker. In a special folder he kept letters from those who had seen her, with the notation "success" or "failure" in the upper-left corner. Apparently he still sought statistical confirmation of his belief, but any remaining doubts must have crumbled when accommodating mediums provided him with supportive messages in order to hold their famous convert.

On one occasion his son Kingsley's spirit came through in a childish scrawl, rejoicing over the "Christ like message you are giving to the World," and William T. Stead's spirit described Doyle's work as "the Review of Divine Reviews." Stead had "looked into the eyes of the Christ with Cecil Rhodes by my side and he said tell Arthur that his work on Earth is holy and divine—that his Message is Mine. . . ."

Accustomed to suffering much good-natured ribbing, as when a railway agent preparing an American itinerary wrote him "in connection with your intended trip to the other side,"[14] Doyle was slow to grasp the dangers of more malicious pranks. Around 1920 he began to exhibit slides made from spirit photographs sent him by sympathizers, as dramatic and conclusive evidence of survival. A few embarrassing incidents of fraud caused Doyle to investigate more carefully the many prints which arrived in his mail. One of these, sent in 1927 by a New Jersey school girl, purported to be a photograph of her brother's spirit taken in a workshop where he had ground lenses for homemade telescopes. Investigation revealed a hoax concocted to discredit Doyle by Albert G. Ingalls, an assistant editor of the *Scientific American* and later the author of several handbooks on amateur telescopes.[15]

More often Doyle's critics did not have to bother tricking him. During what he called "one of the most remarkable" sittings of his life,[16] a succession of variously shaped and costumed spirits entered a seance room from a curtained hallway with "small lockers" along the sides and rear door that was "wired up." When one of the spirits exhibited "the general outline of head and shoulders" of his mother, Doyle cried out, "Is it you, mother?" Taking her cue, she "danced up and down in an ecstasy of delight," leaving her son to arrive at the ambiguous conclusion that there was "no doubt in my mind that the form had reproduced my mother, though I admit that the effect was not an absolutely certain one. . . ."

Eventually vacillation gave way to a more pronounced credulity, as Doyle became no longer concerned with scientific evidence except as a rhetorical device for winning converts. He and Lodge never broke off relations, but their paths diverged. Lodge came to defend the SPR as the "right wing" necessary to convince the "hostile and suspicious" scientific establishment, while Doyle advised inquirers to join instead J. Hewat McKenzie's less discriminating British College of Psychic Science, dismissed by Lodge as a group of "faddists and cranks."[17]

According to his own estimate, Doyle addressed 150,000 people in Britain between 1916 and 1920, often speaking five times weekly.[18] In addition he spread his gospel in several books and in countless newspaper and magazine articles. But he refused formal debate with opponents of spiritualism after an acrimonious and inconclusive encounter with Joseph McCabe of the Rationalist Press Association in March 1920. By that time, in any event, the home front looked secure, and Doyle was planning to lecture abroad. The National Spiritualists' Association in America had invited him to its autumn 1919 convention, but in Doyle's mind the Empire took priority, and he responded to pleas from Australia and New Zealand before launching his first assault on the North American continent, which was, according to Lodge, "ripe for some kind of spiritual development . . . as a sort of reaction against the spirit of excessive materialism and dollar worship."[19]

From the outset of his initial American lecture tour, when besieged by a platoon of reporters before his ship had passed the Narrows in early April of 1922, Doyle exhibited great skill in manipulating the press with his open manner. Even the staid New York *Times*, which editorially attacked his crusade, followed his progress through the eastern United States and Canada with several neutrally-worded articles per week. But Doyle met his match in Harry Houdini, whose publicity stunts, according to a disgruntled believer, were "enough to make poor old Barnum turn in his grave."[20] Houdini's *anti*-spiritualist lectures and demonstrations were induced partly by his outrage that mediums could dupe sitters with tricks whose techniques were common to all stage magicians. It was to obtain introductions to mediums, for the purpose of exposing them as frauds, that Houdini had first met Doyle in 1920, while performing in England. This early encounter impressed Houdini with the gullibility of Doyle, who had marveled at the magician's escape from a locked tank of water through apparent spiritual "dematerialization," a theory advanced by Hewat McKenzie and accepted by Doyle. If he made no other American convert, Doyle wanted Houdini.

Doyle, however, found his opponent difficult to understand. For one thing, Houdini was no gentleman: he invited Doyle to an annual dinner of the Society of American Magicians, neglecting to tell his guest that he had planned for the occasion a demonstration of bogus mediumship. But Doyle had it eliminated from the program as a condition of his attendance. Houdini was also unethical: he would attack Doyle in the press, misquoting him with alacrity, then apologize privately and attribute distortions to the reporters. In fact, Doyle took with him Houdini's rather amazing advice to disregard any future newspaper reports of attacks because the American press was notorious for misrepresentation. But there were times when Houdini seemed susceptible to conversion, as when he appeared to be emotionally overcome by a message from his mother, transcribed by Jean Doyle through automatic writing.

When the puzzled Doyles returned to England in August 1923, after a second American tour, events leading to a final encounter with Houdini were already in motion. In December of the previous year, roused to action by the controversy surrounding Doyle's first tour, the *Scientific American* had pledged $5,000 to any medium who could demonstrate physical manifestations conclusively before a committee of scientists and other knowledgeable judges. Included on that panel, as sleight-of-hand expert, was none other than Harry Houdini. Doyle became involved when, after many months of inconclusive testing, the judges accepted his recommendation that they investigate Mina Stinson Crandon, whom he had met in Boston in 1922.

In his first and only sitting with "Margery" (as she became known), in England on 17 December 1923, Doyle was persuaded that the invisible spirit of her brother Walter levitated a table, juggled furniture, and whistled and spoke in a voice which did not appear to be coming from either of the Crandons. After returning to Boston, the Crandons kept in touch with Doyle through almost weekly letters, and on 2 May 1924 Le Roi Crandon informed him they were "trying frankly" for the *Scientific American* prize. Margery soon began sitting for a few of the committee members, but everyone awaited the time when Houdini, whose schedule kept him away until the middle of the summer, would be numbered among the judges.

If Doyle later seemed personally as well as professionally biased in siding with the Crandons against Houdini, he had good reason. On 13 May Crandon wrote him describing an advance copy of Houdini's *Magician Among the Spirits*. He reported that Houdini had been "not in any way held back by ability or intent to tell the truth." In addition, he had used Doyle's personal letters "as bait and material all through the book, entirely disregarding the usual obligations of civilized society." This must have astonished Doyle, since Houdini on 7 February had requested permission to quote from several of his books but had mentioned nothing about private correspondence. Doyle bracketed portions of Crandon's description and instructed his secretary to include them in a letter to Houdini, in order to confront him with the allegations. But reconciliation became impossible after Doyle himself obtained the book, which confirmed Crandon's remarks. Doyle filled the margins of his copy with exclamations such as "Rubbish!" and "Bunk!" On the title page he summarized his reaction—"A malicious book, full of every sort of misrepresentation"—and abandoned Houdini to the coming slaughter.

Throughout the early summer Margery met in Boston with members of the committee and with a private group of admiring spiritualists who sat in rapt attention through the repeated playing of "Souvenir" on a Victrola, waiting in the dark for Walter to tip the table, tickle their ears, or burst out in song with a coarse verse on Houdini. Had Doyle maintained an open mind in reading Crandon's letters and seance transcripts, he would have seen that the man was planning, as he actually had threatened in regard to certain other committee members, to "crucify" Houdini and thus prove Margery's work "the most extraordinary mediumship in modern history."[21] But in spite of Crandon's increasingly vituperative attacks on committee skeptics Walter Franklin Prince and William McDougall, and his talk of "war to the finish," Doyle maintained until the end of his life that the Crandons were "the most patient and forgiving people in the world, treating the most irritating opposition with a good-humoured and amused tolerance."[22]

On the morning of 23 July Crandon reported that Margery was "vomiting merrilly [sic]" at the prospect of the "general nastiness" expected that evening from Houdini, who had arrived for two days of sittings. At both seances the spirit Walter moved some screens placed around the medium as a cabinet and succeeded in ringing a battery-operated bell in a box on the floor. (Ordinarily a lever that completed the bell's circuit was held out of place by a spring, so that to ring the bell it was necessary to exert pressure on the lever.) Although Houdini made no exposure either night, he rushed into print with a pamphlet claiming, among other things, that Margery had rung the bell herself by tipping her chair until its rung made contact.[23] His proclamation of victory in the first skirmish proved disastrous, since it spurred the equally nasty Crandon to make certain of success in the final round of seances on 25 and 26 August.

The first night Walter's voice came through but the bell would not ring. Then the spirit charged that Houdini was being paid "to stop these phenomena" and insisted that the bell box be inspected. An eraser was found wedged between the lever and its contact plate, rendering the bell inoperative. On the following evening Margery was fastened into a massive padlocked box provided by Houdini as a cabinet, and two minutes after the lights were put out Walter cut in with a whistle: "What did you do that for, Houdini? You God damned son of a [word deleted in transcript]. You cad you. There's a ruler in this babinet [sic], you unspeakable cad. You won't live forever Houdini, you've got to die. I put a curse on you now that will follow you every day until you die." The lights came on, the box was opened, and on the floor of the cabinet Houdini found a folding ruler of the sort that Margery could have used as a rod to effect phenomena. On the subject of these "plants" Doyle concluded that Margery's reputation was saved and Houdini's ruined by the "miraculous" interference of the spirit Walter, "a very real and live entity, who was by no means inclined to allow his innocent sister to be made the laughing-stock of the continent."[24]

But a more balanced reading of the documents would have suggested otherwise. As early as 6 August Crandon had sent Doyle a rude drawing of the bell box and mentioned a suspicion that Houdini might insert his foot or some object beneath the lever to prevent it from ringing. At a private seance on 23 August, two days before the eraser episode, Walter had mentioned his desire "to wipe Houdini off the map as a ghost hunter" and also suggested that the magician might "slip a die into the contact box." More-over, Crandon emphasized in a comprehensive letter written on 22 September that Houdini was the last person to inspect the box before the sitting, but neglected to mention a crucial fact revealed in his own transcript—that the eraser was actually discovered by Daniel Comstock, a sympathetic member of the committee, who had taken the box from the room for inspection.

Although the episode of the ruler is not so clear an indictment of Crandon, the controversy surrounding these two raucous seances ended seri-ous scientific consideration of the Margery mediumship (the *Scientific American* prize was never awarded) and encouraged psychical researchers like McDou-gall and J. B. Rhine to seek the respectable calm of university laboratories, where they experimented with telepathy and clairvoyance under controlled conditions. Widespread public interest generated by Doyle's postwar cam-paign evaporated, returning spiritualism to its prior status as a minor reli-gious cult. As for Doyle, he ignored Crandon's suggestion of 11 May 1926 that he utilize the Margery story as a plot for "a romance of value." On the basis of revelations given through his wife, Doyle had come to interpret his crusade in even more apocalyptic terms, and in that context another attack on Houdini dwindled to insignificance.[25]

The unprecedented scope of the Great War had produced among spiritu-alists and other occultists a substantial revival of interest in Atlantis, the sunken continent whose destruction had resulted from its inhabitants' moral depravity. In the twenties Lewis Spence, a scholarly occultist, suggested that deluge myths found in many cultures derived originally from colonies of Atlantean refugees, and Percy Harrison Fawcett, a member of the Royal Geographical Society, vanished while seeking such a colony in Brazil. Seers like Kentucky-born Edgar Cayce predicted the destruction of modern civiliza-tion in a series of earthquakes and floods similar to those which had destroyed Atlantis, while H. P. Lovecraft, also an American, based a short story on his own troubled dreams of a submerged city rising cataclysmically.

Doyle himself became actively involved when an Arabian spirit called Pheneas, who had announced himself as a personal guide in December 1922, began revealing details of the modern world's Atlantean future.[26] Communi-cating by means of Jean Doyle's automatic writing and trance speaking, Pheneas informed them in 1923 that humanity was "sinking into a slough of evil and materialism" caused by the presence on the earth's surface of thousands of evil spirits who had never progressed beyond the first of the spiritual planes. "God's own light must descend and burn up the evil fumes," he said, and a band of spiritual scientists was already at work "connecting vibratory lines of seismic power" to bring about preliminary earthquakes and tidal waves. The late war would be "as nothing, nothing, nothing, compared with what lies ahead." Doyle's own task, Pheneas said, was "to prepare men's minds so that when the awakening comes they shall be more ready to receive it." Doyle would act as "a battery to others," and the "whole world . . . in its great extremity" would "cling" to his record of the revelations.

In 1924 Pheneas began to provide specific details. The "coming world-surrender to God" would begin at harvest time in 1925 with a great storm moving from west to east, followed by "a tremendous upheaval in Central Europe," "the submerging of a Continent," and then "a great light from on high." Hardly a nation would escape. America would face civil war; Russia, that "black mark upon the map of humanity," would be destroyed; Africa would be flooded; Brazil would suffer "an eruption of an extraordinary kind"; and the Vatican, that "sink of iniquity" from which "countless veins of poison flow to humanity," would be "wiped off the face of the globe." England, however, would be "the beacon light in this dark world." Already Christ had approached the "power-station" being erected around Doyle's home and would soon make his presence known. Then he would withdraw to make final preparations before returning to proclaim himself, after which Doyle would "rally round Him" for the final battle. In a small leather notebook entitled "Prophesied Course of Events," Doyle recorded that "the whole process will take some years, but I shall survive to the end, then pass over with my whole family," a conclusion supported by a Winnipeg medium's prediction that he would "not die in the ordinary sense."

He apparently accepted completely these revelations from Pheneas. Among friends he circulated "A Short Synopsis of Some Corroborations" containing more than eighty prophecies of a similar nature reported by other mediums. When the autumn of 1925 passed without remarkable incident, Pheneas explained that preparations would take longer than expected, since they had underestimated the strength of the enemy. As a measure of concern it might be noted that in 1927 members of the British spiritualist community were seriously considering the problem of how they would distribute their literature in the coming crisis, in the event of "interruption of railway communication."[27] Pheneas had warned Doyle not to publicize his prophecies until after the first definite signs of their fulfillment, but early in 1927 his Psychic Press and Bookshop, located in London, offered an expurgated version called *Pheneas Speaks*, containing excerpts of a generally sentimental, uplifting nature.

A comparison of the book with the original typescript indicates that Doyle was not above helping out Pheneas on occasion. Where the typed transcript had Pheneas stating that "the light will be the greater for the darkness you have passed through," Doyle wrote in ink a concluding phrase for the sentence—"in fighting for truth"—and the book contained the addition (p. 36). But his handwritten interlineations encompassed more than exactness of expression. To previously typed messages received in 1925 he added supposedly prophetic remarks concerning earthquakes and storms in Russia, Jamaica, and Australia, complete with footnotes describing their actual occurrence in 1926 and 1927. These also appeared in the published book (pp. 116, 123, 127). One might suspect Doyle of fabricating all the messages, but it is likely that he hoped to ensure the book's acceptance with a few dramatically fulfilled predictions.

These few pathetic lapses from his customarily strict ethical code do not detract significantly from his record as a selfless campaigner for the world's moral reformation through spiritualism. Shortly before his death Doyle wrote to a friend that he had "broken my heart in the attempt to give our spiritual knowledge to the world and to give them something living, instead of the dead and dusty stuff which is served out to them in the name of religion." By that time Doyle had begun to wonder if he and his wife were "victims of some extraordinary prank played upon the human race from the other side," since none of the Pheneas predictions had materialized, but his faith in survival itself never wavered.[28] He looked forward to his own passage "over there" as a glorious new beginning, and when the event occurred on 7 July 1930, it was a cause for quiet celebration among his family and friends.

Notes

1. See Hesketh Pearson, *Conan Doyle: His Life and Art* (London: Methuen, 1943), p. 174. For biographical data I used Doyle, *Memories and Adventures* (Boston: Little, Brown, 1924); John Dickson Carr, *The Life of Sir Arthur Conan Doyle* (New York: Harper, 1949); Pierre Nordon, *Conan Doyle*, trans. Frances Partridge (New York: Holt, Rinehart, and Winston, 1967).

2. Doyle to Greenhough Smith, n.d. All cited MSS are in the Doyle Spiritualism Collection, Humanities Research Center.

3. As quoted by Nordon, p. 147.

4. *The Stark Munro Letters* (London: Longmans Green, 1895), pp. 21, 258.

5. *Memories*, p. 79.

6. See "List of Members and Associates," *Proceedings* of the SPR, 9 (1893–94), 378. HRC holdings include account books for 1894–1928 with several gaps of a few months.

7. *The Parasite* (Westminister: A. Constable), pp. 83, 85.

8. *Memories*, p. 205.

9. Doyle to a Mr. Strachey, n.d.

10. See *A Visit to Three Fronts* (London: Hodder and Stoughton, 1916), pp. 78–79, and *Memories*, p. 303.

11. Doyle to Greenhough Smith, n.d.

12. Following summary based on *The New Revelation* (Toronto: Hodder and Stoughton, 1919).

13. *Memories*, p. 390.

14. Canadian National Railways to Doyle, 21 March 1923.

15. See Effa H. Maroney to Doyle, 9 Jan. 1927; George E. Merigold to Wilbur B. Grandison, 29 Aug. 1928; Wilbur B. Grandison to Barbara McKenzie, 30 Aug. 1928.

16. *Our Second American Adventure* (London: Hodder and Stoughton, 1924), pp. 107–19.

17. Lodge to Doyle, 3 March 1922, 26 Nov. 1924.

18. *The Wanderings of a Spiritualist* (London: Hodder and Stoughton, 1921), pp. 11–12.

19. Copy of Lodge to Mrs. Henry Sidgwick, 27 May 1920, enclosed with Lodge to Doyle, 28 May 1920.

20. Ernest F. Mansfield to Doyle, 22 March 1926. On Doyle and Houdini see Bernard M. L. Ernst and Hereward Carrington, *Houdini and Conan Doyle* (New York: Boni, 1932); Milbourne Christopher, *Houdini: The Untold Story* (New York: Crowell, 1969).

21. Crandon to Doyle, 6 June 1924; carbon of Crandon to Lodge, 14 Nov. 1924.

22. Crandon to Doyle, 6 June 1924; Doyle, *The Edge of the Unknown* (New York: Putnam, 1930), p. 14.

23. *Houdini Exposes the Tricks Used by the Boston Medium "Margery"* (New York: Adams Press, 1924), p. 25.

24. *Edge of the Unknown,* p. 9.

25. Houdini's sudden death late in 1926 followed curses delivered through several mediums, including Margery. Doyle and other spiritualists claimed the last word when an American medium, Arthur Ford, produced a test message entrusted by Houdini only to his wife.

26. The following quotations come from several series of typed transcripts, each with its own pagination, and all catalogued as "Phineas speaks."

27. J. Engledow to George Vale Owen, 17 March 1927.

28. Doyle to Walter Gibbons, 17 March 1930 (typed copy).

Index

♦